1994

This book uses the Breton experience to address two fundamental historiographical issues: the meaning of absolutism and the nature of early modern French society. Drawing on economic, social, and institutional approaches, Professor Collins develops an integrated analysis of state-building in France.

The classes and their interests are analyzed first, in an examination of the Breton economy, and then the social system and the political superstructure that preserved it. Finally, Professor Collins addresses the question of order itself. How did the elites preserve order? What order did they wish to preserve? His analysis suggests that early modern France was a much more unstable, mobile society than previously thought; that absolutism existed more in theory than in practice; and that local elites and the Crown compromised in mutually beneficial ways to maintain their combined control over society. They imposed a new order, one neither feudal nor absolutist, on a society reexamining the meaning of basic structures such as the relationship of the family and the individual, the role of women in society, and property.

CAMBRIDGE STUDIES IN EARLY MODERN HISTORY

Classes, estates, and order in early modern Brittany

CAMBRIDGE STUDIES IN EARLY MODERN HISTORY

Edited by Professor J.H. Elliott, University of Oxford,
Professor Olwen Hufton, Harvard University, and Professor H.G. Koenigsberger

The idea of an "early modern" period of European history from the fifteenth to the late eighteenth century is now widely accepted among historians. The purpose of Cambridge Studies in Early Modern History is to publish monographs and studies which illuminate the character of the period as a whole, and in particular focus attention on a dominant theme within it, the interplay of continuity and change as they are presented by the continuity of medieval ideas, political and social organizations, and by the impact of new ideas, new methods and new demands on the traditional structures.

For a list of titles published in the series, please see end of book

Classes, estates, and order in early modern Brittany

JAMES B. COLLINS

Professor of History, Georgetown University

CAMBRIDGE
UNIVERSITY PRESS

Published by the Press Syndicate of the University of Cambridge
The Pitt Building, Trumpington Street, Cambridge CB2 1RP
40 West 20th Street, New York, NY 10011-4211, USA
10 Stamford Road, Oakleigh, Melbourne 3166, Australia

© Cambridge University Press 1994

First published 1994

Printed in Great Britain at the University Press, Cambridge

A catalogue record for this book is available from the British Library

Library of Congress cataloguing in publication data
Collins, James B.
Classes, estates and order in early modern Brittany / James B. Collins.
p.   cm. – (Cambridge studies in early modern history)
Includes bibliographical references
ISBN 0 521 44072 6
1. Brittany (France) – Civilization.   2. Monarchy – France.
3. Brittany (France) – Social conditions.   4. Social classes – France –
Brittany.   5. Regionalism – France – Brittany – History   I. Title.
II. Series.
DC611.B851C59   1994
944'.1–dc20   93-18620   CIP

ISBN 0 521 44072 6 hardback

Contents

Preface	*page* ix
List of abbreviations	xii
Glossary of French terms	xiii
Introduction	1
1 The Breton economy in the sixteenth and seventeenth centuries	30
2 Elements of Breton society	71
3 Institutional structures of political control – financial and judicial organization	108
4 The Estates of Brittany and the Crown, 1532–1626	154
5 The Estates of Brittany and the Crown, 1626–1675	187
6 The burden of Breton taxation	229
7 The problem of order	249
Conclusion	271
Appendix	289
Bibliography	292
Index	309

vii

Contents

Preface

My interest in Brittany began half a lifetime ago, during a trip around Europe with one of my college roommates, Gregg Hillman. Gregg's aunt and uncle, Lorraine and Georges de Braux, lived in Nevez and graciously put us up for a few days. Georges, though a Norman, had an infectious enthusiasm for his adopted *pays*. So began my attraction to this strange and somewhat gloomy peninsula, whose people often reminded me of the Irish-American ghosts of my childhood.

One tradition Bretons share with the Irish is that of hospitality. My family and I have received many kindnesses from Bretons in every corner of the province. My greatest debt, both personal and professional, is to Jean Tanguy and his family. Jean has been the most generous of mentors and he and Marie-Claire have sheltered a wandering American historian more times than I dare to admit. No words can express my appreciation to them.

In any long project one builds up a mountain of obligations; indeed, one of the most sobering of deeds is to write a preface because it reminds the often solitary researcher how tied even he is to countless others. Some of those ties are personal, to people who have stood by you in difficult times. My oldest friend, Will Rogers, and his wife Edna, fall into that category, not only for harboring a penniless graduate student during his first month at Columbia, but for a lifetime of joyful memories. Other ties are both personal and professional, such as those to colleagues like Bob Weiner and Don Miller at Lafayette College or Marcus Rediker and Andrzej Kaminski at Georgetown. All historians who read these lines will understand the unique combination of professional and personal support one receives from those colleagues one is privileged to call friends as well.

One's professional obligations are more numerous, both to those in the field and to the unsung heroes of historical scholarship, the archivists. I have benefited enormously from the assistance and professionalism of the archivists all over Brittany; in all five departmental archives, especially those at Rennes and Nantes, in many municipal archives, and even from those with private papers. The municipal archivists at Nantes are a special pair whose good humor has been as much of a tonic as their efficiency has been an invaluable aid. At Rennes, Mme. Reydellet has often gone out of her way to alert me to newly classified materials and to aid me in every conceivable task. The archivists at Rennes and Nantes, M. Charpy and M. du Boisrouvray, can well be proud of their staffs. I would also like to thank Ron Robbins of the Lafayette College library for his special assistance.

The list of colleagues, French and American, whom I might thank is too long to reproduce. In France, Bernard and Ségolène Barbiche have been extremely kind to me (and my family) through the years; Bernard has also offered much sage professional counsel. In recent years, I have been fortunate to come to know Alain Croix and his family. Alain has provided criticisms only he could, while he and Nicole have been most generous to the Collins family.

In America, the Ancien Régime study group in the D.C. area has shared its criticisms and ideas with me. Farther afield, Jon Dewald, Liana Vardi, and Sarah Hanley have provided new insights in their comments to various conference papers related to this manuscript. I have also had the pleasure of discussing a wide range of matters with colleagues at the United Nations Population Fund. Two of them, Hirofumi Ando and Rafael Salas, offered me their friendship and their mentorship. I am particularly saddened that I cannot share this work with Rafael Salas, one of the most outstanding individuals whom I have ever known, a genuine force for good in the world whose life ended far too early.

Three people, however, have a special, albeit unknown to them, relationship to the manuscript. I had come to a dead end with the material and simply did not know where to turn. At the AHA that year, I had a long talk with Bill Beik and Kristen Neuschel; their new approaches to similar material reinvigorated my interest in state-building and social structures. A few months later, we renewed those conversations at the French Historical Studies meeting. The third member of the group, Phil Hoffman, shared there his thoughts about the economy and agriculture of early modern France. After my meetings with Bill, Kristen, and Phil, I was able to come back to my mass of archival data and make some sense of it. I offer them the ritual absolution – all that follows is my responsibility – but I will say that this book would never have seen the light of day without their inspiration.

Several foundations and universities supported various stages of my research and writing. I would like to thank the Ecole des Hautes Etudes, the Economic History Association, the American Council for Learned Societies, the National Endowment for the Humanities, the Mellon Foundation, Columbia University, Lafayette College, and Georgetown University for their financial assistance.

Special thanks as well go to Richard Fisher, my indefatigable editor at Cambridge, and to Frances Nugent, who copy-edited the manuscript.

My ongoing source of personal inspiration, my family, deserves the final thanks. My first book was dedicated to my father and his hands rest lightly upon this one as well, but I would offer this one as a gift to the living. All of them, as it happens, are women. They have broadened my professional perspectives about women in history in ways I would never have imagined fifteen years ago. To my mother and my sisters I offer thanks for their support (and to Mom for the doggedness gene so essential in the archives!). To three special little girls – Anna, Liz, and Margaret – their dad says thanks for being such good sports about going to a strange country and, well, just for being who you are.

And the first shall be last: Nancy has been with this project from the beginning, from the miserable hovel we occupied in Rennes to the frantic scrambles between town archives to the family trips to France, with their incredible childcare burdens. She has shared the hopes and travails of this book; it is only fair that it be dedicated to her.

Abbreviations

AC	Archives communales
AD	Archives départementales
AM	Archives municipales
AN	Archives nationales
BM	Bibliothèque municipale
BN	Bibliothèque nationale
CN	Côtes du Nord
F	Finistère
IV	Ille-et-Vilaine
LA	Loire Atlantique
M	Morbihan
Mss Fr	Manuscrits français
NAF	Nouvelles acquisitions françaises

Glossary of French terms

Whenever possible, I have tried to translate the French terms into English. Certain words or phrases, however, make no sense in a straightforward translation, so I have kept them in French. The principal ones appear below.

alloué   Second ranking judge at Breton seneschalsy courts.

bêtes vives   Export tax on livestock leaving Brittany. Throughout the period in question here, the king leased this tax farm in conjunction with that of the *ports et havres*.

brieux   Royal (seigneurial) right to salvage of shipwrecks. Leased jointly with the *ports et havres*. Some Breton seigneurs, notably the Rohan family, had such rights in certain parts of the coastline.

élection   Local financial district. In the fourteenth century, the French state created a tax system based on local districts supervized by an elected official (*élu*). He gave his name to the district he supervized, the *élection*, even though, after the 1360s, these officials ceased to be elected. Please note that Brittany did not have any tax officials called *élus*. Unfortunately (for the sake of clarity), Brittany did have *élus*; the province used that name for the "elected" (i.e. selected) parish member of the royal militia, for which the king levied a direct tax in the sixteenth century.

feu   Literally, a hearth. In fourteenth-century Brittany, the duke fixed the fiscal *feu* as three real households. Over time, this relationship disintegrated but the fiscal *feu* never represented an actual hearth.

fouage   Hearth tax. In Brittany, the main direct tax was the *fouage* rather than the *taille*. Through most of the period in question here, the *fouage* had a fixed rate of about 8.6 livres per *feu*.

généralité   Regional financial district. The districts took their name from their chief officer, the *général*. Most *généralités* had a large complement of officers, organized into a *bureau des finances*. Brittany provided the lone exception, as it had only two *généraux*. Francis I merged the offices of *général* and treasurer of France (the latter responsible for oversight of the king's demesne). In the text, these officials are referred to as treasurers of France.

lieutenant particulier   Local military commander. Brittany had a royal governor, a royal lieutenant general (on occasion, two lieutenants general, one for

Nantes and one for the rest of the province), and three *lieutenants particuliers* – one each for the bishopric of Nantes, for Upper Brittany (bishoprics of Rennes, Saint-Malo, Dol, and Saint-Brieuc), and for Lower Brittany (bishoprics of Vannes, Quimper, Léon, and Tréguier).

livre   French pound (known as the *livre tournois* or pound of Tours). The *livre* was a money of account, not a real coin.

livre breton   Breton pound. Five Breton pounds equalled six French pounds. The *fouage* rate was always listed in Breton pounds (after the 1540s, as 7.35 Breton pounds per *feu*), as were most of the transit and export–import duties, thus a given commodity might pay 8 Breton pence (*deniers*) per barrel. Like the *livre tournois*, the *livre breton* was, throughout our period, merely a money of account. The *livre breton* is also known as the *livre monnaie*.

noblesse d'épée   Nobility of the sword, that is, those from an old (i.e. medieval) noble family. In Brittany, many members of this group owned judicial offices (especially at the Parlement), so the distinction robe/sword does not provide much insight.

noblesse de robe   Nobility of the robe, that is, those ennobled by virtue of their office. Referred to in the text simply as the *robe*; the members of the group are called *robins*.

pays d'élection   The area covered by *élection* districts, that is, the regions under the authority of the Estates General of Languedoil that voted taxation in the 1360s. Only Normandy among the original *pays d'Etats* also had *élections*, although Dauphiné and the southwestern regions received them in the first half of the seventeenth century. The king levied the standard royal taxes, notably the *taille*, in the *pays d'élection*.

pays d'Etats   Provinces that still had Estates in the sixteenth and seventeenth centuries. The main ones were Béarn, Brittany, Burgundy, Dauphiné, Languedoc, Normandy, Provence, and the small regions (*pays*) of the southwest, such as Quercy and Périgord. The southwestern regions lost their estates in 1621, Dauphiné lost them in the 1630s, and Normandy in the 1650s.

ports et havres   Export–import duties of the eight Breton bishoprics other than Nantes. The Rohan family possessed these duties in one small area of the bishopric of Léon and the duke had abandoned the export–import duties of Saint-Malo to the town itself in the fourteenth century.

prévôté de Nantes   Export–import duties of the bishopric of Nantes, covering products leaving/arriving by sea as well as those coming from France (by land or by river).

seigneur   Landlord. I have used this term throughout to indicate a landlord who possessed feudal rights. In so doing I am following the practices of early modern writers in an effort to simplify terminology. In reality, the terms *seigneur* and *sieur* could overlap. *Seigneurs* are often listed in documents merely as *sieur* of "x"; a simple *sieur* was never called a *seigneur*. A *seigneur* owned a *seigneurie*.

sieur   Landlord. I have used this term to refer to landlords who did not possess feudal rights. Some *sieurs* possessed relatively small estates but others could have quite substantial properties, called *sieuries*. Many *seigneurs* (indeed probably a majority of them) owned *sieuries* as well as *seigneuries*.

Money   1 *livre*=20 *sous*=240 *deniers*

From 1576 until 1602, the state used the *écu* as the money of account; during that period one *écu*=3 *livres*. (Please note that the value of the *écu* varied over time, as it was a real coin.) The people used a wide variety of real coins, both French (*liards* worth 3 *deniers*, *francs*, half *francs*, *écus*, and others) and Spanish (*réales*, *pistoles*). Spanish coins were so prevalent in western France that peasants continued to use the *réal* as a money of account until the twentieth century.

Introduction

The spring of 1675 was a time of turmoil in western France, with public discontent rising rapidly against the battery of new taxes enacted to pay for the war with the United Provinces. In early April the rumor spread to Brittany that rioters in Bordeaux had conducted an *auto-da-fé*, using his wares to incinerate the chief *traitant* of the new stamped paper tax. The forces of order everywhere stood on edge. The First President of the Parlement, Florent d'Argouges, wrote to the mayor and aldermen of Nantes that "authority must always be preserved." Mindful of the constant conflicts between the municipality and the seneschal of Nantes, he reminded them that "service is better carried out when the main officers are united."

D'Argouges presents us with the primary policy goal of the early modern French state, the preservation of order, and with its necessary enabling condition, unity among the ruling elites. In this new world, the focus of divine benediction shifted from the hierarchical social order itself to a combination of the sovereign state and the newly moral individual. The king himself was the first such individual, giving law binding on all his subjects, although not on himself. How hard it must have been to maintain the necessary unity when the order around which elites had to rally lacked clear definition. The old social, economic, and political hierarchy, which was still an organic reality in France, was that of the society of estates. The new hierarchies were economic (the society of classes) and political (the sovereign state). The structure of inquiry about such a society must examine both hierarchies to show how they formed a new order based, above all, on the defense of property.

The king provided confused leadership in the search for the new order. On the one hand, he defended the social status quo by supporting its two defining institutions, the family and the society of orders hierarchy. On the other hand, he attacked the political status quo by seeking to move French governance outside the framework of contract and into that of law, that is, into the area in which the king had unlimited authority. Order thus had contradictory meanings. The network of orders codified inequality into a divine social cosmos, yet the king wanted to treat everyone as an equal before him, to make all subject to his laws. The framework of orders preserved the hierarchical structure contemporaries believed society needed to function, yet the government demanded

I

freedom of action outside that structure in order to preserve the social peace and protect that most important of all social elements, property. In a society both unstable and stable, the government had to be a combination of absolute authority, to preserve order (that is, enjoyment of property) and limited power, so as not to threaten property. The government could not threaten the property of elites and simultaneously maintain its legitimacy in their eyes. Contemporaries made no bones about the connection between property and order: as the bishop of Saint-Malo wrote to Colbert (1675), "the bourgeois and principal inhabitants are well intentioned as much for the service of the king as for the preservation of their goods." The good bishop did not fail to remind them that the two went hand in hand.

How best to analyze this disorderly society obsessed with order? This book has three sections: on classes and their relationship to the Breton economy; on the society of estates, as seen through its institutions, above all the Estates of Brittany; and on the problem of order itself. Before turning to the Breton case, however, we must first establish the broader French context within which Breton developments took place. Let us start with classes and estates and then turn to an examination of the problem of order and the nature of "absolutism."

CLASSES AND ESTATES

The two "scholasticisms," the society of orders and the society of classes, have defined the historiographical parameters of inquiry about early modern France for more than a generation. As Pierre Goubert has suggested, each model has its utility, yet neither can satisfactorily explain the complexity of early modern French society. To be restricted to either is "the negation of the greatest and dearest of all liberties, that of the mind, and the negation of historical research itself."[1] To understand early modern France, we must consider classes (classifying people by the nature of their economic activity and by their level of wealth), estates (or orders) (classifying people by culturally determined legal categories), and order. We need also to relate these categories to gender and age because of the destabilization created by rapidly changing gender relations and attitudes toward the social peace.[2] The Breton network of classes and estates reflected the province's particularism in certain ways, yet the Breton pattern broadly resembled the larger French one.

---

[1] P. Goubert and D. Roche, *Les Français et l'Ancien Régime* (Paris, 1984) I, 31.
[2] S. Amussen, *An Ordered Society: Gender and Class in Early Modern England* (New York, 1988); S. Hanley, "Engendering the State: Family Formation and State Building in Early Modern France," *French Historical Studies*, 16, (1) (Spring 1989): 4–27. Hanley cites the relevant edicts in note 9. See also her "Toward a Reassessment of Political Culture through Gender Concerns in Early Modern France," a paper presented to the Annual Meeting of the Society for French Historical Studies, 1991. My thanks to Professor Hanley for permission to cite a work in progress.

Introduction

Brittany, like France as a whole, had three distinct elites: the titled nobility, the legal and judicial elite, and the merchants.[3] Individuals rarely moved from the mercantile elite directly to that of the titled nobility; the middle group, primarily the officers of the royal judiciary, served as a mechanism for upward social mobility. The nobles possessed all the marks of social and political esteem: they had unquestioned social precedence; they were the military; they rendered (or had rendered in their name) local justice. The legal class, like the nobility, owned land, but save for some Parlementaires, most Breton legists held a *sieurie* rather than a seigneurie. They had to cede social and political precedence to the nobles, although they shared political power by means of their offices. The nobles often judged (or rather had others, lower ranking lawyers, judge for them) in the first instance but the sentence went to a royal court on appeal. These two noble worlds intersected at the Parlement of Brittany.

The second elite, the judicial officers, came from legal families: almost all Breton judges were the sons of judges, lawyers, or petty officials. Among the lesser judiciary, the grandfathers had often been merchants but among the higher ranking judges grandfathers, too, were usually (lower ranking) judges. Once one had chosen the legal path, one cut off ties to the world of commerce and finance. In Nantes, as elsewhere, the royal judicial officers and the lawyers lived in one section of the city, while the merchants and financiers lived in another. They followed highly endogamous patterns of social interaction, for instance in marriage and godparenting. The Parlement provided one noteworthy Breton particularity: some of the highest echelons of the royal judiciary came from old "sword" noble families, from families already noble in the fourteenth or early fifteenth century. These noble Parlementaires, however, tended to be the descendants of nobles who had moved to a city and taken up a legal career in the late fifteenth or early sixteenth centuries.

The third elite, the merchants, shared urban power with the royal officers in the sixteenth century; in the seventeenth century the judicial officers tended to obtain a monopoly on mayoralties and to dominate the town councils. Even though thirty or more Breton towns sent deputies to each session of the Estates in the seventeenth century, those deputies came overwhelmingly from the legal class, either royal officials or lawyers. The merchants therefore had very little political representation. Their chief political allies came from among the royal financial officers, a much smaller group in Brittany than elsewhere. Breton merchants and financiers had less political power than their compeers in many other areas, even though Brittany had a thriving commerce. Unlike the legal group and the nobles, the merchants rarely owned land, except in the areas around the richest commercial towns such as Morlaix, Saint-Malo, or Nantes.

The monarchy rested on the cooperation of these three elites, whose interests

---

[3] On the legal group, see the provocative essay by G. Huppert, *Les bourgeois gentilshommes* (Chicago, 1977).

3

tended to be more consonant than conflicting. Simplistic class-based analyses of the French monarchy tend to emphasize the conflicts more than the consonance, so that the king becomes the ally of the bourgeoisie against the nobility or the ally of the nobility against the bourgeoisie – the "absolutist" state as the last stage of the feudal monarchy. Perry Anderson, in *Lineages of the Absolutist State*, gives the classic formulation: "Absolutism was essentially just this: *a redeployed and recharged apparatus of feudal domination*." In his view, this absolutist monarchy was primarily (although not exclusively) a mechanism for the protection of "aristocratic property and privileges."[4]

Robert Brenner, in his wide-ranging articles comparing England and France, takes essentially the same line, seeing the absolutist state as a replacement for the old structures of "surplus extraction" but operating for the benefit of the same class.[5] William Beik, in his outstanding book on *Absolutism and Society in Seventeenth-Century France*, comes to a similar, albeit more nuanced, conclusion about Languedoc: "Absolutism was the political manifestation of a system of domination protecting the interests of a privileged class of officers and landed lords." Beik even goes so far as to suggest that the "'society of orders' did not exist as a system, but only as one aspect of a distinctly early modern form of a society of classes." For Beik, the society of orders is based on "the social esteem accorded to the mystical or real function which each group performs and which has *no necessary connection* to the group's economic role."[6] In one sense, Brittany bears out Beik's observations about Languedoc because the two hierarchies – classes and orders – overlapped so much; however, in another sense, the social (and political) esteem of the dominant groups had a very real connection to their economic role as landlord.

The consonance of identity between the dominant economic class, large-scale landlords, and the dominant order, the titled nobility, meant that their political, social, *and* economic interests combined to make a formidable and coherent ruling class. The richest Breton landlords of the mid 1660s, those with a *landed* income of 30,000 livres a year or more, were all titled nobles: princes

---

[4] P. Anderson, *Lineages of the Absolutist State* (London, 1974, 1979), 18. Anderson's argument resembles that of B. Porchnev, *Les soulèvements populaires en France avant la Fronde, 1623–1648* (Paris, 1963), 572, which claims that the state had to become stronger (achieve absolutism) to maintain feudalism. I would emphasize here that I am not disputing Anderson's contention that the "aristocracy" remained the dominant political and economic class, although the adjective "feudal" is, in my view, somewhat misleading. These people certainly were "feudal" lords but their main independent source of income was ground rent, not feudal dues.

[5] R. Brenner, "Agrarian Roots of European Capitalism," *Past and Present*, 97 (1982): 80. Brenner's original (1976) article on this subject, together with the revised version and a variety of related articles are available in *The Brenner Debate. Agrarian Class Structure and Economic Development in Pre-Industrial Europe*, ed. T. H. Aston and C. H. E. Philpin (Cambridge, 1985, 1987).

[6] W. Beik, *Absolutism and Society in Seventeenth-Century France. State Power and Provincial Aristocracy in Languedoc* (Cambridge, 1985), 335 and 7.

(Rohans), dukes (Brissac, Cambout-Coislin, Retz, la Trémoille, Vendôme), marquises (Coëtquen, Goulaine, Rieux, Rosmadec), and counts (Assérac-Rieux, Avaugour, Boiséon). All of these families had superior seigneurial jurisdictions: the Rohans – the principalities of Léon and Guémené, the county of Porhoët, and the baronies of Coat-Méal and La Roche Mochan – and the la Trémoilles – Quintin, Goëllo, Paimpol, Châteaulaudren, and the great barony of Laval – held the most important ones.[7]

These titled families dominated the military hierarchy. In the sixteenth and seventeenth centuries, a member of one of these great families usually held the office of lieutenant general for the three major military divisions of the province (Upper Brittany, Lower Brittany, and Nantes). The two most powerful families, la Trémoille and Rohan, produced national military leaders. The great families provided the military governors of the major cities: Rieux at Brest, Boiséon at Morlaix, Coëtquen at Saint-Malo, Goulaine or Rosmadec at Nantes. They dominated the Estates: Rohan and la Trémoille above all. In the first quarter of the seventeenth century a Rohan invariably served as the president of the Second Estate; in the second quarter of the century the function shifted to the la Trémoille family. The other major families often assisted at the Estates; some, such as Cambout, served as royal commissioners to the Estates or deputies to Court for the Estates, or even both (in 1636–7).[8]

A given prominence on one scale *required* equal prominence on the others. The richest landlords had to have titles that matched their landed prominence; thus, the richest parvenus, such as Gilles Ruellan in Brittany, obtained elevated noble titles – in his case that of marquis. The king had to make Ruellan a marquis because he owned so much land and because his daughters married into the apex of Breton society – Brissac, Goulaine, Guémadeuc, Coëtlogon, and Barrin de la Galissonnière – that is, to a duke and four marquises.[9] A royal army commander of a certain rank virtually had to have an equivalent social rank; a lieutenant general had to be a duke or a marquis, lest one of his military subordinates be his social superior. A duke or a marquis had to have a certain landed revenue to maintain himself, a landed revenue that placed him at the apex of the economic hierarchy as well. The military commander, after all, had to maintain a certain standing, a certain state of living; the king officially recognized this necessity by granting all officers of a given rank an *état* to help

---

[7] Incomes are taken from the estimate of Charles Colbert de Croissy, investigating commissioner of 1665, whose report has been published: *La Bretagne en 1665 d'après le rapport de Colbert de Croissy*, ed. J. Kerhervé, F. Roudaut, and J. Tanguy (Brest, 1978).

[8] See below, ch. 5, on Cambout at the Estates of 1636–7. Although he was a relative-client of Richelieu, Cambout's position in Brittany, as baron of Pontchâteau, created local prominence in its own right.

[9] On Gilles Ruellan, see the entry on his son in F. Saulnier, *Le Parlement de Bretagne de 1554 à 1790* (Rennes, 1909), 3 vols., and the story about him in G. Tallement de Réaux, *Historiettes* (Paris, 1960), I, 154–6.

them maintain the standing required of their position.[10] At a royal court, the First President had to set the social tone. At the Parlement of Paris, a First President (Potier de Novion) even resigned (1724) because he could not maintain the social schedule expected of him.[11] At the Estates the leaders of the nobility *had* to offer evening banquets to the lesser nobility (banquets at which they lobbied effectively for support).

The nobility dominated society by means of the three related attributes of title, seigneurial land, and military office. Most nobles (many Breton ones) did not serve in the military, so that their personal relationship to that function was indeed mystical, but most military officers (and cavalrymen in the *compagnies d'ordonnance*) were nobles. Military service might have been a "mystical" function for a specific individual noble, but it was a very real function for the nobility as a group.[12] Although a specific noble might have held a very small amount of land (most did), the largest seigneuries, and the largest share of the land, belonged to nobles. In Brittany, very few non-nobles obtained seigneurial rights although a considerable group of them, especially near large towns such as Rennes or Nantes, bought the land of the fiefs to which the rights were attached.[13]

The nobility dominated the Breton economy as landlords (that is, as part of a class) and as seigneurs, a function that set them apart from other landlords. In the sixteenth and seventeenth centuries royal officers and lawyers bought substantial amounts of land. These people had family roots in the mercantile elites of the towns, but it would be a mistake to connect them *as a class* with the merchants, and to call the combined group the bourgeoisie (in the modern sense of a specific economic class; in the vocabulary of the Ancien Régime, urban dwellers living from their rents were "bourgeois"). They were, virtually without exception, *sieurs*: owners of rural estates without seigneurial rights.[14] Those who reached the highest judicial offices, such as judge in the Parlement or president

---

[10] The king gave an *état* to an officer to enable him to maintain a level of living appropriate to his rank. He expected military officers to use this money on expenses such as dinners for their subordinates. A marshal of France, for example, received an *état* of 10,000 livres a year. An *état* was not the same as a pension; it was a fixed amount determined by the *qualité* of the position one held.   [11] J. H. Shennan, *The Parlement of Paris* (Ithaca, 1968), 33.

[12] Goubert and Roche, *Les Français*, 120 and ch. 4 in general. P. Contamine, *Guerre, état et société à la fin du Moyen Age* (Paris, 1972) and A. Corvisier, "La noblesse militaire: Aspects militaires de la noblesse française du XVe au XVIIIe siècles: état des questions," *Histoire Sociale – Social History* 11 (1978): 336–55. Although most nobles did not fight in the army, the fact remains that the officer corps (and parts of the cavalry, such as the *compagnies d'ordonnance*) remained noble preserves.

[13] See, for example, the *francs fiefs* list of 1539: Mss. Fr. 22,342, fols. 193v and ff. For 1566, see, ADLA, B 3023. H. Sée, *Les classes rurales en Bretagne du XVIe siècle à la Révolution* (Paris, 1905) notes that the phenomenon was particularly marked around Rennes, Nantes, and Saint-Malo.

[14] The term is that of J. Gallet, *La seigneurie bretonne, 1450–1680. Le cas du Vannetais* (Paris, 1983), although it can be found in the writings of contemporaries, such as Charles Loyseau (*Traité des seigneuries*, 3–4). A *sieur* did not share in public political power; a seigneur did *own* a share of such

Introduction

of the Chamber of Accounts (or of one of the four presidials), did traverse this last barrier: they eventually bought (or obtained through royal letters) seigneurial rights. Our modern difficulty in placing the judicial officers in the social and legal hierarchy of Ancien Régime France is not surprising, given that contemporaries had precisely the same problem. There was a strident disagreement about the place of the royal officers within the framework of estates: at the Estates General of 1614, after a long dispute, the deputies even assigned the Parlement of Paris to sit with the Third Estate.[15] The upper levels of the hierarchies of class and order blended closely together:

Order	Class
titled nobles	seigneurial landlords (superior)
untitled nobles	seigneurial landlords
royal judicial officers	non-seigneurial landlords
royal financial officers	mixed interests
rentiers	mixed interests
wholesale merchants	merchants
retail merchants	

The groups tended to overlap at certain interstices, such as that of non-seigneurial landlord: judicial officers and nobles alike owned *sieuries*. Some financial officers, *rentiers*, and merchants (especially around Morlaix, Saint-Malo, and Nantes) also owned *sieuries* but much of their money tended to be invested in trade or tax farming. Some judges, such as those in the Parlement of Brittany, even owned seigneuries (not only around Rennes but in the Vannetais and in western Brittany). These judges tended to come from families that held seigneuries *before* they joined the court but certain families, notably those of presidents of the court, obtained them after joining the Parlement in the late sixteenth or early seventeenth centuries.

The capitation classifications of 1695 demonstrate the overlap between economic class and social order, if one examines them carefully. Almost all of the 500-plus categories concern royal officers, so they provide a neat hierarchy of rank within segments of the royal bureaucracy and, to a lesser extent, among those segments. The massive list of such offices, however, tends to obscure the broader social categories to which the vast majority of taxpayers belonged. The highest Bretons would have ranked in the second of the twenty-two "classes": dukes, the provincial governor, and the prince of Rohan (all paying 1,500 livres). The next class included the lieutenants general, the First President of the Parlement of Brittany, the treasurer of the Estates, and the receivers general

---

power. Thus a *sieur* invariably (except in the south) had a seigneur to whom his holding subordinated him (among other obligations, he would owe *lods et ventes*). In the Vannetais, old nobles virtually monopolized the seigneuries: Gallet, *La seigneurie bretonne*, esp. 305–8.

[15] J. M. Hayden, *France and the Estates General of 1614*. (Cambridge, 1974).

(these latter three would certainly not have ranked so high fifty years before). The fifth, sixth, and seventh "classes" would have included the other major political figures of the province: fifth, the First President of the Chamber of Accounts, the intendant, governors of frontier fortresses; sixth, the presidents *à mortier* of the Parlement and the governors of the major towns; seventh, marquises, counts, viscounts, and barons, and the presidents of the Chamber of Accounts.

Within the twenty-two classes the list invariably starts with the military, moves to the judiciary, and then to the financial officers. Economic categories appear only in the tenth and eleventh classes, with bankers (tenth) and wholesale merchants (eleventh). The list essentially follows the general categories laid out above. Only merchants and *rentiers* appear before class 15, when rural agents show up (those leasing lands for an annual value of 3,000 livres rent). In the towns, we see wholesale merchants, then retail merchants (sixteenth). Artisan masters (those who had journeymen) from large towns appear in class 18, small-town artisans without help in class 20. The twenty-second class lumps together cottagers, day laborers, married shepherds and servants, journeymen, apprentices, unmarried shepherds and servants, and small-town servants, listed in that order. They all pay 1 livre.

This list can be simplified as follows, for the towns:

Order	Class
master craftspeople	small occupiers
journeymen	workers
day laborers and other unorganized workers	

In the countryside, the peasantry had three major groups: ploughmen (*laboureurs*), cottagers (*manouvriers*), and day laborers (*journaliers*).[16] The village artisans belonged to the two lower groups. The capitation categories mention farmers of 3,000 livres of lands and 2,000 livres of mills in category 15, but these people were not peasants. The richest *laboureurs* appear in category 16 – "some farmers and ploughmen" – paying 30 livres; others appear in categories 17, 18, and 20, along with some wine growers (*vignerons*). The day laborers and servants show up in the last category. Ploughmen often owned a small plot of land and *always* had a plough team (usually leased) and a rented farm. Cottagers could own a house or, rarely, a tiny plot; they usually rented a small holding. Day laborers owned only their labor and usually rented a room or a part of a room from others (although some day laborers had their own rented houses).

The hierarchy of orders made it difficult to move from one group to the next, but some forms of movement proved easier than others. The two sharpest breaks came between the artisans and the merchants and between the judicial

[16] The French terms did not have a universal meaning; in some areas *laboureur* meant day laborer not ploughman. See the discussion of these terms in Goubert and Roche, *Les Français*, I, ch. 2.

and financial officers. Many families used royal office (and other techniques) to ascend to nobility during the period between 1550 and 1625 but after 1625 the process slowed considerably. The consolidation of a new order, one in which the three elites had well-defined places they all willingly defended, greatly facilitated the increased stability.

The social and economic hierarchies had few points of dissonance. Some of the titled nobles and many of the untitled ones had relatively modest economic resources; others among them had few (or no) seigneurial rights. Consider the different capitation payments expected of these groups: dukes and princes – 1,500 livres (class 2); marquises, counts, viscounts, and barons – 250 livres (class 7); fief holders (untitled gentlemen) – 40 livres (class 15); gentlemen without fiefs – 6 livres (class 19). The overwhelming majority of nobles fell into these final two categories, indeed most of them probably came from the last one. These people had political weight only as members of a faction at the Estates; the large retinues of the great, sometimes numbering more than a hundred, gave them additional authority (and more votes) in the deliberations of the Estates. In practical terms, however, the royal officers, especially the higher judicial officers – Parlementaires, the leaders of the presidial courts, the seneschals – had far more political and economic power than petty country squires. In general, such officials also owned far more land; some of them also held seigneurial powers. Presidents *à mortier* ranked in class 6; regular councilors of the Parlement and masters of accounts in the Chamber fell into class 9 (150 livres), the mayors of Nantes and Rennes in class 11 (100 livres), the aldermen of those two cities and mayors of all others in class 13 (60 livres). Although the capitation categories rely on several different elements – political, institutional, economic – these differences – Parlementaires well above untitled nobles, even those holding fiefs, presidents in the Parlements on about the same level as titled men below dukes – represented something like the real overall social structure of the province.

The break between judicial and financial officer families provides one of the more striking elements of Breton social structure. Judicial families often achieved nobility; they also intermarried with old noble families. Judicial and financial families rarely intermarried. Financial officers, except those of very great wealth, married endogamously or with the daughters of merchants. The dividing line between rural and urban interests, between those who kept their economic holdings in land or in commerce/capital, ran between the two sets of officers, with the judiciary aligned with the nobles on the rural side and the financiers allied with the merchants on the urban one.

The next social chasm lay between merchant and artisan. Artisans produced what they sold; merchants did not. Movement from one social/economic group to the other happened as rarely in Brittany as in Dijon.[17] Among the artisan class

[17] J. Farr, *Hands of Honor. Artisans and Their World in Dijon, 1550–1650* (Cornell, 1989).

a barrier ran between journeymen and masters, but many journeymen could reasonably aspire to becoming masters. The dividing line between journeymen and masters often involved age and marital status: masters had to be married; they also tended to be in their thirties or older. We see the same divisions in the countryside. Day laborers were generally young and unmarried; cottagers were usually married and in their late twenties or early thirties; ploughmen were always married and tended to be over 35. At these levels of society, whether rural or urban, the three factors – class origin, marital status, and age – together determined one's place in the economic and social hierarchy.

The class and estate interests of these groups usually overlapped. The landlords, noble or non-noble, seigneurs or not, favored low direct taxation; the merchants worried about high indirect taxation. In Brittany the choice between direct and indirect taxation provided the main political issue. Unlike Dauphiné, Brittany had both real and personal exemptions, so that the political dispute about taxation centered not on order-based distinctions (*taille réelle* versus *taille personnelle*) but on economic interests and the relationship of the tax system to land.[18] The dividing line lay not, as in Dauphiné, between the Second and Third Estates, but between landlords and merchants. The peasants sided with the landlords; the artisans, who paid the lion's share of the indirect taxes on wine, sided with the merchants.

The considerable order-based solidarity about indirect as against direct taxation should not obscure the class basis of this economic issue. One's economic relationship to the land determined one's stand on direct taxation. Many landlords were not nobles: indeed, in some regions the legal families, many still commoners, held a substantial share of the land.[19] In Brittany landlords sat as deputies to the Third Estate as well as the Second: the two orders had the same vested interest in protecting their tenants from direct taxation. Breton politics, after 1598, revolved around a class issue: how much direct taxation would the cultivators have to pay?

The (noble and *roturier*) landlords' common possession of land meant that they had a shared class interest. Economically, landowners dominated early modern France. Agriculture produced by far the largest share of the economic output but, beyond that, land itself held an almost mystical power over the people of the time. As with so many mystical powers, this one had important rational roots: land meant political and social power.[20] Those without land could not hope to aspire to prominence in either sphere.

The merchants had a complex relationship to the land-based systems of

---

[18] D. Hickey, *The Coming of French Absolutism* (Toronto, 1986).

[19] Especially in the bishopric of Rennes, near the Parlement, but Colbert de Croissy implies a considerable concentration in the bishopric of Vannes as well: *La Bretagne en 1665*, 245–47.

[20] Goubert and Roche, *Les Français*, 31, stress the essentially rural nature of French society "qui s'organise en fonction de la terre."

hierarchy. Their families could gradually move higher in the order hierarchy by a careful strategy of changing profession, buying land, and adopting a new cultural outlook. This strategy involved changing classes as well, because their main economic interest had to shift from commerce to land. Even as merchants, however, they received many benefits from the social and political structure. Town police officials could (and did) protect local merchants from outside competition and from disorder; provincial Estates could (and did) oppose mercantile monopolies and new taxes on commerce or manufacture. The Estates of Brittany, a body made up almost exclusively of landlords, opposed mercantile monopolies as unceasingly as did Breton merchants.[21] Merchants and landlords frequently did not have opposing class interests; such opposition rarely provided the driving motor of class conflict in early modern French politics. Each group owned property; the preservation of such property (order) was the primary purpose of the state in the Ancien Régime, so that the state could simultaneously serve the main interest of each of these two classes.[22]

Historians often juxtapose two conflicting systems of values, one based on older notions of loyalty and order, the other based on the more "modern" foundation of economic interest. As Kristin Neuschel's analysis of noble culture demonstrates, however, the dichotomy "affection" (i.e., action based on *fidelité*) and "gain" (action based on material interest) – the artificiality of the distinction between estate- and class-based actions – makes little sense. She notes the extent to which "the bonds noble men formed with each other and with the state were complementary; they were flexible, nonexclusive, and episodic."[23] Early modern society had both estates and classes. People acted, had to act, according to several stimuli: concerns about honor, about property, about order. To say that we can single out one element to the exclusion of others is fundamentally to misunderstand early modern France. To speak of a "society of orders" is to miss the point that when early modern French people said "orders" they meant "order." Many solidarities overlapped class and order boundaries: did noble landlords defend their interests as an order (nobles) or as a class (landlords)? They invariably referred to their order-based interests in defending their

---

[21] J. Collins, "La flotte normande au début du XVIIe siècle: le mémoire de Nicolas Langlois (1627)," *Annales de Normandie* (1984): 161–80, on the anti-mercantilist feelings of Norman merchants. On the Estates of Brittany, ADIV, C 2777–84, papers of the Estates from 1651 to 1679. The Estates attacked monopolies in the Great Banks, in linen trade, and generally defended the "liberty of commerce."

[22] Anderson, *Lineages*, and Brenner fully recognize the point that the French seventeenth-century state protected many mercantile interests.

[23] K. Neuschel, *Word of Honor. Interpreting Noble Culture in Sixteenth-Century France* (Ithaca, 1988), provides an in-depth look at the relationships among nobles, particularly those in the circle of the Condé family. In her introduction, Neuschel attacks the notion of *fidelité* (as promulgated most prominently by Roland Mousnier, in *Les institutions de la France sous la monarchie absolue, 1598–1789* (Paris, 1974, 1980), translated as *The Institutions of France under the Absolute Monarchy, 1598–1789* (Chicago, 1979, 1980), I, ch. 3) and the entire practice of "dichotomizing nobles' political behavior generally – ideal versus reality, faithfulness versus gain" (p. 15).

actions, but this hardly explains their genuine reason for action. First, they were accustomed to using the rhetoric of orders; second, in a society obsessed with custom, it made more sense to couch an appeal in terms of violation of ancient norms, which were defined in terms of orders.

The most important class issue revolved around the division of the output of the main means of production – land. The landlords wanted more rent; the king wanted higher direct tax payments. In their *cahier* for the aborted Estates General of 1649–51, the nobility of Périgord put the matter quite bluntly in article 2: "That the demesnes, mills and farms of gentlemen be exempt from all *tailles* and contributions."[24] They based their claim on their noble (i.e., order-based) privileges. The tax collector assaulted the noble's sense of honor and subverted the local political order, which rested on the protection that the powerful offered the weak. Bercé and Mousnier rightly argue that such grievances provide evidence of the nobles defending their honor (and thus their political interest), but we must also recognize that, in so doing, they defended their economic interest.[25] Pay the rent or pay the taxes – surely the landlord wished to have that dilemma resolved in his/her favor. In fact, the noble complaints on this matter specifically stated that the peasants could not pay their rents and dues because of the high taxes.[26] Protection of tenants from taxation was primarily class interest, as the position of the sovereign courts clearly shows, but taxation was a political issue, quite aside from its economic ramifications. To be defenseless before the tax collector was both an economic liability and a socio-political one, a class issue but also an order one.

The bourgeois financial officers and the king allied to overcome the nobility (and other landlords) on this fundamental issue. It was an order-based conflict in the sense that the inability to protect one's "vassals" (as the Breton nobility refered to their peasants) from higher taxation carried heavy political and social cost: if the seigneur was powerless with respect to the state, why continue to be loyal to him or her? Yet it was also a class issue, one in which the financial administration was the class enemy of the landlords, while the judiciary were their class allies. The royal courts invariably opposed new royal taxes: their class interest, as landlords, was to preserve their access to peasant surplus production.[27] Everyone wanted access to peasant stocks of cash: the king obtained the cash through the direct taxes, the landlords through higher entry fees for leases

---

[24] Y.-M. Bercé, *Histoire des Croquants* (Paris, 1974), II, appendix.

[25] R. Mousnier, *Fureurs paysans* (Paris, 1967), takes this position with respect to the southwestern rebellions. Bercé, *Histoire des Croquants*, 146, takes a similar view, but the rest of his text demonstrates a far more nuanced perspective on these complex issues.

[26] Y. Durand, *Cahiers de doléances de la noblesse des gouvernements d'Orléanais, Normandie et Bretagne* (Nantes, 1971), 75 (complaint of nobles of Orléanais), 99 (similar complaint from Normans).

[27] R. Bonney, *The King's Debts* (Oxford, 1981), gives many examples. ADLA, B 65–80, papers of the Chamber of Accounts, for Breton ones. See below, ch. 3–5. The available literature on other royal courts demonstrates the same phenomenon. See, for example, A. Hamscher, *The Parlement of Paris after the Fronde* (Pittsburgh, 1976).

or in higher rents.[28] Higher direct taxes meant less liquid capital for paying entry fees, rents, and, perhaps most critically of all, for investment. The military nobles and the civil administration (legal men), although paid by expanded royal revenues, stood to lose financially if their tenants could not pay their rents due to overtaxation. The landlords had a clear class interest: low direct taxes on their tenants, so that they could collect greater income in rents; a free market for their grain; the maintenance of order. The key issue was the first: rates of direct taxation. To argue that the French state was the feudal ally of the nobility is to ignore that on this most important of class issues – the distribution of the surplus value of the main means of production – the interests of the state and of most of the nobility were incompatible.

ORDER AND ABSOLUTISM

The main guarantor of order in early modern France was the king. The king relied upon the Church to sanctify this order and upon the nobility and the royal officers to enforce it. The Church continued to sanctify the traditional three orders, yet it also specifically sanctified the king as a special individual. The change in the *ordo* of coronation under Charles V (made normative only under Charles VIII) moved in this new individualist direction.[29] The king became, particularly under Francis I, the Machiavellian prince of *virtù*, the man who relied on reason for his actions: in Francis's case, action meant making, not discovering, law.

In the old system, in which the judge discovered the law, the judge held pride of place; Hugh Capet's seal showed him as a judge, not as a fighter. By the sixteenth century, French practice and theory shifted the emphasis of kingship, of law, and, by extension, of the political order itself. The new *sovereign* king – of l'Hôpital, Bodin or Richelieu – defined himself as a lawmaker. Francis I took the necessary first step: he carried out the plans of Charles VII to write down the customary laws of every bailiwick in the kingdom. He then issued a wide range of edicts to fill in the gaps in those customs. At the theoretical level, l'Hôpital and Bodin spelled out the new order: l'Hôpital told the Parlement in 1561 that "the true office of a king . . . is to consider the times and to augment or mitigate the laws accordingly." Bodin summed up the changes in one of his most famous sentences: "la premiere marque du Prince souverain, c'est la puissance de donner loy à tous en general, et à chacun en particulier."[30]

---

[28] D. Dessert, *Argent, pouvoir et société au grand siècle* (Paris, 1984), on the special importance of *cash* in this period. On financiers and cash, F. Bayard, *Le monde des financiers au XVIIe siècle* (Paris, 1988) and "Manière d'habiter des financiers de la première moitié du XVIIe siècle," *XVIIe Siècle*, 162 (1989): 53–65, on one particular aspect of that life in Paris.

[29] On changes in the coronation oath, see R. Jackson, *Vive le Roi! A History of the French Coronation from Charles V to Charles X* (Chapel Hill, 1984), 26, 37–40.

[30] J. Bodin, *Les six livres de la république* (Paris, 1583, Geneva reimpression of 1961), 221.

That definition of sovereignty, shifting away from judging and toward legislating, weakened seigneurs and strengthened the king. The definition assumed equality rather than the customary inequality before the law. These contradictions on equality and law meant that Ancien Régime France contained characteristics of both a state based on law binding on all, which lent itself to grouping by class because it denied the efficacy of the privileges on which the society of orders rested, and of a state based on custom and contract (and, by extension, efficacy of privilege), which lent itself to a society of orders. Despite this shift in the king's chief function from *interpreter* to *maker* of law, he continued to define himself in terms of a relationship to law, for which he therefore maintained the greatest respect.

The king's relationship to the law was the central reality of absolutism. Absolutism was not a system of government nor was it the simple process of state building: absolutism was the belief that the king had absolute ability to make *positive* law.[31] The monarchy of the seventeenth and eighteenth centuries was "absolutist" only in the sense that it constantly sought to rule France by means of promulgated laws, thus placing political discourse squarely in the area of unimpeded royal authority. The systematic undermining of alternative centers of authority, be they seigneurial or municipal, formed part of that process. The king did not want to destroy these elites or to eliminate their power; he could not want such a thing, because his power rested on their power. He wanted their power to emanate from him, rather than from some independent source. In the fifteenth and sixteenth centuries, the king systematically removed the three great attributes of sovereignty from all other French authorities, save the Church. He eliminated their power to tax; he eliminated their ability to render sovereign judgments; and he usurped lawmaking ability by changing the definition of law. In the seventeenth century, he often, as in Brittany, relocated the legitimation source of their power; for example, the real

---

[31] R. Bonney, "Absolutism: What's in a Name?" *French History* 1 (1987): 93–117 and Bonney, *L'absolutisme* (Paris, 1989). On absolutism's sixteenth-century origins, two brief introductions to major positions on these issues are found in G. Pagès, "Essai sur l'évolution des institutions administratives en France du commencement du XVIe siècle à la fin du XVIIe siècle," *Revue d'Histoire Moderne* (1935): 8–57, 113–38, and M. Antoine, "L'administration centrale des finances en France du XVIe siècle au XVIIIe siècle," in *Histoire comparée de l'administration. IVe–XVIIIe siècles* (Munich, 1980). My thanks to Bernard Barbiche for a copy of this article and for sharing his thoughts on this matter. J. Russell Major's views on the "renaissance monarchy" were first set out in "The Renaissance Monarchy: A Contribution to the Periodization of History," *Emory University Quarterly* (1956): 112–24. Major's grand synthesis is his *Representative Government in Early Modern France* (New Haven, 1980). R. Mettam, *Power and Faction in Louis XIV's France*, (London, 1988), 34–41, has a fine synopsis of the distinction between "absolute monarchy" and "absolutism." On the issue of the king's subordination to divine or natural law, Bodin is unequivocal: "la puissance absolue des Princes et seigneuries souveraines, ne s'entend aucunement aux loix de Dieu et de nature." Elsewhere, he states: "tous les Princes de la terre sont subjects aux loix de Dieu, et de nature, et à plusieurs loix humaines communes à tous peuples" (*République*, 133 and 131).

police power of Nantes shifted from the mayor to the provost and seneschal after 1600. The seneschal *was* often the mayor but his police power now came from an unmistakeably royal source rather than from the more ambiguous municipal one.[32]

Contemporary elites accepted the king's absolute ability to make law because they believed it guaranteed order, that is, both property and inequality.[33] The king remained within the framework of law itself, because that framework included, indeed rested upon, divine (in some later formulations, natural) law. The king had one main restriction on his freedom of action: his obligation to respect divine law and thus contracts, most particularly the property of his subjects. This restriction comforted the French elites because the Decalogue includes full respect for contracts, and French society rested on a mass of contracts.[34] The Estates of Brittany well understood the importance of contract protection: they sought, and obtained, a written contract with the king to cover each grant of tax money. That the king's power was both absolute and limited is only, as Nannerl Keohane has suggested, an apparent paradox.[35]

Bodin's definition of kingship satisfied the ruling elites of early modern French society. The strong king preserved order – above all, property. Bodin unequivocally stated that the king has no right to interfere with the private property of his subjects.[36] Ordinary lawyers, such as Yves Laurente of Quimperlé, concurred:

Le conseil des deffandeurs ne voulant donner aucunes bornes ni limites à l'aucthoritté des Roys on demeure d'accord que s'ils en usent de toute leur absollue puissance que sans doute Ils ne puissent tant sur le bien et la vie de leurs subjects mais quelque pouvoir qu'ils ayent Ils n'en ont Jamais agy de cette manière ont sçaist que dans la France les Roys y ont tousjours traité leurs subjects avec justice qu'ils ont laissé à leurs subjects les moyens d'augmenter leurs biens et leurs fortunes sans les leur oster par aucune viollance ... Ils n'ostent pas au particullier la pocession de ses biens ...[37]

Individual members of given groups suffered in the process of the king establishing positive law, but other individual members of those same groups benefited. The king did not strike out wildly at privilege, seeking to replace one elite with another, or cleverly playing off one elite (the bourgeoisie) against another (the nobles). Early modern Frenchmen debated how best to adapt to

---

[32] J. Collins, "Police Authority and Local Politics at Nantes, 1550–1680," a paper given at the Annual Meeting of the Western Society for French History, 1990.

[33] Hence the ultimate confusion of the two roles was proprietary dynasticism, on which H. Rowan, *The King's State. Proprietary Dynasticism in Early Modern France* (New Brunswick, 1980).

[34] R. Doucet, *Les institutions de la France au XVIe siècle* (Paris, 1948), 35–6.

[35] N. Keohane, *Philosophy and the State in France. The Renaissance to the Enlightenment* (Princeton, 1980), 26. Keohane also has an excellent discussion on Bodin and property on pp. 69–73.

[36] Bodin, *République*, Book V, ch. 2, even doubts the wisdom of confiscating the property of condemned criminals. The key passage on property is found in Book I, ch. 8 (140): "il n'est en la puissance de Prince du monde, de lever impost à son plaisir sur le peuple, non plus que prendre le bien d'autruy."   [37] AD Finistère, 5 H 37.

changing circumstances. The state needed a great deal of money, primarily to pay for military expenses (including debt). Local elites wanted order: political, religious, social, economic, and moral. Like it or not, the king provided the best, indeed the only, means of obtaining such order.[38]

Order could mean many things. It could mean protection of the status quo with its hierarchy of estates. It could mean simple obedience to the state, which those same estates often perceived to be violating their sense of the "real" order. Different members of one group and different groups had different ideas about the "real" tradition and about the meaning of order. The king's new order – his legislative role, his effort to rule outside of contracts – violated some basic principles of the old order.[39]

French elites had achieved a compromise definition of order by the time of Louis XIV. First, order meant the protection of property. The rising social elements improved their standing through the accumulation of property, so respect for property satisfied them. The existing social inequality rested essentially on an unequal distribution of (landed) property; respect for that unequal division of property protected the landlords' most vital interest as well. Early modern France had several forms of property, one essentially similar to our modern notion of private property, another what we might call feudal, still a third that belonged to the community. The most powerful members of society possessed both property in our sense (usually land) and feudal property, such as lordship rights. Their feudal property established them as the ruling elite of society, so the rising importance of private property, particularly commercial wealth, threatened the social status quo. Even for the old ruling elite, the private property element of their income came increasingly to dominate over the feudal property one. Almost all nobles received the bulk of their income from simple land rent, not from feudal dues or obligations; moreover, the percentage of income coming from land rent rose continuously.

Order also meant the preservation of patriarchy. The state would do everything in its power to protect male dominance of society. French society had long been patriarchal but underlying social and economic forces combined to offer new threats to the traditional patriarchy. Families weakened *vis-à-vis* individuals and some women demanded more rights – to choose husbands, to control property, to run businesses. The French state passed one law after another between 1550 and 1700 in an effort to prevent these women from obtaining their goals. These laws generally gave fathers (male guardians) much

---

[38] Beik, *Absolutism and Society*, explains how this process worked in Languedoc (see esp. ch. 12, 13 and conclusion).

[39] S. Collins, *From Divine Cosmos to Sovereign State. An Intellectual History of Consciousness and the Idea of Order in Renaissance England* (New York, Oxford, 1989), ch. 1 and 4, on similar changes in England. M. Raeff, *The Well-Ordered Police State* (New York, 1982), discusses the theoretical impact of this ideology, although his specific points of reference are eighteenth-century German states and Russia.

greater authority within families and removed women's economic rights but women systematically got around the new restrictions, as we will see.

These two elements, property and control of women, went hand in hand. Those who belonged to the real civil society had both; indeed, they often obtained their critical mass of property at marriage. The people who mattered in society, the real society, called themselves the *gens de bien*. Who were, or rather who were not, *gens de bien*? The boundary line was the small shopkeepers and the artisan masters of the towns, the ploughmen of the villages.

To the elites, the urban people below the level of the guild masters had no real place in the social order: such people did not participate, as a corporate group, in official processions.[40] Elite descriptions of revolts reinforce this failure to make social distinctions among the lower classes. Elite observers always described the crowds involved in urban revolts as the *canaille* or the *gens de néant*, as *inconnus* – those foreign to the community. Those prosecuted for participation were journeymen, small masters, and others with an actual tie to the community. The dissonance demonstrates the social perspective of elites but it also shows us the frontier of order.

That frontier lay along the dividing line between the small shopkeepers, the artisan masters, and the laboring classes (both journeymen and day laborers). The shopkeepers and artisan masters were the decisive group in the maintenance or breakdown of urban order; in the countryside, the ploughmen played the same role. When these groups upheld order, as they usually did, order prevailed; when they opposed the existing state of affairs, order collapsed. Little wonder that the elites should direct their accusations at the "unknowns" and the propertyless. Elites did not wish to admit even the possibility that the small holders had abandoned the party of order. Artisan masters and shopkeepers felt themselves to be *gens de bien*; elites rarely regarded them as such, yet relied on them to protect the universe of the worthy people, of those with property.

The key distinction lay between the *gens de néant* and the *gens de bien*: those who held property belonged to the community – they were *gens de bien*. The term plays on the dual meaning of *bien/biens* (good/goods): these people were literally the worthy people, but the overtone implied by the plural (*biens*) is that they were also those with property. The connotation is all the stronger because the antitheses of the *gens de bien* were the *gens de néant* – those with nothing, that is,

---

[40] P. Benedict, *Rouen during the Wars of Religion* (Cambridge, 1981), 1–7, for a delightful description of the society of orders on parade. The complexity of the problem is neatly demonstrated in R. Darnton, "A Bourgeois puts his World in Order: The City as Text," in *The Great Cat Massacre and Other Essays* (New York, 1984), 107–44. For the views of other contemporaries, see: J. Ménétra, *Journal de ma vie*, ed. D. Roche, (Paris, 1982), trans. as *Journal of My Life* (New York, 1986) and, for a more theoretical presentation, C. Loyseau, *Cinq livres du droit des offices; les seigneuries; les ordres* (Paris, 1613, 1644). Roland Mousnier has long relied on Loyseau as the theoretical cornerstone of his arguments about the nature of Ancien Régime society. See, most recently, his remarks in *Institutions*, I, 14–24 and 499–524.

without *biens*.[41] In Spain, too, as the proverb cited in Lazarillo de Tormes informs us, one should seek out the society of the *buenos* to become like them. The original meaning was, of course, purely moral, but Lazarillo takes *buenos* to mean those with earthly goods.[42]

In France, the social order revolved around this distinction over property. The *gens de néant*, because they had no property, did not fully belong to the community: hence the term *inconnus* to describe them. Every element of French life revolved on this most basic distinction. In court, witnesses had to be "worthy of faith" (*digne de foi*); in the village assembly, as in the communal assembly of the towns, what mattered was the opinion of the "plus saine et meilleure partie des habitans." In a literal sense, this meant the wisest and best of the inhabitants; in a practical sense, it meant those with the most property (here again, the comparative term "best" brings to mind its simple equivalent, good, and, by extension, goods). The focus on property relations cannot obscure the fact that Ancien Régime society had many layers of political and social conflict. First, the centrality of the distinction propertied/propertyless meant that the deepest political and social problems often represented a conflict between those two groups. Second, the dissonance between the economic order and the legal structure of society meant that some political conflicts opposed different orders rather than broad economic groups (such as the propertyless) or even more narrowly defined classes. Third, we can clearly distinguish local power struggles, in which a coalition of members from various orders and classes allied against a similar multi-class/multi-order coalition. These clientage conflicts remind us that practical political conflicts, then as now, often pitted social coalitions against one another, rather than bloc class or order groups.[43] Fourth, ordinary people had a conception of how society *ought* to function. When it did not they protested, sometimes violently, in what might best be termed populist politics.

The changing roles of women and the determinative function of age make gender and age essential categories of analysis about early modern French society, categories that further complicate any analysis beginning with classes and orders.[44] Women, as we shall see below, played a very prominent role in

[41] My thanks here to Mack Holt, whose paper on "Wine, Community and Reformation in Sixteenth-Century Burgundy," given to the D.C. Area Ancien Régime Study Group, has so helped me to clarify my conception of the category of *gens de bien*.

[42] A connection pointed out to me by one of my students, Elena Foley, in her excellent seminar paper on Lazarillo.

[43] S. Kettering, *Patrons, Brokers, and Clients in Seventeenth-Century France* (Oxford, 1986), esp. 3–39, which contains a very useful discussion of Ancien Régime patronage networks as an example of a larger historical phenomena. Mettam, *Power and Faction in Louis XIV's France*, offers a penetrating analysis of the impact of factional politics on royal policy and capacity for action.

[44] On gender redefined, see, for example, F. Poullain de la Barre, *Of the Equality of the Two Sexes* (Detroit, 1987, reimpression of English translation of 1663); on age, D. Troyansky, *Old Age in the Old Regime* (Ithaca, 1989), which argues for a dramatic shifts in attitudes toward old age in the eighteenth century.

Breton politics, in the economy, in social relations, and in popular unrest. They typically shared the interests of their male partners (husband or other family members) but they had special roles and interests as well. Age also determined one's relationship to the system. The young, particularly those between 15 and 28, had fewer ties to the system because they rarely had any property. Before we ascribe a class basis to conflict between the journeyman and the master, we must remember that the 25-year-old journeyman's social place reflected his age as often as his class. These young men were much more rowdy than their elders. The relative toleration of that behavior shows the converse of youthful rowdiness, which formed part of the system, not a threat to it. A crowd of journeymen and day laborers (most of them under 30) was a nuisance; a crowd of journeymen, day laborers, master artisans, and shopkeepers was an insurrection.

The small shopkeepers, the day laborers and journeymen, and the master artisans made up 80 percent (or more) of the urban population, yet they had little to say about the manner in which society operated. They had some negative input – riot, rebellion, tax strikes – but very few mechanisms for positive action. The (young) laborer class lived on the margins of society, in fairly constant conflict with it. The small occupiers had one foot in society and one foot out; their assistance could turn the dissatisfaction of the laborers into a local crisis. The problem for the forces of order in early modern society was to prevent a general alliance of these groups against the ruling elite. When order broke down we see an alliance of these groups and, usually, of one (or more) segment(s) of the elite against the existing political order. The authorities of the day called this effort to preserve order the "police." At its simplest level, "police" meant the administration of a given area, yet we must take care to consider the full contemporary meaning of the term "police" as elaborated by early modern writers and civil servants. They took such administration to be not only political, but social, economic, and *moral*. Historians often overlook this final element, yet early modern authorities thought it the most important. As Nicolas de la Mare put it in his *Traicté de la police* (1705), "the Police includes in its objective all those things that serve as a foundation and a rule to the societies that men have established among themselves." He added that "Religion is the first and principal, one might even add the unique object of the Police."[45]

Breton authorities felt the same way. A 1721 pamphlet on the "Police Générale de la Ville, Fauxbourgs, Banlieue et Comté de Nantes" began with a prohibition against swearing and "blaspheming the Holy Name of God, of the Virgin Mary, and of the Saints." Seven of the first eight articles concerned moral issues, most of them relating to behavior on Sundays and holy days. The pamphlet regulated a wide variety of activities, such as latrines, butchering,

---

[45] N. de la Mare, *Traicté de la police* (Paris, 1705), 267.

selling of various products, and even the price of wine.[46] The authorities knew full well where morality broke down: the fourth article demanded that cabaret and tavern keepers prominently post the prohibition against blasphemers.

Civil society fought the forces of disorder in the taverns because public and private space overlapped there. To its customers, the tavern formed the very center of the community; to the authorities, the tavern meant debauchery, moral decay, and potential political discontent.[47] In 1650, when the journeymen tailors of Nantes plotted a strike, they met at the tavern of the Croix Blanche. The police records of Nantes are filled with visits to taverns for collection of unpaid taxes and for violations of the prohibition against sales of wine during Sunday high mass. The same people always filled these taverns: unmarried men between the ages of 15 and 30. The police sought always to keep such men under surveillance. When these single young men allied with the shopkeepers and masters, as in the case of insurrection on the rue Saint-Léonard in Nantes (1667), the situation transcended the simple case of police; it became a breakdown of order itself.

The political order of early modern France rested on property, especially landed property. The landless found this system irrelevant in one way, oppressive in another. Their discontent was a constant of the system; the purpose of the police was to keep the discontent manageable by denying the laboring class any allies. To look at it from another perspective, the purpose of the system was to keep the critical mass with some stake in the system – the small occupiers and the ploughmen – sufficiently satisfied with the system to support it. Most of the time, the police did so quite effectively. The problem for the historian is not one of classes versus orders but rather one of classes and order. How did the forces of order maintain the existing class system? The remainder of this book examines the province of Brittany in the period 1532–1675 in order to offer an answer to that question.

ORGANIZATIONAL FRAMEWORK

The particularism of Brittany remains a historiographical commonplace, yet particularism, not homogeneity, served as the rule in early modern France. The *pays d'Etats* held about 40 percent of the French population and the *pays d'élection* were by no means the homogenous mass they are often made out to be. Most French provinces, even parts of provinces, had individualized tax systems and local customary law. Brittany had two key differences: 1) it had a specific contractual agreement (signed in 1532) to which it could legitimately claim the

[46] Pamphlet on "Police générale de la ville, fauxbourgs, banlieue et comté de Nantes," published by Nicolas Verger at Nantes in 1721. Copy found in AM Nantes, FF 119.
[47] T. Brennan, *Public Drinking and Popular Culture in Eighteenth-Century Paris* (Princeton, 1988), on the important role of the tavern in community life.

king was bound; and 2) its collection of provincial institutions – Parlement, the Chamber of Accounts, the Estates, a special fiscal system – provided it with an exceptionally strong defense against royal initiatives. After 1628 the province had the further advantage of being well removed from the main sectors of military activities, so it suffered less from troops than most other areas – a state of affairs frequently cited by the king in his demands for higher taxes in the 1660s.[48]

Granting that Brittany was more particularist (and better able to defend that particularism) than other provinces, we can see that it had basic structures very similar to those of other provinces. The landlords formed the ruling class in Brittany, as everywhere in France. Brittany's public opinion came from the same groups so identified by Villeroy in a 1614 memoir to Marie de Médicis about the nation as a whole: "great nobles, officers of the Crown, governors of provinces, gentlemen and lords of all conditions, as well as the Parlements, the other sovereign courts, and royal officials, along with the magistrates and corporate organizations of the towns."[49]

Nobles, royal officials, the upper levels of the corporate structure of the towns – in order to accomplish anything, the government needed the support of these people. In order to maintain their local power, these people needed the support of the government. It was a singularly convenient marriage. Brittany offers an ideal province in which to study both the consonance of interests and the major discordancy: the conflict over division of peasant production. The landlords wanted low direct taxes because their tenants (and, in regions of *métayage*, they themselves) paid most of the money, yet some of them (the most powerful) also depended on royal payments for a substantial portion of their income.[50] The ideal solution was to make someone else pay the taxes.

Brittany proved exceptional only in the degree to which the landlord class could protect its interests. This exceptionalism provides us with an excellent opportunity to observe the basic outlines of the relationship between that elite and the Crown, because they more openly worked out their conflicts and because the Breton elite so effectively preserved its position: low direct taxation, high retail wine duties, and unusually harsh seigneurialism. Brittany followed a different political path from most French provinces in the seventeenth century; it also followed a different economic path in the eighteenth. The two are related:

---

[48] Letter to de la Meilleraye, 27 November 1651. ADIV, C 2777. "I can say that there is no other province in the kingdom, nor any other in any of the kingdoms of Europe, which has been succored or is rich like theirs." The king went on to relate this prosperity to the absence of troops (both the enemy and his own forces).

[49] J. Sawyer, *Printed Poison* (Berkeley, 1990), 39.

[50] J. Collins, *Fiscal Limits of Absolutism: Direct Taxation in Seventeenth-Century France* (Berkeley, 1988), ch. 3. See also ch. 4–5 below. Brenner emphasizes such income as a major stake of the aristocracy in the absolutist state. Beik, *Absolutism and Society*, Tables 11 and 19, gives examples for Languedoc.

the one-sided resolution of the political conflict in Brittany was a significant element in the economic catastrophe of the period 1680–1780. The taxing policy of the Estates, so wedded to the interests of the landlords, provided one key factor in the growing imbalance of the province's economy and in its collapse between 1660 and 1690, after a century of highly diversified growth. The higher rents, combined with higher royal taxes after 1625, severely cut into peasant capital stocks. The fall off in peasant investment probably caused the dramatic economic downturn so evident after 1660.[51]

Brittany (like France itself) consisted of a patchwork of local economic zones; these Breton zones often had closer ties to other parts of France or to foreign countries than they did to one another.[52] Brittany had a more diverse economy than other French provinces, with highly fertile grain regions, a broad manufacturing base, a wine-growing area, widespread livestock rearing, an extensive fishing fleet, its own supply of salt, and considerable foreign trade. Chapter 1 describes these Breton economic zones, and their evolution in response to the policies of the elite in the sixteenth and seventeenth centuries. It also provides definitions of the different economic classes of early modern Brittany (and France).

Chapter 2 shifts to the social system of the province: patterns of interaction and dominance. Here again, we find many similarities to France as a whole: considerable professional and geographic endogamy; ritualized networks of godparenting; extensive and elaborate systems of deference and patronage. The seigneurs and *sieurs* dominated these systems and, with them, political life. In chapter 3, we examine the institutional framework of political life, particularly the way in which the king raised money. Here we can see one of the major differences between Brittany and the rest of France: Brittany had very few financial offices, so that mercantile families could not use such offices to share in the expansion of royal power. In Brittany, financial offices rarely provided a step toward nobility; they were an investment, or rather part of a pattern of investment in the profit-making activities of the government. The other exceptional areas – above all, Languedoc, Burgundy, and Provence – preserved similarly particularist financial systems that enabled their local ruling elite to maintain its position. Burgundy and Brittany also had the two severest seigneurial regimes in France.[53]

---

[51] The only exceptions to the economic decline were the linen trade, which remained prosperous into the 1680s, the cod fisheries, and the colonial trade.

[52] Nantes had very close ties to Spain (prior to 1636), to Holland, to Hamburg, and, to a lesser extent, England. Saint-Malo and Morlaix traded primarily with England, Bordeaux, and, to some degree, Spain. On Nantais trade, see: J. Collins, "The Role of Atlantic France in the Baltic Trade: Dutch Traders and Polish Grain at Nantes, 1625–1675," *Journal of European Economic History* 13 (2) (Fall 1984): 239–89.

[53] T. J. A. Le Goff, *Vannes and its Region* (Oxford, 1981); J. Meyer, *La noblesse bretonne au XVIIIe siècle* (Paris, 1966), 2 vols.; Gallet, *Seigneurie bretonne*; Sée, "Les classes rurales." On Burgundy, see the conflicting views of P. de Saint-Jacob, *Les paysans de la Bourgogne du nord au dernier siècle de*

From the institutional, we move to the political: the role of the Estates from the middle of the sixteenth century until 1680. Chapter 4 covers the Estates up to 1626, chapter 5 the Estates of the period 1626–80. The 1626 meeting, with Louis XIII present, marks a convenient dividing point: annual meetings soon ceased, the wine tax went up permanently, and Breton clientage shifted into Richelieu's network after he became governor (in 1630). The Breton pattern here is entirely typical of France as a whole: a significant change in the king's relationship to each *pays d'Etats* and a massive increase in taxation between 1625 and 1634.[54]

The Estates provided a key mechanism by which the landlords protected their class (and order) interests. The main class interest was low direct taxation: regular Breton direct taxes scarcely changed from 1551 until 1643, when they doubled (although individual assessments remained extremely low even then). The Estates taxed wine, raising the levy from 2.5 livres to 40 livres per pipe of imported wine between 1588 and 1641. They avoided taxing goods produced in the western countryside – grain, linen, hides – and prevented royal taxes on the latter two. In return for this protection, the peasants of the west had to submit to a seigneurial regime of great harshness: *corvées*, *champarts*, rapidly rising rents and entry fees (after 1620), and the widespread use of the *domaine congéable*, all enforced by the combined seigneurial and royal judicial systems.[55] Chapter 6 offers an overall perspective on the division of the tax burden among areas of the province, among parishes, and among ordinary people. The chapter examines both taxation raised for the Estates (primarily on retail wine sales) and all other forms of royal taxation, most notably the hearth tax.

Chapter 7 brings us to the problem of order, taken in the sense of the maintenance of everyday stability and of the prevention of massive civil disruption. First, we will focus on the methods of social and moral police, and on

l'ancien régime (Paris, 1960) and H. Root, *Peasants and King in Burgundy. Agrarian Foundations of French Absolutism* (Berkeley, 1987). J. Bart, *La liberté ou la terre* (Dijon, 1985), provides extensive evidence of the survival of serfdom in eighteenth-century Burgundy. In the seventeenth century, serfdom was a dominant social and economic reality in many parts of the province (a conclusion I reach based on extensive use of the tax records and analyses of notarial documents in Series C and 4 E 49, 12–15 of the AD Côte d'Or).

[54] On Languedoc, Beik, *Absolutism and Society*, ch. 11; on Provence, R. Pillorget, *Les mouvements insurrectionnels en Provence de 1595 à 1715* (Paris, 1975) ; Collins, *Fiscal Limits*, ch. 2–3.

[55] Here disagreeing with Gallet, *La seigneurie bretonne*, who believes that the peasants had a relatively light burden. The peasant living under *domaine congéable* paid the landlord one-third of the gross, but had to pay all other charges (seed and tithe included) from his own share. Given seed ratios of 4:1 or 5:1 and a tithe rate of about 8 percent, these two items (shared with the lord in *métayage* systems) would consume 28–33 percent of the net crop. The peasant would therefore get 100 (= gross) minus 33, minus 28 to 33, or return, after straight rent, tithe and seed of 34 to 39 percent. In *métayage*, with the same assumptions, the peasant would get 100 minus 28–33, divided by two, or 34.5 to 36 percent. The real difference came in taxes and upkeep: in *métayage*, the landlord shared in these costs; in the *domaine congéable*, he or she did not. Overall, therefore, the *domaine congéable* system was more onerous, and became progressively worse as the direct tax burden increased.

the population's manner of expressing disgruntlement, short of rebellion. The authorities of the day lived in mortal fear of the lower classes; the obsession with a society of orders was one method of trying to get the lower "orders" to behave in a manner deemed suitable by their social "superiors." The extensive moral police of the lower classes, a moral police intimately related, as we have seen in the quotation from de la Mare, to the elite's perspective of the maintenance of order, formed one element in the protection of the existing system. Political conflict in Ancien Régime France usually took place at the margins of society, in the everyday relationship between the forces of order and those viewed as a threat to that order. The behavior of individuals in non-normative situations, such as carnivals or cat massacres, can show us the underlying social tensions present but less visible in daily life; such tensions could lead to open rebellion, as at Romans, but they usually did not.[56] The second part of chapter 7 examines the great Bonnets Rouges revolt of 1675. Breton distinctiveness shows in the timing of its great revolt, so long after the other peasant rebellions, and in its uniquely strong anti-seigneurial elements.

The overall impression of Brittany is that of a province completely dominated by the landlords. In Brittany, as in Languedoc, the absolute monarchy was an unfailing ally of the landed nobility (whether military or judicial, seigneur or *sieur* made little difference). Beik is right: the compromise of Louis XIV was that he agreed to give the landed elites in the *pays d'Etats* precisely what they wanted – order, money, power. They, in turn, gave him money and obedience.[57] In so saying, however, we must still ask: what was the meaning of this bargain? If the absolutist monarchy was not the last stage of feudalism, if the absolutist state was not a renewed repressive and extractive apparatus of the landlord class, what was it?

If we look at the *pays d'élection*, we can see, with Pagès, Mousnier, and others, the king allied with the mercantile bourgeoisie (i.e., their offshoot in the financial bureaucracy) against the "aristocracy."[58] Does this mean the king and the bourgeoisie allied to break the power of the nobles in the *pays d'élection* but that the king and the nobles allied to prevent the rise of the bourgeoisie in the *pays d'Etats*? Such a policy is too Machiavellian even for a master such as Richelieu.

The contrast between the *pays d'Etats* and the *pays d'élection* demonstrates the conflicting elements of a state based both on law and on custom. The king sought to rule according to promulgated law; because he had an unlimited right to make such laws, elites generally opposed this policy. They demanded that he

---

[56] Darnton, "The Great Cat Massacre of the Rue Saint-Severin," in *The Great Cat Massacre*; N. Davis, *Society and Culture in Early-Modern France* (Stanford, 1975); E. Le Roy Ladurie, *Carnival in Romans* (New York, 1974), in which a carnival turned into a struggle for political control of Romans.   [57] Beik, *Absolutism and Society*, 331–5.

[58] In one article, Mousnier even goes so far as to use the title, "Monarchie contre aristocratie dans la France du XVIIe siècle," *XVIIe Siècle* (1956): 277–81.

rule according to contractual agreements, which did protect them from arbitrary behavior. The distinction shows us precisely what was revolutionary about the political discourse of the eve of the Revolution itself: in 1789 elites, as they demonstrated in their *cahiers*, had accepted the idea that a society based on positive law, and in which they had a permanent legislative body to limit the king's ability to make law, was a better way to defend their interests than a society based on custom.[59] Although the focus of divine sanctification for the social order had shifted from the society of orders itself to the person of the king, the social order of the Ancien Régime remained legitimate in the eyes of elites because, even in that modified form, the sacral nature of monarchy protected them. The desacralization of the monarchy removed that form of protection and created a profound unease among French elites in the second half of the eighteenth century.

The nobles shared power through the military; the legal class shared power in the royal judiciary; the mercantile bourgeoisie shared power in the financial bureaucracy. Is it so surprising that in those areas, such as Languedoc or Brittany, in which there was no financial bureaucracy, the king's power rested primarily on the other two legs of the triad? The Breton mercantile elite's lack of levers of power made it relatively useless to the king as an ally: the king allied with the strong, not the weak. The weak political position of the merchants was obvious throughout the sixteenth and seventeenth centuries: in the early sixteenth century, when the towns could not keep control of the *billots*; in the 1570s, when the first two Estates overruled the Third in a major tax controversy; in 1613, when the nobles got the king to go along with their request that the Estates had to approve all town requests for levying taxes before the towns could ask the king for his (mandatory) approval; in the general pattern of Breton taxation. The overall weakness of the merchants as a group, however, did not preclude the accumulation of great power by individual merchants, indeed the relatively small, weak financial apparatus of provinces such as Brittany or Languedoc may have facilitated the rise of particularly powerful financiers such as André Ruiz, Gilles Ruellan, or the Pennautier family.

Even the effort to rule according to promulgated royal acts required the cooperation of some members of the elites. The king and elites resolved the apparent contradiction between expanding royal power and maintaining local elite control by using each of the three groups – military nobles, legal men, and merchants – to control an element of the expanding state apparatus. The massive growth of taxation certainly increased the power of the third group, but much of the revenue produced by the system went to the other two.

The effect of this consolidation of power by the existing elite, within the newly

---

[59] Here disagreeing with F. Furet (among others) in the reading of the "revolutionary" content of the *cahiers*. I would argue that the insistence of the *cahiers* on rule by law promulgated by a *legislative body* (not the king) and on a constitution was a political revolution of the first order.

invigorated structure of central government, was to reinforce the position of the nobility and the legal class. Given the overwhelming preeminence of agricultural production in the French economy, any other form of political power structure would have failed. The fundamental dichotomy of interests between the state as the defender of the class interests of the landlords and the state as a corporate entity unto itself is clearest with respect to direct taxation. The state and the landlords both wanted more of the surplus value produced by the means of production (that is, the cash stocks of the peasants); that the state wanted this money primarily to protect the political and social interests of the landlords did not make the landlords any more willing to endure the immediate economic loss entailed by higher direct taxation.

Brenner and Beik both point to the considerable income nobles received from the state (see also below for Breton examples) as evidence that the state was a mechanism for an extra-economic means of extraction of surplus value from the peasants.[60] They argue that the old feudal mechanism had lost its effectiveness, so that the noble landlords turned to the absolute state as an alternative means of obtaining these resources. Such nobles had three ways to obtain income in early modern France: 1) land rent; 2) feudal income (*banalités*, death and transfer fees, etc.); and 3) money from the state. To the extent that direct taxation funded source number 3, it directly reduced income from source 1 (and, to a lesser extent, source 2). Tenants of landlords paid the vast majority of French direct taxation (certainly two-thirds or more); the largest peasant taxpayers were often *métayers*. The available evidence suggests that the (noble) landlord paid half of the *tailles* on a *métairie*: did he get as much return in payments from the state as he lost in paying out the *tailles* (or in reduced rent, adjusted to allow the peasant to pay the *tailles*)?[61] The privileged powerful few did, but the vast majority almost certainly did not. The evidence from the noble *cahiers* of 1614 (or 1649) and of the various provincial Estates makes it quite clear that the nobles themselves did not think they were getting an equal return. The interposition of the state in the transferal of this money to the nobles also greatly reduced landlord independence.

The three forms of income competed with each other. *All landlords* opposed higher direct taxation because it reduced their income from land rent. Seigneurs also opposed higher direct taxes because taxes reduced feudal income. *Sieurs* objected to feudal dues because they reduced land rent. There were three sets of interests; the argument that the state system of direct taxation was simply a reorganized mechanism for transferring, by extra-economic means, the wealth produced by the peasantry to the landlords ignores the fundamental economic

---

[60] Beik, *Absolutism and Society*, conclusion; Brenner, "Agrarian Class Structure," in *Brenner Debate*, 55.
[61] Collins, *Fiscal Limits*, ch. 4. Philip Hoffman has told me that his research on *taille* rolls in the Lyonnais has found the same phenomenon there.

reality that lower direct taxation would mean that these same landlords could expand their capitalist income (based on land rent itself) without the slightest need of state intervention. In fact, Breton landlords did precisely that in the first six decades of the seventeenth century. Although feudal dues provided a very useful supplement to seigneurial income, the largest share of noble income came from a "capitalist" source: land rent. Furthermore, the percentage of income they received from rent *grew* substantially between 1550 and 1650.[62] The landlord, whether seigneur or *sieur*, was, in class terms, primarily a landowning capitalist. Seigneurs had an additional form of property, feudal rights, but feudalities created more political and social than economic differences with other landlords. They were an order issue, not a class one.

On the main political issue, the maintenance of order, the king and the local elites shared the belief that protecting the apparently stable, sedentary world of the ploughmen, the corporate society of the towns, and the upper classes from the unstable, mobile world swirling around them was the main purpose of the state. The contrast between the two societies created the obsession of early modern authorities with the problem of order. When one faction of the elite became dissatisfied with the local system of order, that order collapsed (often in a manner that shifted local political control to the rebellious faction).[63] Local elites took a different attitude toward the rebels when they threatened elite political and social control. In Brittany we can see the distinction between the urban revolts of 1675, aimed at royal tax bureaux, and the rural risings, aimed at the landlords and legal men. One of the key elements in changing elite attitudes toward the former was the widespread belief that it had spawned the latter.

The main threat to order came not from rebellion but from passive resistance and "disobedience": refusal to pay taxes or to perform *corvées*, smuggling, collusion with tax fraud, a general sullenness against authority. One of Louis XIV's most important acts to strengthen the central government was to admit its limitations and to reduce drastically the level of direct taxation (which was then paid in full). For all of his absolutist rhetoric, Louis XIV did not threaten but *enhanced* elite control of local affairs; he sought to obtain elite cooperation in advancing their mutual interests.[64] To that end, he spent locally a large share of local tax revenues: local elites got much of this money in pensions, in remuneration for military and civil offices, and in interest payments.

---

[62] Examples in Gallet, *La seigneurie bretonne*.
[63] S. Kettering, *Judicial Politics and Urban Revolt in Seventeenth-Century France, the Parlement of Aix, 1629–59* (Princeton, 1978), offers some excellent Provençal examples.
[64] On the revision of absolutism, R. Bonney, *Political Change in France under Richelieu and Mazarin* (Oxford, 1976); Beik, *Absolutism and Society*; Collins, *Fiscal Limits*. The most extreme statement of the anti-absolutist position is that of Mettam, *Power and Faction*. On the importance of clientage, see especially Kettering, *Patrons, Clients, and Brokers*. The most intriguing element in Kettering's work is the contrast between the processes she describes and those described by Neuschel, who, in (partial) contrast to Kettering, sees considerable independence of action by

27

Classes, estates, and order in early modern Brittany

Orders or classes – either is too limiting, too narrow for a serious examination of early modern French society. We must also abandon several other historiographical paradigms that are intimately related to the society of orders framework. The acceptance of the idea that France was, above all, a society of orders, makes it easier to believe that, prior to 1750, France was a "stable, sedentary society" and an "absolutist" state. It was neither, insofar as we use the current descriptions of those paradigms. By expanding our categories of analysis to include gender and age, as well as more carefully defined classes, we can use new evidence to question some of our most fundamental assumptions about the nature of early modern French politics and society.

When I began this project, I took as given the conventional wisdom that heavy royal indirect taxation caused the 1675 revolt in the Breton towns, the Papier Timbré, but that taxes had little to do with the revolt in the countryside, the Bonnets Rouges. Higher royal taxes certainly did lead to the Papier Timbré revolt but they also played a much more significant role in the Bonnets Rouges than I had anticipated. The rural rebellion took place almost entirely in the region of the *domaine congéable*, that is, in an area in which the landlord did *not* share in the tax burden (he received one-third of the *gross* production rather than one-half of the *net*, as in the regions of *métayage*). Peasants in the *domaine congéable* area therefore paid the considerable increases in Breton direct taxation after 1643 and again after 1670 on their own. The peasant attack on seigneurialism there is an ideal example of Brenner's argument that the nature of French taxation (noble exemptions, etc.) severely retarded the development of capitalism in France; alas, the very exceptionalism of the land tenure arrangement and the very different target of the rebellion – the seigneurs rather than the royal tax bureaucracy – shows that Brenner's thesis does not work in the rest of France.[65]

The seven chapters encompass several varieties of history – economic, social, institutional, financial, and political – in an effort to bring these different approaches to bear on one French province. I believe that the study of other provinces' police records, local administrative correspondence, and tax rolls would show, as it does in Brittany, that the monarchy had far less power than we think, that absolutism was not a form of government, that social mobility was fairly common in early modern France, and that large segments of the peasantry were not rooted permanently to one village. What we are likely to find is a society

clients. The implication of such a distinction may be that the increased centralization of the state made the clientage system work better. The greater power of the state, combined with the clientage system used to make that state function, gave patrons greater control over clients in the late seventeenth century than in the sixteenth century. The so-called "absolute" state then becomes a mechanism by which the high nobility increases its control over the lesser nobility, rather than a mechanism by which the king breaks the power of the high nobility.

[65] Brenner, "Agrarian Roots of European Capitalism." See also the critique by E. Le Roy Ladurie, "A Reply to Robert Brenner," reprinted in *Brenner Debate*, 101–7.

rooted in instability and a political order based on the preservation of the power of the dominant economic class: the landlords. Most of all, we will find a social order marked not by deference punctuated with rebellion but by permanent hostility within a fragile framework of carefully imposed social, economic, political, and moral order.

The Breton economy in the sixteenth and seventeenth centuries

"Brittany resembles the head or crown of a monk, whose borders are
ornamented with hair and the summit and middle of which is naked, as the
coasts of Brittany are its hair and ornaments, the rest being naked and sterile."
François-Nicolas Baudot, sieur du Buisson et d'Aubenay, 1636.[1]

Early modern Brittany has often suffered from the long shadows cast by our
image of the province in the nineteenth century. The backwardness of
nineteenth-century Brittany, both in economic and social terms, has often been
projected back into early modern times. Nineteenth-century Breton historians
and antiquarians neglected the royal period because of their nostalgic yearnings
for the independent Breton state of the fifteenth century, for the Golden Age of
duke Pierre II and of the duchess Anne.[2] In recent years, the early modern
period has come into its own. There have been remarkable studies of the Breton
nobility and of Breton medicine in the eighteenth century and of various aspects
of the history of Nantes in both the sixteenth and eighteenth centuries. Breton
institutions are well treated only from the time of Louis XIV, but the recent *thèse*
of Alain Croix on life, death, and faith in sixteenth- and seventeenth-century
Brittany provides an unparalleled mass of information about demography,
morbidity, and popular attitudes towards life and death in an early modern
French province. The largest gaps in our knowledge remain in the economic,
political, and social spheres. The only comprehensive work on the Breton
economy is that of Henri Touchard on Breton maritime commerce in the
Middle Ages (that is, in the proverbial Golden Age of the dukes).[3]

Brittany had a relatively dense population in the sixteenth and, especially,

---

[1] F.-N. Baudot, sieur du Buisson et d'Aubenay, *Itinéraire de Bretagne en 1636* (Nantes, 1898,
1902), 2 vols., II, 241 (cited hereinafter as Dubuisson-Aubenay, *Itinéraire*).

[2] The most prominent historian of this school was Artur de la Borderie, who published countless
documents from the ducal period, as well as many articles about it. His general views are set forth
in his six-volume *Histoire de la Bretagne* (Rennes, 1896–1904), the later volumes written by
B. Pocquet.

[3] H. Touchard, *Le commerce maritime breton à la fin du Moyen Age* (Paris, 1967); A. Croix, *La
Bretagne au XVIe et XVIIe siècles* (Paris, 1981); J. Meyer, *La noblesse bretonne au XVIIIe siècle* (Paris,
1966); J.-P. Goubert, *Malades et médecins en Bretagne, 1770–1790* (Paris, 1974); J. Tanguy, *Le
commerce du port de Nantes au milieu du XVIe siècle* (Paris, 1956).

seventeenth centuries. As Alain Croix and Roger Leprohon have demonstrated, the Breton population grew rapidly in this period, particularly during
the seventeenth century (in contrast to the broader pattern in France).[4] By the
seventeenth century, many Breton parishes had very large populations:
the bishopric of Léon, in particular, had a rapid growth between 1600 and 1680.
Leprohon found, in a sample of fourteen parishes, that the annual average
number of baptisms doubled between the period 1600 to 1619 and that of 1665
to 1684. As a result, many "rural" parishes in Léon had populations of two to
four thousand people. Léonard parishes often formed an amalgam of rural and
urban elements; indeed, the merchants who dominated the local linen trade
were often peasants.[5]

Some parts of Brittany had a quite substantial level of urbanization. Croix's
figures suggest that the bishopric of Rennes had more than thirty towns or
bourgs with 1,000-plus inhabitants. Of these, perhaps twelve to fifteen had
2,000 people or more, seven more than 3,000, topped by Rennes with 45,000
(1650), Vitré with some 11,000, and Fougères with 10,000 or so. The
agglomeration continued into the bishopric of Saint-Malo, including that city,
with its 19,000 inhabitants (if one includes the suburb of Saint-Servan) and
Dinan, with some 7,500. In the bishopric of Rennes, Croix's estimates imply
that nearly half of the population (roughly 46 percent) lived in an urban setting.

If we confine ourselves to traditionally defined towns (that is, to places so
defined in early modern times), we find the western bishoprics substantially less
urbanized than the eastern ones, if the various tax levies on towns are any
indication. There was a nesting of towns around the Gulf of Morbihan –
Vannes, Auray, Hennebont, Port Louis – but the remaining Breton towns were
strung out along the coast or in the interior. Even Nantes, whose population rose
from about 14,000 in 1500 to 25,000 in 1605 and 40,000 by 1650, did not have
a substantial network of towns with which to make common cause, either
economically or politically.

There are several tax sources on Breton levels of urbanization between 1425
and 1693, beginning with the assessments of the *aide des villes*, the forfeit paid by
towns exempt from the hearth tax (*fouage*) (table 1). This list excludes Fougères
(because it was drawn up in 1425, before the duke had purchased the barony of
Fougères) but it gives some indication as to where the urban areas were: the
bishoprics of Rennes, Nantes, and Saint-Malo. By way of contrast, Léon paid
virtually nothing. A second list, of towns assessed for a special tax in 1584 (listed
by bishopric only), shows a similar pattern, although Tréguier jumped from 7.8
percent of the *aide* to 11 percent of the special tax: given what we know about the
growth and prosperity of Morlaix in the interim, the change would make sense.
Subsequent lists for special taxes, in 1630 and 1693, suggest that roughly one

---

[4] Croix, *La Bretagne*, I; R. Leprohon, *Vie et mort des Bretons sous Louis XIV* (1984).
[5] Leprohon, *Vie et mort*, table on p. 195.

Table 1: *Indicators of urban population, 1425–1693; percentage of Breton urban population, by bishopric*

Bishopric	1425	1584	1630	1693
Rennes	27.9	18.6	26.8	26.1
Nantes	19.3	21.7	19.1	15.2
Vannes	13.5	13.7	7.2	11.0
Cornouaille	5.6	9.4	7.65	9.6
Léon	1.0	5.0	4.8	8.3
Tréguier	7.8	11.0	7.65	10.4
Saint-Brieuc	9.5	6.0	7.65	5.9
Saint-Malo	13.4	14.4	16.3	12.8
Dol	1.9	*a*	2.9	0.7

Note:
a Included in Saint-Malo figure.
Sources: ADLA, B 12, 871; C 415; C 696, number 26, *côte* 1.

urban Breton in four lived in the bishopric of Rennes, with its three large towns: Rennes, Vitré, and Fougères.

The comparison of percentage of urban population to percentage of total population is instructive. Rennes and Saint-Malo had much higher urban percentages: combined they held only 27 percent of the Breton population in 1660, yet they consistently paid 40 to 43 percent of the urban contributions. Léon and Cornouaille, by way of contrast, held some 21 percent of the population, yet paid only 13 or 14 percent of the urban taxes in 1584 and 1630. Léon shows a rapid increase in urban population between 1630 and 1693, no doubt due to Brest: its share of the urban tax of 1630 was only 4.8 percent; in 1693, Léon contributed 8.3 percent. Croix estimated the total Breton urban population as 280,000 in 1696, of whom 37.5 percent lived in the bishoprics of Rennes and Saint-Malo and only 28.6 percent in all of Lower Brittany. The 1630 tax assessed Rennes and Saint-Malo for 43.1 percent of the total, all of Lower Brittany for 28.3 percent.[6]

The bishopric of Saint-Brieuc would seem to have been the big loser in the sixteenth and seventeenth centuries. Its towns – Lamballe, Saint-Brieuc, and Guingamp – declined in importance and the overall population dropped. Saint-Brieuc had a much higher percentage of *feux* than of the total population, indicating a relative deterioration after 1501 (table 2); the share of Breton wine taxes paid by the bishopric declined steadily, from 11 percent (1578) to 7.1 percent (1650s). The share of urban taxes paid by Saint-Brieuc dropped from the 9.5 percent of the *aide* to a mere 5.9 percent in the tax of 1693.

[6] ADLA, B 12,871; C 415; C 696, number 26, *côte* 1. Croix, *La Bretagne*, I, 152.

The Breton economy

Table 2: *Comparison of population and* feux *counts: population in 1660;* feux *counts, 1617, 1642 (in percentages)*

	Population in 1660	*feux* 1617	*feux* 1642
Rennes	14.3	12.6	12.5
Nantes	17.1	17.7	17.5
Vannes	14.6	13.5	13.9
Cornouaille	13.0	12.9	12.4
Léon	8.0	6.1	5.8
Tréguier	8.0	11.1	10.9
Saint-Brieuc	9.3	10.7	11.1
Saint-Malo	12.9	12.8	13.3
Dol	2.8	2.6	2.5

Sources: ADLA, B 3009; B 2990; Croix, *La Bretagne*, table 18a.

Croix's demographic description of the province is entirely borne out by the tax records. Eastern Brittany had a broad urban nesting between Rennes and Saint-Malo and the south a large, isolated Nantes; towns dotted the coastline – among them the most important were Morlaix, Quimper, and Vannes; there were isolated sub-regional centers, such as Ploërmel, and many small towns of two to four thousand people sprinkled everywhere. Most Bretons lived in a rural parish; however, these parishes, especially in Léon, often contained several thousand, rather than several hundred people.

The economic structures of the province closely reflected its population distribution. Brittany was an extremely rich area in the sixteenth and seventeenth centuries, with a growing economy and rapidly expanding population. The province did not form an integrated economic unit. It had four principal economic zones: the coastal region running from the bay of Bourgneuf to the Crozon peninsula, with its fulcrum at the great port of Nantes (and with a sort of adjunct on the northern coast, in parts of the bishoprics of Tréguier and Saint-Brieuc); the linen-producing region of Léon, with its export center at Morlaix; the Saint-Malo–Rennes urban agglomeration; and the vast *landes* or heaths of the interior, notably the eastern portion of the bishopric of Cornouaille and the contiguous parts of the bishoprics of Saint-Brieuc, Saint-Malo, Vannes, and Rennes. These regions often had areas of specialization, such as the vineyards east and south of Nantes, or the salt marshes of the mouth of the Loire and the Bay of Bourgneuf. The three main littoral regions, focused on Nantes, Morlaix, and Saint-Malo, had relatively little contact with each other; their maritime commerce usually involved non-Breton partners such as the English, Spanish,

33

Dutch, and Bordelais.[7] Let us examine each of these regions in turn, beginning with the *landes*, in order to get a better understanding of the economic interests at stake in Breton social and political developments. Then we can try to establish workable definitions of Breton economic classes.

THE *LANDES*

Dubuisson-Aubenay's observation that Brittany resembled the head of a monk had some justice in 1636–7, as the population density was much higher on the coast than in the interior, yet he over-simplified the complicated local geography and the economic vitality of the interior heaths. Certain interior regions, such as the linen-producing area of Léon, were extremely prosperous. Brittany had many local economies and a broad spectrum of local political societies that reflected the economic differentiation.

The political and social structure of Brittany reflected the difficulties of balancing the varied economic interests of the main economic zones. These zones could reflect a symbiotic relationship, such as that between the wine-growing *pays Nantais* and the grain lands of the bishopric of Vannes. The economic ties of the Léonard linen parishes, however, stretched outside the province – to its main market in England – so that the peasants living on the *landes* of Léon and Tréguier had direct connections with international markets. This particular trade grew substantially in the late sixteenth and seventeenth centuries, bringing tremendous prosperity to Léon. The physical evidence of this prosperity remains in the church closes of Saint-Thégonnec and the other linen-producing parishes: almost all Léonard parish closes date from the period 1580–1680, a testimony to the successful trade in linen (the *crées* of Léon). Many parishes near Morlaix grew by 75 percent between 1600 and 1650.[8] These interior parishes, seemingly so remote, were, in fact, at the mercy of international events: when Louis XIV banned trade to England, the trade of *crées* collapsed, destroying the economy of the region. It quickly became poverty-stricken, because the high population density encouraged by linen production

---

[7] J. Collins, "The Role of Atlantic France in the Baltic Trade: Dutch Traders and Polish Grain at Nantes, 1625–1675," *Journal of European Economic History* (1984): 231–80; E. Trocmé and M. Delafosse, *Le commerce rochelais de la fin du XVe siècle au début du XVIIe* (Paris, 1952). At Bordeaux, see, for example, AD Gironde, 6 B 213, register of 1640, showing the extent of Breton trade with the city. The register gives quantities only for wine, but often shows Breton ships arriving with butter, *toiles*, sardines (and other fish), and caskwood. On Breton grain at Bordeaux, see A. Leroux, *Inventaire sommaire des registres de la jurade de Bordeaux* (Bordeaux, 1916), XI. For Saint-Malo, J. Delumeau *et al.*, *Le mouvement du port de Saint-Malo, 1681–1720* (Rennes, 1966).

[8] Croix, *La Bretagne*, graphs 31–2. On the linen trade, see: J. Tanguy, "L'essor de la Bretagne aux XVIe et XVIIe siècles," in *Histoire de la Bretagne et des pays celtiques*: III, *La Bretagne province, 1532–1789* (Morlaix, 1986), graph on p. 27. Both Tanguy and Leprohon, *Vie et mort*, also have extensive statistics on population growth in Léon.

and economic growth could not be supported by the meager agricultural output of the region.

The interior zone, the naked crown of Dubuisson-Aubenay, had a much lower population density than the other regions of the province. An investigation by the intendant in 1733 showed that 42.3 percent of the land in Brittany lay uncultivated, most of it in the interior of the province.[9] Croix hypothesizes that the interior was lightly inhabited even in the Middle Ages because the largest Breton parishes were those of the interior, especially in Cornouaille; in 1650 the average parish in Cornouaille contained nearly 50 square kilometers, while those in the bishopric of Rennes averaged just over 25 square kilometers.[10] Croix's maps for population density in 1667, 1696, and 1770 show that some interior parishes had fewer than twenty-five inhabitants per square kilometer but that many of them had between twenty-five and fifty inhabitants per square kilometer.

The underpopulated regions of the seventeenth century were heaths – in the bishopric of Cornouaille, in the southern part of the bishopric of Saint-Malo, and in the northern reaches of that of Nantes. These heaths, while underpopulated by Breton standards, supported a population density greater than that of France as a whole. Market towns strung out across the peninsula – Ploërmel, Josselin, Carhaix, Pontivy, Loudéac – show that the region, despite its apparent desolation, had extensive ties to the larger Breton economy. The one true zone of isolation was eastern Cornouaille: the quadrilateral defined by Morlaix, Saint-Brieuc, Auray, and Quimper had only one town in its interior – unwalled Carhaix, whose population was estimated at 2,000 in the 1697 inquest. Carhaix had 266 taxpayers in 1603, of whom 32 were single women, so the town then probably held some 1,000 to 1,200 people.[11] The rest of the interior looked isolated only in comparison with the remarkably dense urban networks connecting Rennes and Saint-Malo, or with the trade network of the southern coast from Quimper to Vannes, and, by sea, to Redon, La Roche Bernard, and Nantes. The interior heaths had connections with the three littoral networks, providing products related to livestock trade, such as horses, cattle, and butter.

These *landes* supported an extremely varied economy. They provided grazing

---

[9] H. Sée, *Les classes rurales en Bretagne du XVIe siècle à la Révolution* (Paris, 1906), 371–3.

[10] Croix, *La Bretagne*, maps 12–14 (1667, 1696, 1770) and the map *hors texte*. On the earlier development of the population, see J.-P. Leguay, "Les fouages en Bretagne ducale aux XIVe et XVe siècles," (D.E.S., Rennes, 1961), 125–7: Leguay found, in Léon and Saint-Brieuc, that there were more *feux* in the littoral parishes (59.3 and 56.7) than in the interior ones (only 40.3 and 47). In the eighteenth century, the situation was much the same: 42.3 percent of the land, most of it in the interior, was uncultivated: Croix's hypothesis follows the methodological principle developed by Georges Duby in "La carte, instrument de recherche: les communes de France," *Annales* (1958): 464.

[11] ADF, 2 E 1501; Croix, *La Bretagne*, table 18, taking the figures provided by the intendant, Béchameil de Nointel. His memoir of 1696 has been published by J. Berenger and J. Meyer, *La Bretagne de la fin du 17e siècle d'après le mémoire de Béchameil de Nointel* (Paris, 1976).

ground for both cattle and horses, two of the mainstays of the Breton economy. In 1651, tavern keeper Joseph Faure and his wife, Ollive Dunord, told the wine duty clerk that their establishment, near Saint-Brieuc, served wine and cider (in substantial quantities) to the "merchants of Normandy," who were going "to the fairs and markets of Lower Brittany to buy horses, oxen and other animals, as well as all [sorts of] other merchandise."[12] In the west, the great horse fair of Le Folgoët attracted merchants from all over western France, particularly Normandy. Charles Colbert de Croissy wrote of this fair in 1665: "There is a great trade of horses in the said region, which has 12 fairs per year, the largest of which is at Forgouet. It lasts 15 days and the inhabitants of Normandy come to it. Up to 2,000 horses have been sold in a single fair. But this commerce is much diminished; this livestock activity relies solely on the stalling and feeding of animals carried out by the local peasants." The twelve-day Le Folgoët fair was not even the largest of the Léon region, an honor that fell to the fair of La Martyre. Béchameil de Nointel, the intendant at the end of the seventeenth century, when the trade had fallen on hard times, said that Brittany exported some 12,000 horses each year.[13]

Léon and Tréguier were particularly renowned for their horses but other regions also had substantial horse fairs. The cities of Rennes and Nantes, and the two bishoprics, levied long-standing local taxes on the export of livestock.[14] In 1636, Dubuisson-Aubenay mentioned the horse fair of Saint-Julien-de-Vouvantes (near Châteaubriand) and that of Pontivy, in the *landes* of the Vannetais, as two of the most important in the province.[15] In the early sixteenth century, the lease price of the export duty on livestock (the *traite des bêtes vives*) indicates minimum exports of about 5,500 head in 1503, of 7,500 head in 1523, and of nearly 17,000 animals in 1533. At some point in the mid sixteenth century, the livestock duties became part of a general lease with the *ports et havres* and the *brieux*; this joint lease price increased between 1610 and 1630 but then declined until 1660, indicating a pattern similar to that offered by the hearsay evidence of Colbert de Croissy.[16]

While it is impossible to determine the overall amount paid for the *bêtes vives* in the seventeenth century, we do have evidence about sub-leases for the duties in several bishoprics. These leases indicate (if the ratio between the two duties remained constant) minimum exports from Rennes, Dol, and Saint-Malo of over 12,500 animals in 1612 and of 18,500 in 1638: 12,500 head over the bridge

[12] ADCN, B 107.
[13] J. Kerhervé, F. Roudaut, and J. Tanguy, *La Bretagne en 1665 d'après le rapport de Colbert de Croissy* (Brest, 1978), 182. Berenger and Meyer, *La Bretagne de ... Béchameil de Nointel*.
[14] ADLA, C 781, *côte* 5; *ibid.*, *côte* 2, on duties levied for the *bêtes vives*.
[15] Dubuisson-Aubenay, *Itinéraire*, I, 5.
[16] BN, Mss. Fr. 22,330, fols. 679–700v (*état de la valeur*) and Mss. Fr. 22,342, fols. 135–40v, on 1533 and 1535. For 1503, ADLA, E 212; for 1523, R. Doucet, "L'état des finances de 1523," *Bulletin Philologique et Historique du Comité des Travaux Historiques* (1920): 3–120.

at Dinan (2,500 livres) and another 6,000 animals from the other border towns of the bishoprics of Rennes (Fougères, Vitré, La Guerche, Châteaugiron, Bazouges, Saint-Aubin, Liffré, and Rennes) and of Saint-Malo (Combourg).[17] The lease prices continued to go up until the mid 1640s, peaking at 2,700 livres for 1642 at Dinan. If we allow for the costs and profits of the tax farmers, we can estimate that at least 26,000 head of livestock left the province each year in the 1620s and 1630s. The Dinan figure probably represents exports from the western bishoprics, so that annual exports from that area reached some 15,000 head in the late 1630s and more in the early 1640s.

The export figures exclude all internal Breton sales, that is, sales from one Breton to another. We know from other records that Bretons slaughtered many animals, producing meat, hides, tallow, and lard for local trade. Quimperlé, in a region not noted for its livestock production, had a duty on the export of hides. It shipped 100 untanned cattle hides in eight months of 1644 and the 1631 port register of Nantes shows imports of tallow and butter from Quimperlé and nearby Le Conquet to Nantes.[18] At Pleyben (near Quimper), the receipts in kind of the *fabrique* of the parish in 1633–4 also show the importance of livestock in Cornouaille: calves ranked second, after grain, while butter came in third and pigs fourth. In 1692–3, however, while calves and butter had retained their prominence (and declined less in value than other in-kind receipts), pigs had disappeared entirely.[19]

The import–export figures for Nantes in 1631 show that the interior must have provided most of the livestock for export. While fewer than 1,000 calfskins entered by the port, Nantes exported, mostly to Spain, more than 6,500 tanned calfskins. The *Saint-Martin* of Le Poulinguen, for example, shipped 89 dozen tanned calfskins to Spain on 28 February 1631. While Nantes obtained hides from as far away as Russia (the 1631 port register includes the importation of 477 "peaux de vaches de Roussy," by way of Dutch intermediaries), most of the raw materials for its tanning industry came from the *landes* of the northern bishopric of Nantes and, perhaps, from the Ploërmel region.[20] At Nantes, in 1611, the tanners paid the second highest guild assessment, after the merchant drapers, for the confirmation of their privileges. At Rennes, the tanners shared the highest assessment with the merchant drapers and the large-scale mercers, while the *parcheminiers* ranked next.[21]

The cattle produced a wide variety of products to sell. The Breton preference

[17] AD Loire-Atlantique, 4 E II 20; 4 E II 98, fols. 276, 299, 302, 542, 565. 4 E II 1713, fol. 2; 4 E II 98, fols. 294, 345, 380; 4 E II 100, fols. 59, 85. Jean Tanguy gathered this material, which he kindly shared with me.
[18] ADF, 5 H 37 and ADLA, B 2976, port register of 1631.
[19] J. Tanguy, supporting documents for a history of Pleyben, private communication.
[20] ADLA, B 2976; J. Tanguy, "Le commerce nantais à la fin du XVIe et au commencement du XVIIe siècle," (Rennes, 1965, thèse de troisième cycle).
[21] ADIV, B 3276, glorious accession tax for Louis XIII.

(one might say mania) for butter can be seen in the extent of the butter trade in the sixteenth and seventeenth centuries. In 1631, Nantes imported some 15,000 lb. of butter from Ireland and western Brittany. Some of this butter was for the elite, such as the 100 lb. that passed duty free for the personal consumption of the marquis de Goulaine, but much of it was consumed by the lower classes. In fact, importation by sea furnished a very small portion of total Nantais consumption. In 1568–9, some 335,000 lb. of butter passed through the gate of Saint-Nicolas, in small carts or on mules or horses. This butter came from the heathlands immediately north of the city and from central Brittany: it was roughly thirty times more than the amount imported by sea in the same period.[22] The *traite domaniale* of Nantes listed butter first among the goods assessed (1537). In fact, it listed two categories of butter: butter that had received a *brevet* (a passport indicating that duties had been paid) from Ploërmel, and butter that had not. Ploërmel is well over 100 km. from Nantes, yet there was a substantial road leading, by way of Redon, from the one to the other; the existence of the special category of butter from the Ploërmel region on the *traite domaniale* implies that the area had long supplied Nantes with much of its butter.[23]

Breton *métairie* leases, whether they are from the *pays Nantais*, the bishopric of Rennes or Vannes or Cornouaille, list many animals. The *métairie* of Landerotte (near Rennes) listed six calves among the lessees' obligations in 1550 and, as late as 1711, required them to "prennent soin des boeufs à graisser de l'abbaye et les entretiennent de litière." The nearby *métairie* of Fayel owed fifteen days of harness labor and 100 lb. of butter on each of its leases, clear signs of livestock. The *métayer* of Chantepié, also working for the abbey of Saint-Suplice-la-Forêt, received five milk cows, one heifer, two bulls, three calves, a horse, five pigs, and two oxen (*boeufs*) in 1560. The rents included 100 lb. of butter, twelve chickens, and a dozen capons.[24]

In the Nantes region, the situation looked much the same. Although small holdings, such as the *bordage* of La Robinière (in Valets, southeast of Nantes), had no livestock noted in the lease, they often owed livestock products as part of their rent: La Robinière carried a charge of 6 lb. of butter (as well as assorted poultry).[25] The leases did not always mention the livestock, but we find out about the extent of peasant herds in other ways. At the *métairie* of La Chapelle-

[22] Tanguy, "Le commerce nantais," 214.

[23] ADLA, C 780, *côte* 2, first item is butter from Ploërmel, taxed at 16.67 *d.m.* per 100 lb.; other butter was taxed at only 13.33 *d.m.* per 100 lb. The *pancarte* made a like distinction with respect to *toiles*, but the duties were the same.

[24] P. Anger, "Cartulaire de l'abbaye de Saint-Suplice-la-Forêt," *Bulletin de la Société des Antiquitaires d'Ille-et-Vilaine*, 39 (1909): 1–207. See also the materials published by H. Sée, "Un bail de métayage dans le pays de Rennes en 1537," *Annales de Bretagne* (1931): 297–300 and "Cheptels de métairies au début du XVIe siècle," *Annales de Bretagne* (1931): 523–4.

[25] ADLA, H 275, *côte* 1: four chickens at Pentecost, two capons at All Saints' Day, often planting six apple or pear saplings.

aux-Moines, near Nantes, the 1611 lease required the lessee to plant fruit trees and to provide two sheep and a pig each year; it made no mention of cattle. In 1709, however, a later group of lessees went bankrupt. The forced sale of their livestock, for 572 livres, included six oxen, two bulls, six cows, thirteen ewes, eight lambs, and assorted other animals: in all seventeen head of cattle and twenty-one sheep, excluding the animals pastured for the landlords by the lessees.[26]

The typical *métairie* in the Nantes region had a substantial supply of livestock, to fulfil its labor or cartage obligations (as at Coudray or La Chapelle-aux-Moines in 1611). The lessees often had to pasture the landlord's cattle on nearby *landes* set aside by the landlord (Coudray, 1624). As in the Gâtine region of Poitou, the landlord and tenants split the increase in the number of livestock.[27] The other regions of Brittany put their *landes* to similar use. Even if we exclude specialization, such as the raising of horses in the *landes* of Léon, livestock contributed substantially to the Breton economy. The *landes* of the interior, far from being a source of poverty and ruin, provided both a means to diversify the economy and a solid core area of livestock production.

All of the taxes of the province, usually established in the fourteenth and fifteenth centuries, assessed livestock products as a special category, indicating that livestock raising had been a major economic activity in the Middle Ages. The *ports et havres*, for example, usually levied a flat rate tax on goods (5 percent), but had special tax rates for grain (30 sous per ton on wheat, 20 sous per ton on other grains), fish, iron, wine, salt, and the three most important livestock products – meat, fats (including butter and tallow), and hides.[28]

The tax mechanism for livestock products tells us something about the political ramifications of the economic importance of cattle. The absence of a substantial grouping of towns explains in part the one-sided political and social atmosphere of the central heaths: the great nobles, particularly the Rohans, dominated the region. The Rohans had large castles in both Pontivy and Josselin, dominating the two towns in a physical as well as a political sense. (Politically, they expressed their domination through their superior seigneurial courts in each town.)

The creation of ducal taxation in the province illuminates the Rohan domination because duke Jean V issued special letters about the creation of the new taxes in the lands of the Rohan family; the duke often allowed the Rohans to

---

[26] ADLA, H 275, *côte* 3.
[27] L. Merle, *La métairie dans la Gâtine poitevine* (Paris, 1956); local examples in ADLA, H 9, lease of 1613 to *métayer* of Gavre; H 275, *côte* 2 (Coudray), *côte* 3 (La Chapelle). As for other Breton regions see, for example, the *prisage* done at Hennebont in 1634: the peasant had two steers, two cows, a heifer, a calf, and a pig (ADM, B 2778).
[28] ADLA, C 788, *pancarte* of *ports et havres*.

levy indirect taxes for their own benefit.[29] The tax packages demonstrate the importance of livestock in the regions dominated by the Rohans. When duke Jean V granted (1420) the Rohans a special tax for the repair of their chateaux of Rohan, Josselin, la Chèze, Blain, and la Roche Maurice, they levied duties on wine, on cloth (three categories), and on "hooved animals," horses, pigs, butter (and other fats), wax, skins and hides (both tanned and untanned).[30] In 1420, as in 1620, the region's economy depended on livestock rearing and cloth production. The tax also shows the extraordinary power of the Rohans over the central *landes*, a power that continued (albeit in a lesser form) into the seventeenth century.

The only political interests that mattered in the *landes* were those of the nobles. Jean Meyer found, for the eighteenth century, that most of the nobles of this region obtained the largest share of their income from seigneurial privileges, while those of the western littoral relied on land rents.[31] Both sets of landlords had strong interests in keeping the taxes on the peasantry to a minimum, to maximize their ability to extract money from their tenants and "subjects." At the Estates, the most powerful families, such as the Rohans, could rely on their clients to support tax packages that would fall more heavily on the towns than on the countryside: this meant levying only the traditional taxes on grain and livestock products, keeping direct taxation to a minimum (also, as we shall see, by fixing the tax in custom), and levying heavy duties on wine consumption. For the Rohans and the other seigneurs of the *landes*, this tax package was ideal because there were few towns in the region and the chief sources of its wealth – livestock and, in certain areas, grain or cloth production – remained undertaxed. Even the wine taxes came to have less impact, as the mass of the population shifted from wine to cider consumption in the early seventeenth century.

THE LITTORAL REGIONS

The other landlords of the province shared the interest in maintaining low direct taxes, but the agricultural systems of the littoral regions were quite different from those of the *landes*. The southern littoral from Redon to Quimper exported

[29] G.-A. Lobineau, *Histoire de Bretagne* (Paris, 1707), I, 521. Similar agreements are noted elsewhere in M. Jones, "Les finances de Jean IV, duc de Bretagne (1364–1399)," *Mémoires de la Société d'Histoire et d'Archéologie en Bretagne* (1972): 26–53; 37. See also R. Blanchard, *Lettres et mandements de Jean V* (Nantes, 1889–95), 5 vols., piece 1,133. On Josselin, piece 2,525. Later in the century, for similar grants, see: ADLA, B 2, fol. 116 (1462); B 8, fols. 111–13 (1477); BM Nantes, Mss. Fr. 1722, fols. 279 (1467) and 281 (1471). The Rohans continued to have a special *ports et havres* they levied in the viscounty of Léon as late as 1549: BM Nantes, Mss. Fr. 1560 (13 Oct. 1549); AD Loire-Atlantique, C 788 on the *ports et havres*. My thanks here to Yair Seltenreich for information and leads about the Rohan family.

[30] Blanchard, *Lettres*, piece 1,401.

[31] Meyer, *La noblesse bretonne*, has many references to noble incomes in the eighteenth century.

grain to Nantes, La Rochelle, Bordeaux, and even Iberia.[32] Most of the ports in this region specialized in the export of rye. Quimperlé and Hennebont were the two most common sources of rye for Nantes in 1631 and 1644, while Auray ranked second to Hennebont in 1643 (the port register did not list Quimperlé for any rye) and third to the others in both 1631 and 1644. Auray differed in its mix of grains in 1643 and 1644, as it exported substantial amounts of wheat as well as rye (unlike Hennebont and Quimperlé, which shipped very little wheat). Quimper also shipped wheat in these years, but rye was usually its main staple.[33] The *apprécis* of grain prices at Nantes between 1656 and 1676 listed rye from Hennebont, Quimperlé, Quimper, Vannes, Redon, Auray, Pontchâteau, Châteaubriand, Nozay, and the "pays" (presumably the area immediately around Nantes). The wheat came from Donges, Retz, La Roche Bernard, Redon, Nozay, Lavau, Frossay, Saint-Nazaire, Barbatic, and "la plaine" (again, this would imply the area immediately north of the city).[34]

In the eighteenth century, the interior regions produced rye and buckwheat, the littoral ones, except for the region around Hennebont and Quimperlé, produced wheat.[35] In the sixteenth and seventeenth centuries, the pattern looked somewhat different. In the investigations of the royal demesne, done in 1583, 1617, and 1643–4, the commissioners found that thirteen demesnes provided all (or nearly all) wheat, six provided equal amounts of rye and wheat, three split two rye : one wheat, one produced only rye, and one produced equal amounts of wheat and "gros blé." The wheat areas ran along the north coast – demesnes of Goëllo, Lannion, Lanmeur; on the Quimper to Vannes coast – demesnes of Quimper, Pontecroix, Pont l'Abbé, Quimperlé, Auray, Vannes; in Léon – Brest, Saint-Renan, Landerneau (in both cases, tiny amounts), Lesneven (with the "gros blé"); and in two interior demesnes – Huelgoat and Ploërmel. The rye regions were the *pays Nantais*, Hennebont, and Muzillac (near Vannes), while the split regions included two demesnes in Nantes, the Rhuis peninsula, and three interior demesnes.[36]

Other evidence, such as revenues from tithes in kind, allows us to see that the wheat regions were Cornouaille, a small area near Vannes, the northern coast, and parts of the bishopric of Nantes. Around Quimperlé, the tithes of one local abbey produced two-thirds wheat and one-third rye, those of another, Chambrières, were all rye in both 1617 and 1621, but included buckwheat in 1637 and 1642. By 1668, the hamlet also produced wheat: the tithes of 1668, 1670,

---

[32] Trocmé and Delafosse, *Le commerce rochelais*; Leroux, *Jurade*; Collins, "The Role of Atlantic France in the Baltic Trade," for the interference of the Dutch in this trade after 1600.

[33] For 1631, ADLA, B 2976; for 1643, B 6685; for 1644, B 12,901.

[34] ADLA, B 8612; see also, AM Nantes, series FF (152, 154, etc.) for other citations; AM Nantes, HH 1 (1570s, 1630s, 1640s, isolated years).

[35] Meyer, *La noblesse bretonne*, 500.

[36] ADLA, B 12,871 (1583), 715 (1613), 720 (1643) on the demesne.

and 1678 were let for an average of 20.3 *muids* of rye and 6 *muids* of wheat.[37] In the Vannes region, at mid century, in a group of twenty-eight parishes between Vannes and the Rhuis peninsula, eleven produced only rye, five equal amounts of rye and wheat, seven half rye and a quarter each of wheat and oats, and five primarily wheat. In all, the tithes of these parishes produced 110.5 tons of rye and only 19.5 tons of wheat.[38]

Various police investigations of grain stocks, either due to famine or to inventories after death, reinforce the picture of the relatively equal stature of the two grains. At Hennebont, in inventories done in the 1630s, we find one case in which there were 10 *minots* of rye and 3 *minots* of wheat, others in which the authorities found only rye and oats.[39] Nearby, at Vannes, an investigation of stocks of grain traders in 1598 found that they held 156 tons of wheat and 145 tons of rye.[40] At Nantes, a check of bakers in 1643 found some 15.3 tons of wheat as against only 8.95 tons of rye.[41] In fact, despite the overwhelming preponderance of rye in the import figures for Nantes in 1631, 1643, and 1644 (all famine years), the investigations of bakers' shops tell a different story. The loaves weighed by the provost, to verify their marked weight, usually consisted of wheat, occasionally of a mixture of wheat and rye; he found very few loaves of pure rye bread.[42] The clear implication is that Nantes obtained its wheat from the surrounding countryside. Brittany thus follows the larger French pattern in which the inhabitants of towns usually ate wheat bread, while peasants (and often those in small towns) ate rye bread.

The Nantais records indicate that northern Brittany specialized in wheat more than rye. In 1631, the city received regular shipments of wheat from Paimpol, Guingamp, and Saint-Brieuc. In a 1630 investigation of stocks in Guingamp, the police found some 143.5 tons of wheat and only 80 of rye and 10 of buckwheat.[43] When the Sauvagets sought to buy grain for Nantes during the famine of 1630–1, they turned to the north for wheat, to the Quimperlé-Hennebont region for rye.[44]

Brittany shipped extensive amounts of grain to Bordeaux, La Rochelle, and

---

[37] ADF, 5 H 115. Yet another nearby abbey received its tithes in the early sixteenth century in wheat (two-thirds) and oats.   [38] ADM, 38 G 5, region of Sarzeau.
[39] ADM, B 2778, B 2780, B 2789.   [40] AM Vannes, HH 1.
[41] ADLA, B 6662. In 1590, on the other hand, an investigation of 13 February found 200 tons of rye as against only 30 of wheat, with another 120 listed as mixed (AM Nantes, FF 186).
[42] ADLA, B 6649–63. One example among many: B 6655, investigations of 12 September, 9 October, and 27 October 1634, show almost all loaves short in weight to be "pain de chapitre" (finest white) or "tiré à sa fleur" (wheat bread, more grey than white). In famine years, however, the overwhelming majority of imports were rye.
[43] ADIV, 1 Bh 8 (7 March 1631).
[44] AM Nantes, FF 188. Sauvaget's exports touched off a riot in Saint-Pol-de-Léon (8 December 1630). His ship there had 17 tons of wheat and 2 of rye. By way of contrast, a list of twenty-three other ships coming to Nantes for his effort to supply the city shows only one, from Pontecroix (near Quimper), shipping wheat.

Iberia. The western part of the province traded its grain for Bordeaux and Rochelais wines, rather than those of Nantes (shipped, in Brittany, primarily to the southern coast). These Breton barks brought grain in return, trading both rye and wheat to Bilbao, Lisbon, Bordeaux, and La Rochelle.[45] This trade went back to the Middle Ages and formed a considerable portion of the activities of sixteenth-century merchants such as André Ruiz.[46] In the seventeenth century, Bretons remained active in the Bay of Biscay, despite severe competition from the Dutch. Brittany imported more than 32,000 tons of wine from Bordeaux in 1672 and averaged about 16,000 tons of Bordeaux wine between 1698 and 1716, roughly 25 percent of all exports from Bordeaux.[47] The intendant in Bordeaux wrote, in the late 1680s and early 1690s, that Bordeaux traded only with Bretons and foreigners and that its grain came from Ireland, Holland, and Brittany (in 1692).[48] The governor of Brittany in that period, the duc de Chaulnes, told the controller general in 1688 that the "meilleures bourses" of Brittany were all in the grain trade.[49]

The landlords of western Brittany had little interest in taxing this grain and, as we shall see, they were largely successful in limiting taxation on grain to the *ports et havres* duty of 30 sous per ton of wheat and 20 sous per ton of other grain. While these duties had been substantial in the early fifteenth century, perhaps as high as 10 percent, by the seventeenth century they were derisory: in ordinary years, a ton of wheat sold for 80 to 90 livres, so the tax came to less than 2 percent.[50]

The peasants of the west also had vested economic interests, but they did not always revolve around grain (marketed largely by landlords and the clergy). The great linen-producing region of Léon provided an oasis of peasant prosperity: save for its export, peasant merchants controlled the linen trade, employing peasant craftspeople to do the labor. One clear sign of their economic prosperity in this period remains visible today; the many churches built in the sixteenth and seventeenth centuries have neither seigneurial arms nor special seigneurial

---

[45] On Lisbon, see: J. Gentil da Silva, *Stratégies d'affaires à Lisbonne entre 1595 et 1607* (Paris, 1956), 125.

[46] H. Lapeyre, *Une famille des marchands: les Ruiz* (Paris, 1953), esp. appendix on grain shipments.

[47] C. Huetz de Lemps, "Le commerce maritime des vins d'Aquitaine," *Revue Historique de Bordeaux* (1965): 25–44, provides a table with a neat summary of the figures from the author's subsequent monograph on Bordelais commerce. We might also cite here the opinion of Henry IV, writing to the Estates of Brittany in 1609: "la plus grande partie des vins que se debittent aulx autres villes de lad. province sont vins de gascoigne" (ADIV, C 3467). AD Gironde, series 6 B, has the port registers for several years, all of which paint the same general picture of Breton commerce (with the exception that grain appears sporadically, in part due to fluctuating local demand and in part due to the Dutch).

[48] A. Boislisle, *Correspondance des contrôleurs généraux avec les intendants des provinces* (Paris, 1874), I: 1683–1699, pieces 710, 980, 1072 (reports from 1689, 1691, and 1692).

[49] *Ibid.*, piece 638.

[50] Prices are those at Nantes, although they are comparable to prices at Vannes, Hennebont, and Quimperlé. On the latter, in 1680, see: AM Quimperlé, piece 2.

doorways.[51] The extensive carvings and decorations of the churches also bespeak the presence of peasant artists, working with the local granite to produce art that responded to the tastes of their clients – the peasantry. The peasants of Léon seem to have been a remarkably privileged lot: they had two substantial sources of non-arable income – horse rearing and linen production – and they were not subject to the typical leasing system of Lower Brittany, the *domaine congéable*.

The peasants of the nearby bishoprics of Cornouaille, Tréguier, and Vannes were not so fortunate. Each of these areas had important centers of linen production (such as Locronan in Cornouaille), yet the peasants were subject to the *domaine congéable* and the economies were often less varied than that of Léon. The rent structure of a *domaine congéable* was different from that of a *métairie*. The entry fees tended to be much larger on a *domaine congéable* and the annual rent came to one-third of the *gross* revenue rather than half of the *net* revenue. Peasants renting a *domaine congéable* (called "tenanciers") were therefore much more vulnerable to increases in direct taxation than were *métayers*, whose landlord typically shared the tax payment with them.

The *domaine congéable* did much to stifle the peasants' ability to innovate because no alterations in the crops, buildings, or vegetation could take place without the landlord's permission. In a lease under *domaine congéable*, the landlord kept possession of the land, while the tenant got possession (usually for nine years) of all the buildings and trees (excluding those of a certain size). Because the landlord had to repurchase all buildings and trees, and therefore would have had to pay for any improvements, no improvements could be made without his permission. This system limited the peasant's ability to make material improvements in buildings and slowed the spread of new crops to Lower Brittany. For example, apple trees spread rapidly through Upper Brittany in the sixteenth and early seventeenth centuries, but did not make their way extensively into Lower Brittany until much later.[52]

Cider spread in an east-to-west pattern between 1600 and 1640. The larger towns, such as Morlaix and Quimper, taxed both cider and beer (as well as wine) by the end of the sixteenth century, but the smaller towns of the western half of the province only began to add cider to their duties after 1610: Josselin, Guingamp, and Malestroit by 1615; Ploërmel and Saint-Brieuc in 1615; Quintin in 1619; Pontivy and Moncontour sometime between 1619 and 1646. In the far west, towns such as Brest, Concarneau, Saint-Pol-de-Léon, and

---

[51] Tanguy, "L'essor de la Bretagne." Jean Tanguy pointed out to me, on a guided tour of the closes, the absence of the armorial doors. On the marketing of grain by the landlords, lay and ecclesiastical, see J. Gallet, *La seigneurie bretonne (1450–1680). Le cas du Vannetais* (Paris, 1983), 564–70, and, especially, purchasing network of merchant Regnard of Vannes, table on 566–7.

[52] H. Bourde de la Rogerie, "Introduction," in *Inventaire sommaire des archives départementales du Finistère*, series B, III (Quimper, 1902).

Lesneven did not tax cider even in the 1640s.[53] In 1626, the Estates added cider (and beer) to the beverages covered by their wine tax, an indication that those two beverages had spread to a good part of the province.[54] Yet Dubuisson-Aubenay tells us, in 1636, that Lower Brittany did not grow its own apples, rather it bought them at the fair of Montfort.[55]

The landlords and peasants of the western part of the province opposed new taxes on grain, on livestock, and on linen production. In addition, the landlords and peasants alike opposed higher direct taxes (which, as in France, would have fallen on the peasants). There remained two important local products that might support higher taxation: salt and wine. Brittany did not belong to the general *gabelle* system: it retained its exemption from royal salt taxes (save small demesne fees levied in the marshes) until the Revolution. The enormous differential between the Breton and French prices of salt (easily 30:1) encouraged widespread salt smuggling, particularly in the parishes bordering on Anjou, Maine, and Normandy, and in those lining the waterborne transport routes, such as the Vilaine River.[56] Salt production declined in the seventeenth century, but the Estates never made a serious move to tax salt, so local taxation had no bearing on the decline.

How could the Estates raise substantial amounts of money without harming the trade in any of the western products and without raising direct taxes? They could tax wine, more specifically, the *retail* sale of wine. The wine growers of the province formed a powerful lobby against wine taxes. In the sixteenth century, vineyards existed in many parts of Brittany: in the bishoprics of Rennes, Tréguier, Vannes, and Nantes. The harsher climate of the late sixteenth century confined vineyards essentially to Nantes (with other small regions such as the Rhuys peninsula producing a very low-grade product).[57] One reason for the shift from taxing a broad variety of products (and from using surtaxes on the *fouage*) to taxing wine exclusively may have been this disappearance of vineyards from most of the province. The winegrowers of Nantes became increasingly isolated in their opposition to wine taxes, losing the support of their compeers in Rennes, Tréguier, and elsewhere.

The vineyards of Nantes expanded in the sixteenth and seventeenth centuries, to meet both greater Breton demand and expanded foreign (Dutch and German) interest in Nantais wine, but exports declined after 1645. The

---

[53] The requests for new taxes are filed with the papers of the Chamber of Accounts, ADLA, B 64–82, for example, B 69, fol. 30, renewal of the duties of Vitré in 1610.

[54] ADIV, C 2764, assizes of Estates of 1626.

[55] Dubuisson-Aubenay, *Itinéraire*, I, 9. In the bishoprics of Dol, Saint-Malo, and part of that of Rennes, fruit trees were so important that they gave rise to a special leasing arrangement, the *bail à détroit*, described in Meyer, *La noblesse*, 679–83.

[56] This was a constant complaint of the Estates under Henry IV and in the early part of the reign of Louis XIII. See the *cahiers* of these years, ADIV, C 2750–62.

[57] J. Delumeau, *Histoire de Bretagne* (Toulouse, 1969).

Nantais obtained special reduced rates for Nantais wine, rates that kept Nantais wine at a reasonable price until the 1630s. By the early 1640s, however, the duty reached 3 sous per *pot* (1.8 liters) of Nantais wine.[58]

The agricultural economy of Brittany rested on grain, wine, and livestock. The regions producing these commodities had something of a symbiotic relationship, so that the interior *landes* provided meat and livestock products, along with a small amount of grain, in return for grain, wine, and salt. The *pays Nantais* sold its wine – over 20,000 tons in 1631 – to the southern littoral (up to Quimper) and to part of the northern (from Saint-Brieuc to Saint-Malo), in return for grain from these regions – rye and some wheat from the south, wheat from the north. The littoral ports reexported the wine to the interior (for example, Redon served as the advance port of Rennes and Ploërmel). Two regions did not fit into this agricultural framework, the westernmost bishopric of Léon (and part of Tréguier) and the region between Saint-Malo and Rennes. These two industrial regions exported cloth, the *crées* of Léon and the *canevas* and, later, *noyales* of Saint-Malo and Rennes.

In the sixteenth century, Vitré dominated the production of *canevas* and Locronan, in Cornouaille, that of the *olonnes*; in both cases, the cloth had a hemp base. Hemp continued to be an important Breton product, both woven (Locronan, Saint-Brieuc, Nantes region) and raw (the north coast). Saint-Brieuc and Paimpol often shipped hemp to Nantes. In the seventeenth century, however, the balance shifted sharply to flax-based production. In the Saint-Brieuc region, we find the tithe collector of the parish of Saint-Michel noting, in 1636, that "since a little while ago, flax has been brought from Danzig and Flanders in much greater abundance than it was before." He added that the peasants of Saint-Michel (and other parishes) planted more and more flax. Another tithe collector stated that flax had never been planted until "three or four years ago" and that the peasants refused to pay the tithe on the new crop.[59]

The production figures of these new cloths rose sharply in the late sixteenth and seventeenth centuries. Jean Tanguy has shown that the export of linen from Morlaix rose from about 2,000 *pièces* in the mid fifteenth century, to 14,000 *pièces* in the 1540s and to 20,000 *pièces* in the 1560s. After a decline during the League War, production reached 15,000 *pièces* by 1600, 25,000 *pièces* in the 1640s, and peaked at 66,000 *pièces* in 1680. Tanguy estimates that total production in the Léon–Tréguier region must have been close to 90,000 *pièces* (9 million *aunes*) by 1680.[60] At Saint-Malo, minimum exports rose from 14,720 *fardeaux* in 1621 to 29,120 *fardeaux* in the 1630s, 32,000 in the early 1640s, and peaked at 60,000 *fardeaux* (12 million *aunes*) in the early 1650s[61] (table 3). The

[58] See below, ch. 4 and 5 for details.   [59] ADCN, B 1135.

[60] Tanguy, "L'essor de la Bretagne," graphs on 27 and 51.

[61] ADIV, G 274. The number of drapers followed a similar evolution, up from thirty-two in 1624 to forty-eight (1626 to 1642) and to sixty-four (1642), then seventy-one (1649); in 1701, it was back down to thirty-one.

Table 3: *Evolution of the linen trade at Saint-Malo,*
1621–1706

	Linen tax in livres	Licensed drapers
1621–2	460	40
1623–4	610	38
1624–5	600	32
1626–7	600	43
1633–4	910	48
1634–5	910	48
1635–6	910	52
1636–7	600	52
1637–8	600	51
1639–40	600	48
1640–1	1,000	47
1641–2	1,000	48
1642–3	1,000	64
1649–50	1,875	71
1650–1	1,875	69
1651–2	1,875	68
1652–3	1,700	70
1653–4	1,700	64
1701–2	not leased	31
1702–3	500	32
1703–4	500	32
1704–5	500	32
1705–6	488	32

Sources: ADIV, G 276–7.

royal prohibition on trade with England ruined the linen trade of both cities. At Morlaix, exports dropped from 66,000 *pièces* in 1680 to under 15,000 *pièces* in 1715; at Saint-Malo, there are no figures between 1654 and 1701, but the drop-off between the two dates was from 54,400 *fardeaux* to 16,000. The number of registered drapers, which had risen from thirty-two (1624) to seventy-one (1649), dropped back to thirty-two by 1702. There is little reason to believe that the Malouin decline antedates that of Morlaix, so that the linen trade probably continued strongly into the 1680s and then collapsed.[62]

The linen trade formed another vested interest the Estates had to protect;

[62] Delumeau *et al.*, *Saint-Malo*.

they did so successfully until the prohibition of trade with England in the 1680s. The Estates fought off several attempts to establish a tax of 32 sous per *pièce* of linen, under Henry IV and under Louis XIII. Louis XIII had even sold the offices of inspectors before the Estates purchased the abolition of the tax (and the offices).[63] Many textile industry towns sat at the Estates: Rennes, Saint-Malo, Dinan, Fougères, Vitré, Hédé, Quintin, Morlaix, Lannion, Tréguier, and lesser centers as well. As producers, these towns carried more clout than Nantes, which had few natural allies in the Estates, so their production – linen cloth – received the protection of the Estates. Yet the Estates willingly allowed the consumers, particularly the lower class consumers, of the western towns to bear the brunt of the burden of the wine taxes.[64]

The economically powerful towns clustered in the triangle between Vitré, Rennes, and Saint-Malo and along the coast – Morlaix, Nantes, and a few others. The absence of large towns in a given area did not mean, however, the lack of an urban presence. In many parts of Brittany, small towns (often with only 1,000 inhabitants) played a much larger role in the local economy than one would suspect. The middle-sized towns, those of 5,000 or more inhabitants, had long tentacles reaching out to the surrounding countryside. They controlled commerce into and out of such areas, and the legal class of such towns often bought considerable amounts of land in the surrounding countryside.[65] Away from the towns, however, the old landlord class continued to dominate possession of the land.

The small towns ringing the coast had three major related industries: maritime commerce, fishing, and shipbuilding. Most shipbuilding centers built barks of 20 to 40 tons displacement but certain ports, such as Pénerf in the north and Montoir-de-Bretagne, specialized in slightly larger ships, in the range of 50 to 70 tons. Merchants used the smaller ships for the *cabotage* trade within Brittany and for trade with Bordeaux and La Rochelle, while the larger ones braved the Channel, shipping goods to Picardy, the Low Countries, and Hamburg. In the second half of the sixteenth century, it became much rarer for Breton ships to export goods to Holland, but they remained quite active in commerce with Hamburg. Small boats (French and English), generally under 40 tons, carried the cross-Channel trade with England, conducted primarily out of Saint-Malo and Morlaix.[66]

Given regions or towns also specialized in certain fisheries. At the end of the seventeenth century, Saint-Malo and Nantes ranked first and second among Breton ports sending ships to the Newfoundland banks for cod, but Nantes

---

[63] ADIV, C 3300.   [64] Croix, *La Bretagne*, 148–50 and table 18.
[65] ADLA, B 2461, sale of "terres vaines et vagues" in 1640–1, shows a wide range of buyers, with members of the robe the most active group, but other urbanites buying as well. These merchants also became very active in tithe farming in the 1640s in the *pays Nantais* (G 244–5).
[66] Collins, "The Role of Atlantic France in the Baltic Trade"; Tanguy, in *La Bretagne province*.

came late to this fishery. Breton sailors had flocked to the Grand Banks in the early sixteenth century; virtually all of these sailors came from the northern coast – Saint-Malo, Saint-Brieuc, Pénerf, Brehat. The southern coast, particularly Audierne and Douarnenez, specialized in sardines.[67] Some ports engaged in all three activities: the fishing ports such as Audierne, Penmarc'h, Pénerf, and Saint-Malo were also the home ports of the ships trading with Bordeaux. By way of contrast, the home ports involved in the trade between Nantes and the bishopric of Vannes were not notable fishing centers.

What was the evolution of this economy, or rather these economies in the sixteenth and seventeenth centuries? We have already seen that the textile areas focused on Morlaix and Saint-Malo prospered mightily between 1550 and 1650 and that the livestock trade grew rapidly as well. The fairly continuous growth in the Breton population is evidence of this prosperity, as are the upward trends in parish offering curves.[68] The Nantes region, too, prospered in the late sixteenth and seventeenth centuries. In all cases, we must make allowances for the trough of the 1590s, due to war and to the catastrophic harvests of 1596 and 1597. The areas with ties to non-Breton markets expanded such ties, so that the trade with England (through Morlaix and Saint-Malo) grew rapidly, as did that with Holland (through Nantes). Only the salt marshes seem to have declined in the early seventeenth century; they lost their position as a primary source of salt for northern France to the marshes around Brouage.[69] The regions not tied to foreign markets also prospered because they usually traded with areas, such as Nantes, that grew with the increase in foreign trade.

The evolution of the Nantais network demonstrates the level of integration reached by some parts of the Breton economy. Nantes' chief trading partner in the sixteenth century was northern Spain, to which it exported cloth and paper. The southern littoral, so closely tied to Nantes, exported rye and wheat to Iberia (through La Roche Bernard, Vannes, Redon, Hennebont, and Quimperlé). In the early seventeenth century, the pattern of trade shifted dramatically at Nantes, with Holland replacing Spain as the chief foreign partner (and Hamburg an important second). The Dutch brought a broad variety of products

---

[67] Bourde de la Rogerie, "Introduction," clix, on northern fishing; H. Moret, *Le Croisic* (Rennes, 1917), 162, claims that port reached its apex under Louis XIII.

[68] J. Tanguy, documentation for a private monograph on the history of Pleyben. Professor Tanguy also showed me several M.A. theses done under his direction that used this technique. See also, Tanguy, "L'essor de la Bretagne," graphs on p. 45. On general French population trends, see J. Dupaquier, *La population de la France au XVIIe et XVIIIe siècles* (Paris, 1979). On Brittany, Croix, *La Bretagne*, I, ch. 3; on Languedoc, Beik, *Absolutism and Society*, 34. The contrast between the Breton economic pattern and that of France as a whole is clear in E. Labrousse, ed., *Histoire sociale et économique de la France* (Paris, 1965), following the local studies of Goubert, Deyon, and others. I do not entirely agree with their French scenario; I would suggest that the French economy as a whole grew strongly between 1600 and 1640 and that the decline set in then (allowing for slight variations here and there) in all but a few areas, such as Basse-Provence and most of Brittany. On the former, R. Baehrel, *Une croissance: La Basse-Provence rurale (fin du XVIe siècle–1789)* (Paris, 1961). [69] Tanguy, "Le commerce nantais," table XIX.

– naval stores, cheese, colonial products, and, in famine years, rye; they purchased wine. This important new market for wine (the Dutch took more than 8,000 tons in 1631 and Hamburg another 4,000) led to greater prosperity for the wine growers and to the expansion of vineyards in the bishopric of Nantes. The expansion of the vineyards created a larger market for grain from the southern littoral; the greater prosperity of the Nantes region led to increased consumption of various goods, such as fish (fresh and salted). More fish consumption led to greater demand for fishing boats and equipment (reexported from Nantes to the western ports). Save for the products introduced by the Dutch, the commercial network consisted essentially of subsistence commodities – grain, wine, fish, salt. The internal trading network for such commodities was extremely old (dating back easily to the twelfth century) and involved widespread use of barter, such as the officially sanctioned (tax-free) exchange of salt for grain practiced in the salt marshes of Guérande and the hinterlands of Cornouaille. In 1631, for example, we see Olivier Le Mitrailler of Guérande bartering 18 *muids* of salt for 30 tons of rye and buckwheat from Châteaulin.[70]

In the 1640s, this Nantais prosperity began to wane. There were more quarrels between the Dutch and the Nantais; the heavy wine taxes reduced Breton consumption of wine (especially Loire wine and Nantais wine sold outside of the bishopric of Nantes); the wars in the Baltic reduced trade (and therefore exports of wine, especially Loire wine) to that area. The result was a catastrophic decline in wine exports from Nantes after 1642 or so.[71] The hard times in the *pays Nantais* led to problems elsewhere, problems compounded by local disasters such as the massive fishing fleet losses of Audierne and Penmarc'h in the 1630s and 1640s.[72] When Nantes recovered from the mid-century malaise, it was not within the framework of this old trade network of subsistence products, but as a center of the new colonial commerce. Nantes' trading partners in Brittany did not adapt so well to the new economy; they continued to export the old subsistence goods (especially grain). The result, in the eighteenth century, was a situation in which Nantes grew rapidly (its population reaching 80,000) and prospered, while its old partners dropped further and further behind.[73]

We can get a sense of the overall movement of trade by looking at lease prices for the major transit tax farms (table 4). The export–import duties at Nantes produced steadily greater income in the sixteenth century and, after a sharp decline during the League War, in the first third of the seventeenth century.

[70] AD Loire-Atlantique, B 9230.
[71] Collins, "Atlantic France" and Collins, "Les impôts et le commerce du vin en Bretagne," *Actes du 107e Congrès National des Sociétés Savantes* (Brest, 1984), I, 155–68.
[72] H. Le Carquet, "Le Cap-Sizun, la morue du Raz de Fonteroy," *Bulletin de la Société des Antiquitaires du Finistère*, 37 (1908): 8–26.
[73] J. Meyer, *L'armement nantais au XVIIIe siècle* (Paris, 1976); T. Le Goff, *Vannes and its Region in the Eighteenth Century* (Oxford, 1981).

Table 4: *Leases of the* ports et havres *and* prévôté de
Nantes, *1606–72 (in livres)*

Year	Ports	Prévôté
1606	34,600[a]	58,000
1609		56.000[b]
1615		60,000[c]
1618	59,910	58,000
1621	61,487	59,000[d]
1624		63,000[c]
1627–8	58,000	60.000[c]
1630	65,300	
1633	64,000	
1636	58,500	
1639	60,000	
1642–3	57,000	70,000[f]
1649	51,700	66,000
1652	52,500	70,000
1656–2		70,000
1661–2	52,000	75,000
1664	56,800	
1667	56,700	
1670	57,700	

Notes:
[a] Substantial portions of revenues alienated.
[b] Rebate of 10,000 livres.
[c] Rebate of 10,000 livres.
[d] Large rebate, unknown size.
[e] Part of *Cinq Grosses Fermes*, no separate lease.
[f] Part of *Cinq Grosses Fermes*, official estimated value
given by Chamber of Accounts.
Sources: AD Loire-Atlantique, B 66–83, registration of
leases at the Chamber of Accounts.

The revenue from the duties of the other bishoprics also rose steadily into the
1620s. In each case, we see a decline in the middle of the seventeenth century –
at Nantes after 1640; elsewhere, after 1630 – and a recovery after 1660
(although not to earlier levels, particularly when prices are adjusted for currency
devaluation).[74] The actual receipts were much higher than the lease prices, if

[74] Lease prices on the farms are available in various places: on 1503, ADLA, E 212, piece 20; on
1533 and 1535, BN, Mss.Fr.22,330, fols. 679–700v and BN, Mss.Fr.22,342, fol. 135; on 1578,
ADLA, B 60, fols. 98 and ff.; on the early seventeenth century, ADLA, B 61, fols. 183 and ff.,
232–7, 303–9v.

the situation of 1631 was at all normative: in that year, the lease of the *prévôté de Nantes* had an estimated value of 70,000 livres and receipts were 83,000 livres.[75] The income from the duties levied for the city of Nantes reinforces the image taken from the evolution of the *prévôté* receipts: they show steady growth in the port traffic in the sixteenth century, with a tremendous jump in the 1560s and 1570s, followed by a decline in the war years, rapid recovery after 1600, and a steady increase until the 1660s, when the traffic drops sharply.[76]

The slightly different curves of the *prévôté* and the *ports* between 1620 and 1670 indicate that the products taxed by the *prévôté*, mainly wine, followed a different market evolution than those – grain and livestock products – taxed by the *ports*. Livestock exports continued to go up into the 1640s, declining only after 1650, so that the decline in the *ports* lease was probably due to the erratic grain trade of the 1640s and to the sudden incursion of the Dutch into the Nantais market in 1643. They had already interfered on the Iberian markets and those of Bordeaux and La Rochelle. This greater Dutch presence in traditional Breton grain markets, and consequent lower sales for Breton grain, may have led to the decline in the receipts of the *ports*. When livestock exports declined as well, around 1650, the overall lease price (for the *ports* and *bêtes vives*) dropped sharply.[77]

The evolution of the wine trade was more complex than the *prévôté* figures would suggest. The most heavily taxed item at Nantes was wine, which provided over half of the receipts in 1631. The overall lease price evolution would suggest that the wine trade continued strong into the 1660s; such was not the case. The most severely damaged trade was that of Loire wine exported through Nantes. The lease price of 5 sous/pipe of upstream wine passing under the bridge at Nantes declined by 90 percent between 1644 and 1695[78] (table 5). The actual tonnage of upstream wine coming through Nantes rose from about 7,000 in 1505 to double and triple that figure in the late sixteenth and early seventeenth centuries, peaking at about 28,000 tons in 1631.[79]

The leases for general wine farms in the province bear out the overall decline of the wine trade in the 1640s. If we take 1610 as an index of 100, we can show long-term trends based on the great duty of the Estates and on their "little duty," raised to help pay the Parlement. The latter is particularly interesting because the lease price remained constant; farmers competed to offer the lowest possible duty to achieve the fixed price[80] (table 6). The general movement of

---

[75] ADLA, B 2976, register of the *prévôté*.
[76] Tanguy, "Le commerce du port de Nantes au début du XVIIe siècle," appendix tables, reproduced in his "L'essor de la Bretagne," 27, 40–3, and 51.
[77] ADLA, B 82, fols. 146–51; lease of *ports* in 1664 to local syndicate in ADLA, B 82, fols. 182–5; B 80, fols. 33v–7v for 1652, B 83, fol. 46v for 1667.   [78] ADLA, G 87.
[79] J. Tanguy, "Le commerce du port de Nantes au début du XVIIe siècle," appendix tables.
[80] ADIV, C 2749 and continuing, papers of the Estates. Rebillon offers a confusing description of the *petit devoir*. At its origin (1601), the Estates levied it to pay for the extra session of the

Table 5: *Shipment of wine past Nantes, 1613–1713*

Year	Minimum shipments of upstream wine (tons)
1613	11,134
1617	12,600
1621	14,000
1625	17,000
1631	20,000
1633	8,000
1644	18,200
1650	13,300
1656	13,800
1671	4,500
1674	4,600
1687	6,000
1695	1,810
1704	2,820
1707	2,280
1713	3,000

Note:
A ton of upstream wine contained about 775 litres.
Sources: AD Loire-Atlantique, G 87; B 71, fol. 250
(1613); B 2976 (1631, actual shipments); B 75, fols.
94v–95 (1663).

both indices is quite similar: after 1610, an increase until the early 1620s, followed by a leveling off or a slight decline until 1640, when both drop precipitously. For the great duty, there is a marked recovery in 1661 – indeed to an almost euphoric level – followed by a return to the typically reduced level of the period in 1664. The unadjusted level then moves steadily upward, reaching 90 by 1675, only to fall again in the immediate wake of the rebellions of 1675.

The great duty did not remain constant, nor did the product mix remain the same, so that we must remain aware of other influences on the evolution of its returns. The Estates added cider and beer taxes in 1626 and a tax on eau-de-vie in 1637. Each time the duty rose sharply, the proportional returns declined (a time-honored phenomenon of all taxation). The great duty was also subject to constant interference from the provincial notables in the leasing arrangements: in the 1670s, the bishop of Dol accused the duke de Chaulnes, the governor of

Parlement. The price, 27,500 livres, remained fixed; the size of the duty to raise the money was allowed to fluctuate. After 1653, the Estates changed the *petit devoir* into a large wine tax, one that they consistently "doubled" in the 1660s and 1670s. In 1678, for example, the *petit devoir* was 5.5 livres per pipe on imported wine (and pro rata); the Estates had even alienated 26 sous/pipe in 1673 to raise 600,000 livres.

Table 6: *Evolution of the great and little wine duties of
the Estates (1610=100; ratio of 1610 was duty of 10
livres/pipe=400,000 livres receipts)*

	Great duty		Duty in livres/pipe	Little duty
1611	100		10	100
1612	98		10	100
1613	111		7.5	100
1614	111		7.5	100
1615	119		6	101
1616	119		6	113
1617	142		5	unknown
1618	142		5	96
1619	133		5	100
1620	133		5	116
1620	125		5	
1621	125		5	116
1621	112	(101)	7.5	ª
1622	112	(101)	7.5	105
1622	97		2.5	
1623	97		10	100
1624	104		10	116
1625	85		15	122
1626	99		10	110
1627	103	(87)	15	110ᵇ
1628	103	(87)	15	90
1629	100		15	97
1630	100		15	101
1631	100		15	101
1631	100	(98)	5	
1632	100	(98)	20	97
1633	100		20	97
1634	100		20	84
1635	108	(106)	20	84
1636	108	(106)	20	unknown
1637	94		20	98
1637	111	(102)	1.67	
1638	94		20	98
1638	111	(102)	1.67	
1639	94		20	95ᶜ
1639	111	(102)	1.67	
1639	83		5	
1640	83		32.5	95
1641	83		32.5	95
1642	75		40	95
1643	75		40	68
1644	93	(69)	40	68
1645	93	(69)	40	62

Table 6: *contd*

	Great duty		Duty in livres/pipe	Little duty
1646	71	(66)	40	62
1647	71	(66)	40	55
1648	68		35	55
1649	68		40	50
1650	68		20	50
1650	71		20	
1651	71		40	53
1652	71		20	53
1652	66		20	
1653	66		40	*d*
1654	66		10	
1654	58		40	
1655	58		40	
1656	58		10	
1656	68		25	
1657	68		40	
1658	68		40	
1659–60	69		40	
1661–2	103		40	
1663–4	69		40	
1666–7	67		40	
1668–9	75		40	
1670–1	79		40	
1672–3	79		40	
1674–5	85		40	
1676–7	90		40	
1678–9	81		40	
1680–1	78		40	

Notes:
[a] Figures in parentheses are corrected for rebates.
[b] In 1627, the Estates taxed cider and beer for the first time.
[c] In 1639, the Estates taxed eau-de-vie for the first time.
[a] The manner of levying the little duty was changed in 1653, so that it can no longer be used to construct a similar index.
Sources: AD Ille-et-Vilaine, C 2765–86, assizes of the Estates; C 2940–2, 2887–9, 2930, 2969, 2980–2, accounts of the Estates; AD Loire-Atlantique, B 79–83, registration of contracts of Estates and king.

the province, of taking a bribe of 700,000 livres during the leasing process; if added to the lease price, it would raise the index over 100.[81] We must also consider the currency devaluations of the period 1637 to 1663, which would sharply depress the index in constant silver equivalencies.

The local wine duty returns of various Breton towns show the same patterns. At Hennebont, the sou/*pot* of wine sold in the town and suburbs produced 5,080 livres in 1607 and 6,050 livres in 1632. In 1641, however, the price dropped to 3,375 livres; it remained at approximately that level for the next thirty years.[82] Vannes's pattern of consumption resembled that of Hennebont: 9,000 livres in 1624, up to 11,500 livres by 1634, but down to 7,900 livres in 1645 and to 6,500 livres in 1672.[83] At Roscoff, on the northern coast, the receipts from the duties rose from 600 livres in 1595 to 1,600 livres in 1638, but then dropped to 800 livres in 1643.[84] By 1665 the town had discontinued the wine tax because its receipts (then under 500 livres per year) did not cover the costs of registering the royal letters patent and of auditing the accounts.[85] At the mouth of the Loire, at Guérande, the duty produced between 2,000 and 2,300 livres a year in the 1620s and 1630s, but declined to 1,720 livres in 1641 and to 800 livres in 1653.[86] Here we see the clear decline of the salt marsh region, evident as well in the reduced salt shipments through Nantes.[87]

The general lines seem clear: rapid increase between 1610 and 1620, steady overall performance in the 1620s and 1630s, with certain crisis years causing problems (notably 1622 and 1627), catastrophic decline in the 1640s and 1650s, recovery to earlier levels (although below the peaks) in the 1660s and 1670s. Loire wines suffered the most, losing their Breton markets. Nantais wine does

---

[81] On the evolution of the Breton wine trade, see: Tanguy, "L'essor de la Bretagne," 34. C. Huetz de Lemps, "Le commerce maritime des vins d'Aquitaine de 1699 à 1716," *Revue Historique de Bordeaux* (1965): 25–43, has a very useful table on exports of Bordeaux wine for those seventeen years (summarizing the author's findings presented in his later monograph on this subject). The intendant of Bordeaux, in 1691, claimed that the city sold only to foreigners and Bretons (Boislisle, *Correspondance*, piece 710). This consumption pattern was noted by the king in the early seventeenth century – Bordeaux wine in the west, Angevin and Nantais wine in the Vannetais and Rennes region. See also, Collins, "The Role of Atlantic France." Outside developments, such as the wars in the Baltic, could have an important influence on Breton wine exports: the farmer of the 5 sous at the bridge of Nantes asked for a rebate for the late 1650s on the grounds that "la Guerre du Nort qui auroit beaucoup contribué à l'anéantissement de lad. ferme, ayant faire cesser le commerce et transport des vins aux royaumes de Suède, Dannemarck, Pollogne et autres pays estrangers..." (ADLA, G 87, piece 21).

[82] AM de Hennebont, CC 2.   [83] AM de Vannes, CC 3–10.

[84] ADLA, B 79, fols. 193v–4 (lease of 1643), claiming they had received 1,600–1,700 livres before. In 1642, the lease price was 1,200 livres (B 78, fols. 73v–4). B 76, fol. 153, lease of 1634 for 1,600 livres, claiming that the highest previous level was 1,700 livres.

[85] Colbert de Croissy, *La Bretagne en 1665*, 179.   [86] ADLA, B 9230.

[87] Tanguy, "Le commerce de Nantes"; Collins, "The Role of Atlantic France in the Baltic trade," 239–80, table III: receipts from salt shipments dropped from 33.6 percent of total revenue at the *prévôté de Nantes* in 1603 to 21.6 percent in 1631.

not seem to have had a similar decline and total exports of Nantais wine may have reached earlier levels. There was also, until the 1660s, an increased export of Nantais eau-de-vie (each ton of which consumed about 7 tons of wine). In the 1680s and 1690s, the intendant of Tours argued that Nantais eau-de-vie had completely destroyed that industry in Anjou because of its tax advantages.[88] The overall impression, after 1640, is of a troubled sector. Breton consumers turned increasingly to cider and overseas markets tended to dry up. The Dutch bought less Nantais wine after 1660 or so and virtually no Loire wines. Exports of wine to Holland dropped sharply in the second half of the century and continued to decline in the eighteenth century (when wine had long since been replaced by sugar as the main Nantais export).

The indicators of other economic sectors show a similar pattern of increase followed by stagnation or decline after 1640–60. The tithes throughout the province rose rapidly from 1610 until the mid century. Taking a sample of thirteen parishes in the Nantes region, we find that their collective tithes produced 4,174 livres for the cathedral chapter in 1610 but 9,580 livres in 1650.[89] Entry fees (variously known as the "denier à Dieu", the "commission", the "droit d'entrée" or "pot de vin") had been minor annoyances – at Chantenay, near Nantes, two capons in 1601 – but rose to become enormous *cash* burdens – at Chantenay, 32 livres by 1620 and 100 livres by 1640. The *pays Nantais* was entirely typical in this pattern: at Chambrières, near Quimperlé, at Theix and "Suhiriac" (perhaps Sulniac), near Vannes, at Plouvara and Gourin on the north coast, the tithes jumped sharply after 1620, fluctuated wildly in the 1650s, and levelled off or declined after 1660.[90]

Rents, like tithes, rose rapidly in the first half of the century. At the *bordage* of La Robinière, near Nantes, the rent increased from 30 livres (1624) to 60 livres (1647) but dropped back to 30 livres by 1698. At Coudray, a *métairie* near Nantes, the rent jumped from 40 livres (plus *corvée* and other duties) in 1611 to 150 livres from 1645 to 1664; it dropped to 120 livres in 1685 and stayed there until 1732. At a third property of the Chartreux of Nantes, the *métairie* of La Chapelle-aux-Moines, the rent moved from 180 livres in 1629 to 260 livres by 1651 and 330 livres by 1662, but it declined slowly to reach 270 livres in 1683, a

---

[88] Boislisle, *Correspondance des contrôleurs généraux*, pieces 417, 1478. Piece 1283, a letter from the intendant of Brittany, de Nointel, in February 1694, claims that the lease price of the 45 sous/*barrique* (quarter-ton) of eau-de-vie passing Ingrande-s-Loire dropped from 25,846 livres in 1694 to 17,333 livres for the period 1695–1710 (lease newly signed in 1694, for fifteen years). These figures would represent 2,872 tons of eau-de-vie in 1694 and 1,926 tons in 1695. By way of contrast, Nantes exported only 1,752.5 tons of eau-de-vie in 1728, the highest year in the eighteenth century (and the figure includes Nantais as well as Angevin eau-de-vie): P. Jeulin, *L'évolution du port de Nantes* (Paris, 1929), table 3*bis*, 243.

[89] ADLA, G 244–5.

[90] ADF, 5 H 115 (Chambrières); ADM, G 43, G 131, 38 G 5 (Theix); ADM, 38 G 5 (Suhiriac); ADF, 66 G 60 (Plouvara); ADF, 1 G 335 (Gourin).

level at which it would remain until 1714.[91] In the Vannetais, the evolution was virtually identical.[92]

The interconnectedness of much of the province – Nantes and the southern littoral – meant that trouble in one area would lead to trouble elsewhere. A recession in the Nantes region meant recession for the areas tied to Nantes, particularly the southern littoral. Less wine to sell meant less money; less money meant fewer grain purchases, fewer fish consumed. A decline in fish sales meant a decline in sales of naval stores; the process spiralled steadily downward. After 1660, the cargoes of ships bound from Nantes to Brittany and elsewhere took on a very different character. In 1631, for example, virtually every ship going to Vannes or Redon carried wine only (a few carried building materials or naval stores); in 1701, the bill of lading for a ship delivering goods to M. Felot at Vannes included prunes, herring, almonds, muscat grapes, cloth, iron goods, planks, English wool, Nantais wine, faience, cod, and wine from the Canary Islands.[93] We know from the work of Jeulin, Meyer, and others, that such was the typical pattern – colonial goods taking the place of Nantais wine.[94] These goods were expensive and there is little evidence that they were sold to a broad clientele, save for sugar. The poorer classes of the Vannetais were no longer part of the Nantais commercial circuit as they had been in the early seventeenth century.

Whom did taxes and other methods practiced by elites for getting a share of surplus production affect? In the long run, almost everyone in the province; in the more immediate sense, the richer peasants and the lower classes (both tradespeople and day laborers) of the towns suffered most. The richer peasants were hurt most by the rising rents, particularly by the sharply higher entry fees, which had to be paid in *cash*. These rich peasants, perhaps 20 percent of the total, were the ones able to invest. They received a double blow, from higher direct taxes and from the higher entry fees and small cash dues, which took cash out of their pockets and made investment more difficult. The poorer peasants, the bottom half of those on the tax rolls, paid very little in direct taxes. The increased assessments of the period after 1637 had little direct effect on the poor but these rising taxes did have a powerful indirect impact on such individuals, because they meant that those who monopolized the land had less available capital and therefore might employ fewer laborers. As half to two-thirds of the heads of households relied on such income for part of their sustenance, this posed a serious problem. Rising rents meant that their cottages and tiny plots cost more, further squeezing their limited resources.

The economies of the different regions of the province faltered at different

---

[91] ADLA, H 275, pieces 1–3. ADLA, G 244–5.
[92] Gallet, *La seigneurie bretonne*, 360–1.   [93] ADM, B 820.
[94] Jeulin, *L'évolution*, table 3*bis* gives a good summary. He estimates that 80 percent of the sugar processed at Nantes that went to Europe went to Holland.

times in the seventeenth century. The salt marshes went first, at the end of the sixteenth and beginning of the seventeenth centuries. The Vannetais and the fishing industry of the southern littoral seem to have been next, running into problems in the 1640s. The vineyards of Nantes began to have problems in the 1640s but the period 1640–60 was more one of erratic economic evolution than of complete collapse. By way of contrast, the vineyards of nearby Anjou suffered dreadfully in this period, in large measure due to the Breton tax system. The entire province, except for the linen manufacturers, seems to have had problems after 1660, with perhaps a generation of uncertainty, as we have seen in the evolution of tithes and rents.

The last to go were the linen manufactures of Morlaix and Saint-Malo but they, too, collapsed shortly after 1680, wiping out all of the growth of the century. In the case of the linens, the king's prohibition of trade with England killed the market; the Estates argued strongly against the prohibition, claiming that while England sold many goods in France, the French sold far more in England, so that the country received a net gain from the exchange. The king was unmoved. The evidence of the parish vestrymen's accounts is clear on the timing of the decline in the west: Cornouaille starts to slip in the 1660s, Léon, the linen-producing area, slips only in the 1680s and 1690s.[95]

By 1700 most of Brittany had a severely depressed economy. The port of Nantes and, to a lesser degree, Saint-Malo prospered in the colonial trade and in Grand Banks fisheries but the economy of the rest of the province stagnated or declined. The wine trade did not recover; the grain trade remained at a much reduced level; the local manufactures did not recover their overseas markets. Save for Nantes and Brest, Brittany's population did not grow as fast as that of the rest of France; in a dramatic reversal of earlier migration patterns, Bretons now moved to France.

The much higher rents, higher tithes, and higher royal taxes after 1626 gradually dried up the capital resources of the peasants and prevented the sort of investment that had been so successful in the late sixteenth and early seventeenth centuries. The richer peasants, the ones who monopolized the land, had to pay the bulk of all three exactions. The upper classes and the state were a bit too greedy in their efforts to obtain more of the surplus production of the peasantry, so that the wealthier peasant farmers no longer had the resources necessary for investment and improvement. If we consider our examples from the Nantes region, the rents doubled between 1610 and 1650, the tithes doubled in the same period, royal direct taxation doubled in 1643, and the Estates' duty on local wine went from 4 deniers a *pot* (1.8 liters) to 2 sous a *pot* between 1624 and 1642. There is no evidence that wages increased in anything

---

[95] Tanguy, "L'essor de la Bretagne," 45 and 74. J. Tanguy, "La production et le commerce des toiles 'Bretagne' du 16e au 18e siècles," *Actes du 91e Congrès National des Sociétés Savantes* (1966): 105–41.

like this proportion; in fact, the available evidence suggests that they remained absolutely stable, at roughly 10 sous a day, throughout the seventeenth century.[96]

Over-taxation of certain groups within the population contributed to this economic decline. The sectors that suffered most – wine, livestock, linen – were those whose production was most strongly in the hands of the peasants, and here one must be specific and say the richer peasants. There were many factors involved in the decline of the Breton economy after 1660: the loss of markets to the Dutch, the loss of Dutch markets, the prohibition on trade with England, the changing nature of European patterns of consumption of alcohol. Two local factors stand out: the taxing policies followed by the Estates of Brittany between 1583 and 1675, overloading one of the province's most important economic sectors and thus putting an intolerable strain on the traditional commercial economy; and, more importantly, the unrestrained political control of the landlords, which enabled them to tighten the screws on the peasants beyond the pressure the latter could bear.

Brittany had a remarkably varied economy in early modern times. It produced a wide variety of agricultural goods – different grains, livestock products, fruits (apples, pears, plums, even melons), wine, industrial crops (flax and hemp), pulses (beans were particularly widespread); it had a broad industrial base, focused on textiles woven from hemp and flax; it had a thriving merchant marine and fishing industry; it had an extensive international trade in textiles, wine, paper, salt, and fish. The greater Dutch penetration of the Breton market in the early seventeenth century expanded the number of products available in the province and tied ever larger portions of it to market production; that is, in the early seventeenth century, more and more Bretons produced for the market and broke away from subsistence agriculture. The collapse of those markets in the late seventeenth century, combined with the heavy burdens placed upon the better-off peasantry by the landlords and the Crown, ruined the province's economy and reduced the Breton peasantry to a penury from which much of it would not escape for over two centuries.

CLASS AND ECONOMIC INTEREST

The various socio-economic groups, which may loosely be termed classes, had different stakes in the Breton economy. The seven major classes were: 1) the rural and urban workers, whose chief economic resource was the sale of their

---

[96] Prices and wages from AM de Nantes, series CC, accounts of the town government, and DD, accounts of the Hospital. BN, Mss. Fr. 22,311, fols. 267–9, repairs of Douarnenez in 1615–17, shows masons and carpenters getting 12 sous a day, helpers and laborers 10 sous a day. The hospital paid as little as 8 sous a day, plus midday meal in the 1650s, but the usual rate was 10 sous a day for unskilled work.

labor; 2) the small occupiers – shopkeepers and artisan masters, many of the fishermen, 3) the medium-level peasants, those with a holding too small to support a family; 4) the rich peasants; 5) the merchants; 6) the legal people (many of them *sieurs*); and 7) the noble landlords (including the seigneurs).

The main interest of the working classes was simple survival. This meant, first of all, low or reasonable grain prices. This group was the largest, numerically, and the other groups recognized its right to survive. Survival depended on the grain supply, usually satisfactory in Brittany (with some exceptions, such as the savage famine of 1597 or the dearth years of 1631 and 1661).[97] The town authorities rigorously supervised the grain trade, both to ensure an adequate supply and to maintain certain price and quality controls (the latter focused largely on bread). The ruling authorities also supplied charity when necessary, so that charity took on sharply political overtones. These poor workers, both urban and rural – and many of them worked in both sectors – worried about job availability as well, so that it was in their interests that the economic sectors in which they worked – livestock or arable farming, manufacturing of textiles – be protected from taxation or restriction. These people, in Brittany as elsewhere in France, had relatively few grievances against royal *direct* taxation; they were far more sensitive to increases in *indirect* taxation, which struck either their means of earning a livelihood or their daily consumption. While they had very little direct political clout, they did have significant indirect political influence, because the ruling groups usually did not wish to drive them to rebellion and because the economic elites needed their labor to make the system function.

The small shopkeepers and artisan masters of the towns and the middling peasants of the countryside shared some economic interests but had very great differences as well. Both groups had ties to the market, but their markets were limited in scope. The shopkeepers and artisan masters usually sold to local customers (although, at the top of each scale, there were exceptions); many of the artisans, such as the linen weavers of Léon, lived in villages rather than towns. These crafts and shops had many women owners and workers; the budgets of families in this category often included two incomes. At Nantes, for example, a wife-and-husband team ran most taverns: the husband often carried on a separate profession (such as master craftsman), while the wife ran the tavern.[98] On the middling farms, the family produced goods – eggs, vegetables, industrial crops – for the market; the woman managed such activity. The husband had primary, but by no means exclusive, responsibility for the few fields and also hired himself out as a laborer. The shopkeepers, masters, and

[97] Croix, *La Bretagne*, 367. The highest price for bread I have found for seventeenth-century Nantes was 4 sous a pound in 1631.

[98] ADLA, B 6782, piece 72. J. Collins, "The Economic Role of Women in Seventeenth-Century France," *French Historical Studies*, 16, (2) (Fall 1989): 436–70; details on 461–2.

middling peasants shared the concern of the wage laborers with respect to grain prices, because they all purchased grain on the market.

These middling groups prospered in the late sixteenth and early seventeenth century because of the expansion of local commerce. Consumption of a wide variety of products – wine, oranges, fish – went up, and it is likely that the greater prosperity of this middling group had much to do with the increase.[99] The urban members of this group paid an inordinate amount of taxation because they could afford to drink wine, yet probably did so most often in taverns, thus paying the retail sales tax. The workers also fell into this category, as they drank in taverns, both urban and rural. In the *pays Nantais*, in 1625, roughly one person in 100 or 150 ran a tavern: the percentage was highest in small towns like Ancenis, where there were thirty-nine taverns to serve the roughly 2,000 inhabitants, but even villages such as Massérac or Anetz had four taverns for populations of 500–650 people.[100]

In a rare case of the enumeration of the clients of a tavern, that of Claude Marcan, cooper, and his wife, in the Fosse of Nantes, we find men, most of them between 18 and 30 (ten of the fourteen whose ages are known), all of them from our two bottom groups, half of them from a single trade – shoes.[101] These people had a strong interest in keeping down the duties on alcohol. In western Brittany, this goal was unmet, as the duties on wine rose sharply after 1620. In Rennes and Nantes, the two towns with the greatest capacity for causing problems, special rules limited the duties on the main beverages of popular consumption (cider in Rennes, an advantage shared with the other eastern towns; Nantais wine in Nantes, taxed at a lower rate there than elsewhere).[102] The political treatment of these people, therefore, was that they were protected as producers but, save for those in Nantes and the cider-drinking regions, they were heavily taxed as consumers of alcohol.

There were four key differences between these two groups, otherwise so similar. First, the small peasants held land (in some cases even owned a tiny bit of it). Second, the small peasants produced some of their own grain, so were less dependent on that market. Third, the small peasants often supplemented their income by doing manufacturing work in the putting-out system. They supported the liberty of commerce – that is, fewer guild and production restrictions – while the shopkeepers of the towns generally opposed a liberty of commerce that would destroy their monopolies. Fourth, the peasants opposed higher direct taxation, because they paid it; the artisans opposed higher wine taxes, which *they* paid.

The third group, the rich peasants or ploughmen (*laboureurs* and some *métayers* and *tenuyers*) had close ties to the market. They produced very little

---

[99] ADLA, B 2976. Nantes imported over one million oranges in 1631.
[100] ADLA, B 6782, piece 149; Croix, *Nantes et le pays nantais*, 202.
[101] ADLA, B 6784.   [102] See ch. 4 for details.

grain for the market – that was sold almost exclusively by landlords and the Church – but they produced many other goods for markets near and far. Here we must allow for local variation, because the poorer peasants of certain regions were also tied to such markets. In Léon, for example, many peasants produced linen cloth, usually bought by peasant merchants, who then sold it in Morlaix.[103] In the *pays Nantais*, the peasants marketed most of the wine: the leasing system, the *complant*, allowed the peasant to keep either two-thirds or three-quarters of the crop; they sold this wine to Nantais merchants who exported it to western Brittany and abroad. Their situation was a sort of early imperialism, in that they became tied into a large international market, producing one special commodity – wine. When the demand for that commodity declined, they were in serious trouble. A memoir of 1645 showed the nature of their dependence on the merchants; they complained of receiving very low prices for their wine (and for being forced to deliver it to Nantes, rather than to the customary "flowing water"), while the same merchants supplied them with inferior grain (linseed, barley, oats, peas mixed in with the rye) at inflated prices.[104] The situation in Léon was much the same; when the market for linens collapsed in the late 1680s and 1690s, the area went into a dramatic economic and demographic tailspin.

These rich peasants could also market other goods. It would seem likely, based on the information about livestock holdings on various tenures in the province, that some (probably a considerable portion) of the livestock marketed in the province was sold by peasants. The customary arrangement was for them to split the increase in livestock with the landlord (who had supplied the original stock); we have seen how large the peasant herd could be in the case of the *métairie* of La Chapelle-aux-Moines. These peasants, like the middling ones, also marketed subsidiary goods: poultry and poultry products, butter, cattle by-products, flax and hemp, beans, some fruit (notably in the eastern part of the province). Their economic interests dictated low direct taxes because they paid the bulk of such taxes – 60 percent in an average parish. As consumers, they also felt the wine taxes and, in the 1660s and 1670s, the increasingly high legal fees and taxes (because they were the ones needing legal contracts). This group was not heavily taxed by French standards, but it did bear the brunt of Breton direct taxation and paid a goodly portion of the indirect burden as well. They were also squeezed by the higher rents, especially entry fees due in cash, of the period 1620–60.

The merchants formed a heterogeneous group, ranging from small traders to enormously wealthy individuals at Nantes, Saint-Malo, and Vitré. The richest merchants traded in cloth, grain and wine during the seventeenth century, with

---

[103] Tanguy, "L'essor de la Bretagne." As for the socio-cultural gap between peasants and artisans, see, J. Ménétra, *Journal de ma vie* (Paris, 1982) which contains many examples of his utter contempt for the peasants. The journal makes it clear that Ménétra finds peasants to be almost another order of human being.   [104] ADLA, B 6663.

a shift into the colonial trade after 1660 (and a new group of merchant families, at least at Nantes). The wine duties did not affect the export of wine to foreign countries, a prime concern of the Nantais, but they did harm substantially the consumption of both Nantais and Angevin wine in western Brittany. The sharp decline in exports of Angevin and Loire wine visible after 1640 or so reflected the impact of the higher tax rate of the post-1635 period.

Merchants sought protection from the government, both in the sense of maintaining a strong royal navy (especially from the 1570s to the 1620s, to combat Rochelais pirates) and in the sense of keeping the government from interfering with commerce. They constantly petitioned the Estates to prevent new manufacturing, export, and sale taxes; they were, in most cases, successful. The merchants, and their allies in the financial bureaucracy (made up of men from mercantile families), also wanted to keep Breton tax farms in Breton hands. These farms provided a substantial source of income, not only for those directly involved, but also for those who invested the background capital. Again, with occasional exceptions (the 1630s and 1640s, in particular), the Estates did manage to protect Breton access to tax farms.

The merchants' interests were usually protected when they were compatible with the existing socio-political system. When there was a conflict, as in the case of higher direct taxes versus more retail wine taxes, the landlords followed their own interest. The chief point of dispute, other than wine taxes, was the free export of grain outside the province. The Nantes region was the only large-scale importer of grain, so it sought to protect its supplies by limiting shipments outside the province; the grain-producing regions sought to broaden their markets, so they wanted free export. Barring a severe famine, the free export forces won out.

What about the interests of the ruling elite, the landlords, both noble and *roturier*? These people dominated the possession of the land. Jean Gallet's figures on eighteen parishes in the Vannetais are startling in this regard: peasants and others held only 11 percent of the land held in tenures, *sieurs* (noble and *roturier*) held the other 89 percent. The range of peasant ownership was from zero (Plumergat, 0 of 130) to 47.6 percent (10 of 21 in Pluherlin), with one cluster (7) of parishes around 5 percent and another one (6) around 15 percent.[105] These figures *exclude* much of the landlords' property, such as mills, *métairies*, and manors. The peasant holdings tended to be quite small. In the eighteenth century, Henri Sée found that half of all peasant holdings contained under 5 *journaux* (a bit over 2 hectares) and 80–90 percent under 10 *journaux*.[106] Gallet has found, in examining land sales in the Vannetais between 1480 and 1598, that most of those selling land (102 of 193) were peasants and that they sold very small parcels. The buyers, of course, were *sieurs* (147 of the 193

---

[105] Gallet, *La seigneurie bretonne*, 523–7.   [106] Sée, *Les classes rurales*, 62–9.

cases).[107] The figures of Sée and Gallet strongly imply that while the peasants of Upper Brittany owned a considerable share of the land (for the most part in tiny plots), those of Lower Brittany owned almost no land because of the extensive use of the *domaine congéable*.

The landlords did not form a homogenous group. We can distinguish between two basic groups: those with feudal rights, the seigneurs; and those without such rights, the *sieurs*. The latter were primarily people from the judicial system (judges, lawyers, notaries), but many old noble families owned *sieuries*. Even among the seigneurs, we must be careful to distinguish between the rich, middling, and poor. The capitation lists of 1695 provide sharp differences among the different ranks of nobles: dukes – 1,500 livres (class 2); marquises, counts, viscounts, and barons – 250 livres (class 7); untitled gentlemen holding fiefs – 40 livres (class 15); and untitled gentlemen without fiefs – 6 livres (class 19). Many ploughmen paid more than the last category of nobles, and we can see the extraordinary range of difference among nobles – dukes paid 250 times as much as an *hobereau* (quite a reasonable proportion when one considers the overall incomes of Breton dukes). Although it is impossible to provide any sort of exact count or estimate of noble incomes in the sixteenth or early seventeenth centuries, Charles Colbert de Croissy, the visiting royal commissioner of 1665, provided a list of major nobles and their landed incomes for seven of the nine Breton bishoprics (he left out Nantes and Rennes).[108]

Colbert de Croissy enumerated some forty-five to fifty families whose landed income came to 20,000 livres a year or more, as well as another thirty-five to fifty whose landed income exceeded 10,000 livres a year. He did not consistently go into details on those whose income was under 10,000 livres, although he mentioned about thirty such families by name, as well as indicating that thirty to forty other families existed in the bishopric of Cornouaille and "many others" in the bishoprics of the north coast. The people whose income exceeded 30,000 livres all held a title (marquis, baron, even prince or duke); their seigneurial jurisdictions usually extended over broad areas (and had lesser seigneurial courts under their purview); family members were or had been governors of local towns or local royal military commanders. Because he did not include the bishoprics of Rennes and Nantes, most of the highest judicial officers are not represented in his report.

The most powerful families included some of national, even international stature: Rohan, la Trémoille.[109] Immediately behind them, we find the Rieux,

---

[107] Gallet, *La seigneurie bretonne*, 323 ff.
[108] Colbert de Croissy, *La Bretagne en 1665*. See the list of such families in the appendix.
[109] The Rohan family even conducted marriage negotiations with the families of foreign rulers (Sweden, the Palatinate). The most elaborate social classification scheme in the available literature is that of Roland Mousnier, set out in volume I of *Les Institutions*. He also gives a detailed explanation of his views on social divisions in *Recherches sur la stratification sociale à Paris aux XVIIe et XVIIIe siècles* (Paris, 1976), ch. 2. Contemporaries were clear on the idea that the

Rosmadec, Coëtquen, la Moussaye, Carman (Maille), Cambout-Coislin, Coët-logon, Guémadeuc, Goulaine, Avaugour, and Boiséon families. Some French families, such as Brissac or Vendôme, had large Breton holdings and served as local military commanders (Brissac was lieutenant general, Vendôme the governor). In the group of forty major landlord families, we find five about whom it is difficult to know any details, and two others who were local royal judicial officers (seneschals). All of the remaining thirty-three families held military office (national, regional or local), all of them save four held a superior seigneurial jurisdiction, and all played a significant role at the Estates (see appendix).[110]

These families often intermarried: the count of La Bellière (Boiséon), governor of Morlaix, was the son of Jeanne de Rieux, daughter of the governor of Brest, and the husband of Françoise de Coëtquen, daughter of the governor of Saint-Malo. Malo II de Coëtquen, brother of Françoise, governor of Saint-Malo, married Marguerite of Rohan-Chabot. In the Rieux, Rosmadec, and Rohan families, cousins intermarried to keep the family estates intact. The marquis of Locmaria, Vincent du Parc, married Claude de Nevet, from one of the forty families; she was the widow of Gabriel, marquis de Goulaine, member of another such family.[111] The Goulaine family intermarried with the Rosmadecs and other leading old noble families, yet also arranged alliances with leading families at the Parlement and even with one of the daughters of Gilles Ruellan, the parvenu financier marquis.

These families also sold land to each other. The la Trémoille family sold two seigneuries in the bishopric of Saint-Brieuc: Quintin, in 1638, to la Moussaye; Plélo, in 1663, to Maurille de Bréhant (another of the forty families). The Rohans sold the county of Crozon to Sébastien de Rosmadec. These families also produced many of the leading Breton ecclesiastics: Rosmadec, bishop of

financiers and the judicial officers were two different classes. E.-M. Benabou, *La prostitution et la police des moeurs au XVIIIe siècle* (Paris, 1987), 384, speaking of the police of Paris, states: "'L'épée, la robe et la finance', est une distinction que font nos inspecteurs." On the peasants, see Goubert and Roche, *Les Français* and P. Goubert, *The French Peasantry in the Seventeenth-Century* (Cambridge, 1986). There is an enormous literature on Marx's (and Marxist) definitions of class, and on the conflict between Marx and Weber with respect to class definitions. Beik, *Absolutism and Society*, 6–9, esp. note 3 on pp. 6–7, gives some of the relevant literature. Marx himself has two distinct general categorizations of classes, one on the theoretical level (bourgeoisie versus proletariat) and the other more analytical (as in the *Eighteenth Brumaire of Louis Napoleon*).

110 Here defining national military office as a position in the royal army, such as marshal of France (Brissac), or as a post as lieutenant general or governor of Brittany (Vendôme, Brissac, de la Meilleraye), regional military office as that of *lieutenant particulier* of Upper or Lower Brittany or of Nantes, and local military office as the command of the local (bishopric) militia, governorship of a town, or temporary royal command (as in 1675). The information on such offices comes from the notes to the report of Colbert de Croissy and from the many encounters with such people in a wide variety of archival records (such as the papers of the Estates).

111 Colbert de Croissy, *La Bretagne en 1665*, 78, n. 57 (Coëtquen), 156, n. 44–5 (Boiséon), 162, n. 72 (Locmaria).

Vannes in 1665; Coatjunval, bishop of Quimper until 1665; Coëtlogon, bishop of Quimper after 1665; Guémadeuc, bishop of Saint-Malo. Several other families, about whom Colbert de Croissy does not give full information, certainly belonged to this group as well: the Lannion family, governors of both Auray and Vannes and intermarried with Pontcallec; the Visdelou family, whose members included Jacques, *chevalier de l'ordre de roi* and purchaser of the seigneurie (later castellany) of Hilguy, from the Rosmadecs, and François, bishop of Léon and, later, Cornouaille.

The most powerful families all held superior seigneurial jurisdictions; some of them, such as the Rohan, la Trémoille, Carman, Avaugour, and Vendôme-Penthièvre families, held several. In 1675, when the peasants of Lower Brittany rose up against their seigneurs, the members of the forty great families led the forces of order. In Cornouaille, the king's lieutenant was the marquis de la Coste; when he was wounded, the baron of Nevet took his place. The local governors were Boiséon (Morlaix), Rieux (Brest), Lannion (Vannes), Kernezne (Quimper), Rosmadec (Nantes), and Coëtlogon (Rennes). The marquis of Cludon commanded the noble militia of Tréguier. Aside from the governor, de Chaulnes, the single individual most active in the struggle against the peasants was Sébastien de Guémadeuc, bishop of Saint-Malo.[112] Some of these people were also the direct targets of the peasants: Mme. de Rohan, at Josselin; the marquis of Trévigny, whose chateau of Kergoët the peasants sacked. Rioters at Châteaulin wounded the marquis de la Coste; his own peasants murdered the marquis of Kersalaun, whose income Colbert de Croissy estimated at only 7–8,000 livres.

Kersalaun is representative of a much larger group: noble landlords with an income under 10,000 livres. Colbert de Croissy named eight such families in the bishopric of Saint-Brieuc and more than a dozen others in that of Dol. He tells us that "many others" in Saint-Malo and Léon had incomes of 4–6,000 livres or less, and that thirty to forty families in Cornouaille met this criterion. In Vannes, he divided the nobility into two classes, seventeen families in the first class (Rohan, etc.) and twenty-two in the second (many of them Parlementaires).

The clear impression is four (perhaps five) distinct groups within the landed nobility: 1) the very rich regional lords, who combined large landed incomes with seigneurial power and royal military office; 2) a second tier of families just below this level, whose incomes were usually in the range of 20–30,000 livres, and who were less likely to have superior seigneurial jurisdictions or high royal office; 3) the squirearchy, with their incomes of some 10,000 livres a year and

---

[112] J. Lemoine, "La révolte dite du Papier Timbré ou des Bonnets Rouges en Bretagne en 1675," *Annales de Bretagne*, 12–14 (1894–6): 315–59, 523–50, 180–259, 346–408, 524–59, 109–40, 189–223, and 438–71. The last five sections are entirely made up of documents, as is the section 197–259 of volume 13. On Guémaduec, see, for example, his report to Colbert, document XCIII, pp. 394–400.

their local seigneurial courts; 4) the poorer nobles, those who had 6,000 livres a year or less (sometimes much less – this group, who could have incomes as low as 500 livres a year, might be a fifth division within the nobility). The most successful social climbers, those who made it to the Parlement, joined categories 2 and 3. The truly spectacular social climbers, like Gilles Ruellan, used their money to buy into the very apex of Breton society: his daughters married into the Brissac and Goulaine families, as well as three other powerful local clans.

How did these landlords make their money? They sold grain – again, following Gallet, we see that most of the grain furnishers to the merchant Gabriel Regnard of Vannes were *sieurs*, including several Parlementaires and sword nobles. There were also three priests and two canons of Saint-Gildas of Rhuys. The landlords, then, sold the grain. They always favored free export of grain and opposed taxes on its sale or shipment. They could be expected to support campaigns against La Rochelle because the city's pirates cut off trade with one of their main clients, Bordeaux. In addition, landlords sold livestock and some wine.

They had some interest in the welfare of the peasants because they needed to obtain cash income from their tenants. The cash entry fees climbed sharply after 1620, often reaching 100 livres in the Vannetais or the *pays Nantais*.[113] These fees represented a considerable drain on the cash resources of the peasants; it would seem likely that the peasants had to borrow money, often from notaries, in order to come up with the cash, just as they did in meeting the large payments for *affranchissements* in 1638 and 1640 (see chapter 3). The nobles, like everyone else in seventeenth-century France, needed cash. Daniel Dessert argues that there was something of a mania about cash in Court circles in the second half of the century, and the same was probably true in western Brittany.[114] Land rents, especially in the western part of the province, came in largely in kind – the landlord usually got a third of the gross crop – and marketing the produce was time-consuming and costly. Cash entry fees produced immediate income and did not depend on the vicissitudes of the harvest of a given year.

Many landlords supplemented this income with cash from other sources. The legal people obtained revenue from offices, from legal practice, and from lending money. Many nobles worked for the royal army, at first in the *compagnie d'ordonnance* of Mercoeur or, later, Brissac, then in the local garrison network or regular army of the 1630s and after. The larger towns had a governor, who was entitled to an *état* and to funding from the town. The main military officers collected a sizeable pension from the Estates each year (see chapter 5), as well as an *état* from the king. These people were invariably powerful nobles such as the duke of Mercoeur, the duke of Brissac, members of the Rohan and Rieux

---

[113] Gallet, *La seigneurie bretonne*, 361.
[114] D. Dessert, *Argent, pouvoir et société au grand siècle* (Paris, 1984).

families, the baron (later duke) of Cambout-Coislin and the duke de La Meilleraye (cousins of Richelieu). By the 1630s, the lieutenant general (de La Meilleraye) received 18,000 livres a year from the Estates and the local lieutenants (Brissac, Vertus, Pontchâteau, Rohan) between 5–10,000 livres each. The Estates also tried to help those of lesser station: in 1636, Dubuisson-Aubenay gives the names of those on the list, sixty-two in all, receiving between 90 and 274 livres. Most of those so assisted received 127 livres (fifteen), 150 or 163 livres (twenty), or 200 livres (seventeen).[115]

Many of these lesser nobles also received money from the great nobles. In 1586, the duke and duchess of Mercoeur salaried and pensioned a wide variety of individuals: four squires for the stables, fourteen "gentilles servantes," three "filles de chambre," two "femmes de chambre," valets, and others received salaries ranging from a few livres for the valet to 200 livres each for the "gentilles servantes." This was a large household indeed, with its four cooks, wine steward, and many other regular servants. The accounts indicate that the household consumed more than 42,000 liters of wine, as well as 240 livres worth of Breton butter (for which a servant was dispatched to Rennes, to make the purchase).[116] Here we see one of the alternative ways of making cash income – serving in a more important household.

Again, as in the lower-class households, we must be aware of the possibilities for the two-income family. When the man was off to war, the woman managed the estates. Marie de Luxembourg, duchess of Mercoeur, witnessed the presentation of the treasurer's account and signed it. Both women and men took positions in the households of the great, receiving salaries, sustenance, and, often, pensions. The duchess and duke pensioned the widow of their intendant (and gave her a gift of 6,000 livres as well), various noble women and men, and influential lawyers, such as the *avocat du roi* at the Parlement of Paris.

Many high-ranking nobles kept noble retainers. Magdelaine de Rohan, dying in 1606, left substantial amounts to various servants: René Le Clerc, *écuyer*, her *maître d'hôtel* – 1,000 livres; Louis Lemarne, *écuyer* – 600 livres; *damoiselle* Magdelaine Blondeau – 1,000 livres; *damoiselle* Françoise Le Clerc – 300 livres.[117] The great nobles – the Rohans, the Rieux, the la Trémoilles, the other national families – needed nobles, both female and male, to fill out their households; the lesser nobles of the province needed these positions to make ends meet. The most powerful individuals had a complex position *vis-à-vis* the royal government. As landlords, they wished to keep royal direct taxation at the minimum possible level. As pensioners of the king (Henry III owed Mercoeur over 75,000 *écus* (1586) – about 45 percent of his income – although the duke

---

[115] Dubuisson-Aubenay, "Journal des Etats," 397–9, gives the list of pensioners.
[116] BN, NAF, 21,878.
[117] BN, Mss. Fr. 22,311, fols. 139–41. There were also pensions to the secretary, the nurse of her child, and to a servant to accompany the child for two years.

did not get most of it) or as pensioners and servants of those who were pensioners of the king, the nobles were in no position to allow royal coffers to run dry. The king and, under his authority, the Estates, pumped tens of thousands of livres into the hands of the nobles every year, and this amount rose steadily in the first half of the seventeenth century.

The political relationship of Brittany and the Crown in the sixteenth and seventeenth centuries was about protecting these partly conflicting interests of the most important group, the landlords. The Crown supported the firm control of the political elites over the province. Those elites used the existing political institutions, notably the Estates and the Parlement, to protect their economic and social interests, as well as their political ones. One of the most important means by which they did so was the Breton tax system. The king demanded money from the province, but he allowed the political elites to determine the manner in which they would raise the money. In so doing, he allowed them to influence, by means of fiscal policy, some of the directions the Breton economy would follow in the sixteenth and, more particularly, in the seventeenth century. Those policies had a profound impact on Breton society, on its patterns of interaction and dominance, and of discontent. Before we examine the policies followed by the Estates, let us turn first to patterns of interaction and dominance, to get the social context for the political situation.

2

Elements of Breton society

THE INSTITUTIONAL FRAMEWORK OF SOCIAL CONTROL

The distribution of political power in early modern Brittany followed closely the distribution of economic resources. The province, like all French provinces of the Ancien Régime, had a superficial society of orders structure. This structure formed part of the system of political and moral authority; most importantly, it strongly influenced the perception of power and authority. The language of political discourse in seventeenth-century France was the language of tradition, of respect for custom and, by extension, of an ordered society.[1] While contemporaries certainly thought in such a manner, they often acted according to different systems of societal organization. The Estates of Brittany invariably protected those privileges that had significant economic meaning to provincial elites.

In Brittany, as in Languedoc, the great power of the entire panoply of monarchical institutions – Sovereign Courts, Estates, town governments, seigneurial systems – meant that the limitations on the monarchy's actions retained their efficacity throughout the Ancien Régime. The contract between the Estates and the Crown provides the best symbol of those limitations. This contract placed the king's obligations to the province precisely in the sphere in which contemporaries felt he had the least freedom of action. Although Brittany had no specific constitution, a network of contracts provided Breton elites with guarantees, similar to those of a constitution, against arbitrary behavior.[2]

The lower classes received, in these contracts, some protection from arbitrary royal behavior, but this protection came at the cost of a freer hand for local elites. When the lower classes received real benefits from the contracts, as in the

---

[1] R. Chartier and D. Richet, *Représentation et pouvoir politique: autour des Etats-Généraux de 1614* (Paris, 1982).

[2] E. Burke, *Reflections on the Revolution in France* (New York, 1973), 45, states that: "It has been the uniform policy of our constitution to claim and assert our liberties, as an *entailed inheritance* derived to us from our forefathers, and to be transmitted to our posterity ... we have an inheritable crown; an inheritable peerage; an house of commons and a people inheriting privileges, franchises, and liberties, from a long line of ancestors." Breton elites believed they were protected by a series of "privileges, franchises and liberties" (a phrase constantly used by the Estates in their dealings with the king), although they did not refer to such protection as a constitution.

case of defending Bretons from non-Breton jurisdictions, such as the *gabelle* courts, these benefits usually worked to the advantage of local elites as well. The relationship between elites and the mass of the population relied on a system of deference, but within that system there was a constant undercurrent of disrespect for the authorities. The antagonisms of early modern Breton society were partly class-based, that is, they were related to the individual's relationship to the means of production, but they had other sources as well.

The three most important other factors involved in such discontent were gender, age, and the mentality of an order-based society. Women had a second level of grievance against the prevailing order; that is, they had the same class- and order-based grievances as men, but the gender role division meant that women played a particularly important role in the expression of grievances. Their singular responsibility for food (and their legal immunities) made women particularly prominent in grain riots, of course, but we tend to forget the extent to which women ran market stalls and the financial end of artisan shops. Conflicts between the indirect tax collectors and the civil population, therefore, often involved a woman running a tavern, a market stall, or a shop of some kind.[3]

Young people remained at the margins of society. Those in their late teens or early twenties tended to be unmarried, mobile, and poor. In the towns, they ate in taverns and congregated there for companionship as well. The large numbers of such people in taverns created the duality of the tavern as private space (to the young men, it was part of *their* "home") and public space (to the authorities, taverns were dens of iniquity, in which political discontent, so closely tied to the moral turpitude of tavern life, was ever present). These young people, like young people of all modern societies, cherished their independence from authority and deeply resented the efforts of the authorities and of civil society to force them to conform to its rules. Quite aside from grievances related to gender or age, all people had grievances that can only be understood within the context of a society of orders: matters of precedence, violations of the "traditional" order of things. These order-based grievances were invariably political, yet often unrelated to economic matters.

In order to understand the distribution of political and social power in Brittany, we must first briefly outline the institutional structure of the province (for details, see chapter 3). Breton political society had six major administrative elements: the Estates, the Parlement, the Chamber of Accounts, the lower judicial system, the seigneurs, and the town governments. These institutions tended to overlap, particularly in the case of the seigneurs (who were, of course, a basic economic structure as well). Virtually all deputies to the Estates were landlords, as were almost all royal officers; many of these people were seigneurs. Town administrative structures included two elements: royal officials, such as a

---

[3] J. Collins, "The Economic Role of Women in Seventeenth-Century France," *French Historical Studies*, 16, (2) (Fall 1989): 436–70.

seneschal or provost, and local ones, such as a mayor and aldermen (or, in smaller towns, a *procureur syndic*). Many of these town officials owned considerable amounts of land, although few of them were seigneurs.

The lower levels of the royal judiciary participated in the direct administration of the larger towns, and the individual officers were often municipal as well as royal officials. Such people, the seneschal of Nantes for example, usually represented the towns at the Estates. If it sounds like a very tightly controlled, neatly defined elite, it should; it was. It was not a *closed* elite – there was always room for the successful new family – but it was a fairly well-defined and united one. Some conflict existed between the town elites and the landlords, particularly at the Estates, but, despite the large proportion of Bretons living in towns (likely over 20 percent), the towns never could mount a serious threat to the political and social supremacy of the landed nobility. The two most powerful towns – Rennes and Nantes – often successfully protected their separate interests, leaving the smaller towns to fend, unsuccessfully, for themselves. Even Nantes, however, consistently lost out when its interests clashed with those of the landlords.

The nature of representation for the Third Estate also mitigated against the interests of the merchants, because the town delegates usually came from the legal group. In virtually all cases, the towns sent their *procureur syndic*, a lawyer, and the mayor, who was often a judge at a royal court. At Nantes, the town usually sent these two individuals and the sub-mayor; in the seventeenth century, when no merchant served as mayor of Nantes, the city's deputies to the Estates always came from its legal rather than its mercantile elite. At the Estates of 1619, when there was a long dispute about precedence in the Third Estate, the deputies for Morlaix, the town that most often of any sent a merchant to the Estates, included Yves Gourville, an *avocat*, and Pierre Callouet, a judge; those for Rennes included Guy Mantes, *alloué* (second judge) of the prevotal court. The Estates settled the dispute about precedence in the Third Estate by allowing the president of the presidial in whose jurisdiction the Estates met, to preside over the order. The landlord–legal group ran even the Third Estate.[4]

The Estates are covered in detail in chapters 4 and 5; here we need only provide brief specifics about their make-up and powers. The Estates had three orders: clergy, nobles, towns. The peasants had no direct input into the Estates; the Estates of Brittany reflected the medieval French tradition that landlords represented their peasants. The clergy consisted of the nine bishops, the nine cathedral chapters, and various abbots. Parish priests had no right to representation at the assembly. The right to participate for the nobility had been reserved to fief holders until the middle of the sixteenth century but the practice gradually crept in of allowing all Breton nobles the right to come. The Estates officially

---

[4] AM Nantes, AA 75, for list of some Third Estate deputies.

codified this practice in the early seventeenth century. A fifteenth-century ruling fixed the presidency of the nobility, the dominant order of the Estates, by rank among the nine ancient baronies of Brittany; in the absence of all nine barons, the order elected its own president. In practice, the president of the Second Estate came from one of a handful of families: Rohan, la Trémoille, Cambout-Coislin, Rosmadec, Retz.

The Estates themselves designated the towns with a right to assist at the Estates. The list of such towns varied slightly in the fifteenth and sixteenth centuries, but the Estates finally settled on a list of forty-four towns in 1613. Rarely did deputies from more than twenty or twenty-five towns attend. The leadership of the Third Estate usually rested with Nantes or Rennes, the latter traditionally presiding. The rivalry of the two cities sometimes undercut the solidarity of the order; in 1619, it led to a special ruling on precedence in the Third Estate, in which the president of the presidial in which the Estates met was to preside.[5]

The Estates were supposed to meet annually, on 25 September, to vote all taxes for the coming year. They did meet each year, except in 1615, until 1630, when the meetings became bi-annual.[6] In the 1630s and 1640s, the meetings often took place in December and carried over until January. The Estates had the right to consent to all taxation, although their role as voters of the traditional taxes – the *fouage*, the *impôts* – was purely ceremonial by the late sixteenth century. They gave the king a large grant each year, a grant paid for by a broad package of taxes in the sixteenth century but uniquely by a retail sales tax on wine in the seventeenth (until 1643).[7] In return, the king signed a contract with the Estates, promising to abolish certain offices or taxes and to redress various other grievances. The Estates quite effectively prevented new taxes and offices and obtained action on many other complaints. They did not keep royal taxes from tripling in the first half of the century but they did succeed in determining the manner in which the extra money would be raised.

The two Sovereign Courts fought with each other and with the Estates, although all often cooperated against the king. The Parlement, with its enormous complement of landed noble judges, sat at the apex of provincial society. Many Breton Parlementaires could trace their heritage back to the fourteenth century, so that the distinction robe/sword makes only marginal sense in Brittany. The highest levels of the judiciary, the Parlementaires,

---

[5] A. Rebillon, *Les Etats de Bretagne de 1661 à 1790* (Paris, 1930) has extensive documentation on the number of nobles at many sessions and on the eligible towns (111, n. 51). See below, ch. 4, for the full list.

[6] There was no session in 1627, but there had been two in 1626 and the Estates of 1628 met in January.

[7] There were several small direct surtaxes voted under Henry IV, to pay for specific grants to the count of Soissons, the heirs of the duke of Montpensier, and to others. The main grant, however, was paid for uniquely by the wine duties.

included many judges from old noble families and many of the members of Parlement were seigneurs. The so-called "sword" families at the Parlement had often moved into lesser judicial offices in the early sixteenth, or even late fifteenth, century and had then bought offices after Henry II created the Parlement (in 1554). The Parlement was, in theory if not always in practice, the final court of appeal in Brittany. It registered all royal edicts, thus possessing broad powers of veto by procrastination, oversaw the judicial system of the province, and periodically intervened in its administration, for example, with respect to the grain trade.

The Chamber of Accounts sat in permanence from the early fifteenth century on. Its location, Nantes, made it a natural rival for the Parlement, which sat at Rennes. The Chamber's members came from the legal families of Nantes. In the sixteenth century, many sons of merchants moved directly on to the court, but, in the seventeenth century, that was rarely the case. In the late sixteenth and early seventeenth centuries, the Chamber often served as a stepping stone to the Parlement, but the process virtually ceased among families joining the Chamber after 1600. After 1600, Chamber families, save those of presidents, rarely intermarried with Parlementaire or military noble families.

The Chamber audited all Breton accounts, even those of towns. It also registered all royal financial edicts, here frequently entering into conflict with the Parlement about which court should register a given edict.[8] One peculiarity of the Breton Chamber was that the two treasurers of France (*trésoriers-généraux*) sat as *ex officio* members of the court, ranking just below the presidents. Parlementaire families considered treasurers and their families acceptable marriage partners; many treasurers moved from that office to higher social and political standing in the late sixteenth and seventeenth centuries (details below). It should be emphasized that Brittany was the only *généralité* without a *bureau des finances*, that is, it had only two treasurers, not the ten (later raised, by stages, to between nineteen and twenty-six) of the other *généralités*. The entire Breton financial apparatus consisted of the two treasurers, two receivers general, two controllers general, twenty *fouage* receivers, and a small complement of officials at the *prévôté de Nantes*. The military administration had its own financial officers (fewer than ten in all).[9]

The lower judicial system had several layers. The most prestigious was the presidial courts, created by Henry II, in Nantes, Rennes, Quimper, and Vannes. The lower level of the royal court system included both bailiwicks and

---

[8] Examples in ADLA, B 65–80, papers of the Chamber of Accounts, 1600–50. The Chamber's general position is summed up in B 76, fols. 37v and ff, registration of the contract between the king and the Estates for 1632, in which the Chamber noted that edicts relating to finance were to be registered *only* in the Chamber.

[9] ADLA B 12, 871, full listing by treasurers of all Breton revenues, demesnes, offices, and matters relating to finances, done in 1583, in all likelihood for the Assembly of Notables of Saint-Germain-en-Laye.

seneschalsies (the same courts, merely different local names), as well as two provosties – Nantes and Rennes. The seneschals and provosts were generally the chief law enforcement officials of a given town and they had broad police powers. At Nantes, for example, the provost oversaw the grain trade and all markets, the general security of the city, the port, and the court system. The city government took care of the walls, streets, and bridges, as well as the hospital and, in some cases, such as during the disastrous famine of 1631, of poor relief.[10]

Royal officials, such as the provost or seneschal, invariably came from the leading legal families of the area. This could mean an old noble family that had long served as judges rather than warriors, as was often the case at Rennes, but it usually meant a family of merchant origin that had long since passed from any mercantile activity into the law: notaries, *procureurs*, *avocats* (most often the latter). The highest level of this network, the presidial courts, provided a feeding ground for the Parlement throughout the late sixteenth and early seventeenth centuries.[11]

The lowest level of institution was the town or, in the country, the seigneurie. The town governments had considerable resources at their disposal by the seventeenth century. While one would expect cities such as Nantes or Rennes, with their populations of 30,000 to 40,000 people, to have large budgets, smaller Breton towns also had access to large sums of money. Here, as elsewhere, the League Wars seem to have been a critical breaking point. The enormous debts of the towns, often running over 100,000 livres, forced them to increase their tax bases; once they had a larger budget, they found new ways in which to spend the money. The towns spent this money on civic improvements – new markets, hospitals, colleges, bridges, wall repairs, poor relief, medical emergencies. The larger towns also spent considerable sums on deputations to the Estates, on deputations to the king and to other high authorities, on distribution of wine to local notables, and, in the case of those towns which periodically hosted the meetings of the Estates, on hospitality for the Estates.[12]

Municipal offices, at least at Nantes, became progressively more oligarchic in the early seventeenth century. Between 1565 and 1589, Nantes had nineteen different mayors: five from the legal profession, one each from the presidial and prevotal courts, two each from the Parlement and Chamber of Accounts, and eight from mercantile/financier families. Only one family, the Harouys, provided two mayors: Me. Guillaume Harouys, *greffier* of the Parlement, son of a treasurer

---

[10] AM de Nantes, series CC, accounts of the *miseur* (treasurer) of Nantes. 1605–7=CC 150, etc.
[11] The Parlementaires could come from outside the province – in theory, half of the officers were supposed to be non-Breton – so that the presidials of nearby jurisdictions, particularly those in the Loire valley, also sent magistrates to the Breton Parlement.
[12] AM de Nantes, CC 167, accounts of 1637–8, is one example among many. The Estates of 1636–7 received various sorts of wine from the city: Graves, Spanish, Orleans, Anjou, Gascon, even Muscat.

of France, in 1572, and *écuyer* Charles de Harouys, president of the presidial court, in 1588. Charles's sons, Louis (president at the Chamber of Accounts) and Jan (president of the presidial), served as mayors in 1623 and 1625.

The shift began in 1598–9, when Henry IV intervened directly to name the mayor, Gabriel Hus, scion of one of the rare Breton families that had both financial and judicial officers. Hus was the treasurer of the Estates of Brittany and a reliable supporter of the king. From that point on, no merchant or financier served as mayor of Nantes. The mayors of the period 1599–1610 came from local courts (three), from the Chamber (three), and, in one case, from the local ecclesiastical court. There were no cases of two members of the same family serving as mayor although, beginning in 1603, three consecutive mayors were the sons of previous mayors.

That began a clear trend of mayors being chosen from families that had already served in the office. Of the eighteen mayors of Nantes between 1603 and 1638, we find six whose father had been mayor before 1603 and a seventh, Pierre Bernard, whose father was a sub-mayor and whose mother was a Poullain (Robert Poullain was mayor in 1576). Three other mayors were sons of mayors who served between 1603 and 1615 (Charette, 1619, 1637; Bernard, 1633). Four of the other twelve mayors were members of the Charette family: René, seneschal, in 1609; Louis, his brother, in 1613; Alexandre, son of René, also seneschal, in 1619, and René II, also seneschal, in 1637. A fifth mayor, Jacques Raoul, president of the Chamber, was married to Yvonne Charette. Of the remaining four mayors, two were from the Blanchard family, Jan in 1611 and Guillaume in 1631, the former subsquently rising to be president of the Chamber. The other three mayors, were André Morin (1617), descendant of Jan Morin, mayor in 1571, René Menardeau (1627), and René de la Tullaye (1629). The latter two came from rising families; both would have later mayors of Nantes. The de la Tullaye family was a veritable dynasty at the Chamber throughout the seventeenth and eighteenth centuries; just to make sure, however, René had chosen Isabelle Poullain as his second wife.

While the mayors of Nantes had been chosen from a broad spectrum of the ruling elites in the late sixteenth century, including many merchants or financiers, in the seventeenth century the mayors were invariably judicial officials: between 1611 and 1637 there were ten members of the regular judicial courts and four from the Chamber. They tended to be the top officials of their respective courts: three seneschals; two present and one future president of the Chamber; lieutenants general, presidents, and *alloués* from the presidial and prevotal courts. In the 1580s, three merchants served as mayor of Nantes; between 1599 and 1680 not one merchant held the post.[13] Every mayor of

---

[13] A. Pertuis and S. de la Nicollière-Teijeiro, *Le livre doré de l'hôtel de ville de Nantes* (Nantes, 1873), cited henceforth as *Livre doré*. Abbé Travers, *Histoire civile, politique et réligieuse de la ville et du comté de Nantes*, 3 vols. (Nantes, 1837–41) gives the story of the installation of Hus.

Nantes, save one, serving between 1601 and 1680 was the son of a royal judicial official: the one exception was Pierre Poullain (1639–42), probably the grandson of a mayor, and the father of another, Jean (1661–2).

The town council (the *échevinage*) was more evenly divided, and many of its officer members came from the block of Spanish families that combined royal office and mercantile activity (French families did not, a matter discussed in detail below). The period 1615 to 1631 was one of particularly strong mercantile representation on the council, peaking in 1621 and 1622: in 1621, five out of six councilmen were merchants; in 1622, merchants occupied four out of six places, and the two officers came from the Espinoze and Poullain families, both still engaged in commerce. By the late 1620s, the officers had reasserted control, generally holding four or five of the six slots (later, three of the four). Even these merchants, however, may have held land, as, virtually without exception, they styled themselves "sieur de 'x'."[14]

In the countryside, the lord provided local authority; in western Brittany that meant an old noble, but in the areas around the large towns, it was often someone from another group. Near Rennes, many Parlementaires had seigneurial estates; around Saint-Malo, Colbert de Croissy cites mercantile families buying seigneuries; at Morlaix and Nantes, we see legal families buying estates, although the pattern was similar to that of the Vannetais – they bought *sieuries* not seigneuries.[15] Tiny seigneurial jurisdictions, many with their own little fair or market and their own weights and measures, honeycombed the province. Not all seigneurial jurisdictions were the same: there were several levels of jurisdictions, with the leading (*ménéant*) seigneuries hearing appeals from the lesser ones. These leading jurisdictions invariably belonged to one of the most important families (Rohan, Rosmadec, Coëtquen, Rieux, etc.).

The peasants resented many of the seigneurial demands made of them: *corvées, champarts,* transfer fees. They also resented the limitations placed on their actions by seigneurial rules: lack of access to woods and water, upper-class hunting abuses, dovecotes. In most respects these complaints resembled those of peasants elsewhere in France, with the exception that the general seigneurial system was harsher in Brittany than in most other areas; that is, the seigneur took a larger share of production than in most other regions. In some cases, this share could be enormous. On the Rhuys peninsula, for example, the king was

[14] The mayor and town council are listed chronologically in the *Livre doré*. Most men are also listed with their positions and titles; I have also gone through the town archives, including the civil registers, to get more information on each individual.

[15] J. Kerhervé, F. Roudaut, and J. Tanguy, *La Bretagne en 1665 d'après le rapport de Colbert de Croissy* (Brest, 1978), 149 on Morlaix (work cited hereinafter as Colbert de Croissy, *La Bretagne en 1665*). On Nantes, *Livre doré,* as well as the *francs fiefs* lists of 1539 and 1566 (see below, Conclusion, for details). The most detailed examination of this question is in ADIV, 1 F 36, an eighteenth-century copy of a list of "terres nobles" in Léon in 1536. In the parish of Taullé, for example, of fourteen noble houses, two were in the hands of merchants from Morlaix.

the seigneur; the *champart* on the peninsula was one-third of the crop. This was a bit excessive by customary standards but the typical *champart* was one-sixth of the crop of all marginal lands.[16]

The seigneur combined purely economic exploitation with powers of political oversight. In the countryside, the seigneurial court provided the first line of judicial recourse. Most Breton landlords did not have a seigneurial court; Gallet found the majority of landlords in sixty parishes in the Vannetais were *sieurs*, not seigneurs. He found forty-eight seigneurial courts, most with high justice, two superior seigneurial jurisdictions (Largouet and Rochefort), and twelve ecclesiastical courts in those sixty parishes. This ratio, roughly one court per parish, held true for the province as a whole, although there were important local variations (see chapter 3).

Of the forty-one seigneurs whose origins were clear, thirty-eight were from old noble families. The *sieurs* were a mixture of old nobles and new, even of *roturiers*.[17] As noted in the introduction, we must distinguish between the seigneurs who held tiny jurisdictions (often sharing jurisdiction over a single parish) and those who held superior jurisdictions, such as Largouet or Rochefort. The latter held the real power in the province, but the seigneurial regime as such included all jurisdictions.

The Breton seigneurial regime was harshest in the west, especially in the grain-growing areas of Cornouaille, Vannes, Saint-Brieuc, and Tréguier, and in the *landes* scattered throughout the province. The peasants of Léon were far better off than their neighbors: a tenure system of leasing and *métayage* rather than *domaines congéables*; access to alternative economic activities such as linen production and livestock raising; in the coastal parishes, a ready source of fertilizer (*goémon*). The peasants of the wine-growing region south of the Loire, in the bishopric of Nantes, were also better off in many cases. The customary tenure arrangement there was the *complant*, in which the peasant winegrower kept two-thirds to three-quarters of his crop.[18] In the Dol–Saint-Malo–Rennes

---

[16] See the peasant codes, copied in a non-contemporary hand, in ADIV, 1 F 692, papers of A. de la Borderie; the most famous code, of the fourteen parishes near Douarnenez, is reproduced in many places, most recently in Tanguy, *La Bretagne province*, 109. On the Breton seigneurial system in general, see J. Meyer, *La noblesse bretonne au XVIIIe siècle* (Paris, 1966) 2 vols.; J. Gallet, *La seigneurie bretonne, 1450–1680. Le cas du Vannetais* (Paris, 1983). Gallet does not see the demands of the landlords as particularly great ("la pression restait modérée" – 600) but his evidence suggests otherwise. He argues (601) that rents were relatively light, but the *domaine congéable* allowed the landlord to take one-third of the crop, with no allowances for seed, tithe, or other exactions. This would strike me as more severe than the typical French system in which the landlord took half of the crop but also shared equally in the seed, tithe, and, most often, taxes of the *métayer*. See above, introduction, note 73.

[17] Gallet, *La seigneurie bretonne*, 523–7.

[18] On the general structures of the Breton countryside, see Meyer, *La noblesse bretonne*, 720–55 (particularly the map on tenure systems, 722) and H. Sée, *Les classes rurales en Bretagne du XVIe siècle à la Révolution* (Paris, 1906), 263–300. The demesne investigation in 1583, in ADLA, B 12,871, is also very helpful.

triangle, so much of the population lived in towns (about 40 percent), that it is difficult to speak of the same sort of general noble dominance of the countryside that one can find in the interior heaths or near Vannes and Quimper. This does not mean that individual villages in this region did not bear a heavy burden, with the same sort of seigneurial charges as those of the west.

How does one understand the manner in which these elites dominated the province? It is impossible to discuss in detail each aspect of the institutional structure; the nuances and, with them, the real workings of the system, would escape us in any case. Let us approach two separate aspects of the system: 1) patterns of social interaction; and 2) patterns of social dominance. We will return to the institutions themselves in chapters 3, 4, and 5.

PATTERNS OF SOCIAL INTERACTION

Breton elites conformed to the basic patterns of Ancien Régime social interaction. They had a high level of socio-political endogamy. One can see clear evidence of clientage structures in basic social events, such as baptisms and marriages. These patterns can be seen in almost any French province. Whether it is Châteaudun or Aix, Rouen or Bordeaux, each layer of society shows a strong propensity to interact with its own and to seek protection from higher levels. Noble families intermarry; legal families intermarry; artisan families intermarry; town immigrants marry other immigrants; rich peasants marry rich peasants.[19] These patterns of intermarriage cover a large percentage of marriages, often two-thirds or more of a given group, but endogamy statistics are not the most useful indicators of social or geographic mobility.

The first problem we encounter is that of the stereotypical image of the sedentary society of the Ancien Régime.[20] In this view, most people, especially peasants, married those from the same parish, so that society was geographically (and socially) quite stable. The pattern is less true in Brittany than in the Beauvaisis, where parish endogamy rates of 85–90 percent were typical. In the *pays Nantais*, most parishes had endogamy rates of 70–80 percent; non-resident partners invariably came from surrounding villages.[21] Yet these endogamy rates hid a remarkably high rate of mobility, both geographic and social. This mobility extended from the lowest ranks of society to the highest; in some individual cases, such as that of the famous Gilles Ruellan, one individual rose from the

---

[19] M. Couturier, *Recherches sur les structures sociales de Châteaudun* (Paris, 1969); P. Goubert, *Beauvais et le Beauvaisis* (Paris, 1959); J. P. Poussou, *Bordeaux et le sud-ouest au XVIIIe siècle. Croissance économique et attraction urbaine* (Paris, 1983).
[20] P. Goubert, *The Ancien Régime* (New York, 1970). The revised version of this fundamental work, by Goubert and D. Roche, *Les Français et l'Ancien Régime* (Paris, 1984), 2 vols., takes the same approach (I, 47–8). My objections to this argument are laid out in greater detail in: J. Collins, "Geographic and Social Mobility in Early-Modern France," *Journal of Social History* 24 (3) (1990): 563–77.   [21] A. Croix, *Nantes et le pays nantais au XVIe siècle* (Paris, 1976), 173–90.

lowest ranks (in his case, peddler) to the highest (the Parlement for his son, marriage to the duke of Brissac for his daughter).[22]

If we turn away from endogamy rates, which can be deceiving indices of immobility, we can find considerable geographic movement within the province. In his study of the eighteenth-century Vannetais, T.J.A. Le Goff has distinguished between "insiders" and "outsiders," between those early modern Frenchmen would have called "habitans" and "horsains."[23] Indeed, we can see clearly such distinctions in almost all Breton villages. The insider families remained in the village, often for centuries; the outsiders came and went with regularity. We can see this pattern in Breton towns, such as Audierne, Carhaix, and Lannion, or in Breton villages, such as Massérac. In Audierne, for example, between 1616 and 1618, 28 of the 242 taxpayers dropped off the roll (excluding the nine men replaced by their widows). Who were these individuals? For the most part, the poor: they paid a median *fouage* of about 4 sous. They have another peculiarity. Among the 242 taxpayers, 136 shared a surname with another parishioner, 105 did not (1 unclear): only 7 of the 136 disappeared (5.1 percent), while 21 of the 105 dropped off the roll. Here we see the basic division; those with ties to the village, who remain; those without ties, who leave.[24]

The pattern looked much the same at Carhaix, where 17 of 266 (6.8 percent) contributors disappeared between October 1603 and January 1604. Among this 17, 14 paid less than 1 livre in taxes; these 14 people, 5.3 percent of the population, paid less than 1 percent of the taxes. The pattern of disappearance among those sharing or not sharing a surname is quite striking. There were 254 individuals whose names could be clearly identified as being shared or unshared; of this group, 142 shared a surname, 112 did not. Only 5 of the 142 persons (3.5 percent) sharing a surname disappeared, whereas 10 of the 112 persons (8.9 percent) who did not share their name disappeared. The pattern of single women at Carhaix followed closely that of the men, so that while 54.9 percent of all taxpayers shared a surname, 54.5 percent of the "single" women did so. The rate of disappearance among the women was lower than that for men.[25]

At Lannion, the lapse between tax rolls is longer – 1641 to 1651 – and the overall figure for disappearances, while similar in terms of annual percentage loss, more striking – 75 percent.[26] Lannion was a town of 6,000 inhabitants, so it can hardly be used to demonstrate mobility in the countryside, but it reminds us that urban populations turned over at a bewildering rate. Turning to the other

[22] Biography of the son, and a short bit of material on Ruellan himself, in Saulnier, *Le Parlement de Bretagne*. See also Tallement de Réaux, *Historiettes*, I, 154–6.
[23] T. J. A. Le Goff, *Vannes and Its Region in the Eighteenth Century* (Oxford, 1981).
[24] ADF, 16 G 1. The 1616 roll was published by D. Bernard, "Rôle des fouages à Audierne en 1616," *Mémoires de la Société des Antiquitaires du Finistère*, 38 (1909): 158–66.
[25] ADF, 2 E 1501.   [26] ADIV, 1 F 1640, papers of A. de la Borderie.

end of the spectrum, Massérac is a village marked for its stability and high percentage of shared surnames. It lies in the Vilaine valley, about 15 kilometers from Redon. Here we can see the importance of mobility in even highly endogamous parishes.

At Massérac, we make use of the tax registers for 1665–8 and the civil registers for the entire seventeenth century.[27] There were 238 taxpayers in 1665; 37 disappeared between 1665 and 1668 (16 percent). If we make the same surname categories as at Audierne and Carhaix, we find 188 people sharing a surname, of whom 28 disappeared, and 45 not sharing a surname, of whom 9 disappeared. In fact, the civil registers make it possible to be even more precise. We find, among the 45 individuals not sharing their surname with another parishioner, that 19 did have ties within the village: 11 married a villager (4 of these men came from outside the parish), 8 shared a surname with someone marrying in the village. Of the remaining 26 individuals, 4 were the "possessors of the goods of 'x'," one a widow, two others related to individuals buried in the parish church (a sure sign of local prominence; the poor and middling were buried in the cemetery). Of the remaining group of 19 with no apparent ties to the parish, 7 disappeared: the total contribution of the 7 was 16 sous.

At the other end of the scale were the grand families of Massérac. These twelve families, with eighty-seven taxpayers, paid just under half of the taxes of the village. Just as their social betters at Nantes or Rennes intermarried, so, too, this village elite intermarried. Thus, in 1668, we see the marriage of *noble homme* Jan François Provost and *honorable femme* Perrine De Rennes; the witnesses were *noble homme* Guillaume Macé, seneschal of Massérac, *maître* Jullien Heurtel, *procureur fiscal*, Sébastien De Rennes, the second largest taxpayer, *maître* Jacques Thébaut, Jan Joubier, and Jullien Espye. Sébastien De Rennes was married to Julienne Provost, Heurtel to Renée Le Clerc, Espye to Janne Melin, old and large families all. Those buried in the church had the same names: Joubier, De Rennes, Le Clerc, Provost, Thébaut, Macé, Espye. In some cases, such as those of the De Rennes, Ally, and Hamon families, there were priests or monks in the family. This immobile village was truly remarkable down to the First World War; the stained glass windows of the nineteenth-century church often carry the names of donors from seventeenth-century families – Hamon, Lucas, Guerin – and the *monument aux morts* for 1914–18 shows many of the old families still there in force.

Here, even at the level of the village, we find a pattern of elite intermarriage but it is coupled with access for newcomers to the higher social strata of the parish and to its honors. The greater families were a combination of the local officers – *procureur*, *greffier* – and of the *laboureurs*, with the former, to be sure, in

---

[27] ADLA, G 440 (tax rolls), G 441, papers of the *fabrique*; civil registers prior to 1668 at the town hall of Massérac, unclassified.

real control. We can see this in the records of the *fabrique*. Those running the temporal property of the parish church were from the same group of core families: Hamon, Thébaud, De Rennes. The real oversight of the accounts, however, lay not with these *laboureur* families, but with the local officers; the Thomas, Leclerc, and Macé families invariably witnessed the presentation of the accounts in their official legal capacities.

The temporal possessions of the church were a convenient way for a young man or woman from one of these families to get a start in the world. Thus we find, in 1601, that the common lands owned by the *fabrique* were leased out to Martinne Ally, to a daughter of Me. Mathurin Thomas, to a son of Me. Julien Thébaud, and to a son of Jullien Prévost. In 1606, it was Guillaume Leclerc, *sieur* de la Chesnaye, Guillaume Hamon, Jan Thébault. When the parish needed to borrow money to bribe troops in 1615, it turned to Me. Louis Macé and to Me. Mathurin Thomas. When they needed to use force to collect extra taxes from recalcitrant parishioners, the sergeant was a Thébault. When there was a lawsuit about the use of parish funds in the 1660s, we find the usual families: Le Clerc, De Rennes, Nepveu, Belline, Ally, and Thébaud. We find these same families often running the *fabrique* in the early seventeenth century: a Le Clerc in 1601 and 1604, a De Rennes in 1611, a Nepveu in 1613, a Belline in 1609, an Ally in 1610, a Thébault in 1608.

Yet there were also two newcomers involved in the lawsuit, Louis Jullaud and Me. Jullien Heurtel. Jullaud was likely a monk, as a Dom Louis Jullaud appeared as a witness at a 1667 marriage in Massérac. Perhaps he was a brother of Jean Jullaud, of the nearby parish of Belé, who had married Michelle Thébault in 1665. As for Me. Jullien Heurtel, he had married into the village elite in 1654, wedding Renée Le Clerc. There was some movement within the two elites – the top elite of legal men and the secondary one of *laboureurs*. Certain *laboureur* families of the early seventeenth century, such as Robin, Allaire, and Amosse, died out or declined sharply. New families, such as the Jullaud or Heurtel, moved in from outside, particularly into the legal elite, which was so small that it had to intermarry with outsiders. This legal elite, with the tacit support of the *laboureurs* (many of whom were their tenants, after all), kept control of the village, setting the tax rates, intermarrying, monopolizing the land. In Massérac, their task was easier in that there was no seigneur, a rare situation in Brittany.[28]

The priory of Redon, part of the great abbey of Redon, held overlordship. The only surviving lists of seigneurial rents date from 1608 and from an undated, late sixteenth-century inquiry.[29] In the late sixteenth-century list, Guillaume Robin, Julien Gaultier, Guillaume Gicquel, and Jan de Rennes paid the four largest rents. In 1608, there had been some change: Robin's piece had

---

[28] Ogée, *Nouveau dictionnaire historique et géographique de la Bretagne*, 2 vols. (Rennes, 1843, 1853) (reedition of eighteenth-century work), II, 14, on Massérac. [29] ADLA, H 158.

passed to Me. Mathurin Thomas, that of Gaultier to Me. Guillaume Macé. Guillaume Le Gendre and Jan Thébaud, Me. Sébastien Thébaud and Julien Amosse, and Julien de Rennes held the three largest other emplacements. The general sense one has from the two lists of seigneurial rents is of a significant rupture in the landholding structure of the village at the end of the sixteenth century. Here, as among the elites, the period 1580 to 1610 seems to have been one of dramatic social mobility and upheaval.

There were two related reasons for the sudden change. First, the massive destruction of the League Wars disrupted social, economic, and political continuities. Burgundian tax rolls show simply unbelievable levels of disappearance in the 1580s. Parts of Brittany suffered similar depredations (although Massérac was not one of them). Even in the better-off regions, such as that of Massérac, we can see the dramatic changes. The second factor was the rise of the state. Those directly tied into the state apparatus, particularly the class of legal families, benefited enormously during the late sixteenth century. The royal bureaucracy grew dramatically, both in its judicial and financial branches. The number of lawyers surely grew just as rapidly. In this respect, Massérac is a prototypical parish: the legal elite – Macé, Thébaud – bought out the old farmers. We know from the tax rolls of the 1660s that these legal men did not farm the land themselves, they let it to *métayers*. What is most striking is the discontinuity of the largest landholders in the two seigneurial rolls, yet the continuity of landholders between 1608 and the 1660s. Clearly, in Massérac (and elsewhere, as we shall see), a new elite came to power at the beginning of the seventeenth century.

In 1640, when Jan-Baptiste Coupperie, archdeacon of Nantes, made his episcopal visitation of the bishopric, he found the parish of Massérac in the hands of the curate (*vicaire*), Jan Gicquel. The vestrymen included Jan Couriolle, Pierre Chauvin, Guy Hamon, and René Le Clerc. The curate complained that the parishioners went to taverns instead of attending mass on Sundays and he also provided a list of masses said each week. The patrons of these masses were precisely those one might expect: Julien Rochedreux, Me. Guy Robin (now paid for by the Hamon family), Me. Guillaume Le Clerc, and Me. Jan Couriolle.[30] Archdeacon Coupperie also noted in passing that Allain Marchant and Jeanne Geffrin lived together but had not yet been married. He unsuccessfully demanded an explanation; the parish marriage register is no more informative – no marriage between these two can be found.

Many families overlapped parishes, such as the Ally family, found both in Massérac (they were the most numerous on the tax roll of 1665) and in nearby Guéméné-Penfao. The same is true of the Provost family. We find Guillaume Provost as a *fabriquien* in 1608, Benjamin Provost in 1613, yet Georges Provost,

---

[30] ADLA, G 47.

married to Guyonne Canaud in 1610, came from Guéméné-Penfao. In that same year, also at the church of Massérac, Michelle Provost married Jan Meleran, from Guéméné. The next marriage of a Provost was in 1630, Guyonne marrying Guy Briard, followed by her marriage to Julien Guerin of Brains in 1633. In 1635, Benjamine Provost married Benjamin Ally, of Guéméné; in 1638, *honorable fille* Perrine Provost married *maître* Jan Jarné of Pierre, and Guillaume Provost married Julienne Ally. The Provosts often married those from the second parish as in two of five cases here (and a third to a woman with the same surname as one of the Guéméné partners). Their next round of marriages, in the 1650s and 1660s, took place entirely within the regular village elite – Thébaut, De Rennes (two).

Their social improvement seems to have mirrored a geographic shift as well. In the late sixteenth-century list of rents owed to the priory of Redon, the Provost family can be found exclusively in the hamlet of Le Jardinelaye, paying two rents of 3 sous each and a third one of 9 deniers. In 1608, they lived in several locations: Julien Provost, still in Le Jardinelaye, paying 6 sous, plus 5 deniers for land in Paimbien and 2 deniers for the locks of the port of the Grenier; Benoist Provost, 5 deniers for land in Paimbien and two sous due to the locks at Rolland. On the tax rolls of the 1660s, the Provost family were substantial contributors in the hamlets of Le Plessis and Le Lombardye; no Provost remained in Le Jardinelaye, Rolland, or Paimbien.

The most prominent families, such as the Macé, had their own pattern. We have seen that Guillaume Macé, sieur de la Porte, was the seneschal of Massérac (and, assessed at 5 livres, its largest taxpayer). They had been in legal office since at least the beginning of the century, as we find a Me. Louis Macé, *notaire*, as one of the witnesses for the *fabrique* accounts of 1600, 1601, 1603, 1604, 1607, 1608, 1610, 1611, and 1613. Little surprise that the Macé family were also prominent on the list of tenants of the priory. Me. Guillaume Macé owed 24 sous, 8 deniers, the second largest amount, for the holding of La Porte, from which his descendants would take their title. Although the sixteenth-century *terrier* is partly torn in this section, it is virtually certain that the holding was in the hands of Jullien Gaultier, as guardian of his children by Jeanne Gicquel. Guillaume Gicquel held the next piece listed on the *terrier*, paying 11 sous, 4 deniers. The first piece on the *terrier*, the *clos* Froger, had also changed hands, moving from Guillaume Robin (quite likely the curate of that name, although the *terrier* does not specify his profession) to Me. Mathurin Thomas. The implication is fairly clear; the Macé and Thomas families moved into Massérac at the end of the sixteenth or beginning of the seventeenth century; they dominated the parish throughout the seventeenth century. The Gaultier and Gicquel families, who were *laboureurs* rather than legalists, remained in the village; indeed, four of the thirty-four villagers who participated in the redaction of the *cahier* of 1789 were from the Gaultier family (and three of them could sign their names).[31]

As for the Guillaume Macé of the 1660s, we find him styling himself *noble homme* on the parish register. Members of the Macé family consistently sought marriage partners outside the parish: *demoiselle* Janne Macé marrying *écuyer* Henry de Launay (of la Bouexière, east of Rennes) in 1634 and another *demoiselle* Janne Macé marrying *noble homme* Julien Anger, also of la Bouexière, in 1653; Guillaume himself, whose marriage is not listed on the parish records. The exceptions involved other local families of elevated status. There were marriages of *noble homme* Jacques Macé to *demoiselle* Marguerite Thomas, and of *noble homme* René Thomas (of Derval) to *demoiselle* Bonne Macé. The Thomas also married outside of Massérac on occasion: *demoiselle* Jacquette Thomas, daughter of Jacques Thomas, married *noble homme* Yves Merand of Saint-Similien of Nantes. The witnesses included Jan Macé, various members of the Thomas family, and "many noble and honorable persons."

The manner in which one entered into the village elite cannot always easily be reconstituted. In 1665, for example, Perrine Thébaut paid 62 sous in taxes. She died in February 1666; her place on the tax roll was taken by René Paviot. Paviot had married in 1665, making himself eligible for one of the parish's tenancies. His bride was Anne Le Gendre, from one of the old core families of Massérac: a Guillaume Le Gendre had been one of the treasurers of vestry in 1606. The connection among these events becomes clear only when we see that Perrine Thébaut was the wife of Hugues Le Gendre and that their marriage was immediately preceded on the register of 1632 by that of Félix Thébaud and Louise Le Gendre (she in a second marriage). Perhaps Perrine Thébaud was the daughter of Perrine Le Gendre, who held the "fief" of La Loubinetterie, owing 5 sous, in 1608.

Guy Cherel was not on the tax roll of 1665; he married Julienne Melin in 1665 and we see him listed among the middling contributors of Couesmault in 1666 (17 sous; four other members of his family were on the roll for that hamlet). Perhaps Julienne was the daughter of Jean Melin, of Bas Paimbien – he was one of its two main taxpayers, assessed at about 20 sous a year – or of Pierre Melin, of Haut Bois, who contributed about 70 sous a year. The Cherel family included Me. Guillaume Cherel, married to Perrine Ally and the Melin were intermarried with the De Rennes, Couriolle, and Espye clans.

More modest was the marriage of Maurice Berthelot and Louise Vallée. Was she the daughter of Guillaume Vallée, whose widow lived in Rolland, paying some 4 or 5 sous a year in taxes? Berthelot appears on the rolls of 1665 and 1668, also in Rolland, paying about 4 sous a year. In 1666 and 1667 there was

[31] *Cahiers des plaintes et doléances de la Loire-Atlantique*, XI (Nantes, 1983), 787–91. There were five members of the Etienne family, which was also on the tax roll of 1665, as well as members from the Thomas, Guérin, Provost, Chauvin, Hamon, and Lucas families.

no Maurice Berthelot on the rolls, but suspiciously we find "Pierre" Berthelot on the roll, listed for 2 sous, in Le Plessis in both those years. Although the parish register does not list Maurice Berthelot as an outsider, one Jean Berthelot, of Brains, married Jeanne Vallée, in 1667. There was a second Vallée, Georges, who had married Julienne Melin in 1645; he paid 18 sous in 1665, while a second Georges Vallée paid a slightly lesser amount each of the next three years. Georges I died in 1665 and was buried in the church. Julienne Melin had died in 1664, some twelve days after Félice Vallée, perhaps her daughter. Félice was buried in the church; Julienne in the cemetery. That same year, Guillaume Berthelot died and was buried in the church. Were all of these events related? Given what we know of early modern French marriage practices – children often married immediately following the death of the father of one of the partners – it would seem likely.

This village pattern repeats itself in the city, at higher social levels. If we turn to Nantes, we find a consistent intermarriage of financial robe families, often of precisely the same level. Thus *noble homme* René Drouet, auditor of accounts at the Chamber, married *demoiselle* Renée Madeleneau, daughter of Pierre, auditor of accounts, in 1637. Those in the legal profession will marry the daughters of lawyers or notaries, as in the case of René Rousseau, lawyer, and Katherine Le Moinne, daughter of a notary.[32] In another case, we find *messire* Jacques Huteau, treasurer of France (later president at the Chamber) marrying Charlotte Thévin, daughter of a councilor at the Parlement, yet the Thévin family were not, like so many Breton Parlementaires, from the old sword nobility; rather they were from the judicial robe, at Angers.[33]

Let us take another Nantais case, involving a more famous individual – Nicolas Fouquet. Fouquet's great uncle was a president at the Parlement, his father briefly a councilor (leaving to take a similar position in Paris). The family was of Angevin bourgeois stock, ennobled through Parlementary office in Paris and Rennes. In 1640, Nicolas Fouquet was a *maître des requêtes*; he married the daughter, Louise, of a Breton Parlementaire, Mathieu Fourche (then deceased). Fourche had been a councilor at the presidial of Nantes and was a son of a master of accounts (Jean, also mayor of Nantes). Fourche married the widow of a Parlementaire (Thévin, whom we have met above). Here we see the problem of general statistics about how many Parlementaires married into the "sword" or into other parts of the "robe." We have two cases (oddly a mother and daughter) of *annobli* Parlementaire families intermarrying with other Parlementaire families, yet the Parlementaire was himself of *annobli* origin. To

---

[32] AM Nantes, GG 4, parish of Notre-Dame and Saulnier, *Le Parlement de Bretagne*.

[33] Saulnier, *Le Parlement de Bretagne*. D. Dessert, *Fouquet* (Paris, 1986), gives further details on Fouquet's marriage. Mlle. Fourche's dowry was 160,000 livres in cash and *rentes*, as well as various landed estates.

make the matter more confusing, Thévin's own daughter married a Parlementaire from an old noble family.

Breton Parlementaires increasingly married the daughter or sister of a Parlementaire after 1625. Taking a sample of 170 marriages of Parlementaires entering the court between 1554 and 1675, we can see the clear difference in marriage partner choice after 1625. The 101 marriages of councilors entering the court before 1625 included thirty-two cases of marrying a daughter of a colleague, thirty-four of marrying the daughter of a lower-level judge, twenty-three instances of marrying into a sword noble family, and twelve others (including three merchants – hardly ordinary ones, two daughters of André Ruiz and one of Gilles Ruellan). From 1625 to 1675, however, the sixty-nine judges married thirty-nine daughters of Parlementaires and only fourteen of lesser judges and eleven from sword families.

Taking a reduced sample of forty-two such marriages in the period 1590–1650, we find that twenty-one councilors married within the Parlement: sixteen daughters of Parlementaires, two sisters, one widow, one granddaughter, and the daughter of the *greffier*. The other councilors married eight women from judicial families, seven from old noble families, six daughters of a *noble homme*. If we trace the origins of the councilors themselves, we find that seventeen clearly came from old noble families; in this group, six married the daughter of another councilor – three each from ennobled judiciary and old nobility. Three of these men married someone from an ennobled judicial family, two from an old family, and two the daughter of a *noble homme*. The councilor with the longest pedigree, de la Bourdonnaye, whose family could trace its nobility back at least to 1208, married the daughter of a councilor who had been a merchant before entering the robe.

The general impression one gets from the pattern of intermarriages is that the Parlement served, in the early seventeenth century, as a blending ground for the various elites of the province – judicial, landed, the occasional rich (rather *very* rich) merchant. The merchant families we see at the Parlement are those of the stars of late sixteenth- and early seventeenth-century French finance: Ruellan, Ruiz, Rocaz (this latter also heavily involved in financial offices by 1600), du Bot (married to the granddaughter of André Ruiz), Le Lou, d'Espinoze. The councilors descended from French mercantile families invariably had legist (judge, lawyer) fathers; they themselves, before service in the Parlement, served as legal professionals and judges in lesser courts. The Spanish families – Le Lou, Ruiz – were a bit different in that the father was usually a merchant/banker, and the son an officer in the Chamber of Accounts before moving on to the Parlement.

These great merchant/financier families intermarried. Julien Ruiz wed Jeanne Rocaz; their daughter Isabelle married Roland du Bot (councilor of the Parlement), himself son of a Nantais merchant. Du Bot served as mayor of

Nantes in 1596 and became a councilor of the Parlement in 1598. Marie Rocaz, sister of Jeanne, was married to Michel Le Lou, master of accounts; their daughter Marie, married Maurice Boylesve, who became a councilor at the Parlement in 1576, scion of a long line of Parlementaires. The sister of Marie, another Jeanne, married Bernardin d'Espinoze, also a councilor of the Parlement. D'Espinoze was the son of a Nantais merchant, Pierre, and of Marguerite Poullain, daughter of a major Nantais merchant family that also moved into the financial bureaucracy (three Poullains sat as mayors of Nantes, two others as treasurers of the Estates in the first half of the seventeenth century). Bernardin's son, Michel, became a President of the Parlement and married Jeanne Gazet, daugher of another Parlementaire. Her father, Michel Gazet, descended from a mayor of Nantes. Their son, Michel, received as a councilor in 1656, married Bonne de Renouard, daughter of César de Renouard, master of accounts at Nantes and later treasurer of the Estates of Brittany. Renouard inherited the latter office through his wife, Isabelle Poullain.[34]

Here we have one of the circuits that ran into the Parlement. The richest families of sixteenth-century Nantes insinuated themselves into the Parlement by means of the Chamber of Accounts and the presidial, by marriage, and by purchase of office. These families intermarried frequently and constantly stood as godparents to each others' children. From 1606 to 1609, Bonne de Troyes, wife of Michel Le Lou, master of accounts, stood as godmother to five different children in the parish of Saint-Laurent of Nantes: to Pristin Guischard (whose father was an *avocat* at the presidial of Nantes), to Bonne Desmonty (whose father was a master of accounts), to Bonne Guischard (whose father was a councilor in the Parlement), to Victor Binet (whose father was First President of the Chamber of Accounts), and to Bonne Hus (whose father was also a councilor in the Parlement, first having been a councilor at the presidial of Nantes).[35] The mothers of the children included Marie Fyot, daughter of a treasurer of France, sister of a Parlementaire. The godfathers included Mathurin Guischard (for Binet), François Boux, councilor in the presidial of Nantes and later a Parlementaire, Yves Le Lou, Pristin Le Peletier, receiver of the *fouages* of Nantes, and *messire* Anthoine de Conigan, lieutenant of the duke of Montbazon. These families, with the exception of Le Peletier and de Conigan, all went on to the Parlement in the first quarter of the seventeenth century. They intermarried with the families we have noted above, thus Bonne Hus' father, Audart, was the son of Gabriel Hus, treasurer of the Estates, whose daughter married Michel Poullain. The circularity of marriage and godparenting never seems to end.

The situation changed in the early seventeenth century for several reasons. The extreme flexibility of the late sixteenth and early seventeenth century was

---

[34] Information on marriages from the biographies of Saulnier, *Le Parlement de Bretagne*.
[35] AM de Nantes, particularly GG 1–10 (Notre-Dame) and GG 137–50 (Saint-Laurent).

due to the newness and relatively small size of the courts in question. Access to the Parlement could not be restricted to those with Parlementaire connections when there were so few people who could fit such a description. As the Parlement developed a longer bloodline, so to speak, it became easier to practice endogamy and to exclude those from newly ennobled families. In fact, such proved to be the case, as eighteenth-century Parlementaires were notably more blue-blooded than those of the second half of the seventeenth century who, in turn, were more socially elevated than those of the early seventeenth century.[36] In the period up to 1650, the Parlement served as a kind of elite melting pot, where the basic elements of the Breton elite – ennobled judicial families, old nobles, leading legal families, and a very few wealthy merchants – could form a cohesive ruling class.

We can see this pattern quite easily if we look at a large sample from the Chamber of Accounts. We have complete lists of officers for 1583 and 1588, as well as a complete list of those received into the Chamber in the first half of the seventeenth century.[37] If we take two cohorts, those families serving in either 1583 or 1588 and those families received between 1591 and 1650, we have groups of 45 and 121, respectively. The first group includes twelve families whose members joined the Parlement in the seventeenth century (nine before 1610, two in the 1650s, one in the 1680s) and three more whose members joined in the eighteenth century. The second group includes eight families whose members had previously served in the Parlement: four of these families joined the Chamber of Accounts before 1603, three others had one or two members who had served before 1600 (they had all joined the Chamber after 1625), and only one had a serving member of the Parlement at the time of service in the Chamber. If we exclude these families of previous Parlementaires, we have 113 families, of which only five had members go on to the Parlement. Three of the five were presidents of the Chamber, one was there as *procureur général* (usually a stepping stone to the presidency) for less than three months, and the fifth was a corrector of accounts whose two sons became Parlementaires.

The implications are fairly clear. While the Chamber of Accounts was a common step in the social stairway to the Parlement in the late sixteenth century, it ceased to be so, save for presidents, in the seventeenth century. We still see the Parlement as a melting pot in the early seventeenth century because the rising families of the sixteenth century were completing their climb; by the second half of the century, the Parlement became far more exclusionary, calling increasingly on its own for recruitment.

---

[36] Saulnier, *Le Parlement de Bretagne*, introduction, lxi, n. 2.
[37] ADLA, B 65–80; B 12,871 (1583); B 713 (1588). The complete list of all officers ever accepted into the Chamber can be found in BN, Mss. Fr. 14,399, fols. 19ff. One need hardly say that these lists contain some minor discrepancies.

Even the old noble families serving in the Parlement tended to be judicial rather than military nobles. In examining the biographies by Frédéric Saulnier, one finds half or more of the old noble families, that is, families whose ancestors participated in musters of noble militias in the early fifteenth century (or who could prove by other means their clear descent from nobles of the fourteenth century), had a long tradition (usually several generations) of service in the royal judiciary *before* their entry into the Parlement. The noble ancestry of these families is usually clear enough (all were found of ancient extraction in the great commission of the 1660s) but they had long since passed from their military stage into that of royal judge, while continuing to own landed estates.

There were distinctions, particularly cultural ones, between the judicial and the warrior nobilities. The two groups formed distinct hierarchies, with the military hierarchy the higher one.[38] In Brittany, however, their chief difference was often one of function, not ancientness of nobility. The two groups intermarried and many Breton noble families had both military and judicial officers. Many fifteenth- and sixteenth-century royal bureaucrats came, in fact, from old noble families. The complaints in so many *cahiers* written by nobles for the Estates General of 1560 to 1614 and for the *cahiers* of provincial estates in the same period, that offices should be reserved for nobles, bore some relationship to the reality of the sixteenth century, when many nobles did occupy such offices. In 1614, for example, the Breton nobles wanted the king to fill offices based on the recommendation of the Estates of Brittany.[39]

The nobles (judicial, military, simple landlords) and legal professionals kept in hand all of the institutional elements for controlling the province. At the Estates, the deputies of the Second Estate were landed nobles; the major noble families, such as Rohan, la Trémoille, and Rieux dominated the order. These families belonged to larger, national clientage networks, particularly in the 1630s and 1640s, when Richelieu was governor of the province and his cousin, Charles de Cambout, one of the ranking barons (Pontchâteau) in the Second Estate. Even the Third Estate, as we have seen, consisted primarily of lawyers and officers, with a few merchants from the non-administrative trading towns, such as Vitré. The First Estate represented only the upper clergy, invariably members of these elite noble and legal families.

The Parlement and the Chamber took their members from local elites: in the Parlement, from all elites until 1600, but then restricting access ever more steadily. We have seen above that the mayors of Nantes followed a similar pattern, restricting the top position there to a few select families after 1610. In

---

[38] E. Schalk, *From Valor to Pedigree* (Princeton, 1986), on the primacy of the military group in the sixteenth century. As noted in the introduction, K. Neuschel's criticism that the nobility did not abruptly shift from one value system to another seems well founded; *Word of Honor*, 203. See also Goubert and Roche, *Les Français*, ch. 4.

[39] Chartier and Richet, *Representation et pouvoir politique* and Y. Durand, *Cahiers de doléances de la noblesse des gouvernements d'Orléanais, Normandie et Bretagne*.

the Chamber of Accounts, new members came from the legal elite of Nantes. The lower levels of the royal bureaucracy came from the local legal profession, whose direct attachment to a special class, such as the nobility or the mercantile bourgeoisie, was often tenuous. This is not to say that mercantile families did not rise up socially through the royal bureaucracy – there are some examples of the phenomenon – but the passage from mercantile bourgeoisie to high level royal bureaucracy was not common. The recruitment of the officers was from a professional legal group, which, in Brittany, contained old nobles as well as families that had long been involved in royal (and even ducal) service.

The best example of the non-recruitment of mercantile families into the royal bureaucracy is the Chamber of Accounts at Nantes. The Chamber of Accounts shows a pattern completely contrary to that demonstrated by the Parlement. In the period 1591–1609, 20 of the 52 new members shared a surname with a member of 1583/1588; in the period 1610–50, in contrast, only 19 of 131 new members came from these families. Among the 19, we find two old families moving up to the office of president and nine transfers from father to son. The Chamber, unlike the Parlement, continued to play a significant role in upward mobility in the mid seventeenth century. From 1640 to 1650, for example, forty-four offices changed hands: two from father to son, two other family transfers, three cases of upward mobility within the Chamber, one case of a family that had had an office at the Chamber buying a new office, and thirty-six new families.

The Chamber contained some twenty-one offices of master of accounts and a like number of auditors in 1640, as well as correctors, three presidents, a first president, two treasurers of France, two *avocats du roi*, and two *procureurs généraux*. Between 1640 and 1650, fourteen of the auditorships changed hands, seventeen of the offices of master, both treasurers, two offices of corrector, all three offices of president, and both offices of *avocat du roi* (bought by the same man). The evidence of the old families (of the 1580s) still at the Chamber is rather slight: Roland Morin, president (1642), Salomon de la Tullaye, master (1636), and three others likely still in the Chamber – Marc Boutin, master, Yves Desmonty, master, and César de Renouard, master. Renouard became treasurer of the Estates of Brittany in 1645 and was forced to sell his office. Four other old families – Avril, Juhault, Gaultier, and Fourche – sold offices in the 1640s.[40]

While the information on sellers of offices is incomplete, it is still possible to be certain of the disappearance of many families from the Chamber. Of the families added during the 1590s, eight out of nineteen were definitely gone by 1650; of those added during the 1600s, eight of eleven; during the 1610s, twelve of nineteen; during the 1620s, four of ten; during the 1630s, 10 of twenty-five.

[40] ADLA, B 77–9.

Only nineteen of the eighty-two purchases of office in the period 1630–50 involved a family that had been at the Chamber before 1630: six cases of the office moving from father to son, a seventh from brother to brother, an eighth from uncle to nephew. Three other sales involved an office of president, one of *procureur*, and two of *avocat*. The lesser offices, those of auditor and master, went almost exclusively to new families. Even these families often turned the office over quickly: six of the ten families buying offices of master of accounts in the 1630s had left the Chamber by 1649.

One would expect that the new families came from the mercantile elite of Nantes, which had prospered mightily in the first half of the seventeenth century. A wide variety of sources on Nantais merchants survives, including a list of poor relief tax assessments from 1586 (often with professions), tax rolls from 1593, a list of grain merchants holding stocks in 1596 (70 names), a list of wine merchants involved in a 1609 lawsuit (45 names), the list of members of the *Contractation de Nantes* (the local society of merchants involved in trade with Bilbao consisting of over 70 families), and the list of those paying duties on Angevin wine passing through the city in 1631 (roughly 200 names). There is some overlap on the lists, although there is not much between those belonging to the *Contractation de Nantes* and the wine and grain trades (two definite, two others possible).[41]

The truly remarkable element of the lists is that so few officer families can be found; on the list of wine merchants in 1609, one future Chamber family (1637, auditor), one future receiver general of the *taillon* (1639), and one other possibility. From the *Contractation de Nantes*, we find a considerable representation of Spanish families – de Bourgues (Chamber, 1618), Espinoze (Chamber, then Parlement), Rocaz (Chamber, then Parlement), Ruiz (same pattern), Saint-Domingue (*fouage* receiver in 1618, receiver general in 1648). To this grouping we must add the Le Lou family, not members of the *Contractation* but part of the trading network and also heavily invested in financial offices, then at the Chamber, and finally at the Parlement. Among the French families we find two widespread surnames – Le Coq and Richard – that may or may not have been the same family in the *Contractation* and the Chamber, and three families that were definitely in both – Ollivier (Chamber, 1615), Huet (Chamber in 1583), and Poullain. The Poullain family possessed several local offices in the late sixteenth and early seventeenth centuries; it also widely intermarried with the Spanish network described above. Among the fifty or so French families in the *Contractation*, therefore, we have only three or four that

---

[41] On 1631, ADLA, B 2976; wine merchants of 1609, AM de Nantes, HH 137; grain merchants, 1596, AM de Nantes, FF 187; on the 1586 relief rolls, AM de Nantes, GG 743; on the tax rolls of 1593, AM de Nantes, CC 86; on the *Contractation*, P. Jeulin, "Aperçus sur la Contractation de Nantes," *Annales de Bretagne* (1932): 284–331, 457–505.

moved into the royal bureaucracy before 1650 and two of those were in the bureaucracy before 1580.[42]

If we turn to the broad list of 1631, the results are much the same. Aside from a handful of common surnames – Rousseau, Dupont, Macé, Le Masle, Martin – whose presence on both lists is hardly evidence of the same family in both places, there is only the Boux family on the list of wine merchants and in the Chamber. Who, then, were the new members of the Chamber between 1591 and 1650? To the extent that it is possible to determine, they were from legal families at Nantes. Among the eighty-five new families entering the Chamber between 1591 and 1650, we find thirty-six members of the legal group (an ancestor identified as an *avocat, procureur, notaire*, or judge) and only one from a mercantile family; the others cannot be determined, although there is one family – the Marteneau – who likely rose up from positions as shopkeepers to an office in the Chamber. Among these legal families, a smattering were from the Parlement (five) but most were *notaires, procureurs*, or *avocats* affiliated with local courts (presidial, seneschalsy). It is possible to trace back two generations in only fifteen cases, and we find two old judicial noble families (Parlementaires), two other judicial noble families (Parlement), nine families from the legal profession at Nantes, and one merchant family.[43]

If we shift focus back to the lists of merchants, we find that most of those families that went into the bureaucracy began in the financial aspect of it. Thus the Rocaz, Espinoze, and Poullain families produced receivers of the *fouages* in the 1570s, the Saint-Domingue family did the same in 1618; all moved later to the Chamber, the first two also on to the Parlement. The other mercantile families in the bureaucracy moved into receivers' positions for the *fouages*, for the provosty of Nantes, for the military administration. There is still relatively little movement – possibly Coupperie from the grain merchants of 1596, Saint-Domingue, Ernaud, Le Coq, and, perhaps, Richard, from the *Contractation*, Giraud from the wine merchants of 1609, Sauvaget from the grain merchants of 1631 (the family had long had an office of *fouage* receiver of Cornouaille). Yet these names were not necessarily the branch of the family moving into royal office; thus Mathurin Coupperie was a royal notary in 1594, and is a more likely scion of the Coupperie officer clan than Michel Coupperie of the grain traders' list (Mathurin married in the officer parish of Saint-Denis, to Janne Le Roy, perhaps from the same family that entered the Chamber in the 1630s).

We do see a different pattern in the financial bureaucracy. If we take the *fouage* receivers – twenty possible offices – we find more mercantile families

[42] ADLA 12,871 (1583), B 713 (1588), B 65–80 changes of offices.
[43] *Livre doré* and AM de Nantes, CC 86 and GG 743 on ancestors of various officers (identifications also in AM de Nantes, GG 1–10 and 137–41). ADIV, 1 Ba, contains a list of all officers who served at the presidial of Nantes (including the seneschals and provosts). There is an extensive, although not complete, list of Nantais notaries in L. Rouzeau, *Répétoire numérique des archives notariales sous-série 4 E* (Nantes, 1988).

from all over the province. The Nantais dominated these offices in the late sixteenth century: de Launay, Jallier, Poullain, Rocaz, Morin, Fyot, Hus. Among the *fouage* receivers of 1626 we find the two Nantais receivers – Butet and Caris – from local mercantile families, as well as the receivers of Vannes (Madeleneau), Saint-Malo (Saint-Domingue), and Dol (Serizay). Two of these families entered the Chamber of Accounts, the Madeleneau family with an office of auditor from 1605 to 1649, the Serizay family with an office of auditor in 1633; Bonnadventure de Saint-Domingue, receiver of the *fouage* of Saint-Malo from 1618, sold that office in 1635 to Pierre Ernaud, a fellow member of the *Contractation de Nantes*; Claude de Saint-Domingue would become receiver general of Brittany in 1648.[44]

Some offices rarely changed hands: one office at Nantes had only three occupants from 1583 until 1640. By way of contrast the two offices at Rennes had ten and nine possessors, respectively (in one case despite a twenty-one-year tenure by one holder). Twelve of the twenty offices were held by four to six men in the sixty-seven-year period, one office in Léon having seven and the remaining three (two in Cornouaille, one in Saint-Malo that remained in the same family) had three or two. It would seem that these offices had two basic groups of owners: members of financial officer families and merchants. The financial officer families usually had commercial roots like the Hus family (owning the office of receiver at Saint-Malo from 1583 until 1650, yet also owning an office at the Parlement and serving as treasurer of the Estates of Brittany).[45]

There does not seem to have been much upward mobility from these offices, as only Ernaud, Serizay, and Madeleneau (all from Nantes) moved from an office of *fouage* receiver to a position in a higher court (the Chamber) during the first half of the seventeenth century, and the Henry family shortly after 1650. By way of contrast, none of the other eleven families that held an office of receiver at Rennes moved up to either the Parlement or the Chamber, nor did the four families that held an office at Nantes. If we take the twenty-eight families that held an office of receiver of *fouages* in either 1583 or 1588, we find that only two – Rocaz and Hus – moved to the Parlement. The Rocaz family, of course, is one of the group of Spanish merchant families that moved from mercantile activity through financial office and office at the Chamber of Accounts to the Parlement. Among the French families, only Hus had a Parlementaire (in the court before 1600) and he was the sole member of the family to belong to the court. An office of *fouage* receiver was not likely to be an avenue for further upward mobility; it

---

[44] See, for example, ADLA, B 79, fols. 220v–221v on Saint-Domingue buying office of receiver general from Guillaume Martin.
[45] ADIV, C 2650, 2920, 2940, etc., on Hus at Estates; Saulnier, *Le Parlement de Bretagne*, on one son, ADLA, B 713 on another.

was an investment, a way to make money and to guarantee other opportunities to make money.

When we shift to another important economic activity, tax farming, we see the *fouage* receivers far more prominent. While we have rather limited information about the identity of most Breton tax farmers, the existing records show the Henry, de Launay, Butet, Caris, Sauvaget, Le Coq, Le Breton, Gaudé, and du Val families all involved. In 1622, for example, the duties of the Estates were farmed by a syndicate including Georges Henry (later receiver of Rennes), Jan Gaudé (later receiver of Rennes), Charles Le Breton (later receiver of Dol), Pierre Henry (later receiver of Rennes), and Julien Cochet (payer of the *gages* of Parlement). In 1625, the Estates' farmers included Michel Butet and Jan Caris, the two *fouage* receivers of Nantes.[46] These people were clearly financiers, people whose profession it was to handle the king's money, whether it be in the form of regular direct taxes or in the form of tax farm receipts for indirect levies. The pattern found in Brittany of royal direct tax officials farming most of the indirect taxes was quite typical of France as a whole.[47]

One could achieve nobility by combining these financial offices with other, ennobling ones: the Butet, for example, were maintained in the 1660s because they had held a position of alderman of Nantes. It is rare to find these financial families on the list of those maintained in their nobility. There were some cases, such as Henry, in which one branch of the family went on to a higher court, but the other branches remained *roturier*; the only clear-cut cases of movement into the nobility from this group are Henry, Butet, Saint-Domingue, and Hus (the latter already in ennobling office by the late sixteenth century).[48] By way of contrast, virtually all of the families at the Chamber had moved into the nobility, even last-minute arrivals such as Salomon, Coupperie, and Boux. It should be emphasized that most Nantais families achieved nobility by way of the *cloche*, positions as alderman or mayor of Nantes: Butet, Poullain, Madeleneau, Bedeau, Langlois, and many others (the privilege cost them 1,000 livres).

What patterns can we find among these families seeking nobility and office? It would seem that the traditional picture of mercantile families moving into office must be modified somewhat. There is little evidence of direct movement from the role of merchant to that of member of the Chamber of Accounts (to say nothing of the Parlement, whose noble constitution in Brittany has long been recognized). Very few families took the traditional route of low-level financial office, followed by slightly higher financial office and finally substantial office (such as master of accounts). In fact, what one sees in Brittany is something completely different. There was a large group of professional legal men and it

---

[46] ADIV, C 2752, C 2754.
[47] D. Dessert, "Finances et société au XVIIe siècle: à propos de la Chambre de Justice de 1661," *Annales E.S.C.* (1974): 847–81 and annexes. On the early seventeenth century, F. Bayard, *Le Monde des financiers au XVIIe siècle* (Paris, 1988). [48] ADLA, B 12,882.

was this group, rather than a mercantile one, that sought to move into the nobility by means of office. What is more, many members of the group, particularly those who moved into the Parlement, came from old noble families. The Breton officer class was an amalgam involving old nobles, notaries (rarely), *avocats*, and *procureurs* rather than merchants (although there were a few merchants). These lawyers probably came from mercantile families; at Nantes, many of the legal families of the late sixteenth and early seventeenth centuries had been merchant families in the middle of the sixteenth century. The merchant trained his son or sons in the law, the son became an *avocat* or *procureur* and perhaps bought a low-level judicial office, the grandson bought a judicial office and then climbed through the hierarchy. We see among the consuls of the merchants in the 1560s names such as Lemoine, Le Mercier, Gazet, Drouet, Boylesve – all later legal families, then officers at the Chamber (and often councilmen of Nantes).[49] The wealth of these men, at the time of transfer to office, was likely not in commerce – they are not described as involved in mercantile activity – but in land (all style themselves "sieur de 'x' ") and law practice. It would seem likely, from the sample at the Chamber of Accounts, that almost all members of that body were the sons of lawyers and petty judges, not of merchants.

Moreover, the available evidence strongly suggests that these officers were not simply from one branch of the family, with the other branch remaining in commerce. The complete discordance of the lists of Chamber families and of known merchant families in the first half of the seventeenth century shows that the former were an independent group within Nantes, not an adjunct of the merchant class. The two groups lived in different areas of the city. The lawyers and officers lived in Saint-Laurent and Sainte-Croix, with a few of their number scattered in Sainte-Radégonde, Saint-Léonard, and Saint-Denis; the merchants lived in Saint-Nicolas, often outside the walls, in the Fosse.

These Chamber families also intermarried to a considerable degree, perhaps more so than those of Parlementaires. In the Chamber of Accounts, we can trace forty-one marriages in the early seventeenth century: twenty-nine of these involved a member of the Chamber (or his son) and the daughter of another member of the Chamber. Of the remaining twelve, we find three marriages to financial bureaucrats (to old established Nantais families – the Poullain, Fyot, and Sesbouet), three to a Parlementaire, one to the daughter of a local church official (who had also been the treasurer of the duke of Mercoeur during the League War), one to the daughter of the king's physician, and four to women whose family background cannot be determined. If we consider any marriage between officers to be professional endogamy, then thirty-six of the forty-one marriages (90 percent) meet that description. In the laic world, women were an

---

[49] List of consuls in *Livre doré*, by year.

essential element in the pattern of elite domination because marriage alliance and godparenting (also heavily endogamous) were such important methods of creating social cohesion. These women also brought substantial dowries (matched by the marriage contribution of their husbands) to help make the new couples economically viable.

The higher ranks of the clergy were filled by members of these officer families and by old nobles; again, there is little evidence of mercantile families. At the Estates of 1636, for example, we find the clergy represented by the bishop of Saint-Malo (Parlement of Paris), by archdeacon Poulpry (brother of a Breton Parlementaire), by the brother of the *avocat général* of the Parlement, by Pierre Cornulier, bishop of Rennes (brother of a Parlementaire), by Huart, from a large family of Parlementaires, and by Luigné, himself a councilor, as well as a half dozen others not easily identified.[50] If we turn to the cathedral of Saint-Pierre at Nantes, we find the canons are all from robe families: Macé, Touzelin, Dodieu, Loriot, Robin, Avril, Martin, Bonnier, Le Mercier, Gaultier, Pageot. Many of these men were also rectors of rural parishes; Jan Toutteau, for example, was rector of Goulaine, Philippe Charon was rector of Saint-Sebastien, Mathurin Robin was rector of Assérac.[51] In 1665, the report of Colbert de Croissy paints the same picture; everywhere, the bishops, canons, priors, and abbots are from the families of the local noble families or, in the case of some bishops, from the Paris judiciary.[52]

PATTERNS OF SOCIAL DOMINANCE

These high churchmen and judicial families dominated municipal politics and most facets of municipal life. They ran the hospitals of all Breton towns: at Quimper, the commission consisted of the *juge royal*, the substitute for the *procureur du roi* at the presidial, two bourgeois, the bishop and two canons; at Vannes, it was "messieurs de justice" and "messieurs les gens du roi" (both from the presidial), the *procureur* of the town, and the Cathedral canons; at Vitré, the *procureur du roi*, a deputy and several "nobles bourgeois," and a prior. Most Breton towns adopted the Nantais system: one delegate each nominated by the king's judicial officers, by the town council, and by the bishop and cathedral canons.[53] These were all likely to be people from the officer class, with the possible exception of the town council member (and even he was often from the same group).

Municipal budgets turned increasingly to poor relief in the early seventeenth century, relief that was one more way for this officer elite to dominate the town.

[50] A. Bourdeaut, ed., N. Baudot, Dubuisson-Aubenay, "Journal des Etats de Bretagne en 1636," *Bulletin de la Société Archéologique de Nantes* (1927): 339–99.
[51] ADLA, G 244–5.   [52] Colbert de Croissy, *La Bretagne en 1665*.
[53] Croix, *La Bretagne*, 578–93.

At Nantes, for example, there was a regular weekly expenditure for day laborers, employed as a form of relief that also benefited the community. From 1 April 1606 to 31 March 1607, for example, the city spent about 4,880 livres on such workers, an average of 94 livres per week. The work week varied in length from two days (December 25–31) to the "normal" six (nineteen of the fifty-two weeks); the year had 270 working days. The typical working day saw the city spend from 10 to 15 livres, that is, employ some twenty to thirty workers. Yet there were exceptions: the week of August 21–7, Nantes spent 239.6 livres in five days. After a week of normal spending, the city spent heavily for the remainder of September, an average of more than 25 livres per day. In late 1607 and 1608, however, spending declined sharply, although again with a sharp jump in September and early October. The timing of the increase suggests that it involved work on the port facilities, as the end of September and early October marked the beginning of the heavy wine traffic at Nantes.[54]

The hospitals, too, provided poor relief. The main expense of Breton hospitals was food for the poor confined there. At Morlaix, food expenses often ran over 2,000 livres a year, and usually made up 70 percent of the hospital's budget. Many towns began to shift to payments made to the poor living at home; at Saint-Malo, this expense ran to 3,700 livres a year from 1614 to 1619 (62 percent of the hospital's budget). The money went to aid indigent couples and "femmes honteuses" with children. Croix also points out that as the number of poor aided by hospitals increased, the functions of the hospitals tended to change. Relief outside the hospital became more common and moral, that is religious, and instruction became part of the daily routine of those confined in the hospital. At Saint-Malo, after 1650, the women patients were expected to be "informed in the mysteries of God and of his Church." As two female patients put it when entering the hospital of Guingamp in 1626, "the alms of the worthy people (*gens de bien*) are better employed on the poor who are friends of God and in his grace."[55]

Alain Croix has noted that the use of special levies, *quêtes*, for the poor virtually ceased in the seventeenth century. There is one interesting case of such a *quête*, at Nantes, in 1679. The leading women of Nantais society supervised the collection: each parish had two women in charge, one married, the other a young, single woman. This strongly implies that elite young women were expected to learn the virtues and practical exigencies of raising money for the poor, so that they could practice charity when married. We find many of the leading families of Nantes, including the wife of the seneschal of the Régaires (church court), several families from the Chamber (Monnerays, Mesnard) and even the Parlement (Cornulier). Only in the desperately poor parishes of Saint-Similien and Saint-Clément were the women identified simply as "la dame"

---

[54] AM de Nantes, CC 151.   [55] Croix, *La Bretagne*, 648–9; 667.

and then the husband's surname. The list has one administrative oddity: it lists married women only in relation to their husband. Usually, such documents listed married women first in their own name, followed by the notation, "wife of 'x'." The list even described one single woman simply as "Mlle. fille de Monsieur le général."

In the sixteenth century, the *quêtes* of 1552 and 1578–80 gave rise to two different systems. In 1552, in sixty-five parishes of the Nantes region, all of the collectors were men. In 1578–80, we have only the list of those who collected within the city itself. In some parishes, such at Notre-Dame, men continued to collect the money. The general pattern, however, was quite different. In 1579, nineteen of thirty-one collectors were women; in 1580, it was nineteen of twenty-six. These elite women were again described solely in terms of their relationship to a man: the wives of later mayors Antoine Gravoil and François du Bot, the wives of a wide variety of powerful officials, and one woman mentioned by name, Jeanne Rocaz, wife of Julien Ruiz.[56]

The town officials kept close watch on the morality of the inhabitants. Women presented a particular cause of concern, in part because they were more militant than men in their anti-establishment attitudes. In the examples cited above, one notices immediately that the patients receiving religious instruction were women (not specifically identified by Croix as prostitutes and therefore probably not obvious cases of the forced religious instruction incarcerated prostitutes had to undergo). The document makes no mention of such instruction for men (although all patients had to attend the daily mass). City officials constantly struggled with women, fearing the independence and disorderliness of some women, yet needing the support of other women to make the town function. In the latter case, the city fathers needed the wealthy widows to contribute to the tax receipts and, more importantly, to lend the city money. We see the pattern of women lending money to city governments, and to the king, throughout the sixteenth and seventeenth centuries. At Morlaix, for example, in the 1670s, women held 20 percent of the town's debts.[57] At Nantes, in the sixteenth century, more than a fifth of those holding royal *rentes* were women.[58] When Vannes needed to find money to pay an advance to royal soldiers in 1637, it turned to Catherine de Rozerac and Claude Gosserent for a loan of 6,000 livres, to meet expenses until the necessary taxes could be raised. In 1640, when Guérande had to house a company of soldiers, 20 of the 100 men ended up in widows' homes.[59]

The police activities of the provost of Nantes, or chief law officer of other towns, frequently brought them into conflict with women. One of the most common police actions was the investigation of taverns, either for fraud against the wine duties or for being open during forbidden hours (notably during high

---

[56] AM de Nantes, BB 49, fols. 9v–11, collectors of 1679. AM Nantes, GG 726 on relief of 1579–80.   [57] ADF, 2 E 1505.   [58] ADLA, B 12,871.   [59] ADIV, C 3672.

mass on Sunday). At Nantes and elsewhere women owned many taverns outright, 20 to 60 percent, depending on the town; a woman ran virtually all of the others, although the woman's husband was often listed as co-owner.[60] When the provost arrived at the tavern run by Mme. Bastard on Sunday 14 April 1641, it was she, not her husband, who told them "they should be in church, not visiting taverns."[61] On 20 May 1664, at the tavern of Anne Plessis (a widow), she, with the assistance of her neighbor Henry de la Haye, incited a riot against the inspectors of the wine duties.[62] Three years later, at the tavern of Claude Marcan and his wife, she led a group of those drinking at the tavern in an assault on the inspectors, which led to blows from a heavy stick and a sword.[63] The general attitude of these women was perhaps best summed up by a Portuguese immigrant, Mme. Gomes, who was investigated for selling cloth in violation of Nantes' staple privilege. When asked why she and her husband had left Bordeaux for Nantes six years earlier, she replied that "they could live wherever they saw fit."[64] This was not an attitude encouraged by the authorities of the day.

The authorities sought in every way possible to supervise the moral and political behavior of the population: indeed, they made little distinction between the two areas. Taverns had to be supervised, lest the lower classes drink rather than go to mass or lest the students at the Jesuit *collège* drink rather than attend class.[65] These were moral questions, to be sure, yet one of the two major Nantais strikes of which we know anything, that of the journeymen tailors in 1650, centered on actions decided upon at the tavern of the Croix Blanche.[66] The authorities stood ever vigilant lest other political action set forth from the taverns. In the late seventeenth and eighteenth centuries the moral police of the poor was an integral element in political control. Authorities used hospital workers to investigate infanticides; the provost or other police official oversaw most of the other elements of daily life.

The police activities of the provost of Nantes geographically followed the social distribution of the population. The city had a wide social range in its geographic population distribution: Saint-Laurent had only the rich officers and lawyers, Saint-Nicolas had a mixture of poor and rich (merchants), Saint-Léonard had working people, both shopowners and their workers, and poor, while Saint-Clément, outside the walls, housed primarily poor workers. The provost regulated most facets of daily life: honesty of bakers, sanitation of

---

[60] ADLA, B 9230, list of tavern keepers at Bac and Guérande, 1612; list of tavern keepers at Guérande, 1636 and 1638 (pieces 58, 72). ADLA, B 6782, pieces 149 (1625) and 72 (1652); ADIV, 4 Fc 7 (1696). [61] ADLA, B 6661, 14 April 1641. [62] ADLA, B 6784.
[63] ADLA, B 6782. [64] ADLA, B 6655, 23 March 1635.
[65] ADLA, B 6657, 12 April 1641; this ordinance was published. T. Brennan, *Public Drinking and Popular Culture in Eighteenth-Century Paris* (Princeton, 1988), on the important role of the tavern in community life. [66] ADLA, B 6662.

butchers, moral tone of taverns, operation of grain markets, maintenance of local privileges (such as guild monopolies), mediation of wage disputes.

Yet the provost showed greater interest in some areas of the town than others. If we check the geographic location of taverns investigated for being open during high mass, we find them overwhelmingly in the poor parishes: Saint-Clément, Saint-Donatien, Saint-Nicolas, and the port sections of Sainte-Radégonde and the island of La Saulzaye. On 13 February 1633, the provost fined fifteen tavern keepers for being open during high mass; we can identify nine by location: four in the city, one in Saint-Donatien, four in the Fosse (Saint-Nicolas). Of the four inside the walls, three can be clearly placed in the parish of Sainte-Radégonde, in the poor section near the Hospital and the Port Maillard.[67] On 1 and 2 January 1633, the provost fined two violators in the Marchix, five in Saint-Clément, and one in Saint-Donatien. A year later, on a list of forty-four taverns open illegally, we have the names of fourteen proprietors, and the locations of eleven: four in the same poor section of Sainte-Radégonde, four in the Fosse, and one each in Saint-Clément and Saint-Donatien. Two months later, 12 March 1634, there were four in the Port Maillard quarter, five on La Saulzaye, and two in the Fosse. Table 7 shows the general distribution of taverns fined in 1633 and 1634 for being open during high mass. The other taverns of the inner city may well have been in the poor port districts as well but there is no available information as to their location. There is no evidence of any tavern being fined in the wealthier districts of the city.[68]

The provost scrutinized many important aspects of everyday life, not merely the life of the tavern. He consistently visited bakeries, checking to see that balances were honest and that bread contained the appropriate grain. In 1634, for example, he found that baker Jan Seray had false balances. Bread loaves often had short weight: on 9 December 1621, the provost found seventeen bakers with light bread; in February 1633, it was fourteen of the thirty-four visited.[69] This particular problem was most severe in periods of high grain prices, such as 1631 or 1643; the periodic shortages of the 1640s meant that the provost intervened regularly in this matter (although we do not have the geographic distribution of bakers' shops, so his actions cannot be followed in the same manner as the tavern finings). These investigations often followed specific complaints of inhabitants of Nantes; in June 1641, the provost said he would

---

[67] Comparison of lists in ADLA, B 6782, piece 149, and various citations in B 6655–6.
[68] ADLA, B 6785, shows that the situation was much the same in the 1660s. Among the fifty-four taverns identified by geographic location, we find eighteen in the Fosse, six in the Port Maillard, eight in river suburbs, eight in the Marchix (an island), four in Saint-Clément, and three in Saint-Léonard. Inside the city walls, but not identified by parish, we find twenty-two more taverns fined: four in the Port Barbin, four more in the rue de la Boucherie, and five in the rue des Carmes (which ran down to the port). [69] ADLA, B 6650; B 6655.

Table 7: *Taverns fined for selling wine during high mass, Nantes 1633–4; taverns fined for fraud, 1669*

Location	Number of taverns in 1625	Number fined in 1633–4
Inner city	60	15
(Sainte-Radégonde)	unknown	5
Fosse	28	8
Saint-Clément	27	6
Saint-Donatien	8	2
La Saulzaye	9	5
Marchix	28	2

Location	Number of taverns fined in 1669
Sainte-Radégonde	6
Other inner city	25
Rue de la Boucherie	4
Rue des Carmes	5
Port Barbin	4
Saint-Léonard	3
Rue Sainte-Gueldas	3
Fosse	18
Saint-Clément	4
Saint-Donatien	1
La Saulzaye	2
Marchix	8
Other port areas	7

Sources: AD Loire-Atlantique, B 6782 (1633–4). AD Loire-Atlantique, B 6785 (1669).

"weigh their bread given the public complaints made both by the inhabitants of the said town and suburbs and by others that the said bakers make bread that is very small."[70]

When the provost worried about the spread of plague from Saint-Clément in 1636, he ordered the butchers of Saint-Clément not to "breathe on the meats that they butcher for sale."[71] Violators were to have their meat thrown in the

[70] ADLA, B 6660
[71] ADLA, B 6656, 12 July 1636. The provost also forbade merchants and goods from known places of infection from entering the city: B 6656, 11 December 1636, banning merchants from Redon, Rennes, Angers, and Laval from coming to the meeting of the Estates. In 1632, it was an order to "bien nettoyer les rues" (2 December 1632).

river and to receive corporal punishment. When the provost threatened a large fine (500 livres) for a head of household's failure to report plague in the house, he mandated that those who could not pay would be flogged.[72] When it was a question of breaking a strike by the porters in 1615, first offenses led to imprisonment for three days, second offenses to flogging, third to flogging, branding, and banishment.[73] The pattern of physical punishment for the offenses of the lower classes is clear throughout the records of the early seventeenth century, as is the overwhelming bias of the provost against the lower class districts of the city when it came to combatting moral crimes, such as illicit tavern keeping.

The provost and civil authorities had a love–hate relationship with Nantais merchants. The provost provided their first line of defense against outsiders. He vigorously defended their staple privilege: the requirement that all goods passing through Nantes had to be sold to Nantais merchants. The provost often investigated reports of "foreigners" (i.e., non-Nantais) selling to other foreigners. It could be one Frenchman selling silk to another, as in 1642, or an Angevin selling eau-de-vie to a Dutchman, as in 1636, or grain sold from a Breton to an Angevin. Mme. Gomes, whom we have met above, was being investigated for selling cloth to an Englishman, and as acting as a factor for merchants from Madrid.[74]

In the seventeenth century, the outsiders most feared by the Nantais were the Dutch, although there was an anti-Portuguese riot in November 1636. The city officials blocked off the streets with iron chains and ordered night patrols of fifteen to twenty men. The provost also forbade, on pain of death, the discharge of firearms at night. We know nothing more of this anti-Semitic riot at Nantes, save that the Portuguese Jews were themselves armed in self-defense.[75] At Morlaix and Saint-Malo, the English and, to a lesser extent, the Irish and Dutch, provided the foreign threat. The Dutch were the most serious threat because they interfered with the traditional methods of dependence used by Nantais merchants against local peasants. According to a peasant complaint of 1645, Nantais merchants sold the peasants inferior grain ("linseed, barley, oats, and millet instead of good rye") at inflated prices, and forced the peasants to put up their wine harvests as collateral for the loans used to buy the grain. The merchants paid very low prices for the wine and exacted non-customary cartage services, forcing the peasants to deliver the goods to Nantes.[76] The Dutch purchased wine directly from peasants, bypassing Nantais middlemen. The Nantais claimed the Dutch paid very high prices for the wine at first but, having

---

[72] ADLA, B 6654, 18 March 1632.   [73] ADLA, B 6649.
[74] ADLA, B 6655; B 6662, 26 November 1643 ordinance about the staple privilege.
[75] AM de Nantes, BB 38, fols. 156ff. There appears to be no further information about this incident (a judgment reinforced by a conversation with Alain Croix about the matter).
[76] ADLA, B 6663, 5 November 1645.

once captured the market, then sharply reduced them. The Dutch burned the wine down into brandy or adulterated it (adding sugar) to sell as "Rhine" wine.

The provost did his best to stop every phase of Dutch activity. He tried to force the Dutch to buy only from Nantais merchants; he banned the manufacture of barrels not of the local measure (the Dutch had been making "German-style" barrels to facilitate the fraud about Rhine wine); he banned the use of local firewood for distilling. All of these actions, as well as a massive lawsuit finally settled in 1656, proved of no avail. The Dutch also insinuated themselves into the grain trade in the 1640s, cutting into profits in that sector as well. In 1643, for example, the approach of a Dutch fleet reduced grain prices by 29 percent.[77]

The provost's constant efforts to supervise mercantile activity, which did not always meet with approval from local traders, formed the other side of the coin. The grain trade represented a particularly tricky case, because the provost required all merchants to publicly offer all their grain for three days after its arrival. Merchants seeking to hoard grain therefore kept it outside the city, waiting for higher prices. In June 1633, for example, the provost fined Clément Trébillard, Jacques Bidon, and Guillaume de Nort (the last a perpetual hoarder) for failure to declare stocks and for selling grain before it arrived in the city (a common, though illegal practice).[78] This kind of economic oversight was bothersome, although probably less irksome than the provost's obligations to assist tax collectors, which led to constant violence.

In the rest of the province, the inroads of foreigners were equally unwelcome. Morlaix had many English merchants, although perhaps not the 600 that the locals told Colbert de Croissy had lived there in the 1650s. English merchants sent their sons to Morlaix to learn French and Breton, the latter essential for dealing with the peasant linen merchants.[79] At Saint-Malo and elsewhere on the northern coast, there were pirate problems with the English, leading to seizure of English ships even before the diplomatic break of the 1680s.[80] The Irish presented another problem: the western towns complained of the large numbers of Irish beggars flooding into the province in the 1640s; they also disliked the regiment of Irish troops quartered on the province.[81] On the southern littoral, the merchants most often complained about La Rochelle prior to 1628; they frequently demanded action against the Protestants for purely economic reasons.[82]

In these towns, with the exception of Vannes and Quimper (and their presidials), there was little apparent split between the mercantile elite and local

[77] ADLA, B 6685; the price dropped from 17 livres per *setier* to 12 livres.
[78] ADLA, B 6655, 22 June 1633.   [79] Colbert de Croissy, *La Bretagne en 1665*, 160.
[80] BN, Mss. Fr. 18, 592, seizures protested by Dutch merchants, including ships under both Dutch and English flags.
[81] ADLA, B 79, fols. 121ff., contract of Estates, 1647. AM de Vannes, BB 4, complaint about such troops in 1653.   [82] ADIV, C 2759, Estates of 1621.

officials. In 1594, the community of merchants at Saint-Malo received the right to elect their own three-member "consular tribunal" for judging problems between merchants, leaving the royal and ecclesiastical authorities entirely outside of the procedure.[83] Morlaix had had such a tribunal since 1566, elected by fifty merchants.[84] In both cities, however, the regular judicial officers came from legal families, to judge from the occupants of 1666: at Morlaix, Jean Croueze (son of a mayor of Morlaix) was the seneschal, Jean Thepaut, son of a royal *procureur*, was the *alloué*; at Saint-Malo, René Lesquen, Pierre Pepin, and Estienne Macé were the three chief officials, all *sieurs* de "x" and all *roturiers*.[85]

At Vannes and Quimper, the presidial courts and seneschalsies had far more power than the weaker courts of Saint-Malo and Morlaix. In 1666, at Quimper, we find the seneschal was one *sieur* de L'Honnoré de Keranbiguet, likely the descendant of the town treasurer of 1596 and himself perhaps the same Jean L'Honoré who was *procureur du roi* at the presidial in 1660.[86] Colbert de Croissy claimed that the creation of the presidial court and Jesuit *collège* had ruined the town's commerce, as the young men now all sought to become "priests, lawyers, sergeants, and *faussaires*."[87] Whatever the merit of the causality of his statement, it is certainly evidence of discontent between the merchant and officer groups. One would not find such divisions at a place such as Morlaix, where the highest social group traded in wine and the middling group in linens, if we are to believe Colbert de Croissy.[88] The town tax assessments of 1683, for the parish of Saint-Mélaine, would seem to bear out this observation. The fourth class of assessees, twenty-two individuals, were entirely artisans or widows; the third class, eleven individuals, were mostly women (ten); the second class, thirty-two individuals, included thirteen *sieurs* de "x," eleven women, a wine merchant, a merchant, and five artisans; the first class, eighteen people, included eight *sieurs* de "x," four women, and six wine merchants.[89]

The most exceptional town of all was Rennes, because of the Parlement. The court interfered constantly in the town's affairs, and the construction of its palace put a major burden on the town's budget for more than forty years, beginning in 1610.[90] The Parlement oversaw grain prices in the town (and, on occasion, in the whole province). It was the dominant force of the city, the largest single employer and the center of the city's economy. When the Parlement held for the king in 1589, so did the city. The king recognized the power of the court over the city, and severely rebuked the magistrates for the

---

[83] Colbert de Croissy, *La Bretagne en 1665*, 101, n. 118.   [84] *Ibid.*, 157, n. 53.
[85] *Ibid.*, 100–1, 149. The Pepin family had monopolized local offices since at least the 1620s. See ADIV, tax roll of 1623. They had already been important members of the community in the 1580s, when they participated in town council meetings AM Saint-Malo, BB 7, meeting of 8 August 1583.   [86] *Ibid.*, 204.   [87] *Ibid.*, 212–13.   [88] *Ibid.*, 159–60.
[89] ADF, 151 G 94.
[90] ADLA, B 76, fols. 92–4, request for renewal of duties in 1635, noting that two-thirds of the municipal budget went to the cost of building the Parlement.

uprising of 1636. In the Papier Timbré rebellion, the king held the court sufficiently responsible to banish it to Vannes for fifteen years, where its presence proved a great boon to the local economy and to the city itself, which was able to get much higher lease prices for its tax farms during the presence of the court.[91]

Rennes had little mercantile activity – Dubuisson-Aubenay described its trade as "sad" – other than the supplying of the court, so there was less friction between officers and merchants than at Nantes. The relief tax of 1629 listed some 4,558 individuals, of whom we know the professions of 2,023. There were 570 royal officers and 267 individuals identified only as a *sieur* de "x"; by way of contrast, there were only 241 merchants (this in a city of some 35–40,000). There were an additional 713 craftspeople, a remarkably low number for a city of that size (given that 20 percent of the heads of households usually worked in the food and building trades in any early modern French town).[92] As at Nantes, however, the poor – the *gars de Rennes* as they were called – did have their own quarter of the town, tucked away on the side of the Vilaine across from the palace of the Parlement. It was there that the troubles of 1636 began. Indeed, Dubuisson-Aubenay described them as "drunken and seditious."

The elaborate system of social control functioned effectively in most circumstances. Shortages of grain led to periodic riots (less frequently than elsewhere) but, save for the great rising of 1675, Brittany appears to have had little social discontent in the seventeenth century. As the example of the riots at Rennes and Nantes in 1636 illustrates, however, much of the discontent is invisible simply because it has not left any records. The breakdown of the system of social control takes us to the heart of the problem of order. Before we examine that issue, we need first to examine the political and institutional structures of the province. The central bone of contention between the forces of order and the people was usually money, so that the mechanisms and politics of taxation must be our focus.

---

[91] AM de Vannes, CC 10. The population of Rennes dropped sharply in the immediate aftermath of the revolt, down from about 49,000 to 39,000. When the Parlement returned, in 1690, the population jumped up again to about 47,000. F. Lebrun, "L'évolution de la population de Rennes au XVIIe siècle," *Annales de Bretagne* 93 (1986): 249–56, table on 253.

[92] Croix, *La Bretagne*, table 91a.

3

Institutional structures of political control – financial and judicial organization

Judicial institutions

Henry II created the preeminent Breton judicial institution, the Parlement, in 1554. There had been no permanent high court under the dukes but they created periodic panels to hear their most important cases. The last duke, Pierre II, institutionalized two rival courts, a special king's council and an early Parlement. The duchess Anne (and the king) continued both courts, although the Parlement did not receive official recognition as a permanent court. The king preferred to use a similar French institution, the *Grands Jours*, to hear Breton cases in the first half of the sixteenth century. Many of the judges of these *Grands Jours* sittings became members of the Parlement of Brittany.[1]

The earliest judges of the Parlement came from a mixture of three groups: members of the local legal elite; *maîtres des requêtes* from Paris; and Breton nobles. The edict of creation divided the offices into two categories, for Bretons and non-Bretons. The nobles clustered into the former category, the legal class into the latter. Even the old nobles (those whose heritage can easily be traced back to noble musters of the early fifteenth century or beyond) were often from families that had done judicial rather than military service in the early sixteenth century. For example, François Bruslon, one of the original Breton councilors, came from a family whose nobility can be traced back to the fourteenth century; the investigating commission of 1668 found them to be of "ancient extraction of knighthood." Yet Bruslon's father, Yves, had been *procureur* of the bourgeois of Rennes in the 1480s. Bruslon himself had been a councilor of the *Grands Jours* of Brittany since 1533 and was later (1549) named a *maître des requêtes*.[2] The last president of the *Grands Jours*, René Baillet, became First President of the Parlement in 1555. Baillet's family had been ennobled in 1357, for its services in the judiciary. His father was a president of the Parlement of Paris.[3]

The Parlement shifted its social structure between 1600 and 1625. It played

---

[1] F. Saulnier, *Le Parlement de Bretagne, 1554–1790* (Rennes, 1909), 3 vols. For example, see the biographies of René and Julien Bourgneuf.
[2] *Ibid.*, entry on François Bruslon.   [3] *Ibid.*, entry on René Baillet.

the role of social assimilator for the various provincial elites – old nobles, legal men, extremely rich merchants – until the early seventeenth century. We can see the pattern of the court as a whole in one family, that of councilor Jacques Barrin, sieur du Boisgeffroy and de la Galissonnière, who obtained a non-Breton office in 1564. The family could trace its nobility back to the fourteenth century ("ancient extraction of knighthood"), yet its first prominent figure was Pierre Barrin, *maître d'hôtel* of the duke of Bourbon (1415). Jacques was the son of an archer in the king's guards. Seven years after becoming a councilor, he bought a post as president of the *enquêtes*. At the same time, he bought an office as president of the Chamber of Accounts at Nantes. During his stay at Nantes, he married Jeanne Ruiz, daughter of the great financier André Ruiz and of his wife, Isabelle de Santo-Domingo, also a member of a prominent Spanish mercantile family.[4] In 1575, Barrin left Nantes and bought an office as president *à mortier* at the Parlement.

He passed his office to his son-in-law, Christophe Fouquet, the son of a merchant draper of Angers. His brother, François, became a councilor at the Parlement of Paris; here we see another example of the late sixteenth-century phenomenon of very rich merchant families taking direct access into high judicial office. François' grandson was Nicolas Fouquet, the disgraced superintendent of finances of Louis XIV; Nicolas, as we have seen, married into a wealthy Nantais family, the Fourche. If we return to the direct male line of Barrin, we find his son, Jacques II, became a councilor (1598) and later First President of the Chamber of Accounts. Following his father's wise example, Jacques II married the daughter, Vincente, of the richest Breton financier of his day, Gilles Ruellan. Ruellan married his daughters into the highest levels of Breton society; one of Jacques II's brothers-in-law was the duke of Brissac.[5]

Any effort to establish hard and fast lines of sword versus robe nobility will not succeed in Brittany. A family such as the Barrins intermarried, in the late sixteenth and early seventeenth centuries, with rich merchant financiers, with old nobles, and with judicial officers. There was an evolving world view associated with these high royal officials, but it was an amalgam of the values taken from their legal education and milieu and those taken from the military, chivalric ethos of the sword nobility.[6] When we find that many of the judges of given royal courts, such as the Parlements of Normandy, Brittany, and Provence, were "old" nobles, we must be more careful in our definition of what

---

[4] *Ibid.*, entry on Jacques Barrin. D. Dessert, *Fouquet* (Paris, 1987), 28, casts doubt on this story, arguing that the Barrin family achieved nobility only in Brittany, in the mid sixteenth century. On the other hand, the family does not appear on either of the *francs fiefs* lists of the sixteenth century (1539 and 1566).
[5] G. Tallemant de Réaux, *Les Historiettes* (Paris, 1960–1), I, 154–6. and the information on Gilles II Ruellan, in Saulnier, *Parlement*.
[6] G. Huppert, *Les bourgeois gentilshommes* (Chicago, 1977); on the warrior nobility's ethos, K. Neuschel, *Word of Honor* (Ithaca, 1988).

an old noble was.[7] Many of these so-called sword nobles were men like Pierre Bruslon, Jacques Barrin, or François Harpin (a councilor admitted in 1568, who had been *procureur du roi* at the seneschalsy of Fougères) whose training and previous career experience were in the judiciary, not the military. What is more, they often belonged to families, like the Barrin, who had long traditions of judicial service. Judicial service (*consilium*) was never incompatible with nobility; we must get away from a conception of the old nobility that assumes its only function was military service (*auxilium*). The Parlement of Brittany, prior to 1600 or even 1625, allowed for considerable social mobility and served as the chief center for the amalgamation of the competing noble cultural traditions of military and judicial service.[8]

The Parlement had a chancellery attached to it (one whose existence actually pre-dated that of the Parlement itself). The royal secretaries (*secrétaires du roi*) handled all official correspondence related to the province; they also served as notaries for important political or politico-economic transactions, such as tax farm leases. These offices ennobled their holders and their posterity, so that they brought extremely high prices.[9] The lists of secretaries in 1583 and 1639 both contain many important financier families: in 1583, for example, we find members of the Renouard and Lemoine clans, as well as François du Plessis, one of the councilors of the Parlement itself.[10] In general, the secretaries were not recently rich merchants seeking to make the immediate jump to nobility; they were members of families with a pattern of investment in royal office (usually financial) and tax farms. Save for du Plessis, there was no apparent movement from the chancellery to the Parlement.

The second ranking court, the Chamber of Accounts, sat in permanence at Nantes from the early fifteenth century.[11] Its officers came overwhelmingly from the legal class of Nantes, the Loire valley, and, in rare cases, from Breton towns. We have seen (in chapter 2) the social composition of the court: sons of

---

[7] S. Kettering, *Judicial Politics and Urban Revolt: The Parlement of Aix-en-Provence, 1629–59* (Princeton, 1978); J. Dewald, *The Formation of a Provincial Nobility: The Magistrates of the Parlement of Rouen, 1499–1610* (Princeton, 1980). Donna Bohanon, *Old and New Nobility in Aix-en-Provence, 1600–1696* (Baton Rouge, 1992).

[8] Huppert, *Bourgeois gentilshommes* and Neuschel, *Word of Honor*. E. Schalk, *From Valor to Pedigree* (Princeton, 1986), 160–1, reduces these competing ideologies to a battle of different "professions," but the works of Huppert and Neuschel show clearly that the two groups had very different cultural agendas (and backgrounds). Here we have the famous robe–sword split, but we must be careful not to push it too far. Schalk is quite right when he says that certain judicial officers and military nobles shared nobility, but their order-based antagonisms are abundantly clear in any cursory look at early modern archives (such as those of the Estates of Brittany – see ch. 5).

[9] The Estates complained about the ennobling quality of the office in 1661: granting nobility in the first degree to *secrétaires* "wounds the ancient privileges and diminishes the eclat of the ancient nobility of Brittany in giving this quality *indifferently* to all persons" (ADIV, C 2782, remonstrance 7 of 1661).   [10] ADLA, B 12,871 (1583) and B 79, fols. 237–41 (1639).

[11] List of all officers ever serving at the Chamber in BN, Mss. Fr. 14,399, fols. 19ff.

lawyers and minor officials. The upper offices – master, president, king's attorneys – ennobled their holders; the lower ones – corrector and auditor – did not. The Chamber registered royal financial edicts and audited the books of all Breton receivers. This last power expanded in the late sixteenth and early seventeenth centuries to include town treasurers; by 1605, all town treasurers had to present their books each year to the Chamber.[12]

The lower rungs of the Breton judiciary were quite similar to their French counterparts. Henry II created presidial courts in Brittany, as in France: the four Breton courts sat at Nantes, Rennes, Vannes, and Quimper. These courts heard appeals from the seneschalsies, in an effort to relieve the Parlement of part of its workload.[13] The Parlement traditionally tried to enforce strict limits on presidial jurisdictions, while the latter tried to expand their sphere of influence. One of the chief late-sixteenth-century functions of the presidials was to serve as training ground for future Parlementaires. Many of the higher magistrates of the 1560s through 1610s had previously worked as councilors in presidials. It was much less common for the chief officials of the presidials, the presidents, lieutenants general, and *alloués* to move to the Parlement; in fact, movement in the opposite direction (from councilor in the Parlement to lieutenant general of the presidial or to seneschal) was far more common.[14]

The main line of Breton justice was the seneschalsies, of which there were forty-three (in 1597) and the provosties of Rennes and Nantes. There were twenty-four small jurisdiction seneschalsies, with a narrow complement of officials: a seneschal, a king's attorney (*procureur*), a chief clerk (*greffier*), and relevant support personnel such as royal notaries, sergeants, and bailiffs.[15] In 1611, eighteen of the thirty-five seneschalsies had ten sergeants each, four others had six each, and Antrain had only five. The medium-sized jurisdictions (fifteen) all had a seneschal, a king's attorney, and a chief clerk, as well as an *alloué* and a lieutenant. Roughly half of them also had an *avocat du roi*. The subsidiary personnel were often quite numerous; for example, Ploërmel had 45 sergeants, Fougères and Dinan 30 each. Each jurisdiction also had official pleading attorneys, whose numbers ranged from 10 at Lamur to 21 at Morlaix. The seneschalsy courts at Nantes, Rennes, Vannes, and Quimper were larger than all the others, because of their connection to the presidials. Thus Nantes had 37 pleading attorneys, Quimper 24, and Vannes, 25. Rennes had 125 sergeants at its various courts (*excluding* the Parlement), while Nantes had 90, Vannes 56, and Quimper 58.

The seneschalsies (and provosties) and presidials seem to have sharply

---

[12] ADLA, B 67, fols. 303v–4, 1605 renewal of the town duties of Fougères; the town had to present its accounts to Sully every year, to the Chamber every third year. This matter is discussed in much greater detail in, J. Collins, "Sully et la Bretagne," *XVIIe Siècle* (Jan–Mar 1992): 57–74.
[13] R. Mousnier, *The Institutions of France under the Absolute Monarchy, 1598–1789* (Chicago, 1979), ch. 4.   [14] Saulnier, *Parlement*, has several examples.
[15] ADIV, C 3276 on 1611 listing of lawyers and sergeants.

increased their role in the local police after 1598. Part of the perception of increase is due to the relative abundance of records from these courts after 1600 (and the scarcity before that date), but there does seem to have been a general usurpation of local authority by these courts. The seigneurial courts seem to have been primarily for cases involving peasants against each other; cases involving those higher up the social ladder came before the royal courts. The much higher prices paid for the royal *greffes* of each jurisdiction in 1626 (as compared to those obtained in 1576) strongly suggest that the incidence of recourse to royal justice jumped sharply in the early seventeenth century.[16]

These seneschalsies oversaw a bewildering number of seigneurial courts. The intendant of the late seventeenth century, Béchameil de Nointel, estimated that there were (in 1698) between 2,500 and 3,500 seigneurial courts in Brittany.[17] In fact, it would seem far more likely that there were between 1,200 and 1,500: that is, somewhat fewer than one court per parish. Many parishes did not have their own seigneurial court, others had overlapping seigneurial jurisdictions. In the Vannetais, Jean Gallet found that, in the sixty parishes he studied, there were forty-eight lay and twelve ecclesiastical seigneurial courts, as well as two superior seigneuries (Largouet and Rochefort).[18] Bourde de la Rogerie, examining the venue of the presidial court of Quimper, found a similar general pattern.[19] His figures for the seneschalsies of Brest, Carhaix, Château-lin, Châteauneuf-du-Faou, and Concarneau, indicate 124 parishes and *trèves*, but only ninety seigneurial courts. The courts were least common in Léon (Brest had thirty-seven parishes but only eleven courts), a region noted for the relative weakness of its seigneurial system. The region of Tréguier, noted for its numerous petty nobles, seems to have had the largest concentration of jurisdictions: in 1665, Colbert de Croissy noted seven in the single parish of Tredarzac, three in that of Minihi, and five in Langouat (each had only one court of high justice).[20] Again, we must remember that the many petty seigneurial jurisdictions did not appeal their cases directly to the royal courts, but rather to the higher seigneurial courts of the Rohans or Rosmadecs or some other important Breton family. The seigneurial courts demonstrated the same extreme hierarchy as society as a whole.

Here we see the first line of defense against disorder in the countryside. The courts often went hand in hand with fairs and markets, notably the latter. The landlord would collect small duties on sales, charge for the use of his weights

---

[16] ADLA, B 2966, sale of clerkships in 1626. See also the figures in the accounts of the Estates repurchase, ADIV, C 2920.

[17] J. Berenger and J. Meyer, *La Bretagne de la fin du XVIIe siècle d'après le mémoire de Béchameil de Nointel* (Paris, 1976).

[18] J. Gallet, *La seigneurie bretonne: le cas du Vannetais* (Paris, 1983), 523–7.

[19] H. Bourde de la Rogerie, "Liste des juridictions exercées au XVIIe et au XVIIIe siècle dans le ressort du présidial de Quimper," *Bulletin de la Société Archéologique de Finistère*, (1910): 243–91.

[20] Colbert de Croissy, *La Bretagne en 1665*, 138–9.

and measures, and demand a stall fee from merchants displaying their wares.[21] The number of both fairs and markets jumped sharply between 1575 and 1675 in the Vannetais; there is little reason to believe the evolution was different elsewhere in Brittany.[22] The economic value of the petty seigneurial courts was not very high in the seventeenth century; Gallet shows that most of them took in extremely small amounts of money each year. For a larger jurisdiction, such as that of Largouet, the annual profits continued to be important: roughly 10 percent of total seigneurial revenue in the late seventeenth century.[23] Even for the smaller courts, the continued social prestige and concommitant political power of operating a court were reason enough to keep the sessions open. Peasants provided the clientele of these courts.[24] The larger seigneurial courts, however, must have played a considerable part in the political dominance of the main families, because the courts of lesser nobles fell under the direct supervision of those of their richer, more powerful brethren.

In the towns, the royal courts heard virtually all cases. During the sixteenth century, the municipal authorities continued to play a critical role in the urban police, but they seem to have lost ground to the royal administration after the League War. The courts and the municipality shared responsibility for oversight of the grain trade (their primary concern), for public order, and for poor relief. The municipalities had full responsibility for the upkeep of their walls and thoroughfares, as well as for the day-to-day exigencies of poor relief and public health. The royal courts intervened in criminal cases, in civil lawsuits (inheritance cases, wardships, etc.) and, in cases of dire necessity, in the policing of the poor and of the food supply. At Nantes, in the sixteenth century, we see the city government active in fining those who violated commercial ordinances. In 1573, the municipality handed out fines for offenses ranging from selling wine during forbidden hours to aldermanic truancy.[25] The tavern cases are the most interesting because, as we have seen in chapter 2, seventeenth-century violators had to deal with the provost and the seneschal, not with the mayor.

The general pattern of Breton judicial institutions at the end of the sixteenth century seems clear. There was roughly one seigneurial court for each parish,

---

[21] Gallet, *Seigneurie bretonne*, 65ff.

[22] M. Duval, "Erections de seigneuries et institutions de foires en Bretagne sous le règne de Louis XIV (1643–75)," *MSHAB* (1975–6): 69–94.

[23] Gallet, *Seigneurie bretonne*, 496ff. For example, in 1678, 14 percent of the income came from "justice." Overall seigneurial revenue – justice, casuals (transfer and inheritance fees), and minor seigneurial rents – produced some 40 percent of the total. At Rochefort, in 1661, casuals produced only 7 percent of revenue, but feudal rents 38 percent. In both cases, mills and woods produced about 45 percent of total income. In Aix, Bohanon found that both old and new noble families owned fiefs but that revenues from fiefs held by old families were much higher (Appendix IV).

[24] Gallet, *Seigneurie bretonne*, 450. At the church seigneurial jurisdiction (*régaires*) of Vannes, fifty-two of sixty cases in 1634 involved only peasants.

[25] AM de Nantes, FF 50, list of fines in 1568.

but their geographic distribution was not even. Tréguier had far more jurisdictions than parishes, while Léon had far fewer; the other areas seem to have been more of an even balance. The peasants, like those of Pont Saint-Pierre, had direct access to these courts during market days; the vast majority of cases involved peasants only.[26] Above these seigneurial courts lay the royal seneschalsies, of which there were forty-three. The four presidial courts heard appeals in cases involving 10 livres of *rente* or 250 livres capital (amounts later doubled); the Parlement heard those cases involving higher amounts. At the apex of the judicial system lay the Parlement and the Chamber of Accounts. The general judicial system was remarkably dense, with a personnel of several thousand people, ranging from the thousand or so royal sergeants to the nearly 200 members of the Parlement. Parishes invariably had a lawyer or notary, who often doubled as the seigneurial judge or clerk. The Breton judicial system directly touched the lives of ordinary people; it provided an immediate presence in their lives, a presence that took specific human form in the person of the local lawyer, judge, or *greffier*.

The many tiny seigneurial jurisdictions had little to do with the royal courts, but all seigneurial courts were not the same. Each region had a few very broad and powerful superior seigneurial courts, such as those of Largouet and Rochefort studied by Gallet. In 1665, Colbert de Croissy enumerated many of them during his visit to the province. In the northeast, in the bishoprics of Dol, Saint-Malo, and Saint-Brieuc, we find the large castellanies of Malestroit, Châteauneuf, and Landalle (in Dol), the baronies of Quintin and Plélo (in Saint-Brieuc), and the county of Goëllo.[27] These jurisdictions could be very broad: Quintin included six castellanies, covering the town itself and twenty-seven rural parishes.[28] Everywhere in Brittany, we find such large jurisdictions: in Léon, the principality of Landerneau (owned by the Rohans) covered the town and six parishes and the baron of Carman held two superior jurisdictions, covering thirteen parishes; in Cornouaille, we find large jurisdictions for the Rosmadec and Guémadeuc families; in Vannes, it is again the Rohans and Carman, as well as Pontcallec.[29]

There was an overwhelming correlation among large seigneurial jurisdictions, substantial landed income, and political power in every area. In the northeast, the marquis of Coëtquen was governor of Saint-Malo, the key local fortress. He also held the castellany of Malestroit, the barony of Combourg, the marquisate of Coëtquen, and, through his wife, Françoise de la Marzelière, the marquisate of la Marzelière and the castellany of Bain. Bain alone held jurisdiction over twelve parishes and twelve fiefs, four of them of high justice.

[26] J. Dewald, *Pont Saint-Pierre, 1389–1789* (Berkeley, 1987), 252–3.
[27] Colbert de Croissy, *La Bretagne en 1665*, 78, 116–9.
[28] *Ibid.*, 116–7. Quintin belonged to the la Trémoille family, who sold it to la Moussaye (see note 32). [29] *Ibid.*, 171–2, 205–6, 241–2.

His landed income in the immediate region (five local seigneuries and one in Saint-Brieuc) added up to 61,000 livres a year.[30] The two other major seigneuries belonged to the marquise of Asserac (a member of the Rieux family) and to the duke de Mortemart. Her family traditionally owned the governorship of Brest, as well as extensive lands in the bishoprics of Dol, Saint-Malo, Léon, and Nantes: her annual landed income was 100,000 livres. Her castellany of Châteauneuf included fifty-five fiefs holding high justice and jurisdiction over fifty parishes. All told, there were 127 seigneurial jurisdictions under her authority: Coëtquen himself was one of her vassals.[31]

Moving into the bishopric of Saint-Brieuc, we find that many of the important seigneuries belonged to the la Trémoille family: Goëllo, Châteaulaudren, Plélo (which they sold in 1663 for 100,000 livres), and Quintin (also sold, in 1638, to the de la Moussaye family, for a price Tallement de Réaux considered ridiculous).[32] The d'Avaugour family (the counts of Vertus, traditionally *lieutenant particulier* for the king in Upper Brittany, descended from a bastard of duke Francis II) owned extensive lands and jurisdictions, included Lanvollon, Pontrieux, and La Roche Derien. Two other families, Penthièvre (that is, César de Vendôme, bastard of Henry IV, husband of the daughter of the duke of Mercoeur, and governor of Brittany until 1626) and de la Moussaye (the marquis had an annual income of 40,000 livres in 1665), filled out the local political and economic elite.[33]

Further west, we find the same situation. In the bishopric of Tréguier the

[30] *Ibid.*, 103–4. Malo II Coëtquen was governor of Saint-Malo and king's lieutenant in Upper Brittany. He married Marguerite of Rohan-Chabot (daughter of the duchess of Rohan, note 31). Mme. de Sévigné notes that the marquis de Coëtquen and the duke de Chaulnes detested each other (*Lettres*, II, 62; her husband, writing to their daughter on 17 January 1676, noted that the two men "were openly at swords and daggers" and that Coëtquen had sent the king a memoir detailing de Chaulnes' incompetency as governor). In this context, it is perhaps worth noting that the main accusation of peculation by de Chaulnes came from the bishop of Dol, quite likely a client of Coëtquen.

[31] *Ibid.*, 104, 121, 175, 247. The text is somewhat contradictory, first giving her income (104) as 100,000 livres, then saying that her lands in Léon were worth 21,000 livres plus the income from casual jurisdiction (such as *lods et ventes*), that the duchy of Rohan was worth 90,000 livres, and the county of Porhoet another 22,000 livres, a total of 133,000 livres. The duchess in question was Marguerite of Rohan-Chabot, widow of Henri Chabot; her son Louis was, in 1665, 13 years old. Abbé Guillotin de Coursin, *Les grandes seigneuries de Haute-Bretagne* (Rennes, 1897–1898), 3 vols., II, 103ff. on Châteauneuf.

[32] *Ibid.*, 116–18. De la Moussaye served as the king's lieutenant in Upper Brittany, as well as a leader of the Estates in 1651, during the controversy between Rohan and de la Trémoille for presidency of the Second Estate. The son of Amaury Gouyon and Henriette de La Tour-Auvergne, he married Suzanne de Montgommery. Tallement des Réaux, *Historiettes*, I, 251. "M. de la Trimouille a bien fait de plus fous marchez que celuy-là. La Moussaye, son beau-frère, a tiré de la forest de Quintin, qu'il luy vendit avec la terre de Quintin, les cinq cens mille francs qu'a cousté le tout."

[33] *Ibid.*, 118, 130, n. 1. César de Vendôme married Françoise de Lorraine, daughter of the duke of Mercoeur; he succeeded his father-in-law as governor of Brittany but was stripped of his governorship in 1626. The family tried, unsuccessfully, to sell the Penthièvre estates in the 1660s

captain of the *ban et arrière-ban* was Hercule-François de Boiséon, count of La Bellière. He served as governor of Morlaix (succeeding his father and grandfather, going back to 1590). As we have seen in chapter 1, he was the nephew of the governor of Brest, the son-in-law of the governor of Saint-Malo, and a grand-nephew of the bishop of Léon. Boiséon was also baron of Kerouzere, in Léon, a jurisdiction that covered seven parishes (the barony produced 12–13,000 livres a year). In Léon, we find the area dominated by the Rieux family (the marquis of Sourdéac had a landed income of some 60,000 livres), by Boiséon, by the marquis de Molac (a member of the Rosmadec family; Colbert de Croissy estimated his income at 40–50,000 livres), by the marquis of Trévigny (80,000 livres a year, mostly in the Vannetais; he was governor of Dinan), by the duchess of Brissac (40,000 livres for the barony of Chastel), and by the Rohans, the princess of Léon (21,000 livres plus judicial profits). The Rohan family's holdings throughout the province seem to have produced at least 200,000 livres a year. As for the Brissac family, they had inherited the barony of Châteaugiron through marriage with the Acigné family. The baron of Châteaugiron had been the duke's official chamberlain; he held jurisdiction over twenty-six parishes, including twenty fiefs and the town of Châteaugiron itself.[34]

In Vannes, we find the Rohans again, along with the Rosmadec family (Charles de Rosmadec was the bishop). Other major families – de la Moussaye, Carman, Acigné, Boiséon, Locmaria, Pontcallec, Molac, Guémadeuc, Rieux, Trévigny – had local holdings. In the bishopric of Nantes, many of the same families held the great fiefs. The Condé family (by way of the inheritance of Montmorency in 1632; his family inherited it from the Lavals in 1540) owned the barony of Châteaubriant, with its twenty-three parishes. The other four great holdings also fell to national figures. The duke of Mercoeur bought the barony of Ancenis in 1599 for 600,000 livres (it passed to Vendôme after Mercoeur's death). This barony controlled twenty high justiciars, as well as rights within Ancenis itself. The marquisate of Goulaine belonged to an ancient family. In the late sixteenth and early seventeenth centuries, they intermarried with the great mercantile wealth of the province – Ruellan and Espinoze – with a leading Nantais officer family – Cornulier – and with the Rosmadecs (Michel de Rosmadec became marquis of Goulaine through his grandmother, Anne de

(the king prevented it). After César's death, the duchy passed to his grandson, Louis-Joseph, son of Louis de Vendôme and of Louise Mancini. Jean Meyer made extensive use of the eighteenth-century records of the duchy of Penthièvre in his classic work, *La noblesse bretonne au XVIIIe siècle* (Paris, 1966), 2 vols.

34 Guillotin de Coursin, *Grandes seigneuries*, II, 93ff. *Ibid.*, III, entries on Ancenis, Goulaine, and Pontchâteau. On the Rohan family, see also, Colbert de Croissy, *La Bretagne en 1665*, 172–4. He is again contradictory on the value of specific estates; the prince of Guéméné's holdings in the Hennebont area are listed as being worth 35,000 livres, those in the north some 15–20,000 livres (pp. 121 and 221), yet we are later told (247) that the principality of Guéméné is worth 30,000 livres, not 20,000.

Goulaine). The marquisate contained seventeen parishes, fifteen high justices, and received 2,000 "hommages."

The two other great seigneurs of the county of Nantes were the duke of Retz and the baron of Pontchâteau-La Roche Bernard. The Gondi family purchased the barony of Retz in the sixteenth century; Henry III raised it to a duchy in 1581. The duchy held twelve castellanies and eighty-five parishes. The barony of Pontchâteau passed from the Laval family to that of Rohan in 1540; they sold it to the Cambout family in 1586. It held only seven parishes but it was one of the nine ranking baronies of the province. The Cambout family had the good fortune to be related to Richelieu, no doubt a critical factor in their ability to purchase the barony of La Roche Bernard at a judicial sale in 1636 (for 165,000 livres). It, too, had once belonged to the Laval family. The combination of the holdings of Pontchâteau and La Roche Bernard formed the basis for the newly created duchy of Coislin.[35] Cambout, and Richelieu's other local cousin, the duke de la Meilleraye, lieutenant general of Brittany, gave a distinctly national cast to the local patronage network of the 1630s and 1640s.

Even beyond Pontchâteau-Coislin, however, we find, at the summit of the Breton hierarchy, the Rohan and la Trémoille families, who were among the small group of truly national families.[36] These two families each completely dominated two large regions of the province: the Rohans, the *landes* of the center (whose customs were known as the *usement de Rohan*), and the principality of Léon, centered on Landerneau; the la Trémoille, the region around Saint-Brieuc (although they sold off important holdings there between 1630 and 1670) and the eastern marches of the barony of Vitré. The barony of Vitré contained seven castellanies, including eighty parishes. The barony was the *jurisdiction ménéante* for 120 seigneuries, 60 of them holding high justice.

When we assess Breton institutions, it is essential to understand that these forty or so great families dominated the Estates, held the major local military offices, and had substantial landed estates throughout the province. The most powerful families also held the large superior seigneurial jurisdictions, so that the judicial hierarchy mirrored the political and economic structure of the province. The smaller seigneurs might own a court of high justice, but one whose appeals would go to a more powerful seigneurial court, such as that of the barony of Quintin, the castellany of Malestroit, the principality of Léon or the duchy of Retz. Cases heard in these courts moved directly to the royal system (or, in some cases, to the secular courts of the bishops, the *régaires*). We must

---

[35] Colbert de Croissy, *La Bretagne en 1665*, 245–7.
[36] BN, Mss. Fr. 22,311 contains the negotiations between Henry IV and the King of Sweden concerning the marriage of the "princess" of Sweden and the duke of Rohan. The duke noted that he had *meubles* worth 200,000 *écus* and he expected his wife to bring 200,000 *écus* worth of goods to France. The marriage fell through (fols. 64ff). Catherine de Rohan's marriage negotiations with the "duke" of Bavaria's son (1602) indicates that her dowry was worth 100,000 livres. (fols. 71–2).

recognize two parallel processes with respect to the great seigneurs. Their courts probably lost jurisdiction to royal ones in the seventeenth century, but these seigneurs continued to be the means by which the king expressed his power because they held the major military positions of the province. They were also among the chief beneficiaries of royal largesse.

Finances

The financial system also touched everyone because it reached down directly to every parish. There was no elaborate superstructure, as in France; the Breton tax system had fewer than fifty permanent officers. Villagers collected their own direct taxes (as in France) and paid the proceeds to the *fouage* district receivers. Brittany had ten such districts: the nine bishoprics, plus an extra district for Fougères and Vitré (in the bishopric of Rennes). Each district had two receivers, who served in alternate years.[37] The indirect taxes were leased, either by the Estates (the *impôts*) or by the treasurers of France. Disputes about taxation went to the presidial court or the Parlement, not the Chamber of Accounts.[38]

The roots of the tax system lay in the fourteenth century, just as they did in France. The dukes of Brittany followed much the same policies in building their state as did the kings of France. As in France, the creation of the state apparatus required cooperation between the ruler and the most powerful subjects, particularly the landed nobility. The king did little more than take over the existing Breton system in 1492. Early Breton ducal revenue was primarily seigneurial but the duke had recourse to actual taxation in the middle of the fourteenth century.[39] He levied local hearth taxes (*fouages*) in 1345 and 1357 and general ones in 1365–7, 1373, 1379, and 1380–1. The *fouage* became increasingly frequent after 1380 and commonplace after 1400. Following the French example, the duke of Brittany shared the proceeds of this tax with major nobles, such as the Rohan and Rieux families or Olivier de Clisson.[40] While the duke mollified powerful seigneurs by granting them a share (even 100 percent) of tax receipts from their serfs and tenants, he was able, in 1386, to establish the

[37] The administrative framework of Brittany is clearly laid out in the great report of 1583: ADLA, B 12,871.

[38] P. Belordeau, *Controverses agitées en la cour de Parlement de Bretagne et decidées par arrets du mesme Parlement* (Paris, 1619, 1620), 2 vols., I, 773–4.

[39] M. Jones, "Les finances de Jean IV, duc de Bretagne (1364–1399)," *MSHAB*, lii (1972): 26–53; A. de la Borderie, "Le plus ancien rôle des comptes du duché," *MSHAB*, xxvi (1946): 49–68; A. de la Borderie, "Recueil d'actes inédits des ducs et princes de Bretagne." *BMSAIV*, 19 (1899): 155–285; A. de la Borderie, *Histoire de Bretagne*, III (Rennes, 1899); J.-L. Montigny, *Essai sur les institutions du duché de Bretagne à l'époque de Pierre Mauclerc* (Paris, 1959), 59ff.; J. Delumeau, ed., *Histoire de Bretagne* (Toulouse, 1969), 162.

[40] On sharing with Olivier de Clisson in 1392, and the first count of *feux*, P.-H. Morice, *Histoire ecclésiastique et civile de Bretagne* (Paris, 1750), I, col. 417, which gives the figure of 88,447 *feux*; Morice, *Preuves pour servir à l'histoire de Bretagne* (Paris, 1744), I, col. 1604, 1608, which gives 98,447 *feux*, as does G.-A. Lobineau, *Histoire de Bretagne* (Paris, 1707), I, 763–4.

principle that no seigneur could tax his subjects without the duke's per-mission.[41] The duke readily granted such permission to powerful families, notably the Rohans.[42]

The duke also shared the revenues of indirect taxes. Building on earlier local precedents, the Estates of Brittany voted to extend the import–export duty levied at Nantes, roughly 5 percent, to the entire duchy. In order to get permission to raise this money, however, the duke had to share the proceeds with town overlords, such as the bishop and chapter of Saint-Malo or the bishop of Quimper.[43] By the early fifteenth century, the duke levied import–export duties throughout the province: in the bishopric of Nantes, these were called the *prévôté de Nantes*; in the rest of the province, they were known as the *ports et havres*. The duke doubled the duties on wine and grain in 1424; from 1425 until 1789, save for periodic inflation adjustments of the official prices of goods taxed *ad valorem* and for the minor increases in some duties in 1517, the basic import–export duties of Brittany remained the same.[44]

The third major form of taxation was a sales tax on wine. The duke created the main Breton wine tax, the *impôt*, in 1427 or 1428; several ordinances of 1428 mention a newly-created tax of 10 sous/pipe on all wine sold retail, as well as a tax of 5 percent on the sale of draperies and linens. The tax soon fell on both wine and cider, the rate on the former rising to 45 sous/pipe of non-Breton wine by the early sixteenth century. The higher rates remained in force throughout the seventeenth and eighteenth centuries. The tax on the sale of draperies and linens disappeared in the fifteenth century.[45]

The *fouage* provided the most important source of revenue in the fifteenth century. The duke usually raised a *fouage* to pay for military expenses, but there were a few exceptions, such as the levy for the marriage of Jean V's sister

[41] The 1386 ruling is known from the exception letters for the viscount of Rohan, dated 16 September 1385 (Morice, *Preuves*, II, col 493), while the final letters making the ruling binding on others were issued on 1 February 1386 (de la Borderie, *Histoire*, III, 118).

[42] In 1357, Charles of Blois granted half of the product of a *fouage* to various great nobles. J.-P. Leguay, "Les fouages en Bretagne ducale aux XIVe et XVe siècles," (Rennes, 1961, D.E.S., unpublished), 15–19. R. Blanchard, *Lettres et mandements de Jean V* (Nantes, 1889–1895), 5 vols., shows gifts to many powerful nobles: Rays family (piece 1050), Pont l'Abbé family (158 and 986), Rieux (1415), and, especially, the Rohans – 40 sous/*feu* in 1407 (573); 1441 levy (2502). ADLA, B 7 on the dowry of Marie de Bretagne, marrying into the Rohan family (1476). Other grants to the Rohans can be found in Blanchard, pieces 1133, 1401, and 2525. They also received grants in 1462 (ADLA, B 2, fol. 116) and 1477 (B 8, fols. 111–13), both for the viscounty of Rohan; and in 1467 and 1471 (BM Nantes, Mss. Fr. 1722, fols. 279 and 281) for the Guéméné branch of the family.

[43] Lobineau, *Histoire*, I, 521; de la Borderie, *Histoire*, III, 101; Jones, "Finances of Jean IV," 37. On the earliest wine taxes, P. de la Bigne Villeneuve, "Documents inédits concernant la fondation du couvent de Bonne-Nouvelle de Rennes," *BMSAIV*, 3 (1883): 221–38, pieces 8–10.

[44] AD Loire-Atlantique, C 788, *pancarte* of the *ports et havres*; C 790, *pancarte* of the *prévôté de Nantes*. ADLA, B 53, fol. 220v, cites 8 deniers/livre as the usual rate, but heavily traded goods had special rates.

[45] Blanchard, *Lettres*, pieces 2,678 and 2,679; in March 1432, noting increase as of 1 November 1431, piece 2014; renewals of 1439–42, pieces 2673, 2136, 2236, and 2382.

(1407–8) and that for the purchase of the barony of Fougères (1429).[46] The size of the contribution per *feu* and the total receipts for the *fouage* rose steadily from 1392 into the 1480s: the contribution per *feu* rose from 25 sous in 1392 to 8.5 livres in 1490; the total collection increased from a projected 132,000 livres in 1392 to 300,000 livres in 1476 (and possibly more in 1490). The *fouage* of 1476, 300,000 livres, was about the same as that of 1637, 310,000 livres, even in nominal terms.[47]

How was it possible that the main Breton direct tax, the *fouage*, remained the same in absolute terms in 1476 and 1637? The direct comparison of the two years is a bit misleading, because it implies that direct taxation remained stable in the intervening period, whereas, in fact, it did not. It also ignores the existence of new direct taxes, such as the garrison tax and the *taillon*. These new taxes raised total direct taxation to about 500,000 livres in the seventeenth century, as we shall see, but this was still far below the levels of the fifteenth century. Why did the system change so radically in the late fifteenth and sixteenth centuries? Can we detail the chronology of change, so that some political pattern emerges? As in most such cases, the change was an evolutionary process but one that moved in fits and starts, rather than in a simple linear progression.

The Breton system evolved in much the same manner as the French in the fifteenth century. The *fouage*, originally a tax on all lay commoner hearths, quickly became a tax on rural hearths. Rennes and Nantes received exemptions from the *fouage* by 1407; by 1434, some thirty-one Breton towns held exemptions. These towns paid the *aide des villes*, a fixed lump sum (raised as they saw fit), for their exemption; it was only some 8,750 livres *bretons* in the 1470s, so it was hardly a replacement for the lost *fouage* revenue.[48] By the early sixteenth century, the eleven major towns of the province – Nantes, Rennes, Dinan, Quimper, and Vannes among them – had even obtained exemption from the *aide des villes*. It is clear that the ducal administration believed that the towns contributed by means of the indirect taxes, notably the *impôts* and the transit taxes.

The Breton system differed sharply from the French one in other respects. In Brittany, one *feu* legally represented three real households (*mesnages*).[49] In fact, in a seventeenth-century lawsuit about tax assessments in the parish of Gévezé, all of the parties accepted the idea that a *feu* represented a fixed amount of

[46] *Ibid.*, pieces 573 (1407), 1739, 1770, 1777 (1426), and 2502 (1441).
[47] Morice, *Preuves*, II, col. 1756; III, cols. 119, 166, 222. Leguay, "Fouages," 68–9. The details are given in J. Collins, "Taxation in Bretagne, 1598–1648," (Columbia, 1978, Ph.D. dissertation), ch. 5.
[48] Blanchard, *Lettres*, piece 253; Leguay, "Fouages," 93; ADLA, 12,871. The eleven exempt towns paid 7,704 livres of the 10,488 livres. (73.5 percent). The net revenue from this tax, after paying the receiver and the *rentes*, came to only 1,933.5 livres.
[49] Morice, *Preuves*, II, col. 1756.

cultivable land.[50] Each parish paid an assessment of "x" livres per *feu* multiplied by its official number of *feux*. In 1426, the duke counted 64,358 *feux* (excluding the towns) but this figure dropped to between 45,015 and 48,149 *feux* in the reformation of 1426–30 and gradually declined to 39,547 *feux* by 1481. Most of this decline seems to have taken place in the period 1440–8, based on the figures for the bishoprics of Vannes and Tréguier, which show a loss of nearly 30 percent of their *feux* in those years.[51]

The reductions did not always reflect population loss: the duke sold exemptions to the *fouage*. Because Breton direct taxation was both real (based on the status of the land) and personal (based on the status of the individual), the duke sold both personal and land-based exemptions. Each Breton parish was allowed to have two "métairies nobles," which were exempt from the *fouage*. The sale of exemptions had the effect of removing the richest taxpayers from the rolls.[52] The duchess granted another 2,500 exemptions in 1501–3, primarily in those areas – Dol, Saint-Malo, Saint-Brieuc, Rennes – affected by the French invasions of 1488–91. After the reductions for the *nouvelles provisions*, as they were called, the duchess fixed the total number of *feux* as 36,578 (table 8).[53]

Within the parishes, the inhabitants set their own tax levels (as in France). The Gévezé lawsuit shows that the peasants assessed each *journal* of cultivable commoner land for a fixed amount.[54] The lawsuit involved a taxpayer, Toussaint Cormier, trying to include his commoner lands with his noble (exempt) lands, and thus escape from part of his tax burden. The practices at Gévezé show the problems faced by the peasants *vis-à-vis* the dual exemptions, and they also imply that the working assumption of the system was that the *feu* was a fixed amount of land. Certainly that interpretation makes a great deal more sense than the traditional view linking population to the *feux* count, because the *feux* count remained constant after 1503.

[50] ADIV, series G, Gévezé, number 15, case of 1611.
[51] The *feux* count is one of the most bizarre of subjects, as virtually all commentators have accepted the figure of 98,447 *feux* in 1392. As noted above, Morice gives contradictory figures; the figure in the second book, 88,447 *feux* is, in fact, supported by the internal evidence of the document. From this, we should subtract some or all of the 18,699 *feux* in the area controlled by Clisson, as many were not in Brittany. M. Pougéard, "La Bretagne au XVe siècle: etude démographique," (Rennes, 1965, D.E.S., unpublished), 35–6, gives figures for 1426 and a citation of 45,015 *feux* in 1430. ADLA, B 12,871 gives 47,967 *feux* in 1430, while B 3009 lists 48,149 *feux* for that date.
[52] Blanchard, pieces 2447 to 2556 and Pougéard, "Bretagne," 39. The parishes are Legnac, Saint-Goual, Carnac, Auray, Ploeigneau, Locquanvael, and Goellan. AD Loire-Atlantique, B 12,871, gives 983 exemptions granted in this period throughout the duchy, while B 3009 gives 879. If one accepts the percentage of full *feu* as 1.47, then 44 percent of 983 would reduce the number of full *feux* by 433 from an original 662 (based on 45,000 original *feux*). In Gévezé, the exemptions sold in 1577 were for two full *feu* exemptions, one shared *feu* exemption, and two half *feu* exemptions (ADIV, G Gévezé, number 16).
[53] AD Loire-Atlantique, B 12,871; B 3009. On reductions, see the letters to the Estates of 1501, Morice, *Preuves*, III, col. 847–9.
[54] The parishioners testified that they assessed individuals on the basis of 2.5 sous per *journal* (about 0.5 hectares).

Table 8: *Evolution of* feux *count in Brittany, 1426–1617*

Bishopric	1426	1500	1505	1617
		Feux in:		
Rennes	4761	3629	3272	3131
Nantes	7739	6634	6285	6274
Vannes	6199 (6326)	5217	5089 (5058)	4787
Cornouaille	5540	4948	4612	4588
Tréguier	4880	4225	3953	3953
Léon	2735	2352 (2329)	2191 (2169)	2168
Saint-Brieuc	5232	4399	4029	3796
Saint-Malo	6329	5217	4845	4550
Dol	1775	1257 (1072)	1152 (968)	911
Fougères[a]	2776	1515	1440	1358
Totals	47,966	39,393	36,868	35,516

Note:
[a] Fougères and Vitré formed a separate receiving district within the bishopric of Rennes.
Sources: AD Loire-Atlantique, B 12, 871; B 3009 (figures in parentheses). All other citations from B 3009 are within ten *feux* of the B 12,871 figure. B 3009 omits a figure for Fougères.

Peace and the *feux* reductions combined to reduce Breton direct taxation by about 50 percent between 1490 and 1503. The duchess Anne and King Louis XII levied only 4.8 livres per *feu*, so that the share of the *fouage* in total receipts fell from 67 to 54 percent (table 9). Francis I increased the contribution to 8.4 livres per *feu*, but the ratio of direct to indirect tax revenue remained the same because of higher indirect tax income.[55] This higher income came from greater commercial activity and from the ducal confiscation of the *billots*, a retail sales tax on wine, levied by towns for the upkeep of their walls.[56] The duchess confiscated the *billots* between 1498 and 1508; the Estates continued to oppose the seizure as much as twenty years later. In 1524, they argued that it was "a thing of bad consequence for the country," and in 1526 the clerk of the Estates

[55] The *fouage* of 1481–4 was 7.95 livres, that of 1485, 7.5 livres. (AD Loire-Atlantique, E 212). Morice, *Preuves*, III, 736–7, on a similar levy in 1487; for other years in the period 1485–1501, Morice, *Preuves*, III, 706 (1491) and 742 (1493); A. de la Borderie, "Recueil des actes inédits d'Anne de Bretagne," *BMSAIV*, 6 (1886): 243–9, pieces xvii and xxxvi. Under Francis I, figures for 1523 – R. Doucet, "L'état des finances de 1523," *Bulletin Philologique et Historique* (1920): 5–123; for 1533 – BN, Mss. Fr. 22,330, fols. 679–700v; for 1535 – *Ibid.* and BN, Mss. Fr. 22,342, fol. 135.
[56] C. de la Lande de Calan, *Documents inédits relatifs aux Etats de Bretagne de 1491 à 1589* (Nantes, 1898) 2 vols., I, 13, 52, 55, 63–6, and 74.

Table 9: *Breton revenues in the late fifteenth and early sixteenth centuries*

Revenue source	1481–2	1484–5	1501–2[a]	1503	1523	1533	1535
In percentage of total gross revenue							
Fouage	67.1	65.3	53.7	53.3	57.6	56.3	55.3
Impôts	13.9	16.5	25.9	22.5	20.9	22.3	23.2
Ports and prévôté	9.4	9.3	16.3	18.4	14.3	17.7	17.4
In 000 livres *tournois*							
Fouage	320.2	339.0	461.3	209.5	314.4	316.0	321.3
Impôts[b]	66.1	85.6	201.7	92.5	119.6	131.3	141.3
Ports and prévôté[c]	44.6	48.0	126.7	64.4	69.6	89.0	91.4

Notes:
[a] Figures for 1501–2 are for two years of receipts; all other figures are for one year (1481–2 is a single fiscal year).
[b] The figures for 1523, 1533, and 1535 include the *impôts* and *billots* together.
[c] It is unclear if the 1481–2 and 1484–5 accounts include both the *prévôté* and the *ports*, as the documents say only *ports*. The percentage increase, however, is the same as that for the *impôts*, which suggests both were included.

Sources: AD Loire-Atlantique, E 212, pièce 20 (1503); R. Doucet, "L'état des finances de 1523," *Bulletin Philologique et Historique* (1920): 5–123; BN, Mss. Fr. 22,330, fols 679–700v (1533, 1535); BN, Mss. Fr. 22,342, fol. 135 (1535).

noted that "all of the *procureurs* of the towns opposed the *billot*." Their opposition had little effect, as the king kept the money, and leased the *impôts* and *billots* jointly after the 1540s.[57] This incident was an early example of the relative weakness of the towns at the Estates.

Francis I greatly increased taxation in Brittany, as elsewhere in the kingdom. Following traditional French policy, he rarely tried to impose taxes levied in one area on another. There seems to have been no effort to introduce the *taille*, *gabelle*, or other French taxes into Brittany. When Francis created new taxes, however, he levied them in Brittany as elsewhere. Bretons contributed heavily to his ransom in the late 1520s and early 1530s, and Breton towns had to contribute regularly, throughout the sixteenth century, to the levy for the upkeep

[57] N. de la Nicollière-Teijeiro, *Privilèges accordés par les ducs de Bretagne ... à ... la ville de Nantes* (Nantes, 1883), pièce xxxii. On the *billot* of Rennes, J.-P. Leguay, *La ville de Rennes au XVe siècle à travers les comptes des Miseurs* (Rennes, 1968), 81–3, 92. The *billot* was "x" livres/pipe for every "x" sous/*pot* of the cost of retail wine, except in Nantes, where it was 8.33 percent.

of the infantry. In most years, this contribution ranged from 40 to 60,000 livres.[58] The clergy also had to contribute to the *décimes*.

Francis increased his demands in the 1530s and early 1540s. In 1542, he demanded a *fouage* of 9.6 livres per *feu* but settled for the regular levy of 8.4 livres per *feu*, along with a surtax of 20,000 *écus*.[59] This simple arrangement had profound long-term consequences, because the *fouage* soon became fixed at its "customary" level of 8.4 (French) livres per *feu*, and remained at that level until 1789. Because the number of *feux* was also fixed, the amount levied for the tax could not be altered; the only subsequent changes were due to the forced sales of exemptions in 1577, 1638, and 1640.[60]

The fixing of the *fouage* meant that the king would have to find a new form of revenue from Brittany to meet his ever greater needs for income; it also meant that the Estates' chief official function, voting the *fouage* and the *impôts et billots*, became largely ceremonial because neither they nor the king were in a position to change either tax. The Estates had to find a new form of financial leverage on the king, in order to preserve their position of power within the province.

Henry II was the first French king to tackle this problem, and his solution served as a model for later rulers. He was, not coincidentally, the first French king to be the legitimate heir to the duchy. Henry added the *taillon* (gendarmerie tax) of 56,400 livres to Breton direct taxation in 1552, and he also created a fixed tax for the mounted constabulary (roughly 11,500 livres): in both cases, the new taxes in Brittany were part of kingdom-wide increases. Henry also tried to introduce the *imposition foraine*, a new import–export duty, in 1552. In addition to the tax, Henry created more than 140 new offices to oversee its collection in Brittany. The Estates reacted strongly to the new tax and its bureaucracy, borrowing 120,000 livres from André Ruiz, Yvon Rocaz, Jean Le Lou, and Jullien Motay – all Nantais merchants – to pay to abolish both. Five years later, the Estates paid 60,000 livres to abolish the *convoi de mer*, a tax of 20 sous/ton on all ships, to pay for war vessels to patrol the Bay of Biscay, and 40,000 livres more to abolish newly created offices. The Estates raised the 100,000 livres by a surtax of 10 sous/*feu* on the *fouage*, by an entry fee of 10 sous/pipe of wine, and by export duties on Nantais wine (5 sous/pipe) and on "linens, butters, fats, and

---

[58] AM Nantes, AA 23 for various years: in 1551, for example, the Breton share was 60,000 livres. See also AM Nantes, CC 72 (1523, 1547, 1550), CC 75, showing 52,800 livres. in 1575. In 1582, the king demanded 460,000 *écus* from the closed towns; the share of Saint-Malo, Dinan, and Ploërmel was 6,616 livres. (AM de Saint-Malo, BB 7, fols. 14v–15). In December, the king reduced the Breton share to 45,000 *écus*, and that of Saint-Malo to 2,800 livres (fol. 22). The *décimes* for Brittany are given as 85,000 livres in 1578 in BN, Mss. Fr. 21,479, fols. 18–20v.

[59] Calan, I, 93 (1539), 111 (1542), and 117 (1543). A Breton livre was worth 1.2 French livres. The documents reproduced by Calan are taken from an eighteenth-century copy of the registers of the Estates.   [60] ADLA, B 3009.

other merchandise exported from Brittany."[61] The king also created a Parlement in Brittany (actually the re-creation of the old ducal Parlement), pocketing some 350,000 livres from the sale of its offices in 1553 and 40,000 livres from six new offices created in 1554.[62]

Henry II sold *rentes* on the *fouages* in 1558, completing his efforts to undermine the old Breton system. The Estates protested that the king had no right to create the *rentes*, as the *fouage* was not a permanent tax but only a provisional grant made by each meeting of the Estates, in conformity with the great treaty of 1532.[63] In their view, the *fouage* was not part of the king's demesne and he therefore could not assign *rentes* to it. The king overruled their protests, selling 22,628 livres of *rentes* in 1558, as well as a *rente* on the *aide des villes* of Josselin (prompting objections similar to those about the *fouage rentes*).[64]

The developments from 1551 to 1558 represented a new method of dealing with the Estates of Brittany. Francis I raised the assessment on each *feu* from 4.8 to 8.4 livres and added special surtaxes to the basic *fouage*. He also created the tax for the upkeep of 50,000 infantrymen (levied throughout France) and levied certain special taxes, such as the ransom aids and a tax on belfries. Henry II tried to create new taxes, rather than to raise the existing ones. He successfully added the *taillon* but shifted tactics with the *imposition foraine* in 1553. He allowed the Estates to purchase exemption from this and later taxes; they chose the form of taxation levied to pay for the exemption settlements.

The sale of *rentes* on the *fouage* in 1558 must have alerted the Estates to the point that the king no longer considered this tax an extraordinary grant from the Estates. The extreme pressure applied by Henry II, in the form of the many offices and taxes created in the province during his reign, required the Estates to redefine their role *vis-à-vis* the king. The king was perfectly willing to accept subsidies voted by the Estates (particularly when they were paid in advance, as in 1553), just as he had accepted a composition from the southwestern provinces in return for their exemption from the *gabelle* in 1549 and from other salt taxes in 1553. In return for the grant of money to the king, the Estates selected the mode of taxation. This policy increased enormously the power of the Estates and allowed local elites to make key decisions about tax policy. The contrast between

---

[61] ADLA, B 12,871; B 53, fols. 212–25, especially 222v; Blanchard, *Lettres*, 365 and 372 on an earlier, unsuccessful effort to levy the *convoi* in 1406; de la Borderie, "Anne," pieces l, li, and liii on the *convoi* of 1490.

[62] F. Saulnier, *Le Parlement de Bretagne* (Rennes, 1909), 3 vols., introduction on the sale of 1554. The Estates had asked for the Parlement: Calan, I, 128, remonstrance n. 1. See also, ADLA, B 3, fols. 326v–336v.

[63] M. de Mauny, *1532 – Le grand traité franco-breton* (Paris, 1971) reproduces the treaty and relevant edicts.

[64] ADLA, B 12,871. Some were sold as *affranchissements*, which they were not (Calan, I, 176, complaint of 1566).

a body that merely votes the regular taxes and one which adopts *new* taxes is one between a rubber stamp and a powerful protector of local interests. As one might expect in an assembly dominated by landlords, the Estates opted for indirect rather than direct taxation. In the case of the duties levied to end the *convoi* and abolish the presidial offices (1558 on), the largest share of the money came from indirect taxes on transit of goods and on retail sales of wine.

The Estates had another reason to choose indirect taxation: military taxes on the countryside. The Estates of November 1568, in terms that echo the remonstrances of every meeting between 1561 and 1589, complained about extraordinary military taxes:

not a single year has passed in which they have not had to pay extraordinary subsidies; 160,000 livres in 1562 and more than 300,000 livres in 1567 and 1568; in all, more than 400,000 livres over and above the *fouages*, the tax on belfries for the upkeep of 50,000 infantrymen, the money taken from the parishes for the *élus* and free archers, the individual loans . . .[65]

The Estates of 1575 complained that 300,000 livres had been levied for troops the previous year; those of 1576 mentioned levies of two million livres, including 720,000 livres raised for munitions by troops in 1575 and 1576. In the 1580s it was much the same: the Estates complained of the *francs archers*, infantry *étapes*, garrison taxes, and the "theft, removal and ravishing of their other goods, adding up to an inestimable sum."[66]

The royal policy of levying military taxes on the countryside was particularly onerous for Brittany between 1561 and 1588 because the province was on the front line in the war against the Protestants in Anjou and Poitou (on land) and those of La Rochelle (at sea). The king's troops taxed and requisitioned the goods of the peasants to pay for the land war, while the king forced the towns to outfit ships against the Rochelais.[67] Although the self-interest of the landlords dictated a policy of indirect rather than direct taxation by the Estates, the large military levies of the 1560s to 1590s gave the Estates little alternative.

The situation began to change in the 1570s and 1580s, when the Estates turned to a different package of taxes to raise money. The functions of the Estates will be treated in the next two chapters, so here we will concentrate on

[65] Calan, I, 195. ADLA, C 414, pp. 151ff. The citations to documents of the Estates of 1567–98 can be found in the ADLA, ADIV, and ADCN; they are the eighteenth-century copies used by Calan. The original assizes papers of the Estates begin only in 1610. The *élus* were militiamen elected by their neighbors; they had no relation to the *élection* officials of the same name. In 1572, for example, the parish of Ercé paid 38.85 livres for the "francs archers et élus" (ADIV, G Ercé, number 1). The parish of Acigné paid 211.75 livres in 1574, which it had to borrow at interest (ADIV, G Acigné, piece 8). Parishes had to pay the considerable costs of outfitting these individuals.   [66] Calan, II, 67, 71, and 164. See also ADLA, C 414.

[67] See, for example, the account of the cost of outfitting four ships in 1573 for use against the Rochelais: AM Nantes, EE 221, July 1573. Some of the merchants included our old friends the Ruiz, Rocaz, and Poullain families.

the traditional methods of raising money, and the impact on them of the actions of the Estates. By the second half of the sixteenth century, the king and the Estates had tacitly agreed that both the *fouage* and the *impôts et billots* were fixed by custom. As we have seen, the *fouage* remained fixed both as to the number of hearths per parish and as to the contribution per *feu* (8.4 livres, plus a 5 percent collection surcharge). In order to get around this blockage, the king resorted to expedients such as the sale of *rentes* on the *fouage* receipts and the sale of exemptions in 1577. These two techniques produced 1.78 million livres between 1558 and 1583 but entailed a reduction of 118,000 livres in annual receipts.[68]

The reductions in *fouage* receipts, on paper some 96,000 livres but in reality more like 53,000 livres because most *rentes* were paid at only half their face value (when paid at all), were counterbalanced by the additions to the regular direct taxes noted above: the *taillon* and mounted constabulary tax. In 1554, the Estates asked for, and obtained, a surtax of their own – 3,000 livres – later raised to 8,000 livres. Annual receipts from regular direct taxation therefore remained relatively stable from the 1530s into the 1590s, when Henry IV added the garrison tax (in 1597). The proportion of direct taxation in ordinary revenues, however, declined sharply. Direct taxes had produced roughly two-thirds of Breton revenue in the 1480s and about 55–7 percent in the first half of the sixteenth century. By the 1580s, they produced only 35 percent of gross revenue (table 10).

In 1583, regular direct taxation produced 386,924 livres, while the regular indirect taxes – the *impôts et billots* and transit taxes – produced 372,000 livres (34.5 percent of gross revenue). The figures from the 1583 budget demonstrate some of the enduring elements of Breton taxing and spending. They show the province evolving toward a system in which indirect taxes provided the bulk of the revenue, yet they understate the direct taxes of the time because they leave out the substantial military taxes levied in the field. In the seventeenth century, military surtaxes were unimportant before 1627 and, by sixteenth-century standards, quite low even in the 1630s and 1640s.

The 1583 share of the Central Treasury was 275,334 livres, just over 25 percent of the gross revenue. The regional expenses – the amount carried on the in-place expenses of the *recette générale* of Brittany – included the alienation of all indirect tax revenues to Catherine de Médicis, but the genuinely Breton costs, such as the Parlement, added up to 283,389 livres. The Central Treasury's share of the taxes was not all shipped to Paris; we do not have information on how the money was spent, but it was likely disbursed to a great extent in Brittany itself. Henry III gave substantial annual pensions and gifts to the governor of

---

[68] ADLA, B 3009. There were local variations, so that Bréhat and Belle Ile did not pay the *fouage* but did pay the *taillon*; Bréhat had to pay extraordinary levies, Belle Ile did not.

Table 10: *Breton finances in 1583 (figures in livres* tournois*)*

Revenue source	Percentage of total	Net revenue	Gross receipts
Demesne	6.37	13,719	68,765
Demesne to Catherine		17,500	
Fouages	28.83	207,843	311,298
Taillon	5.21	48,990	56,290
Constabulary	1.05	10,768	11,337
Aide	0.20	1,934	2,192
Estates	23.89	258,000	258,000
Great farms	34.45	to Catherine	372,000
Total	100.00	558,754	1,079,882
Regional charges		283,390	
To Central Treasury		275,364	

Note:

The great farms were the *impôts*, the *prévôté de Nantes*, and the *ports et havres* and its associated taxes. There was also a *décime* on the clergy, likely of some 85,000 livres. *Source:* AD Loire-Atlantique, B 12,871.

Brittany, the duke de Mercoeur, and it was customary for the government to assign Breton revenue to local expenses such as the upkeep of royal ships and garrisons.[69]

The Estates granted large sums to the king in the 1580s; they levied a *fouage* surtax of 40 sous per *feu* to help pay these grants. In fact, the extra direct taxes were much higher; in 1589, for example, the king announced in January that he would levy 120,000 livres on the *fouage* contributors to pay his troops.[70] It is tempting to see the reign of Henry III as a critical period of change in Breton institutional development – for example, the Estates removed grain from the list of taxable goods – but the Breton system had powerful elements of continuity as well. The Estates did not abandon direct taxation as a means of raising money: just under 40 percent of the 1582 grant was to come from the *fouage* surtax and the tax on the urban rich.[71] The great watershed in the institutional evolution of the province came during the League War of 1589–98.

[69] ADLA, B 12,871; B 713. In 1582, for example, the Estates voted Mercoeur 4,000 *écus*.
[70] ADLA, B 713.
[71] Calan, II, 197–202. The king needed money to pay debts to various merchants, including Jean d'Aragon, a Spanish merchant of Nantes, and Swiss troops. It ended up in the pockets of Sebastien Zamet, among others.

Institutional structures of political control

THE LEAGUE AND BRETON INSTITUTIONS, 1589–1598

The French civil wars of the second half of the sixteenth century had very different impacts on the various regions of the country. Although the violence touched most areas, the timing and intensity of the immediate military effects of the wars varied sharply from region to region. In Burgundy, for example, there were massive population dislocations in the late 1570s, continuing until the late 1590s.[72] In Brittany, the early stages of the wars had little direct effect, save in the southern reaches of the bishopric of Nantes – that is, the area bordering on Poitou. Brittany did have to pay heavy, extraordinary military taxation, but the awesome devastation that accompanied sixteenth-century armies remained largely confined to the bishoprics of Nantes and (more intermittently) Rennes.

The death of Henry III changed the situation overnight. The local elite split in its reaction to Henry IV. The ardent Catholics, with a major power base at Nantes, rallied to the governor of the province, Emmanuel de Lorraine, duke de Mercoeur (cousin of the slain Henry of Guise). Mercoeur joined his cousin, the duke de Mayenne, in leading the resistance to Henry IV. Mercoeur found many supporters in Brittany, not only among the nobility but also among the merchants of Nantes. The leading merchants were often of Spanish origin – Ruiz, Rocaz, Espinoze. Those who were not themselves Spanish often traded heavily with northern Spain. There was a permanent Nantais colony at Bilbao, and the two cities had a special trading cooperative, the *Contractation de Nantes*.[73]

The Parlement, which sat at Rennes, remained largely loyal to the king. Some of its members fled to Nantes, just as some of the councilors of the Chamber of Accounts fled to Rennes: in both cases, the runaways established rump alternative courts. The Leaguer Parlement consisted largely of families with an immediate tie to the elite of Nantes. Ten of the twenty councilors were from Nantais mercantile or legal families and three others married into such families.[74] The Chamber of Accounts followed precisely the same pattern as the sovereign courts in Burgundy.[75] The senior officials usually sided with Henry IV:

[72] AD Côte d'Or, series C, hearth counts of various bailiwicks of Burgundy. At Beauvernoy, for example, the number of hearths dropped from 53 in 1578 to 11 in 1598; at Cuisery-la-Ville, the decline was from 109 in 1578 to 30 in 1607. C 4767 and 4768.

[73] P. Jeulin, "Aperçus sur la Contractation de Nantes," *Annales de Bretagne*, xl (1932): 284–331, 457–505.   [74] Saulnier, *Le Parlement*, gives a separate list of the League Parlementaires.

[75] H. Drouot, *Mayenne et la Bourgogne* (Paris, 1937), 2 vols. Drouot shows that the senior magistrates sided with the king, the junior ones with the League. P. Benedict, *Rouen during the Wars of Religion* (Cambridge, 1981), found precisely the opposite pattern at Rouen. Here disagreeing with Robert Harding, whose article, "Revolution and Reform in the Holy League: Angers, Rennes, Nantes," *Journal of Modern History*, 53 (1981): 379–416, argues that Nantes followed the Rouen pattern. I have given a detailed analysis on this issue in a paper, "Police Authority and Local Police at Nantes, 1550–1680," given at the Annual Meeting of the Western Society for French History, 1990. This material forms part of a book manuscript on Nantes in early modern times, under preparation by Jean Tanguy and me.

three of the four presidents, one *avocat du roi*, both treasurers of France, and twelve of eighteen masters of accounts. The junior officials sided with the League: sixteen of the twenty-four auditors were Leaguers and only four clearly backed Henry IV.[76]

Both sides tried to make use of Estates, but the meetings involved a rather limited number of delegates, in part because of the uncertainties of travel. The royalist deputies of Quimper, for example, were captured en route to the Estates of 1592.[77] The military situation meant that extraordinary levies by troops (to say nothing of looting and pillaging) formed the chief burden of the times, but the regular taxes and special grants of the Estates continued to be levied (in theory) throughout the war. The military treasurers have left a sufficient number of accounts to show that the peasants did contribute heavily to troops in the field.[78]

The sums necessary to pursue the fighting were enormous. The package of regular taxation included about 800,000 livres, equally divided between direct and indirect taxes, plus the tax for the upkeep of the infantry (about 60,000 livres a year), and additional revenue from the *décimes* and the royal demesne.[79] The Estates of Brittany supplemented this regular income with special grants raised by means of sales taxes on wine, surtaxes on the *fouages*, urban direct taxes, and import–export duties. The combined total of these resources probably reached 1.3 million livres a year, an amount grossly inadequate for paying the large armies placed in the field after 1588.[80]

The garrisons of the two sides cost between three and four million livres each year: the king spent between 1.5 and 2.9 million livres; in 1593, the League estimated its garrisons to cost 1.2 million livres.[81] The unprecedented sums needed to fund these armies revolutionized Breton political life. It is easy to overlook the fact that the two sides had many common interests. They both worried about social upheaval (particularly after the Croquants rising in the southwest); they both wished to preserve the powerful position of the indigenous elites; they both needed to raise a great deal of money. These common interests often led to quite interesting arrangements, such as the 1595 agreement to split

[76] ADLA, B 151, March 1591 listing of Chamber members, giving the faction to which they belonged.
[77] J. Moreau, *Histoire de ce qui s'est passé en Bretagne durant les Guerres de la Ligue* (Saint-Brieuc, 1857).
[78] A. de Barthélemy, *Choix de documents inédits sur l'histoire de la Ligue en Bretagne* (Nantes, 1880); Comte de Carné, *Les Etats de Bretagne et l'administration de cette province jusqu'en 1789*, 2 vols. (Paris, 1868), I, 230–5.
[79] AM Nantes, AA 23; CC 72–8; AD Loire-Atlantique, B 12,871; B 713, showing *décimes* of about 82,000 livres in 1589.
[80] The Estates of 1583 granted the king a wine tax, a *fouage*, a tax on the rich of the towns, and several other duties to cover the cost of a large grant. In addition, the king levied a military surtax of 120,000 livres in 1588–9 (ADLA, B 720).
[81] BN, Mss. Fr. 22,311, fols. 137ff.; AD Ille-et-Vilaine, C 2645, p. 56. De Barthélemy, *Choix de documents*, has lists of troops in the royal garrisons in 1591 (90–6) and 1595 (179–95).

the proceeds of a *fouage* of 160,000 *écus* levied on the bishoprics of Léon, Tréguier, and Cornouaille, or the equal sharing of the transit duties on wine levied at Ingrande-s-Loire.[82]

Although the eastern and southern parts of the province had zones of great destruction (such as the Vitré area), most of the damage took place in the far west, in Celtic Brittany. The infamous La Fontenelle looted much of Cornouaille in the name of the League; in one "battle" against the armed peasantry of the region, his men slaughtered at least 1,500 peasants.[83] The king pardoned La Fontenelle at the end of the fighting, but he subsequently executed him for treason after a later rebellion. La Fontenelle's depredations are a well-known part of Breton lore (peasants used his name to frighten children for centuries to come), but the king's generals were little better. The chief royal commander in the west, René de Rieux, *sieur* de Sourdéac, levied 24,000 livres a year in and around Brest to feed his troops, and forced the townspeople to build and arm warships. In 1595, he levied a weekly *fouage* of 6 sous per *feu* to pay his troops at Brest and raised very large in-kind contributions as well: 1,700 *boisseaux* of wheat, 10,000 lb. of butter, and 80,000 lb. of lard. When these measures proved insufficient, he seized 15,000 livres from the wine duty receivers and threw them in prison. The list of similar complaints against him (made by the inhabitants of Lower Brittany in a special petition to the king at the end of the war) was virtually endless. Henry granted him a full pardon for all actions.[84]

The main armies required far more than these petty sums. The army of Marshal Aumont needed 12,000 ten-ounce loaves of bread a day in 1593: the Estates estimated that bread alone cost 324,000 livres for a six-month campaign.[85] His other expenses included 36,000 livres for horses and cannons, 80,000 livres for ball and powder, and the proceeds of a *fouage* of 9 livres per *feu* to pay his army of 250 horse and 2,500 foot.[86] In a complaint sent to the king at the end of the war, the parishes of Cornouaille claimed that Aumont levied 480,000 livres in that bishopric alone during six months of 1593. Some parishes claimed to be virtually deserted, ravaged by troops of one side or the other.[87] Other parishes in the area sought relief from the Estates; the parish of "Quergustenoellon" (?), for example, asked for remission of its 1600–03 taxes:

---

[82] BN, Mss. Fr. 22,311, fol. 204.

[83] A description of the slaughter appears in De Barthélemy, *Choix de documents*, fols. 258ff.

[84] ADLA, B 66, fols. 23v–29v, lengthy description of the behavior of Sourdéac in the Brest region. The king granted Sourdéac, his officers, and financial receivers full approval for all their actions taken between 1591 and the signing of peace with La Fontenelle (fol. 29v).

[85] BN, Mss. Fr. 22,311, fols. 137ff. The total given in the *état* prepared by the treasurer of France was 41,362 *écus* per month.

[86] De Barthélemy, *Choix de documents*, 179–95, *état* of February 1595.

[87] ADIV, C 2646, p. 71, Estates voting 600 livres to a delegate from Cornouaille to go to the king to request remission of taxes. He had already granted remission for the period up to 1597 (ADLA, B 66, fol. 62). See also the complaints of individual parishes, such as Kerchrist, ADIV, C 2646, p. 579. Several *fouage* receivers in the north and west went bankrupt between 1600 and 1605.

the said parish having been so worked over and ruined by the late troubles and reduced to such an extreme poverty, finally wishing to escape from it through peace, [but] the plague was visited upon the said parish, the which has so worked them over that, instead of the 600 households that it had before, there are today only 25 or so, so poor and necessitous and so afflicted that as soon as they step out of their houses, they are eaten by the wolves, with which the entire region is filled.[88]

The king acted in 1597–8 to reduce the burden on such people, cutting the garrisons, and the tax levied to pay them. In 1597, the garrison tax declined from 165,000 livres to 65,000 livres per *month*; in 1598, it dropped precipitously, soon to become fixed in custom at 75,000 livres per *year*.[89]

The enormous military surtaxes levied on the countryside left the Estates little choice as to the method of raising money for their grants to the king: they had to levy indirect taxes. The war made this difficult, as trade between areas occupied by the opposing sides was often interrupted. The receipts of the regular indirect taxes declined sharply: at the *prévôté de Nantes*, by 1591, to only two-thirds of what they had been in the early 1580s.[90] The records of the Chamber of Accounts are filled with tax farmers' requests for rebates, despite the generally lower prices they paid for the leases. In such a climate, the proceeds of a transit tax were likely to be irregular. The Estates therefore settled solely on wine sales taxes, which reached 18 livres/pipe of non-Breton wine and 9 livres/pipe of Breton wine in 1597 (as against the 1.25 livres and 0.4 livres of the 1580s).[91] At the end of the war, these levels declined, to 15 livres on imported wine and 7.2 livres, later 5.2 livres on Breton wine (1598, 1599).[92]

In 1597 and 1598, with peace partly then fully reestablished, the Estates and king sought to return the province to its normal situation. The Estates of 1598 eliminated the hearth surtax, while the king sharply reduced both the number of troops in garrisons and the special tax levied to pay them. By 1600, direct taxation was down to some 500,000 livres a year, a level it would maintain, save for occasional military surtaxes, until 1628. The end of the war brought with it the need to raise enormous sums to pay for the king's trip into Brittany and for the costs of his settlements with the League leaders. The Estates continued their wartime practice of raising money through wine sales taxes. They would not raise any money from direct taxation until 1643, and direct taxes would not become a permanent part of their resources until 1661; even then, direct taxes would form a limited part of those resources (see chapters 4 and 5).

The war ended in 1598 but its effects lingered into the 1620s. One of the most important legacies of the war was debt. The Estates agreed to give the king

---

[88] ADLA, B 68, fols. 35v and ff.
[89] ADIV, C 2645–6; BN, Mss. Fr. 10,839, fols. 248–68 on 1606 levies. The registration letters for the garrison tax at the Chamber of Accounts are in AD Loire-Atlantique, B 70–8: B 77, fols. 72v–73, raising the tax from 83,000 livres to 100,000 livres in 1639, B 78, fols. 33v–34 for 1643.
[90] ADLA, B 2972.   [91] ADIV, C 2645, 159–61.   [92] *Ibid.*, 208ff., 518–19.

600,000 livres in 1597 to pay for his trip to Brittany and another 2.4 million livres in 1598 to pay for some of the cost of his settlements with Breton League leaders. In the first case, the Estates borrowed the money from provincial notables; in the second, payments to the king were spread out over several years. The loan was to be repaid from the proceeds of a wine tax levied for the Estates; the grant of 2.4 million livres was also to be met by a wine tax (see chapter 4).[93] The Estates, therefore, had obligations totalling three million livres by 1598; this committed them to long-term taxation, in order to repay their debts.

The Estates were not alone in their indebtedness. Many Breton notables had been ransomed during the war, mortgaging properties to cover the ransom payments. Others had had their estates confiscated. The peace agreements generally returned property to its original owner but many nobles and royal officers sought the help of the Estates in getting reimbursement for ransom payments. The Estates frequently granted such payments, not only for those ransomed in the service of the king but also for those who had fought for Mercoeur. They subsequently assumed many of the debts of Mercoeur's chief treasurer, Michel de Loriot (a member of a well-entrenched Nantais officer family).[94]

Breton towns mortgaged their futures in the 1590s. At the end of the war, virtually every Breton town had debts of unprecedented size. The largest towns, Rennes and Nantes, owed well over 100,000 livres each: Nantes still had debts of 59,561 livres as late as 1611, despite being granted a special new tax to pay its debts in 1599. Although much of the money went to troops, we must also remember that the dismal year of 1597 forced towns to spend enormous amounts of money on poor relief. At Nantes, for example, the town handed out as much as 14,563 pounds of bread a week at the Saint-Nicolas gate in the late spring of 1597: on average, Nantes gave out more than 10,000 pounds of bread each week at the Saint-Nicolas gate alone. The total cost of this generosity between 24 April and 30 June 1597 was nearly 18,000 livres.[95]

The smaller towns (table 11) were often worse off than Nantes and Rennes, neither of which had submitted to extensive sieges. Dinan estimated its debts in 1603 as over 60,000 livres, and claimed that war damages that would have to be paid by the city were about 120,000 livres more. Vannes' debts were 46,000 livres as late as 1609, while Quintin had unpaid debts of 16,877 livres as late as 1611. Quintin also submitted a detailed listing of repair expenses to the church, town hall, and hospital (all damaged during the war) that added up to another 50,000 livres.[96] Collectively, Breton towns must certainly have owed close to one million livres in 1598. These debts forced them to request royal permission

---

[93] See ch. 4.   [94] He received 31,040 livres in 1610 – ADIV, C 2748, 2751.
[95] A. Croix, *La Bretagne au XVIe et XVIIe siècles* (Paris, 1981), ch. VII.
[96] ADLA, B 65–9, papers of the Chamber of Accounts, contains the requests of these towns to levy such taxes, along with justifications and lists of debts to be audited by the Chamber.

Table 11: *Indebtedness of Breton towns in the early seventeenth century*

Town (Year)	Debts (in livres *tournois*)	Causes (if given)
Nantes (1613)	59,561	Remaining of much larger sums due to League War
Nantes (1637)	139,631	Famine relief, 1631, intermittent plague
Nantes (1642)	150,000	Same, plus costs of upkeep of Spanish prisoners
Rennes (1626)	105,102	Plus 60,000 committed to Jesuits over ten years and 415,886 estimated cost of Palais de Parlement
Quimper (1603)	166,230	League War
Dinan (1604)	60,000	Plus repairs of 120,000; League War
Quintin (1614)	16,877	Plus repairs to town hall, church, hospital; total debts and repairs: 122,045
Fougères (1620)	16,854	Plus 36,000 wall repairs
Roscoff (1623)	(66,000)	Replace *quai* destroyed by storm (4 Dec. 1614)
Concarneau (1612)	64,081	League War
Concarneau (1645)	5,306	
Vitré (1592)	72,300	League War (siege of 1590)
Vitré (1599)	40,000	League War (other)
Vitré (1609)	(80,000)	Wall repairs
Vitré (1642)	80,000	Troops, sickness, walls
Ploërmel (1594)	19,974	Walls (siege)
Ploërmel (1622)	(16,000)	Walls
Saint-Brieuc (1606)	(25,000)	Street repair
Saint-Brieuc (1613)	49,000	Debts remaining from League War, down from previous amounts
Morlaix (1603)	54,000	Plus 60,000 repairs; League War
Malestroit (1614)	(36,000)	Walls; League War
Saint-Malo (1617)	150,000	League War

Note:

Figures in parentheses are for estimated repair costs. Some towns did not specify their debts, claiming that they were "immense" (Saint-Malo, 1643) or that "la pluspart des habitans violentez par diverses executions faictes en leurs biens se sont retirez de lad. ville" (Pontivy, in 1619, referring to debts left over from the League Wars). The actual amounts of debt had to be proven to the Chamber before they would approve the taxes: in 1602, Nantes paid 2,310 livres for a Chamber verification commission lasting 110 days.

Sources: AD Loire-Atlantique, B 65–79.

for new taxes, to supplement the inadequate receipts from their traditional town duties. Throughout the province, towns turned to wine and beverage sales taxes to pay off their debts. The king granted them temporary levies (usually for three years, later for nine), subject to later renewal. He also demanded that the towns turn over their books to the Chamber of Accounts each time they renewed their new taxes (and, later, every year). The Estates, or rather the nobles at the Estates, took this opportunity to insinuate themselves into town affairs; they obtained (in 1613) royal sanction for the necessity of Estates' approval of all new urban taxes (including renewals). Sully simultaneously ordered all these towns to turn over their books to him, in his function as *grand voyer*. They did so during Henry IV's reign, but the practice fell into disuse as soon as Sully left the ministry. The Chamber, however, conserved its oversight powers.[97]

Brittany entered a new political and governmental era at the end of the League Wars. The Estates suddenly had an enormous budget at their immediate disposal, and they also had new-found leverage on the king because of the substantial wine tax they levied on his behalf. The towns now had greater resources, again due to wine sales taxes. Nantes, which had spent perhaps 10,000 livres a year in the 1560s and 1570s, now spent 30,000 livres. In certain years, such as 1614 and 1626 (when the king came to Nantes), the amount could go far higher. These large urban resources offered new opportunities to the central government, which would often thrust royal expenses on to town budgets. In the 1630s and 1640s, for example, Breton towns went heavily into debt maintaining large numbers of Spanish prisoners of war.

RECOVERY AND EXPANSION, 1598–1627

Breton institutional structure underwent profound changes in the early seventeenth century. The changes in specific elements of the system took place at different moments, so that we cannot really speak of one period of royal offensive against local power. The ruling elite, the landlords, maintained control over the political system but the manner in which they exercised that power altered dramatically. We have seen above that the mayor of Nantes frequently lost the initiative to the royal provost and seneschal after 1600. Taverns open during high mass in the 1570s were fined by the mayor; such taverns were fined by the provost or seneschal in the 1620s and after.[98] This was part of a general pattern of massive royal incursion into local justice. Before we see this as some sort of overthrow of the power of the local elite, however, we would do well to remember that the seneschal of Nantes was, after 1600, often its mayor. If he

---

[97] ADIV, C 2751–3. Collins, "Sully et la Bretagne."
[98] AM de Nantes, FF 50 and ADLA, B 6649–63. See ch. 2 above and Collins, "Police Authority," for details.

did not hold the office, another top-ranking royal judicial officer – the *alloué*, the president of the presidial, or its lieutenant general – did.[99]

The increase in royal jurisdiction took place at the expense of seigneurial courts. We have insufficient information about the latter to be sure of how badly they suffered, but the clerkships of the royal courts were often sold in the 1570s and again in 1626. The civil clerkship of Auray sold for 3,170 livres in 1576, the criminal clerkship for 3,960 livres. In 1626, the general buyer, François Baret, bought them for 13,545 livres and 16,590 livres; Baret later resold them to a local purchaser. The general pattern of increase is clear in table 12; most clerkships tripled or quadrupled in value between the 1570s and the 1620s. At Ploërmel, we know the alienation prices of the 1570s and 1620s, and the lease prices of the period 1608–18. The clerkships sold for 16,000 livres in 1576 but for 50,925 livres in 1626; in 1608, the Estates leased the clerkships for 2,300 livres, indicating a return of 4.5 percent, if the value remained constant from 1608 to 1626 (and assuming a relatively honest leasing process). Most of the other clerkship prices would indicate an even lower rate of return, often 2 or 3 percent a year, strongly implying that the value of the clerkships increased substantially between 1608 and 1626. The enormous growth in the value of the clerkships can only be attributed to the expansion of royal justice, and thus to the increased revenue one could expect from ownership of the clerkship.[100]

The Parlement, too, expanded. The king extended the sessions in 1601, leading to the creation of a special wine surtax, the *petit devoir*, to raise the necessary 27,000 livres.[101] The two sovereign courts were very active in their efforts to prevent new taxes from taking root in the province: the Parlement and the Chamber both refused to register new taxes on linens, surtaxes on the *fouages*, and the garrison tax.[102] The courts were also quite active in defense of their corporate interests. At the Chamber, we have the case of François de Bruc, who purchased the office of auditor held by Patrice Bizeul. Bizeul sold the office in November 1603 (to Pierre Le Lou, member of a Chamber family), who sold it the same day to Jan Trippart. Trippart sold it, on 29 June 1604, to Sébastien de Bruc. The Chamber refused to seat de Bruc, so he sold it, on 31 October 1605, to Guillaume Marceau, who passed it along immediately to François de Bruc, Sebastien's brother. François registered his letters of office and was "received and accepted" by *maîtres des requêtes* in July 1606; in March 1607, the Chamber was still refusing to seat him. In December 1608, the king sent special letters to the Chamber ordering them to examine de Bruc and receive him. De Bruc had had enough, however; he sold the office to René de

---

[99] List of mayors in the *Livre doré* (see ch. 2 above).
[100] ADLA, B 2966, as compared with values in B 12,871 (1583 or earlier – usually mid 1570s), shows that clerkships tripled or quadrupled in value during the period 1575–1625.
[101] On the *petit devoir*, see below, ch. 5.
[102] ADIV, C 2645–6, papers of the Estates (1598–1609); ADLA, B 65–77, registers of the Chamber of Accounts (1598–1650), each contain many examples.

Table 12: *Value of Breton royal clerkships in livres*

	1626	1608–17 price	1608–17 annual income
Parlement	327,000		
criminal only		25,111[a]	
palace register		12,906	
Chambre des Comptes	26,250	9,329	
Presidial of Rennes			
civil	123,900	(50,886)[a]	
criminal	46,725[b]		
office, inventaries	63,525		
appelations, presentations	99,750		
Provost of Rennes	75,600		
Fougères	45,465		
Hedé	10,185	1,290	
Ploërmel	50,925		
civil		18,718	1,700
criminal		7,250	600
Touffou	4,515		
Presidial of Nantes	133,350	29,397[a]	
Provost of Nantes	47,250		
Nantes			
consulate	17,325		
ecclesiastical court	3,150		
Guérande	18,375		
Presidial of Vannes			
civil	27,195	13,209	500; (1.400)
appelations	12,075	6,866.5	
criminal, office	27,195		
Ecclesiastical court	2,205	568.75	
Rhuys	9,030		
Auray			
civil	13,545	4,642.5	500
criminal, office	16,590		
Hennebont	31,678.5		
Hennebont, seal	1,501.5	931	120
Quimperlé	13,020		
Morlaix	45,360		
office, criminal		7,183	600
Carhais, Gourin,	47,460	8,470	1,250
Huelgoat			1,000
Lannion	34,755		
Lesneven	39,270		

Table 12: *contd*

	1626	1608–17 price	1608–17 annual income
Dinan	45,360	8,777	900
Jugon	9,030		
Quimper	57,750		
Brest	13,655		
Châteaulin	13,650	4,777	400
Concq	11,340	1,125	
Maréchaussée	8,400	6,810	950
Total paid	1,625,652.5	850,805.7	87,538 (1620)

Note:
a half-value.
b another source (B 713) says 122,315.
The 1608–17 repurchase paid either one-half or two-thirds of the value of each clerkship. The individual percentages are sometimes specified as for one-half (as at Rennes or Nantes) but are not usually indicated. The total value of the clerkships, however, is for their *full* worth. The figure from 1620 is for the total revenues from all clerkships. The price paid in 1626 are unquestionably too low, because almost all of the clerkships were bought by one *traitant*, François Baret. He obviously represented a syndicate, who likely resold them at a profit.
Sources: ADLA, B 2966; B 713; B 720; ADIV, C 2969, C 2930; C 2752. BN, Mss. Fr. 16,622, fols. 115–56.

Bruc on 26 January 1609, from whose hands it passed quickly to Louis Hernouet and on to those of Nathan Huzeau (10 March 1609). The Chamber received Huzeau on 18 December 1609.[103]

The Chamber and Parlement were extremely selective about those whom they would seat at the court; the Chamber even refused to seat René Descartes' father, a councilor in the Parlement, as one of its presidents.[104] The Parlement also participated extensively in the administration of the province. The Parlement issued a series of ordinances banning the export of grain, notably in famine years such as 1631 or 1643, and acted in tax cases, such as appeals concerning *fouages*.[105] The Estates had frequent recourse to the Parlement and the Chamber when they sought to delay the implementation of royal edicts in the province. The creation of new offices, in 1616 or 1623, could be long

---

[103] ADIV, B 68, fols. 270–6. H. Carré, "Reception d'un procureur général au Parlement de Bretagne en 1603," *Annales de Bretagne* (1889): 161–89, documents the travails of Jean-Jacques Lefebvre in his efforts to be seated at the Court.
[104] ADLA, B 71, fols. 104–6.   [105] ADIV, G, Gévezé, number 15.

delayed by the two courts, enabling the Estates (successfully in each case) to purchase the abolition of the offices in question.[106] The general impression from the sheer volume of records in the archives of both the Parlement and the Chamber, is that their competence and action expanded tremendously in the first quarter of the seventeenth century.

The financial system, in contrast, evolved very little between 1598 and 1625. There were periodic extra levies for the military – in 1601 and 1614–17 – and the king and Estates agreed to small direct surtaxes to pay for special expenses, such as a debt of 39,000 livres to the count of Soissons.[107] The income from indirect taxes jumped sharply after 1601, but the increase came from commercial expansion, not from an augmentation of duty rates. The tax system itself remained highly particularistic. Local expenses were very small, because there were no *élections* in Brittany. As in the sixteenth century, the financial personnel consisted entirely of twenty *fouage* receivers (serving in alternate years) and another score of receivers and controllers at the *généralité* and at the provosty of Nantes. In 1606, total receipts of regular taxation in Brittany were 568,624 livres (because so much of the indirect taxes had been alienated), of which the Central Treasury got 43 percent. The main regional costs were the Parlement – 114,000 livres plus the money from the *petit devoir* (27,400 livres), the Chamber – 53,370 livres, and the local garrison paid by the *taillon* – 56,400 livres (see table 13). At most local levels, the largest expenses were the *rentes* (diocesan), and the main collection expense, the 5 percent surtax of the parish collectors themselves.

Of the 244,466 livres the Central Treasury was supposed to receive from Brittany, the receiver general sent only 86,679 livres in *cash* to Paris. He had two chief reasons for limiting the shipment of cash: the expense – the costs of shipping this cash were 1,936 livres – and the danger. On 15 November 1606, Jehan Jonneaux, the *commis* taking 19,226 livres in cash to Paris, was robbed at Ancenis. The thieves made off with 3,000 livres, carrying out the operation under cover of darkness (at 5.30 in the afternoon). The Chamber of Accounts held Jonneaux personally responsible for making good the loss because "les deniers du Roy doibvent estre voicturer entre deux soleils." The receiver general of Brittany spent the rest of the money by means of *mandements de l'Epargne* (orders to pay the given amount to the specified individual). The Breton military elite and the garrison troops were the chief beneficiaries of this spending. The duke of Brissac received 18,000 livres for himself and 20,300 livres to pay his officers (himself included) and men; the duke of Montbazon (a Rohan) received 19,000 livres, other officers another 29,000 livres. The governor of Brittany, Henry IV's bastard César de Vendôme (still a child),

---

[106] ADLA, B 70, fols. 83v and ff. on 1616 efforts.   [107] ADIV, C 2646.

Table 13: *Regular Direct Taxation in Brittany, 1606, 1628, 1652 (in 000 livres)*

	1606	1628	1652
Fouage	313.0	313.3	278.8
Taillon	56.4	56.4	54.5ᵃ
Constabulary	11.4	11.7	11.7
Estates	8.0	8.0	8.3
Garrison tax	83.0	95.0	100.0
Total	471.8	484.4 or	453.3 or
		584.4	553.3

Note:

ᵃ In 1628, the king ordered that the *taillon* be raised to 156,000 livres. It is unclear if this was done: the Chamber of Accounts refused to register the letters for more than 56,400 livres. Yet the Estates consistently protested against it and the *état du roi* for 1630 carried the *taillon* for 156,400 livres (as did the *brevets de la taille* for 1634 and 1643). The *état au vrai* for 1628 shows the receiver for the *taillon* got the regular 56,400 livres and an additional 50,000 livres. It is likely that the king raised 50,000 livres more for the *taillon* in both 1627 and 1628 (the former counting as an advance for 1628) and 100,000 livres a year thereafter.

Sources: BN, Mss. Fr. 10,839, fols. 248–68 (1606); ADLA, B 2967 (1628), ADLA, B 3009 (1652).

received 12,000 livres. In addition to the money paid to Brissac, the troops received another 45,972 livres.[108]

Here we see a regular feature of Breton taxation: the extent to which the king spent money raised in Brittany in Brittany itself. The Breton elite got the lion's share of this money: 78,000 livres in direct payments to major nobles; 114,000 livres to the Parlement; 53,000 livres to the Chamber of Accounts; 66,272 livres for troops; 30,000 livres to dismantle a fortress on the Breton–Angevin border; 56,400 livres for the *taillon*. While the garrison and *taillon* disbursements may not seem to fit the category of payments to elites, in fact both usually ended up in noble pockets. The *taillon* went largely to pay *compagnies d'ordonnance*, such as that of Brissac (annual cost, 52,800 livres in 1612), whose members were the nobility of the province. The officers received substantial annual payments: Brissac got 3,280 livres a year and his lieutenant (a Rohan) received 1,380 livres. The men-at-arms received 480 livres a year. As for the garrisons, a list of 1600 shows that 42 percent of the money spent on them was paid to their officers (over 50 percent if one includes Brissac's *état* as marshal of France).[109] Many

[108] BN, Mss. Fr. 10,839, fols. 248–68, *état au vrai* of 1606.
[109] BN, Mss. Fr. 22,311, fols. 6–10 for Brissac's company in 1612; fols. 111–14 for expenses of Breton garrisons in 1600.

Breton towns had a governor, who also received either a royal pension or one paid by the town itself (or both, as at Saint-Malo).

In the late sixteenth and early seventeenth centuries, the Estates of Brittany voted considerable sums to various monarchs in an attempt to forestall methods of imposition – direct taxes, production taxes on linens – they viewed as contrary to the interests of the local ruling elite. This policy was largely circumvented by sixteenth-century kings by means of special military taxes. Under Henry IV (after 1600), there were no longer convenient military excuses for levying the surtaxes, so they stopped. The king became more dependent on the Estates for grants and the Estates, as a consequence, became more powerful. The only major surtaxes of the first quarter of the seventeenth century were those levied for the count of Soisson, the tax to end the sou/livre on linens in 1609, the tax for the destruction of Craon, and special military taxes raised between 1614 and 1617 to help pay for troops used to quell local disturbances. In contrast to this, the Estates furnished the king with over 10 million livres from their wine duty between 1599 and 1625.

Henry IV was perfectly willing to let the Bretons choose their own form of taxation, which sixteenth-century practice had customarily allowed them to do, so long as he received extra revenues. It would seem that this policy was part of a general one of pragmatic compromise with those local elites who could defend their privileges. The king sought to coopt such elites in a variety of ways: creating the *paulette* as part of his compromise with creditors (which involved a partial repudiation of debts); making substantial payments to the League leaders; keeping many nobles on the royal payroll and on the royal pensions list (although the latter declined throughout his reign); compromising with the local political powers in provinces such as Brittany or Provence. In Brittany, the king allowed the elite to defend its chief financial interests by letting it choose the form of taxation and by permitting the Estates and the towns to create their own revenue base with which to finance elite policies.

Peace provided the main reason for the low level of Breton regular taxation in the first quarter of the seventeenth century. The one period of military activity, 1614–17, saw the resumption of emergency military levies. The Estates of 1616, for example, complained that the duke de Retz and the baron de Nevet (commander of the fortress of Douarnenez) had levied 160,000 livres on nearby *fouage* hearths to pay their troops. Two years later, the Estates voted 30,000 livres to pay troops there for 1619 and 1620, taking the money from their wine tax.[110] The garrison had already levied some 16,370 livres in Cornouaille between September 1617 and September 1618, in addition to the 69,185 livres

---

[110] ADIV, C 2649, 53; C 2753, C 2755, C 2941. The group C 2750 and on are the papers of the Estates' sittings (the assizes); the group C 2940 and on are their accounts.

assessed within an unknown area for other costs related to Douarnenez's troops in early 1617.[111]

The events of 1614 to 1616 (an abortive revolt by the duke de Vendôme and related rebellion by fractious Breton nobles) led to other military spending. The king tried to seize half of the revenues of the towns in 1614 and even assigned 100,000 livres in expenses to such revenues, touching off a long fight with the Estates and the Parlement. He tried to assign a further 168,000 livres to the wine duty of the Estates, and the local war treasurer, Jan Charon, even imprisoned the treasurer of the Estates for failure to pay. The Parlement came to the aid of the treasurer, Michel Poullain, forbidding royal sergeants to post on his door the order to pay Charon and threatening those who collected the unauthorized taxes with personal liability for fourfold restitution. These "unauthorized taxes" went beyond the money assigned on Poullain: the Parlement mentions supplements of 50,000 livres and 8,000 livres that had been added to the garrison tax of 1616.[112] There are few other records concerning such supplements, which make them a good example of the larger problem of substantial supplements and local taxes that have left no trace because they were not part of the regular levies.

The only two periods for which we have extensive records of extra levies are 1614–17 and 1627–8. We have seen that the king tried to seize money from the revenues of both the Estates and the towns, and that the garrison at Douarnenez levied substantial amounts on the countryside of Cornouaille. In addition, the Estates of 1614 noted that troops raised money in the bishoprics of Rennes, Nantes, Vannes, Saint-Malo, Saint-Brieuc, and in eastern Cornouaille (Corlay). The Estates asked that such sums be deducted from *fouage* contributions, but the king refused.[113] The count (later duke) of Brissac, son of the old duke, held responsibility for the levies in eastern Brittany. The Estates subsequently voted him 30,000 livres to cover his costs in this campaign, and the king gave him a further 60,000 livres from the royal share of the receipts of the duty of the Estates.[114]

There are even some local records about this military activity. The Chamber of Accounts, acting in late 1615, examined the accounts of the *étapes* receiver of the troops of the duke de Montbazon (a Rohan). He had taken goods worth 7,476 livres in the bishopric of Nantes, yet levied, with the assistance of the *fouage* receiver, only 890 livres to reimburse those who had provided the goods. The Chamber checked his accounts and approved a repayment of 6,586.2 livres, duly levied as a surtax on the *fouage* of certain areas of the bishopric of Nantes in 1616.[115] This was the official, legal way to assess *étapes*, with the *fouage* receivers rather than army personnel collecting the money. In 1629, for

---

[111] *Ibid.*, C 2755; on the expense of Douarnenez, see also BN, Mss. Fr. 22,311, fols. 267–9, account of money spent in 1616–17.   [112] ADIV, C 2753.   [113] ADIV, C 3227.
[114] ADIV, C 2753–4; C 2940.   [115] ADLA, B 70, fols. 128ff.

example, the Chamber refused to approve 9,400 livres in *étapes:* levied by army *commis* because the *fouage* receivers had not gotten commissions authorizing the levy and had not collected the money themselves.[116]

In the parish of Massérac, in the Vilaine valley, the accounts of the vestrymen explain the general procedure. In 1614, we find them borrowing 130 livres from various parishioners to pay for the "fourrage et nourriture" of the company commanded by M. de Chase and to "prevent Captain Pierre and his company setting up quarters in the village." The smaller costs included 15 sous, to pay for a bowl of oats for Chase's horse. The following year, the parish paid 37 livres to Captain Vauldurant to prevent him and his company from moving from the abutting parish of Guéméné-Penfao into Massérac, and another 69 livres to Captain Richerye to keep his troops out of the village. When troops did come to the village, the parishioners paid 412 livres "to prevent the disorder that they might commit in this parish." The parishioners had to borrow the money in the nearby town of Redon, a process that cost them another 7.3 livres for the contracts.[117] Even large cities participated in this process of bribing troops to keep them away: in 1642, we find Nantes offering two regimental commanders eight pipes of wine to keep their troops away from the city and its suburbs.[118] The Estates of 1626 pretty well summed up the attitude of all in their third remonstrance to the king: "Experience makes it known that the great number of garrisons can only be the ruin of commerce, the diminution of your [the king's] finances, and the trampling and oppression of your subjects."[119]

REGULAR TAXATION IN AN AGE OF MILITARY NECESSITY, 1627–1675

The occasional mentions of *étapes* in the archives mask their importance in the period after 1627. There are tantalizing glimpses of the problem at Guérande (1628), at Saint-Brieuc and Quintin (1628), and at Vannes (1637). At Guérande, we find that the town had to put up a company of a hundred soldiers for forty-seven days. The town council apportioned the soldiers among forty different households: each soldier received 5 sous a day for living expenses, for a total of 1,175 livres for the soldiers. The two lieutenants cost 180 livres over the same period. Yet total costs far exceeded these sums: the parishes in the senechalsy of Guérande paid 2,649 livres, 13 sous, 3 deniers in the first month alone.[120]

What happened to the rest of the money? We get some idea from the records at Saint-Brieuc and Vannes. At Vannes, in 1637, the city spent 14,000 livres on the regiment of the duke de la Meilleraye. Vannes borrowed 6,000 livres from Catherine Rogerec and Claude Gosserent to pay its up-front expenses (the *rente* for the loan cost 90 livres and the contract itself cost another 18 livres to draw

[116] ADLA, B 74, fol. 74.   [117] ADLA, G 441.
[118] AM de Nantes, CC 168, accounts of 1641–3.   [119] ADIV, C 2764.   [120] ADIV, C 3672.

up). Vannes spent 2,882 livres on delegations to various authorities, trying to get the troops to move on. The local taxpayers (of the entire bishopric of Vannes, save Redon, given a special exemption by its governor, Richelieu) proved somewhat recalcitrant, and the city had to spend 217 livres on sergeants to force payment. The troops themselves (eight companies of foot) cost 10,640 livres (16 April to 15 July). Where did they go when they left Vannes? Can we multiply this figure by six to get the annual cost to the province? And what of the regiment of Brissac, which cost the town of Ploërmel 12,690 livres in 1637? How much did it cost the province on an annual basis?[121]

At Saint-Brieuc, four companies under the marquis de "Couesquon" (Coëtquen) and the duke of Brissac (the younger) stopped for eight days in the spring of 1628. The town levied 1,288 livres to meet this expense (the records do not stipulate how they raised money, yet they undoubtedly levied it as a surtax on the *fouage* payers of the surrounding parishes), but it was far too little. The town had to buy boards for the soldiers to sleep on, as well as paying a carpenter for making the beds (and paying for his other raw materials – nails, etc.). The account lists 1,200 livres as the expenses of the soldiers, plus another 150 livres given to a company for the costs incurred during a three-day march to Paimpol. The minor costs associated with boarding soldiers included 16 livres for a royal sergeant to keep order, and 8 livres for his assistant. The costs of drawing up rolls, of delivering such rolls to the appropriate authorities, of wood and candles necessary for clerks and soldiers alike, ran to almost 150 livres. Then there were the bribes; 40 livres for wine to give to Coëtquen, 50 livres to the quartermaster to preserve good order among the troops while in Saint-Brieuc and Paimpol, 20 *pistollets d'or* and hotel costs for the emissary of the duke of Brissac – 168 livres. There were two deputations to Brissac and Coëtquen, first trying to talk them out of coming to Saint-Brieuc (193.5 livres) and then complaining of the disobedience of the quartering regulations by some captains (155 livres). Finally, the town borrowed 3,000 livres to raise the immediate cash necessary for the expenses: the account lists interest on this 3,000 livres as an expense, but leaves the amount blank. The total expenses listed came to 2,527 livres, of which only 1,350 livres went for the daily upkeep of the troops.[122]

The records of the Estates also tell us something about the troops of Brissac and Coëtquen in 1628. It seems Brissac levied 35,000 livres on his own authority to pay two companies of troops at Hennebont for two months.[123] The troops in the bishopric of Saint-Brieuc are described by the Estates as being under the command of Coëtquen and marshal Thémines (then governor of Brittany). The Estates received complaints that these troops were ruining both "town and country" in the bishopric of Saint-Brieuc. The reluctance of the

---

[121] ADLA, B 77, fols. 191–5v (Vannes), fols. 190–190v (Ploërmel).
[122] ADIV, C 3672.   [123] ADIV, C 2765, Estates of 1628.

inhabitants of Saint-Brieuc to receive these troops may have been related to an incident involving one of the companies, that of the *sieur* of Châteaudary. According to the official complaint to the Estates:

The *sieur* of Châteaudary, captain of a company of men of war in the regiment of Coëtquen, having run about with the company and ruined almost all of the bishopric of Saint-Brieuc, the people, in despair because of the evils they received daily from the said troops, finally armed themselves and defeated the said company. In the combat, the *sieur* of Châteaudary was wounded, from which he died several days later; two or three of his soldiers also died. The widow of Châteaudary filed a complaint with the Parlement and obtained a decree on more than 100 individuals, so that nine or ten parishes in the environs of Saint-Brieuc and Lanvollon are entirely deserted and abandoned due to the fear of the above-mentioned decrees.[124]

The Estates ordered their *procureur syndic* to obtain a general absolution for the peasants and asked the king to give notice to captains and soldiers "to govern themselves and live modestly and to observe the rulings and ordinances of war, under the threat of the punishment carried by such rulings." The Estates also had some words for the peasants: "and it is forbidden to the populace henceforth to take up arms and to uprise without the order [*commandement*] of the King under the punishments [stipulated in various ordinances]. . ."[125]

Here we have an interesting string of events. The king sends troops into Brittany (probably for fear of an English intervention); the troops set about raising their own pay and requisitioning necessary supplies; the peasants respond by defeating a company of troops in open battle, and killing their commander; the Estates take the side of the peasants against the royal army, although making sure to note that they do so only as an exception and warning the peasantry not to act in this manner again. The troops of 1628 have left records of their activities in many parts of the province – Saint-Brieuc, Josselin, Hennebont, Guérande – and everywhere there is the same sense of violent confrontation between the people and the army. The local nobility often served in these regiments, yet the Estates seem better disposed toward the resistance than towards the troops. The attitude of the towns was purely hostile. It is unclear how widespread the presence of troops in Brittany was in the early seventeenth century. The regular garrisons were there (roughly 300 men at the beginning of the century, perhaps 400 after 1635) but the only periods of other heavy troop activity for which we have accounts or other direct records, were 1614–17, 1627–8, and 1635–7. By way of contrast, the town of Vitré, seeking permission to renew its duties in 1642, noted debts of 90,000 livres and specified the passage of troops as one of the main reasons for the debt.[126] In 1643, seeking renewal of its duties, Dol singled out the expenses of the garrison introduced into the town in 1638; Dinan complained of the costs of troops in

---

[124] *Ibid.*   [125] *Ibid.*   [126] ADLA, B 78, fols. 32–3.

Table 14: *Breton* feux *sale in 1577*

Bishopric	Number of parishes	Number of *feux*	*Feux* sold	*Feux* unsold	Percentage unsold
Rennes	122	3,131	139	162	53.8
Fougères-Vitré	88	1,358	83	49	37.1
Nantes	200	6,275	111	296	72.7
Vannes	163	4,787	271	56	17.1
Cornouaille	181	4,588	0	363	100.0
Léon	96	2,168	0	181	100.0
Tréguier	129	3,953	0	251	100.0
Saint-Brieuc	124	3,796	233	14	5.7
Saint-Malo	152	4,556	297	30	9.2
Dol	67	910	59	45	43.3
Totals	1,322	35,522	1,193	1,447	54.8

Notes:
Fougères-Vitré was part of the bishopric of Rennes but had its own receiving district or *tablier*.

In theory, the sale involved two *feux* per parish, but, as the figures demonstrate, there could be some local confusion as to the actual number of parishes (most notable in Rennes and Fougères-Vitré: the total number of parishes in the two areas, 210, would mean combined sales of 420 *feux*, as opposed to the actual 433, so that the error is clearly in determining which receiving district had jurisdiction over certain parishes). *Sources*: AD Loire-Atlantique, B 3009; B 2987; B 713; B 3010.

1645; Morlaix, Vannes, and other towns protested the presence of Irish troops in the late 1640s.[127] The king did not forget the *fouage* payers of Brittany, in the sense that the government obtained only the regular *fouages* and the occasional levies by troops. The beginning of the Thirty Years War marked the start of a series of financial expedients aimed at the peasantry. In 1638, the king issued an edict mandating that the sales of exemptions ordered in 1577, but only partially carried out, be executed in full (table 14)[128]. The sale of 1577 was supposed to enfranchise two *feux* in every parish, but only 1,193 *feux* bought an enfranchisment. In 1638,

---

[127] The city references again come from the papers of the Chamber of Accounts, ADLA, B 70–82, Dol, for example, in B 79, fol. 207, request of 1649 citing costs for troops and munitions. The largest single military expense of the late 1640s was the upkeep of prisoners of war. Nantes alone spent more than 50,000 livres on them between 1642 and 1647, and virtually every major Breton town complained about their cost in the 1640s. Even small parishes had to pay such expenses. At Ercé, in 1559, the parish spent money on hay, straw, oats, and shipment for the garrison at Saint-Aubin de Cormier (ADIV, G Ercé).

[128] ADLA, B 2994, sale of 1638 in Léon. B 3011 has the *fouage* in Léon, by parish (see also ch. 6).

Table 15: *Regular direct taxes and the cost of*
affranchissements *in Léon, 1652, 1638, selected
parishes (in livres)*

Parish	Direct tax, 1652	Affranchissement, 1638
Mihisac	420	940
Plouarzel	505	1,232
Saint-Renan	99	236
Botgartz	36	118
Treffinenez	36	118
Quilbignon	283	704
Saint-Gouesnou	148	352
Lanillis	409	704
Plouguerneau	904	2,112
Plouguier	590	1,526
Plouzane	808	1,936
Ploudaniel	793	1,936
Ploudalmezeau	664	1,644
Plouyen	829	1,936
Minihi Paul	37	118

Source: AD Loire-Atlantique, B 3011.

Louis XIII ordered that these 1,193 *feux* purchase a full exemption from all direct taxes, and further demanded that the unsold exemptions of 1577 (1,450 *feux*) be combined with a total exemption and sold. The additional *feux* were mostly in the far west, as no exemptions had been sold in Léon, Tréguier, and Cornouaille in 1577. The sales, fully carried out, produced about 772,000 livres in a single year.

In 1640, the king repeated this procedure, selling another 1,640 *feux* exemptions (580,000 livres). The king, recognizing that such sales had not been popular in the past, ordered each parish to pay its assessment within six weeks of being notified of the amount:

in the absence of which, the said time passed, the treasurers and vestrymen and six of the principal inhabitants of the said parishes will be constrained as a group in the accustomed ways.[129]

These sales placed an enormous burden on some parishes, particularly those of the west. The typical parish in the bishopric of Léon paid two to three times its annual assessment for the exemptions. As we can see in table 15, the smaller parishes were usually the hardest hit. The small parishes, such as Minihi Paul or

[129] ADLA, B 77, fols. 15v–16 (1638) and 152–3v (1640).

Elestrec, paid triple their annual assessments; the larger parishes, such as Ploudaniel or Plouguerneau, typically paid 2.5 times their normal assessment, an amount that could run to over 2,000 livres. In all cases, the parishes also had to pay their regular tax assessments.[130]

As the terms of the king's letters indicate, the parishes did not have much time to come up with the money. Few records survive as to how they did so, but the parish of Sizun is likely typical of others. We find that five leading parishioners came to Morlaix to pay the money in 1638 (and received a *quittance* for having paid for 4.5 *feux*, thus 1,584 livres); there is no record of how they obtained this money. In 1641, however, we find the parishioners of Sizun borrowed the money from *écuyer* Hervé Coran, sieur de Launay, syndic of Landerneau. While the cost of exempting 2.35 *feux* was supposed to be 827.2 livres, "costs" added another 17.6 livres and, in fact, the parish had to borrow 903.25 livres from Coran. This discrepancy, roughly 9 percent, includes local costs (above and beyond the 10 percent surcharge for "costs" already factored into the 827.2 livres) and interest on the loan; the peasants ended up paying 25 percent more than the king was supposed to receive (720 livres). This discrepancy between what the king got and what it cost the peasants was a constant feature of all French taxation of the period.[131]

In 1642, the king levied *amortissements* on all of the parish churches of Brittany. The parish records for la Roche-Maurice and nearby Ploudiry imply that the king raised about 300,000 livres by this expedient.[132] Combining the three operations of 1638–42, the king obtained 1.65 million livres from rural Breton taxpayers, in addition to their regular contributions of some 550,000 livres a year. These figures exclude any military surtaxes that may have been raised on the countryside.

In 1643, the Estates were unable to meet their obligations to the king by means of wine sales taxes, so they added a *fouage extraordinaire* of 800,000 livres to be levied over two years (1644–5). This money was supposed to be a loan; there was never any question of repayment, despite the officious exactitude of the Chamber of Accounts in drawing up a repayment schedule, complete with allowances for interest.[133] The Estates returned to this expedient in 1647 and twice more in the 1650s. The *fouage extraordinaire* became part of the permanent direct tax burden, although always assessed separately and accounted for by the Estates, in 1661.[134] The general movement of regular direct taxation in Brittany was therefore from about 500,000 livres per year in

---

[130] ADLA, B 3011.   [131] ADF, 267 G 8.   [132] ADF, 232 G 4.

[133] ADLA, B 78, fols. 166v–173, contract of the Estates for 1644–5; B 79, fols. 11–12, letters for the levy of 1644 (*lettres de dernière jussion*), in which the king noted that he wished this matter to be taken care of, "et ne nous donner occasion de vous en faire expedier aultre plus exprès mandement."

[134] For the period after 1661, A. Rebillon, *Les Etats de Bretagne, de 1661 à 1789* (Paris, 1930), and below, ch. 5.

the early 1600s to about one million livres by the middle of the century. While the figures for proposed collections in France as a whole in the late 1630s and 1640s imply that direct taxation far more than doubled in the country as a whole, in fact, those figures are little more than wishful thinking. The actual collections likely doubled between 1620 and 1634, fluctuating wildly thereafter (both in time and in space). In 1661, for France as a whole, the direct tax burden was about twice what it had been in the 1610s, thus the evolution in Brittany was quite typical.[135]

The indirect taxes, save for those levied by the Estates, remained the same throughout the seventeenth century. The king alienated the receipts of these taxes on several occasions (the *impôts* and some of the *ports et havres* in 1600–1, the *impôts* again in 1641) but he did not change the taxes. Their receipts climbed steadily from 1600 until 1640 or so, when they began to waver; the king no longer had to worry about such fluctuations, because the 1641 alienation of the *impôts* produced 3.6 million livres.[136] Tables 4 and 16 show the evolution of receipts from the three major indirect taxes. The *prévôté de Nantes* became part of the *Cinq Grosses Fermes* in 1624, prompting a long, ultimately unsuccessful effort by the Estates to have it become independent again. After 1649, the *prévôté* was theoretically independent of the *Cinq Grosses Fermes*, but, in fact, one of the *cautions* of the lease, Antoine Peillier, was a member of the *Cinq Grosses Fermes* syndicate and the others were all from Paris.[137]

The king also tried to include the *ports et havres* within the lease of the *Aides Générales* but the Estates successfully blocked this effort. The *ports* remained a purely Breton affair: in the 1660s and 1670s, for example, all of the farmers were from Vannes, Auray, and Hennebont (the *ports* were leased at Vannes).[138] The *ports* also kept the practice of the three-year lease, as opposed to the nine-year lease common among the larger tax farms (such as the *Cinq Grosses Fermes*).

The different outcomes of the Estates' battle to maintain the independence of Breton indirect tax farms shows us the political balance within the province. The tax levied only in the bishopric of Nantes was lost to outside forces, and thus to the king; it was no longer carried on the accounts of the Breton receiver general after 1623. The tax levied in all of Brittany save the bishopric of Nantes, remained in Breton hands. Was it a coincidence that the farmers of the *prévôté* were Nantais, or even Parisian, while those of the *ports* were from Vannes or elsewhere in western Brittany? Was it a coincidence that while the treasurers of France in Brittany (of whom there remained only two throughout the Ancien Régime) received a 3,000 livres fee at each renewal of the *ports*, they received nothing for the lease of the *prévôté*? The political powers of the province had

---

[135] J. Collins, *The Fiscal Limits of Absolutism: Direct Taxation in Early Seventeenth-Century France* (Berkeley, 1988), ch. 3.   [136] ADLA, B 2973.   [137] ADLA, B 82, fols. 146–51.
[138] ADLA, B 82, fols. 182–5, lease of 1664–6, to syndicate from Ploërmel and Vannes; ADLA, B 83, fol. 191, lease of 1671 to syndicate including receiver of the *fouages* of Vannes.

Table 16: *Lease price of the* impôts et billots, *1600–1640*

	Lease price in livres	Remarks
1600	159,562	
1601	161,662	
1602	68,175	Vannes, Tréguier, Cornouaille and Saint-Brieuc only
1603	76,250	As above
1604	86,000	As above
		The remaining five bishoprics brought in 108,000 livres in 1612, after their repurchase.
1618	250,000	
1621	280,000	
1623	284,000	
1624	350,000	
1625	350,000	
1627	337,000	Rebate of 109,250 livres over three years
1630	351,000	
1636	354,000	
1640	390,000 estimated	The *impôts* were alienated in 1640 for 3.9 million livres, which would be 390,000 at the then going rate of 10 percent

Sources: ADLA, B 64–80, records of the Chamber of Accounts.

strong vested interests in the *ports* (one of whose chief sources of income was a tax on grain exports), while they had little interest in the *prévôté* (whose income came primarily from taxes on wine (about 65 percent) and salt (about 22 percent) in 1631).[139] Even when it came to the regular taxes, Nantes was the odd man out. Peasants marketed a great deal of this Nantais wine, so that nobles were much less concerned with reduced wine sales than they were with reduced grain sales.

The judicial and financial systems changed little in the seventeenth century. There was a sharp increase in recourse to royal justice after 1600, so that the competence and activity of the courts grew quite rapidly. Their personnel, in contrast, remained virtually constant.[140] The two sovereign courts became more active in their resistance to royal initiatives – new taxes, new offices – but their increased action in such matters was largely a reflection of increased royal

[139] ADLA, B 2976. Discussed in greater detail in J. Collins, "The Role of Atlantic France in the Baltic Trade: Dutch Traders and Polish Grain at Nantes, 1625–1675," *Journal of European Economic History* (1984): 239–89, Table III.
[140] There were small additions to the Chamber and the Parlement in the early 1630s. On the former, Saulnier, *Le Parlement.*

pressure. The Estates, Parlement, and Chamber also carried out a remarkable degree of cooperation, save during the Fronde, when the Parlement backed the duke of Rohan's efforts to discredit the Estates. There were, to be sure, jurisdictional disputes, but the two courts and the Estates far more often cooperated – on evocations, on abolition of new taxes and offices, on maintaining what they perceived to be the liberties and privileges of the provinces.[141]

The financial system followed a somewhat different evolution. As in the case of the judicial personnel, there was little increase in the overall number of officers.[142] The king's regular income from Brittany was quite stable in the 1620s and 1630s. Direct taxes were stable at about 500–550,000 livres per year, although the great repurchase of alienations carried out by the Estates (1605–18) increased the king's share of the proceeds by about 45,000 livres. The indirect taxes, more than half alienated in 1601, came back into royal hands during the repurchase; the receipts also climbed sharply from 1601–10 because of the economic recovery. In the 1620s and 1630s, the three great indirect tax farms produced about 450–500,000 livres per year. The demesne, also repurchased between 1605 and 1618, added perhaps 70,000 livres in net revenue, as well as paying for almost all of the lower echelon judiciary. Unlike the judicial system, however, the financial system changed significantly in the 1640s, with the creation of the *fouage extraordinaire*, which increased direct taxes by about 80 percent.

The most important fiscal issue was usually the presence or absence of troops in the province. A regiment cost between 1,500 and 2,000 livres a week, solely for upkeep. How many troops did the province have to support at any given time? Brittany had far fewer troops passing through or permanently stationed than did, say, the eastern provinces, but there were troops in the province on a regular basis. The tax burden on the countryside, therefore, was higher than it would appear from the regular levels of taxation. The rate of extraordinary taxation seems to have jumped enormously in 1614–17, due to local political instability, and again in 1627–8, due to the war against La Rochelle. After the full entry into the Thirty Years War, Brittany and the other *pays d'Etats* proved a good source of reliable income. We have seen that the king stationed troops in much of the province in 1637, and that he raised very substantial extraordinary sums in 1638, 1640–1, 1642, 1644–5, and 1649–50. Nonetheless, the Breton countryside supported a much lower level of taxation in the seventeenth century than it did in the late sixteenth century. The only period of extremely heavy

---

[141] The main issue at variance was the question of whether the Parlement should register financial edicts. The Chamber argued that it had sole right to do so; the Parlement ignored this protest, and continued to consider all financial edicts. It would seem that the king sided with the Parlement, because they certainly received the edicts in question.

[142] In 1626, the king added several new offices to the *prévôté de Nantes*: ADLA, B 73, reception of the various officers by the Chamber.

taxation was the League War, and the burden of those years was unevenly distributed within the province (the west bearing the heaviest share).

Breton direct taxation in the period running from 1500 to 1675 (and, in fact, into the eighteenth century) bears witness to the curious double political evolution of the province. On the one hand, the long arm of the king reached into ever remoter areas of the province. The difference between the *feux* sales of 1638–40 and the sale of 1577 is particularly striking in this regard. In 1577, the determined opposition of certain segments of the population, notably the inhabitants of Breton-speaking Brittany, derailed the sale of the exemptions: the king sold no exemptions in Léon, Cornouaille, or Treguier in 1577. In 1638 and again in 1640, the use of collective distraint ("contraint solidaire") proved universally effective: in 1638 the king sold all of the *feux* left unsold in 1577 and then sold a new lot in 1640. There could hardly be a clearer illustration of the strides toward stronger central control made by the government in the interim.

On the other hand, the direct tax burden declined (in real terms) from the late sixteenth to the seventeenth century. The landlords of the province were able effectively to protect their tenants, and, thereby, their own rental income. This golden age lasted until 1637, when the demands of war forced the king to step up his pressure on all French taxpayers. The taxpayers of the *pays d'élection* were already assessed for more than they could pay, and the higher assessments of the late 1630s and 1640s merely raised levels of non-payment: they did little to raise income (in fact, they may have reduced it). In the *pays d'Etats*, it was a different matter.

The king saw the *pays d'Etats* as an untapped (or poorly tapped) financial resource. After 1628, he dramatically raised taxes in all of them. In Dauphiné and Provence, this meant, above all, *étapes*; in Brittany, it meant quadrupling the wine duty of the Estates between 1620 and 1640. These demands strained the existing revenue systems and forced local elites into taxing those whom they had sought to protect. In Brittany, it meant that the wine duty of the Estates had gone as high as it could go (by 1641) and that new resources for the Estates would require a permanent addition to direct taxation. The *fouage extraordinaire* began in 1644, was levied in eight years between 1644 and 1660, and became permanent in 1661. It represented an 80 percent increase in direct taxation.

This increase, while enormous in terms of percentage, still left Breton tax levels absurdly low in comparison to French ones. As we shall see, almost all Breton peasants paid between 0.5 and 8 livres a year in direct taxes prior to 1635, so that, aside from the special one-time assessments of 1638, 1640, and 1642, the annual tax burden remained between 1 and 16 livres. The median assessment went from under 2 livres a year to about 3.5 livres; by way of comparison, the median contribution in the parishes of the *pays d'élection* ranged from about 3.5 livres to over 10 livres a year, to say nothing here of the enormous median assessments of the 1640s, often over 20 livres a year, but usually not paid. Breton peasants still got special treatment, even when their tax burden nearly doubled in 1644. In addition to preserving the special treatment of their tenants, the Breton elites managed to get the lion's share of the increased tax revenues for most of the seventeenth century. The only exception to this pattern, as we shall see in chapter 5, was the 1640s.

In order to understand how it was possible to maintain this protected position, in which the manner of taxation was largely left to the local elite – allowing it to protect effectively its interests as landlords and as marketers of grain – we must turn to the Estates. The local elite also managed to obtain a large share of the king's income in the province, thus strengthening its own position, while simultaneously increasing the power of the king. By looking at the Estates, we can see how they acted to continue an apportionment so favorable to their members, and how they served as a conduit for funneling so much money to the local elite. "Absolutism" is often assessed in terms of how much more the king was able to obtain from the kingdom; in fact, we must first understand from whom he got these greater resources and to whom he disbursed them before we can distinguish the myth of absolutism from its reality.

4

The Estates of Brittany and the Crown, 1532–1626

THE CROWN AND THE *PAYS D'ETATS*

Breton elites, like those in other French provinces, relied upon a dense network of institutions to protect their power. These institutions could be royal, like the courts, local, such as a mayor, or a combination of the two, the Estates. Royal institutions, such as the Parlement, were also local because of the predominance of the local ruling elite in the court; local offices, such as mayor, were royal to the extent that the king granted permission for the office to exist (as at Nantes, in 1565) and ratified the local choice to fill the office. Under Henry IV, the king normalized his practice of choosing one from among the top three vote getters as mayor, rather than simply ratifying the choice of the electoral winner.[1]

The dialectic royal–local existed in all early modern French regional institutions but it is most clearly demonstrated in representative bodies, provincial and local Estates. The local elites sought direct redress of grievances at their Estates; the king sought money and political cooperation. The Estates that survived the period 1550–1650 were those that effectively carried out their dual function of redress of local grievances and provisioning of the royal treasury. Although one of the famous aphorisms of this period was, "no money, no Swiss," we might just as accurately say "no money, no Estates." Before we consider the Breton case, we can briefly summarize events in the other *pays d'Etats* to show the extent to which the Breton example conformed to the general pattern, rather than being the exception it has so often been held to be.

Late sixteenth-century France had seven major *pays d'Etats*: Burgundy, Dauphiné, Guyenne, Languedoc, Normandy, Provence, and Brittany. By 1650, Dauphiné, Guyenne, and Normandy had lost their Estates, while those of Provence had lapsed into an Assembly of the *Communes*. Why did these Estates die out, when those of Brittany, Burgundy, and Languedoc continued to flourish? How does the peculiar solution of Provence fit into the general pattern?

The *pays d'Etats* shared a certain institutional framework. Each had a Parlement and all, save Guyenne, had a Chamber of Accounts. Five of the provinces also had a *Cour des Aides*, although the form varied from one to the

---

[1] A. Finlay-Crosswhite, "Henri IV et les villes," in *Quatrième Centenaire d'Henri IV. Colloque de Pau*, ed. P. Tucoo-Chala (Pau, 1990). On the specific case of Nantes, Abbé Travers, *Histoire civile, politique et réligieuse de la ville et du comté de Nantes*, 3 vols (Nantes, 1837–41), III.

next.[2] Their primary dissimilarities came in financial matters. Normandy and Guyenne had *élections*; the other five did not. The existence of these *élections* created a mechanism by which the Crown could raise money in these two provinces without the real intervention of local Estates. In Normandy, the king gradually undermined the power of the Estates between 1568 and 1586. He removed the right of the Estates to take part in the general distribution of the tax burden among the *élections* and then expanded the network of *élections*.[3] By 1600, Henry IV's royal commissioners told the Estates that, pending the king's consideration of the Estates' remonstrances (which included a demand for lower taxes), that the original demanded sum would be levied provisionally.[4] The demise of the Norman Estates followed soon afterward.

In Guyenne, the local Estates were much more important than the episodic Estates of Guyenne. The individual *pays* of the southwest – Quercy, Rouergue, Périgord, and the others – each had local Estates, who held the real power of voting on taxation. Here, too, the *élections*, already present in the Bordelais, were the mechanism by which the king broke the power of the local Estates. The first assault took place under Henry IV, who introduced *élections* into the entire region; after the usual rescinding of the creation, and re-creation and second rescinding, Louis XIII permanently added the *élections* in 1621. The locals, particularly in Quercy, did not take kindly to the *élections* or their personnel. A large popular rebellion broke out (one of whose first actions was to sack and pillage the houses and offices of the *élus*), one overcome only in the late 1620s.[5]

In Dauphiné, the second and third Estates divided so violently over tax policy that they destroyed the Estates.[6] The king eventually intervened on behalf of the Third Estates' interpretation of tax rules (the *taille* was to be real rather than personal) but, in the process, he abolished the Estates and introduced *élections*. The weakness of the Estates of Dauphiné is clear from their failure to eliminate *élections*, when the other provinces in which the king created them between 1628 and 1630 – Provence, Burgundy, and Languedoc – all succeeded in having them abolished. Yet other local institutions, such as the *assemblée du pays*, the local (bailiwick) Estates, the assemblies of the nobility, and even assemblies from several bailiwicks, survived. Daniel Hickey indicates that the Crown

---

[2] R. Mousnier, *Les institutions de la France sous la monarchie absolue, 1598–1789* (Paris, 1974, 1978), 2 vols., on the various institutions. For the sixteenth century, R. Doucet, *Les institutions de la France au XVIe siècle* (Paris, 1948), 2 vols.

[3] J. Collins, *Fiscal Limits of Absolutism: Direct Taxation in Early Seventeenth-Century France* (Berkeley, 1988), 39–41.

[4] H. Prentout, *Histoire des Etats de Normandie* (Rouen, 1925), 3 vols., II, 154.

[5] J. R. Major, "Henry IV and Guyenne: A Study Concerning the Origins of Royal Absolutism," *French Historical Studies* 4 (1966): 363–84; J. R. Major, *Representative Government in Early-Modern France* (New Haven, 1980), 266–305; and Y.-M. Bercé, *Histoire des Croquants* (Paris, 1974); AD Gironde, C 4832, for details on sacking of houses and offices of the *élus*.

[6] D. Hickey, *The Coming of French Absolutism: The Struggle for Tax Reform in the Province of Dauphiné, 1540–1640* (Toronto, 1986).

attacked these institutions cautiously in the 1630s, often restored them in the 1640s and 1650s, and then attacked them with renewed vigor in the 1660s.[7]

In Provence, the Estates acted vigorously until 1633; in that year, they refused to grant any money. The king suspended the Estates until 1639. When the 1639 meeting again refused a grant, the king called an Assembly of the *Communes*, which voted a grant of 1.3 million livres.[8] After 1639, even that Assembly became sporadic, and the Estates ceased to exist. The king had little need for grants of money in Provence because the main expense, the sutlering of the troops, was paid for by local requisitions. The taxes reimbursed those who had had goods requisitioned. The king had no need to ask for grants of such money; he had only to go directly to the taxing authorities who raised the money. In Provence, that meant the *communes* themselves, not the Estates.[9]

In Languedoc and Burgundy, the Estates consistently voted substantial sums of money to the king. The Estates of Languedoc voted large grants of direct taxation, a regular sales tax package, and occasional salt taxes.[10] The Estates of Burgundy used salt taxes to raise most of their money in the sixteenth century (although troops in the field raised far more in direct levies) but had to switch to direct taxes when Henry IV shifted the *gabelles* of Burgundy into the *grandes gabelles* farm.[11] Both Estates maintained an excellent credit rating and each borrowed extensively to meet its obligations to the Crown. In the early 1630s, for example, the Estates of Burgundy, Languedoc, and Provence all bought out the *élections* for a combined total of more than 7 million livres.[12]

The king willingly listened to the complaints of such bodies because he had a

---

[7] *Ibid.*, 179–82.

[8] R. Busquet, *Histoire des institutions de la Provence de 1482 à 1790* (Marseille, 1920), 201–6; R. Pillorget, *Les mouvements insurrectionnels en Provence entre 1595 et 1715* (Paris, 1975), 321–48.

[9] In addition to Busquet and Pillorget (esp. 113–17), see Abbé de Coriolis, *Dissertation sur les Etats de Provence* (Aix, 1867), an apology written in 1788 by a member of one of the leading local families. On the period from 1629–59, see S. Kettering, *Judicial Politics and Urban Revolt in Seventeenth-Century France* (Princeton, 1978).

[10] On Languedoc, there are three sources for the Estates of the late sixteenth and seventeenth centuries: Doms C. Devic and J. Vaissette, *Histoire générale de Languedoc* (Toulouse, 1876–89), 14 vols., notably vols. xii–xiv; P. Dognon, *Les institutions politiques et administratives du pays de Languedoc du XIIIe siècle aux guerres de religion* (Toulouse, 1986); and W. Beik, *Absolutism and Society in Seventeenth-Century France* (Cambridge, 1985).

[11] G. Weill, "Les Etats de Bourgogne sous Henri III," *Mémoires de la Société Bourguignonne de Géographie et d'Histoire* (1893): 121–48; J.-L. Gay, "Fiscalité royale et Etats Généraux de Bourgogne," *Travaux et Recherche de la Faculté de Droit ... de Paris*, 8 (1961): 179–210; H. Drouot, *Mayenne et la Bourgogne* (Paris, 1937), 97–109, and H. Drouot, *Notes sur la Bourgogne et son esprit public au début du règne de Henri III, 1574–89* (Dijon, 1937), 123–35.

[12] Provence paid 2 million livres, Burgundy paid 1.6 million livres, and Languedoc at least 4.2 million livres. The figure for Languedoc is based on BN, 500 Colbert 289, fols. 53–63. Beik (130) gives a figure of 2.3 million livres. The Parisian documents list 3,885,000 livres that had to be paid to the *traitant* who was selling the offices, plus damages of 200,000 livres (to the king), plus 200,000 livres for assorted other minor offices, plus interest (the 3,885,000 livres was to be levied over four years). In addition, the king redefined the local tax levies as 2.25 million livres per year.

vested interest in their continuation. Corporations such as the Estates of Languedoc that could borrow money to meet royal obligations were extremely useful to the Crown; the king had no reason to abolish such groups. Indeed, he had a powerful practical motive for keeping them in place: their superior credit ratings allowed them to borrow money at a much lower rate of interest than the king himself. In Languedoc or Burgundy, as in Brittany (see below), the Estates often advanced the tax money to the king by borrowing against prospective receipts, typically at 10 percent interest. The king invariably had to pay large up-front rebates (generally one-sixth) to tax farmers and usually had to pay far greater amounts to anticipate tax revenues.[13] Why change the system in the *pays d'Etats* when that system was so advantageous to the royal treasury? In the 1640s, the *pays d'Etats*, in direct contrast to the *pays d'élection*, paid their taxes.

The Crown's evident interest in groups who could provide it with money illustrates one reason for the survival of some Estates – those who voted large sums of money and who could also borrow it – but the effective Estates also met the needs of local elites in a way that the doomed Estates did not. What was the interest of local elites in an institution that provided them with no tangible benefit? If they could safeguard their position by means of other institutions, did they lose interest in Estates? One problem with the image of sixteenth-century Estates as tremendously vibrant, effective institutions is that we need to know more about their size before coming to such conclusions.[14] We also need to consider *who* went to the Estates: did the leading nobles of the region attend? In Brittany, the pre-1576 Estates were tiny gatherings, usually including a small (fifteen or so) group of high nobles. Local interest rose sharply in the late 1570s and 1580s, and even more rapidly in the seventeenth century. When the Estates began to vote large amounts of money to the king, and to select the *forms* of taxation that would raise this money, they became powerful in a way they had not been in the days of the simple approval of the customary *fouage* and wine taxes.

The power to choose the form of taxation gave the Estates leverage over the king *and* over the local elites. The Estates of Normandy, for example, essentially argued over the size of the royal *taille* in Normandy. As the *taille* in Normandy was a relatively fixed percentage of the total *taille* levied in France as a whole, they did not have much to argue about. The king had little reason to satisfy the remonstrances of such a body; the local elites had little use for a body whose remonstrances had so little demonstrable effect. What mattered in Normandy was that the viscounty assemblies should continue to have input into local tax

---

[13] F. Bayard, *Le monde des financiers au XVIIe siècle* (Paris, 1988) and R. Bonney, *The King's Debts* (Oxford, 1981).

[14] Major, *Representative Government*, offers an exhaustive look at the various provincial and general Estates, including some figures on numbers of deputies (Languedoc, 61–2; Dauphiné, 74; Burgundy, 81; Provence, 89–90; Normandy, 142). The methods or composition varied from place to place, but it is worth noting that only in Brittany and Burgundy did the numbers of nobles at the assemblies jump sharply around 1600.

assessments, even in years in which the Estates of Normandy did *not* meet. In fact, at the very moment at which the Estates of Normandy ceased to exist, the king reaffirmed the role of the viscounty assemblies in local tax assessments.[15]

The question of the survival of Estates is a complex one because the practical exigencies of governing a given area necessitated an institutional framework of some kind. In a province with a large royal bureaucracy, both legal and financial, there was much less need for Estates and local assemblies. Such was the case in the *pays d'élection*. In the *pays d'Etats*, there was no financial bureaucracy to speak of. The dual regions, such as Normandy, moved in the direction of the *pays d'élection*; the areas that were able to keep out the *élections* – Burgundy, Brittany, and Languedoc – needed to have Estates in order to be governable. The Provençal case, seemingly so exceptional, in fact fits the general model: the real local ruling institutions in Provence were those of the *communes*. They kept their remarkable powers (including the right to levy local taxes without royal permission) down to the Revolution.[16]

These general concerns lead us to the specific case of the Estates of Brittany. There we can see the king's demands on the province; there we can see the resistance of the elites. The Breton situation was quite normative in this respect; the period 1575–1650 was a critical one throughout the *pays d'Etats*. The successful Estates were those that provided money to the king, safeguarded the interests of the local ruling elite, and enabled the two forces to compromise effectively to maintain order in the province. In the entire kingdom, only the Estates of Languedoc were as successful as those of Brittany. We turn now to the Breton success story, to learn what it can teach us about the nature of the French state and society in early modern times.

THE KING AND THE ESTATES BEFORE THE LEAGUE WAR

The relationship began, in a certain sense, with the great treaty of 1532. The province had passed into French control with the marriage of the duchess Anne to King Charles VIII but there remained lingering uncertainties about the nature of Brittany's precise relationship to France. Anne's daughter, Claude, married to Francis I, would actually pass Brittany to the king of France in a personal sense, as their sons (Francis and then Henry) inherited the duchy from her. The Breton elites wanted a place in this transference of political control and Francis I, following long-standing precedents in such matters, signed an agreement with the Estates in 1532. Bretons kept their own laws and institutions (such as the Chamber) and received royal guarantees against violations of their privileges or, as the elites would prefer to call them, their liberties. The most

---

[15] C. de Robillard de Beaurepaire, *Cahiers des Etats de Normandie, règnes Louis XIII et Louis XIV* (Rouen, 1877, 1888).

[16] Pillorget, *Mouvements insurrectionnels*, gives many examples of local taxation in Provence.

important of these guarantees protected Bretons from French courts and promised to obtain the permission of the Estates before levying taxes. The first promise proved difficult to carry out because the Breton *Grands Jours* did not meet often enough. In 1552, the Estates requested that the king establish a Breton Parlement, which he did the following year.[17]

The second promise was much simpler. The first clause of the edict of Plessix-Macé stated unequivocally:

that henceforth, as has been done before, no sum of money can be imposed if it has not previously been demanded from the Estates of this region and voted by them.[18]

Because the Estates voted the *fouage* for only one year's duration, they had to meet each year: the traditional date was 25 September. The Estates voted a *fouage* (hearth tax) and the *impôts et billots* (wine taxes). The leases of seigneurial impositions, such as the import–export duties, often took place at the Estates, although these duties did not require the consent of the assembly. In the late 1530s, Francis I sought higher direct taxes from the Estates. In 1539, he raised the *fouage* from 7.2 to 8.4 livres per *feu* and levied a surtax to pay for dredging the Vilaine river.[19] Three years later, the convocation letters specified a *fouage* of 9.6 livres per *feu*, but the commissioners, on their own authority, changed that to 8.4 livres plus 20,000 *écus* to prevent an "increase of the *fouage*." The Estates opposed the surtax but quickly relented when the commissioners revealed the king's original convocation letters.[20] This seemingly innocuous agreement had dramatic long-term consequences: the Estates and the Crown came to agree that 8.4 livres per *feu* was the customary level of direct taxation. Because the number of *feux* was also fixed by custom, Breton direct taxation ossified at this level. This development meant that the king would have to seek a new form of revenue from Brittany to supplement a *fouage* that rapidly became inadequate for his needs.[21]

Henry II attacked this problem in earnest, creating the *taillon* in 1551 (56,400 livres) and trying to add a new export–import duty in 1552. This duty was most unpopular and the Estates purchased its elimination for 132,000 livres.[22] Here again we have a major innovation: the negotiations over the *imposition foraine* established the pattern for Crown–Estates relations for the remainder of the

[17] F. Saulnier, *Le Parlement de Bretagne, 1554–1790* (Rennes, 1909), 3 vols., introduction and biographies of individual members. The *maîtres des requêtes* in the original court included René Bourgneuf and Julien Bourgneuf, who was earlier the president of the *Grands Jours*, François Bruslon and several other councilors who had belonged to the *Grands Jours*. C. de la Lande de Calan, *Documents inédits relatifs aux Etats de Bretagne de 1491 à 1589* (Nantes, 1898), 2 vols. I, 128, remonstrance 1 of 1552.
[18] M. de Mauny, *Le grand traité franco-breton* (Paris, 1971), 110.
[19] H. Sée, *Les Etats de Bretagne au XVIe siècle* (Paris, 1895). This work also appeared as a series of articles in *Annales de Bretagne* in 1894: pp. 3–38, 189–207, 365–93, and 550–69.
[20] Calan, *Documents inédits*, I, 93 (1539), 111 (1542), 117 (1543).
[21] Custom fixed the *fouage* at 7 livres 7 sous *bretons*, that is, at 8 livres 16 sous 5 deniers *tournois*, including the costs of collection (5 percent). [22] ADLA, B 53, fols. 212–25.

Ancien Régime. The king would demand more money from the province because its regular taxes were fixed in custom, and therefore produced too little revenue. In some cases, as in 1552 or 1557, the king had a specific tax package in mind; the Estates would purchase exemption from these taxes in return for revenue from other taxes, which they selected. In other cases, as in 1582 or 1616, the king would create new offices and the Estates would agree to repurchase them, again with the proceeds of taxes of their own choosing. The king would also ask the Estates to repurchase his alienated demesnes in the 1570s and again from 1605 to 1618. In the sixteenth century, the king sometimes sought money for local military costs, a pattern followed in 1598, 1614, 1616, and 1621 (as well as throughout the League War of 1589–98). The request for a lump sum, for indeterminate purpose, was not part of sixteenth-century practice; it became general only in the 1620s (at which time the phrase "don gratuit" came into use, replacing the earlier "secours extraordinaire").

The sixteenth-century meetings of the Estates often attracted few deputies: in 1569, the assembly included only ten deputies from the clergy, thirteen nobles, and representatives from eleven towns.[23] The 1570 Estates had six clergymen, twenty-eight nobles, and deputies from seventeen towns (twenty-six deputies). In the twelve meetings between 1567 and 1575 (including four extraordinary meetings with limited attendance), the number of nobles ranged from thirty-two (1567) to eleven (1574). If we exclude the meetings of 1567 and 1571 (twenty-four nobles), the other ten meetings had between eleven and eighteen nobles in attendance. Nor were the clergy a dominant force: only four to ten members of the First Estate attended any given meeting. The towns had better representation, with between ten and seventeen towns present at any given meeting (save the special meeting of 1571, when twenty-five sent deputies). The deputies became desperate in their efforts to hold off the demands of the king; they felt the lack of representation limited their effectiveness. In 1572 they demanded of the king that:

It will similarly be required that Bishops, abbots, chapters, and the Barons and other grand and notable seigneurs of the said region will henceforth come to the meeting of the said Estates ... on pain of loss of their votes at the said Estates.[24]

Two years later they complained that no one came to the Estates (in fact, this meeting had only ten deputies from the clergy, twelve nobles, and deputies from fifteen towns). The Estates requested that the king require all bishops, chapters, abbots, barons, bannerets, *écuyers* and other gentlemen, and the procurators of the towns to come to the Estates. In 1576, the Estates noted with satisfaction that the king was now sending individual letters of invitation to barons and

---

[23] ADLA, C 414, Estates of 1569 at Nantes.
[24] *Ibid.*, Estates of 1572 at Nantes. Numbers of deputies from ADLA, C 414 and 415.

requiring that those receiving a pension from the Estates actually attend the meeting.[25]

The turning point came in 1576, at the meeting to elect deputies to the Estates General. The meeting attracted 115 nobles. They dominated the Estates, forcing the other orders to send six deputies each to the Estates General (rather than four, as the Third wished). There had been a lingering dispute between the Third Estate and the two others in the early 1570s about the nature of a repurchase of the king's demesne; the Estates settled the dispute in favor of the privileged orders, although the Third received some satisfaction. The tax package remained varied; the Estates did not focus entirely on the tax on the urban rich or on the special subvention levied on walled towns for infantry as sources of revenue. The Estates enacted a compromise similar to that achieved in the 1550s. The main source of revenue would be indirect taxation (largely on wine) but the duty package would include a new tax on grain exports. There would also be new taxes on the countryside and on the rich of the cities. The town council of Nantes was not pleased with the result – their deputies noted that the Estates "had deliberated on the sum and [decided] to impose it on wine only" – and they sought to have the new taxes levied on the same basis as the surtax for the 50,000 infantrymen, that is, as a direct tax. They were unsuccessful.[26]

To be fair to the Estates, they had little choice but to levy indirect taxation. The 1560s and 1570s were a difficult period for many Breton areas, as the constant warfare along the border with Poitou led to substantial military activity and forced taxation. The Estates of 1568 complained that more than 300,000 livres had been levied in 1567 and 1568; those of 1575 claimed that troops raised 300,000 livres in 1574; the meeting of 1576 claimed the overall figure for extraordinary taxation ran to two million livres in the recent past, including 720,000 livres in 1575 and 1576 alone.[27]

Nonetheless, the fiscal policy of the Estates shifted markedly in the 1570s; it can reasonably be dated from the meeting of 1576, when the nobility first took over the Estates. In the period 1568–75, an average of 16 nobles attended each meeting; in the period 1577–82, at least 32 nobles attended every session and the four regular sessions averaged 42 nobles. The pattern intensified in the seventeenth century. In 1598, with the king present, and in 1607, 59 nobles attended; in 1608, 146 nobles showed up. For the first half of the century, attendance remained substantial, with more than 75 nobles at virtually every

---

[25] *Ibid.*, Estates of 1576 at Rennes, 740–3.   [26] *Ibid.*, 778ff. AM de Nantes, AA 72.

[27] *Ibid.*, Estates of 1567–76; for example, p. 695, Estates of 1575 at Nantes on recent levies: 40,000 livres on belfries; 100–120,000 livres for the *francs archers*, 100,000 livres on the "rich," forced sales of *rentes* on the *fouages*. There is evidence about the *francs archers* in 1572 and 1574 (ADIV, G Ercé and G Acigné); the list of *rentiers* appears in ADLA, B 12,871.

meeting. In the second half of the century, the meetings became larger still.[28]

The lists of nobles attending the meetings between 1567 and 1575 indicate that a small number of the leading seigneurs attended each meeting. In 1567, at Vannes, the leaders were Jean de Rieux, René de Tournemine, baron of la Hunandaye and of La Guerche, the marquis of Coëtquen, the marquis of la Marzelière, Julien Botherel, viscount of Apigné, and Marc de Rosmadec, baron of Pontecroix. The following year, at Nantes, Apigné and la Hunandaye were joined by the marquis de Goulaine and Jean, marquis d'Acigné. The special sessions of the Estates, quite frequent in this period (1571, 1572, 1573, 1574) were often little more than *in camera* gatherings of the elite. In 1573, the extra Estates meeting at Rennes included only fifteen nobles: Rieux, Méjusseaume (Coëtlogon family, but temporarily held by a son-in-law, François du Gué), la Moussaye, d'Acigné, la Marzelière, and a handful of others.

In 1576, all of the leading families came to the Estates, in order to select the deputies to the Estates General. Henry de Rohan, prince of Léon, led the Second Estate, assisted by the other great barons: Vitré, Châteauneuf, Coëtquen, Guémadeuc, la Marzelière, Garo (Kermanon), Apigné, Méjusseaume, la Moussaye, Pontecroix. These families held virtually every major local military office; they also extensively intermarried. The barony of Laval, broken up at the death of the last member of the family in 1547, passed in rapid succession to the Rieux, Maure, and la Trémoille families. The la Trémoille family ended up with the Laval, Vitré, and Saint-Brieuc region territories, but the holdings at the mouth of the Vilaine (La Roche Bernard, Pontchâteau), passed to the Rohan and Cambout families (the latter buying out the former a generation later). The la Marzelière male line died out in the seventeenth century; the lands passed by means of Françoise de la Marzelière to Malo de Coëtquen. The Rieux family inherited Châteauneuf, Assérac, Sourdéac, and La Guerche; in the sixteenth century, they temporarily held Châteaugiron (later passed to Acigné) and Vitré. Châteaugiron moved from the Rieux family, to that of Laval, and then to Acigné. Jean, marquis d'Acigné, last of the male line, died in 1573; his daughter, Judith d'Acigné, passed the marquisate to Charles de Cossé-Brissac, who would later become lieutenant general for the king in Upper Brittany and the dominant figure of Breton politics in the first decade of the seventeenth century. It is hard to escape the conclusion that a small coterie of great barons dominated the Estates and that the other nobles merely added weight to decisions presented by the Second to the Third Estate.

The Third Estate remained at the same level throughout the period 1567 to 1582, save for the special meeting of 1571, convened to levy 300,000 livres over three years on Breton towns (that meeting had deputies from twenty-five towns).

---

[28] ADIV, C 2647, Estates of 1607 and 1608, C 2645, Estates of 1598. This pattern also held true in Burgundy: Major, *Representative Government*, 81. The meetings of the 1620s and 1630s are difficult to estimate because of the vagueness of the records.

The average number of towns at the Estates went up from fourteen in 1567–75 to fifteen in 1577–83. In the seventeenth century, however, the number of towns represented at the Estates also rose sharply; in most years, deputies from some thirty-odd towns attended the Estates. The core of representation remained the same in the sixteenth and seventeenth centuries. In the sixteenth century, Nantes, Rennes, Vannes, Quimper, Saint-Malo, and Vitré attended all (or all but one) meeting; Dinan, Saint-Brieuc, Morlaix, Fougères, Quimperlé, and Ploërmel came to most meetings; Hennebont and Le Croisic attended more than half of the meetings. In the seventeenth century, all of these towns came to each meeting, along with deputies from fifteen or twenty other towns, the most important of which were Lannion, Guérande, and Auray. After 1613, the towns had a very important reason to attend the Estates: all town *octrois* had to be approved by the Estates when they came up for their periodic (usually six- or nine-year) renewal.

The dramatic change came long before 1613, in the troubled period 1576 to 1598. The nobles, as we have seen, entered the Estates in much greater numbers and increasingly came to dominate its sessions. In 1582 the number of nobles at the regular meeting of the Estates was twice the normal figure for 1577–81: fifty-nine nobles attended, including Rieux-Châteauneuf, Rieux-Sourdéac, the marquis de Goulaine, and duke of Retz and his son. The Estates approved a new package of extraordinary taxation, levying 37,500 livres on the rich of the towns, 72,000 livres on the *fouage* payers, new wine consumption taxes (1.25 livres on a pipe of non-Breton wine, 0.4 livres on Breton wine), and a variety of very small export–import duties. These new duties no longer included taxes on grain or on linen, the two most important products of the western part of the province. In fact, the king was already using one of his favorite pressure tactics on the Estates: he would forbid the export of grain from Brittany, agreeing to lift the prohibition only after receiving a grant.[29] The enormous increase in grain prices in the period 1560–80 made grain a tremendously profitable export commodity; the nobles, who profited most from this increase, logically sought to keep their grain competitive on non-Breton markets (such as Lisbon or Bordeaux).[30]

The nature of urban representation at the Estates also mitigated against the interests of the merchants and lower classes of the towns. The deputies were usually the *procureur syndic* – always a lawyer – and one other local notable. In the four presidial cities, it was customary to send the president of the presidial; in

[29] The king used this maneuver in 1572, ADLA, C 414, p. 411, and again in 1582, C 415, p. 410–11.

[30] J. Collins, "The Role of Atlantic France in the Baltic Trade: Dutch Traders and Polish Grain at Nantes, 1625–1675," *Journal of European Economic History* (1984): 231–80; E. Trocmé and M. Delafosse, *Le commerce rochelais de la fin du XVe siècle au début du XVIIe* (Paris, 1952). A. Leroux, *Inventaire sommaire des registres de la Jurade de Bordeaux* (Bordeaux, 1916), XI; AD Gironde, 6 B 213, register of 1640, showing the extent of Breton trade with Bordeaux.

fact, when Nantes and Rennes disputed the presidency of the Third Estate between 1614 and 1620, the final solution was to allow the presidial president of the jurisdiction in which the meeting took place to chair the Third Estate. At Nantes, there was also a dramatic shift in the composition of the municipal government after 1598. Whereas four of the mayors of the 1580s and 1590s had been merchants, no mayor who served after 1598 was a merchant. Similarly, the town council, which had been about 60 percent merchants and 40 percent royal officials, took on precisely the inverse proportions.[31] How sensitive to merchant demands was a royal judge (himself invariably the son of another judge, living, at Nantes, in the highly segregated official quarter of the city) likely to be? Even if a Nantais mayor tried his utmost to protect local mercantile interests, he would have had problems succeeding: in 1581, *maître* Jacques Rousseau, *procureur* at the Chamber, deputy to the Estates, wrote to the town council that he found "all of the towns banded against us."[32]

THE COMPROMISE OF HENRY IV

The financial situation worsened in 1588, as Henry III desperately tried to obtain money from any conceivable source (see above, chapter 3). When the civil war broke out in 1589, the administrative superstructure of the province collapsed as well. The Parlement and Chamber split in two, a rump Parlement moving to Nantes, a rump Chamber setting up in Rennes. The two sides would each fill vacant offices for the next eight years.[33] The Estates met as two separate bodies, one for the League at Nantes or at Vannes, one for the king at Rennes. They voted extremely heavy new taxation, both in supplemental *fouages* and *étapes* for troops, and in sharply higher wine sales taxes. We have seen (chapter 3) the enormous increase in direct taxes; in royalist areas, the wine sales taxes jumped from 1.25 and 0.4 livres per pipe of non-Breton and Breton wine, respectively, to 18 livres and 9 livres.[34] The Estates ceased to tax any other commodity.

When the war ended, the Estates of 1597 and 1598 had to face up to enormous financial responsibilities. In 1597, they voted the king 600,000 livres to come to Brittany; in 1598, they voted him 2.4 million livres to pay off Mercoeur and the other Leaguers and end the war. How would they raise this money? Would they go back to the compromises of the 1560s and 1570s, with extra taxation spread across a variety of groups, or to those of the 1580s, with a somewhat narrower but still fairly broad base, or to those of the 1590s, with

[31] A. Pertuis and S. de la Nicollière-Teijeiro, eds., *Le livre doré de l'hotel de ville de Nantes* (Nantes, 1873).   [32] AM de Nantes, AA 72.

[33] The registers of the rump Chamber of Rennes are in ADLA, B 65 and 66.

[34] Duties of 1583 – ADLA, C 415, pp. 46off. and Calan, *Documents*, II, 197–202. On duty after the war, ADIV, C 2923.

exclusive use of wine taxes? They chose to tax wine: 15 livres per pipe of non-Breton wine, 7.2 livres per pipe of Breton wine. The Estates continued to levy small direct surtaxes under Henry IV, surtaxes dwarfed by the revenues from the wine tax; after Henry IV's death, direct surtaxes virtually disappeared until 1643.[35]

These taxes institutionalized the new relationship between the Estates and the king. The king could now obtain substantial regular sums from the Estates, in return for which he could grant them satisfaction to certain remonstrances. The Estates could thus act on behalf of certain interest groups within the province, either by direct action, such as by buying abolition of a given tax or office, or by indirect action, such as general expression of support in their *cahiers*. The grants of 1597 and 1598 dramatically altered the traditional Breton pattern of extra taxation for the king: there were no supplementary direct taxes, no levies on the rich, no import–export duties, only the wine sales tax. In fact, as we have seen in chapter 3, direct taxation dropped substantially in 1597 and 1598.

The first grant, of 600,000 livres, necessitated a tax of 3 livres per pipe of non-Breton and 1.2 livres per pipe of Breton wine. The immediate cash came from a forced loan on provincial notables (table 17). The army, the Sovereign Courts, the clergy – all contributed to help pay for the king to come to Brittany to end the war. All did not go smoothly, however, with the collection. The duke of Brissac and his staff, who pledged 54,000 livres, seem not to have paid anything. In the western bishopric of Léon, the *fouage* receiver could only obtain 60,000 livres of the 105,000 livres assessed to the diocese because of "rebellion, mutiny, and disobedience to justice of various seigneurs, gentlemen, ecclesiastics and inhabitants of parts of the towns, parishes and commanderies of the said bishopric of Léon." The total shortfall was 111,810 livres; the king had still not received 40,000 livres of his money as late as October 1601 and 15,875 livres remained due in 1603.[36] The Estates made up the shortfall with the proceeds of the wine duty.

The loan and the tax levied to repay it gave the Estates extraordinary new powers. They could determine the order in which the notables would be repaid, a process begun in May 1599, long before the king had received the full amount due to him. The Parlement received the first payment in May 1599, obtaining full restitution of its advance; Marshal Brissac obtained 30,000 livres in January 1600, despite the fact that he had not even paid his original assessment; the Chamber of Accounts was reimbursed in 1600 as well. Yet the reimbursement, without interest it should be noted, lingered on and on. The wine duty of the Estates raised 659,000 livres for them between 1598 and 1605, yet only 132,000 livres of this amount went to reimburse the loan of 600,000 livres and another

---

[35] Henry IV levied several extra direct taxes, to repay his debts to the duke of Montpensier's heirs and to the count of Soissons, among others.   [36] ADIV, C 2920.

Table 17: *Expenditure from the revenues of the Estates of Brittany (200,000 écus loan account) 1598–1612, in percentages*

Expense	1598–1605	1606–9	1610	1611	1612
Loan repayment	49.0	17.0	19.6	15.5	13.5
Military expenses	11.0	2.0	6.7	13.4	13.9[a]
Governor and provincial officers	15.0	14.0	37.2	40.5	43.4
Parlement, special session	9.5	–	–	–	–
Treasurer, for debts	7.5	2.0	–	–	–
Rebates to farmers	8.0	–	–	0.4	5.9
Suppression of officers	–	13.0	–	9.1	7.6
Carryover to 1610	–	25.0	–	–	–
Other, including carryover on second account	–	8.0	–	–	–
Michel Loriot, treasurer of League armies	–	–	24.3	–	–
Debts to treasurer/treasurer's widow	–	–	0.9	12.2	1.1[a]
Deputies to court	–	–	3.9	8.4	9.2

Note:

[a] These two amounts are mixed on the accounts because the debts to the widow of Gabriel Hus were for miltary expenses.

Sources: AD Ille-et-Vilaine, C 2920 (1598–1605); C 2889 (1606–9); C 2748-51 (1610–12).

112,000 livres to meet its shortfall. The repayment of the loan lasted until the early 1620s and the final repayment of all of the Estates' responsibilities for the League War came only in the 1640s (see chapter 5).[37]

The second grant, of 2.4 million livres, required even larger taxation in 1598. The Estates settled on a tax of 12 livres per pipe of non-Breton and 6 livres per pipe of Breton wine and agreed to a new salt tax of 24 livres per *muid* to be levied at Ingrande. The lion's share of the revenues was earmarked for Leaguers: 1.572 million livres for Breton Leaguers and an additional 600,000 livres to the king of Spain for the evacuation of Blavet (Port Louis). The Estates leased the taxes separately at first but merged the two duties in 1603 (effective 1604), reserving one-sixth of the proceeds for their own needs and giving the king the remainder as part of the grant of 2.4 million livres. The merger allowed the Estates to reduce the overall level of wine taxes to 9 livres and 4.2 livres on the two varieties of wine. The meetings of 1599–1604 voted supplemental sums to the king so that his final receipts from these various duties were 2,977,500 livres (plus additional money from the Estates' own duty). We can see in table 18

[37] ADIV, C 2920, C 2923; J. Collins, "Taxation in Bretagne, 1598–1648," (Columbia, 1978, Ph.D. dissertation), ch. 6 for details.

Table 18: *Spending from the grant of 2.4 million livres (1598)*

Recipient	Amount (livres)	Percentage
Central Treasury	799,662	28.34
Sébastien Zamet	769,137	27.26
César de Vendôme	420,573	14.90
Duke of Mercoeur	306,570	10.86
War expenses	225,252	9.06
Leaguers	225,000	7.98
Total	2,746,194	98.39

Source: AD Ille-et-Vilaine, C 2887–8.

that the king did not spend all of the money on Breton Leaguers but that debts left over from the League Wars did consume about 70 percent of the receipts, if we count the money paid to the duke of Mercoeur's son-in-law, César of Vendôme, as part of his share, and consider the debts to Sébastien Zamet to be left over from the war.[38]

The Estates of 1605 had to consider the manner in which to redefine their relationship with the king outside of the framework of the civil war. The grant of 1598, and its adjuncts, had been repaid and the king demanded new subsidies. The grant of 1605 started a new process, one in which taxation would be used for the general expenses of the Estates and of the Crown. Regular extraordinary taxation, if such a paradox is possible, began in Brittany with the grant of 1605. The first agreement on the division of the spoils of the new tax established the incidence rules, terminology, and accounting procedures that would be followed until the end of the Ancien Régime. The Estates changed the classification of wines, adding a third category: the new duty was one sou per *pot* of non-Breton wine, 6 deniers per *pot* of wine grown in Brittany but consumed in a bishopric other than that in which it grew, and 3 deniers per *pot* of wine grown and consumed in the same bishopric. The change was a considerable blow to the bishopric of Nantes, the only Breton area to export significant amounts of wine to the rest of the province. It is perhaps indicative of the weak position of Nantes at the Estates, often isolated from the other towns, as we have seen in the letter of the deputies of 1581.[39]

The terminology quickly became normative. The wine tax would henceforth be known as the "sou pour pot," despite fluctuations in the level of the duty.

[38] ADIV, C 2920. ADIV, C 2887–8, accounts of the king's share of the great duty, by Gabriel Hus, treasurer of the Estates.
[39] ADIV, C 2645, pp. 161–3. ADIV, C 2646, pp. 549–50, 554–8. AM de Nantes, AA 72.

The accounts for the king's share and that of the Estates remained separate, as in the days of the separate taxes: the two accounts, named for the proportion of the receipts held by each party, were the "three-fourths" and the "fourth." Again, even when the proportion changed (in the 1620s), the terms remained. The Estates established the rule that 200 *pots* equalled a pipe, for tax purposes. The Estates and the king agreed to divide the money on a 1:3 ratio.

How could the king get the Estates to agree to levy such a tax? What excuse could serve to make such a grant? The repurchase of alienated royal demesnes, so long demanded by the Estates in the sixteenth century, provided a perfect excuse for new taxation. The king had first broached the matter in 1602, and repeated his demand in 1603 and 1604. In the latter two years, the Estates agreed to examine the possibilities if the king would grant their remonstrances.[40] In 1604, the king required the treasurers of France to examine the demesne alienations and they reported to the Estates of 1605.[41]

The king placed the Estates in a philosophical dilemma by proposing the repurchase of his demesnes. They could hardly refuse to help repurchase alienated crown lands, whose sale they had so often decried in the sixteenth century. The repurchase was also to include the alienations of portions of the indirect taxes, notably the *impôts*. The Estates found it very awkward to have the *impôts* alienated because they were, in theory, levied on a yearly basis only with the approval of the Estates; the alienations implied they were permanent and levied without consent. The Estates agreed to repurchase some 808,538 livres of alienated revenues. The largest benefactor of this repurchase was the duke of Brissac, lieutenant general of Brittany (and, given the age of the governor, César of Vendôme, effectively the governor of the province). Brissac held liens on various demesnes and taxes: he received 310,250 livres in two years.[42]

After two years of effective action on this front, Henry IV and Sully were anxious for more. The Breton repurchase campaign was part of a larger effort in all of France.[43] In 1608, the king demanded that the Estates expand the scale of the repurchase agreement; in a tumultuous meeting, attended by 146 nobles (by far the record attendance to that point), the Estates refused. The king responded by signing a *traité* for the purpose with Antoine Desmontz, a *secrétaire du roi*.[44] Desmontz's contract stipulated a repurchase of 3.6 million livres, including demesnes, *rentes* on the *fouages*, and all remaining alienated indirect taxes. The contract was to run from 1609 to 1617. The Estates subrogated themselves to the contract on 15 February 1609, paying Desmontz 200,000 livres for the privilege.[45] They would receive the income (*jouissances*) from the

---

[40] ADIV, C 2646, pp. 17 (1602), 208 (1603), 466–504 (1604).
[41] ADIV, C 3228, report of the treasurers on the demesne and alienations. [42] ADIV, C 2748.
[43] Examples in B. Barbiche, *Sully* (Paris, 1978). [44] ADIV, C 2647, p. 370.
[45] *Ibid.*, pp. 415ff.

repurchased revenues during the life of the contract and the king would get back all alienated revenues in 1618. The money involved in *jouissances* was substantial; the *greffiers*, for example, agreed to accept only one-half payment of the value of their *greffes* in return for keeping their *jouissances* until 1617. The Estates would also keep their "traditional" one-quarter of the proceeds from the wine tax for their own needs.

Matters were not so simple as this bland description would lead one to believe. Desmontz was not the real *traitant*; he was the front man (*homme de paille*) for Gilles Ruellan, an old "friend" of the Estates. He is worth a brief digression because his involvement shows the real intricacy of the relationship between the Estates and the Crown, and the sort of pressure the Crown was able to bring to bear.

Gilles Ruellan was one of the most remarkable men of his age. He began his career as a peddler, went into tax farming with a widow from Saint-Malo, rose up through the ranks of Breton tax farming to become the lessee of the duties of the bishopric of Saint-Malo and then to be the chief farmer of the *impôts*.[46] Like most tax farmers, he lent money to the king; in return, the king honored him by creating two fairs and a market at his seigneurie of Rocher (letters registered at the Chamber in 1600, but forbidding the market), by ennoblement (1603, registered, after a protest, in 1607), and by raising his holding of Tieregault into a barony (1611) and later to a marquisate.[47] In a spectacular feat of social mobility, Ruellan's daughter married the eldest son of the duke of Brissac. One of his sons bought an office of councilor at the Parlement.[48]

Ruellan held the lease of the *impôts* in 1608. The king had alienated some of them in 1600 to meet obligations to the Swiss. The Swiss, anxious for cash, sold their interest to various bankers, such as Florent d'Argouges and Sébastien Zamet. These bankers had sold their liens to . . . Gilles Ruellan.[49] According to the Desmontz contract, Ruellan also held the lease for the duty of the Estates. Imagine the possibilities for fraud: Ruellan collects the *impôts*; he collects the tax levied to free the liens; he pays himself for his liens against them. The Estates had an understandable reluctance to go along with such an arrangement. In short, the king left them little alternative but to subrogate themselves to the repurchase agreement and thus to commit themselves to long-term taxation. By agreeing to the contract, the Estates insinuated themselves into the chain of transactions performed by Ruellan and thus achieved a measure of control over

[46] On Ruellan, G. Tallemant de Réaux, *Les Historiettes* (Paris, 1960), I, 154–6.
[47] ADLA, B 66, fols. 241–2, letters about the market and fairs; B 68, fols. 124–25v on ennoblement; B 69, fol. 89v on the creation of the barony.
[48] Saulnier, *Parlement*, entries on Ruellan family members.
[49] On Ruellan's leases of various farms, ADIV, C 2748; ADLA, B 73, fols. 236v–42v; ADIV, C 2753, notarial contract among Ruellan and his co-lessees of the Estates' duty in 1617. The details of this matter can be found in Collins, *Fiscal Limits of Absolutism*, 56–7.

those transactions, which amounted to over 700,000 livres in the next eight years.[50]

The great demesne repurchase contract ran until 1618. In its early stages, the chief beneficiaries were Ruellan, the heirs of Charles d'Halluin (creditor of Henry III – 400,000 livres), the duke of Brissac (50,102 livres), the duke of Retz (77,580 livres), and the duke of Montbazon (45,000 livres).[51] The Estates' own share of the money often went in the same directions. At the Estates of 1605 part of the king's coercion on the deputies was the threat of a check on the accuracy of the hearth count for the *fouage* (a possible catastrophe, given the massive population growth of the sixteenth century) and an edict to levy the *francs fiefs*. The Estates bought off the first by agreeing to the demesne repurchase and bought off the second with a grant to the beneficiary of the *francs fiefs*, the heirs of the duke of Montpensier. The Estates suppressed new taxes on barrels, linens, and hides, as well as the office of *greffier* for the treasurers of France and new officers and men for the mounted constabulary. In all cases, these settlements with the king (or, more commonly, one of his creditors) came from either the Estates' duty receipts or from a special levy on the *fouage* hearths.[52]

These payments represented a change in the apportionment of the Estates' own resources. In the period immediately after the League War, the Estates spent most of their money on obligations due to the war. They spent some 242,000 livres repaying the 1597 grant between 1598 and 1605; they also spent another 65,000 livres on military debts from war, and 56,643 livres for a special session of Parlement in 1601.[53] They allocated money for pensions for local officers – the duke of Brissac got the largest share, usually 6,000 livres a year – and for the remuneration of their officers and deputies to Court. In 1605, the pattern began to shift toward the special payments to the Crown or to its creditors.

In 1610, with the death of the king and the ensuing power vacuum, the pattern shifted again, away from special grants to the king and toward larger pensions for local notables. Pensions for the great local nobles – Brissac, Rohan-Montbazon, d'Avaugour, Vendôme – had consumed only 15 percent of the Estates' budget between 1599 and 1609, but took 37.2 percent in 1610 and 43.4 percent in 1612.[54] The budget of the Estates, which ran in the black until 1610, showed a deficit by 1612, one that reached 48,578 livres by 1614. The Estates tried to correct the problem by voting, on 29 October 1617, to ban all "gifts, gratifications, presents or other diversion of their monies." They even

---

[50] ADIV, C 2930 and C 2969, accounts of the king's share, 1608–14 and 1614–16, respectively. The two accounts overlap.   [51] *Ibid.* and ADIV, C 2752.
[52] ADIV, C 2889 on Montpensier; see Collins, "Taxation in Bretagne," ch. 6 and 8 for details.
[53] ADIV, C 2920 and C 2923.
[54] ADIV, C 2645–7, C 2751–8, C 2920, C 2889, C 2940–1. The papers and accounts of the Estates for relevant years. This matter is treated in detail in ch. 6 of Collins, "Taxation in Bretagne."

asked the king for a royal edict banning pensions or gifts to anyone who was not an officer of the province, such as the governor or lieutenant general. Such efforts were in vain: their debts soared to over 300,000 livres by 1620.[55]

In 1614, in Brittany as in the rest of France, Marie de Médicis moved to strengthen the hand of the central government. Louis' half-brother, César de Vendôme, made this easier in Brittany by involving himself in Condé's rebellion. Condé and Vendôme sent letters to the Parlement of Brittany, letters the Parlement forwarded, unopened, to the king. Louis and Marie made a tour of the provinces in 1614, prior to the Estates General, in order to reestablish order. They came to the Estates at Nantes; as in the case of Henry IV in 1598, the king asked for a special grant to defray the costs of his trip. The Estates voted to give the king 400,000 livres from the proceeds of the wine duty and to give Marie de Médicis another 50,000 livres.[56] The Estates were supposed to pay the money over two years, but Louis received an advance of 300,000 livres in 1614; the rest of the money came to him and Marie in 1615, as did the reimbursement for the financier, Beaulieu, who had made the advance.[57] The Estates did not meet in 1615 but in 1616 they voted another 400,000 livres for the king's urgent necessities. He spent much of the money in Brittany: 60,000 livres to the count of Brissac for military expenses of 1614; 60,000 livres to Rohan in return for him renouncing rights against the casual demesne revenues. In all, 35.3 percent of the proceeds went directly to Bretons.[58]

The Estates made a tremendous contribution to the king's coffers during the repurchase agreement. They freed at least 400,000 livres worth of revenue (not new taxation, merely the return of the revenue of existing taxation to the king) and also voted substantial other sums to the king: 1.16 million livres in 1608, 1614, and 1616.[59] The Estates had been worried about their inability to vote extra money to the king during the duration of the repurchase contract and they foresaw dire consequences in their *cahier* of 1608.

During a nine-year period, the way will be open to all sorts of edicts, creations of new offices and new impositions, and that which will prepare His Majesty to do this . . . is that during this nine-year period he will enjoy neither the demesnes nor the *sou pour pot*, thus he will not receive any present commodity of our good work . . . [making it] singular and easy to forget, and occurring necessities will make him lose the memory of it . . . it is to be feared that little effort will be made to have the Estates assembled, if it is not to make new demands on the province. It cannot be denied that the *partis* made of our contributions (*deniers*) bring with them an extreme prejudice to the public, in that they reduce our privileges, rights and franchises into traffickable, commercial goods. And as soon as we have consented any money this will be a foundation on which to raise the hopes of individuals to make a *parti* covering many years and to perpetuate by this means a duty

---

[55] ADIV, C 2757 and C 2920.   [56] ADIV, C 2752, papers of the Estates of 1614.
[57] ADIV, C 2969, account of the king's share, by Michel Poullain, treasurer of the Estates.
[58] *Ibid.* and ADIV, C 2753, papers of the Estates of 1616.   [59] ADIV, C 2920 and 2923.

only consented to for a certain time and to a certain purpose. It is better to oppose ourselves at the beginning to such inventions still unheard of in Brittany than to let them take on even more authority.[60]

The Estates clearly understood the negative aspect of their new relationship to the king. The king did call the Estates from 1609 until 1614 and his failure to do so in 1615 could be explained (and was explained in the convocation letters of 1616) as being due to the representation of Brittany at the Estates General of 1614–15. The annual meetings lasted until 1626, when the Estates met twice, and, if one juggles the calendar, until 1630. After 1630, the Estates met only in alternate years.

Despite the king's ability to obtain just about whatever he wanted from the Estates or rather *because* of his ability to do so, the Estates of Brittany became a far more important body in the seventeenth century than they had been in the sixteenth. Part of this transformation, as we have seen, was due to changes under Henry III, particularly the meetings of 1576 and 1582, but the greater part of the change can be traced to the period 1605–1618. The end of the civil war and the end of the need to pay off debts incurred during the war moved the Estates, and the rest of Breton (and French) society toward a new definition of their roles within the polity. The reign of Henry IV, with its relatively orderly management of the kingdom, greatly facilitated this process. Henry IV, for reasons both of circumstance (peace) and intent (a genuine desire to reform the kingdom), was able to eschew the more odious devices used by his predecessors and to try to put his finances, in Brittany and elsewhere, in order.[61]

He obtained the assistance of the Estates of Brittany in his demesne repurchase but this assistance meant increasing the power of the Estates. As the king became more powerful, those who served him and those who were associated with his power (such as the Estates) became more powerful as well. The grants of 2.4 million livres and of 600,000 livres established the Estates as an important medium for obtaining money and as a powerful financial body in their own right. While the Estates of the late sixteenth century had had occasional amounts of money at their disposal (always voting the governor a pension, for example), the Estates had an annual budget that reached 115,000 livres by 1608. They had some voice in the amount of money the king was to receive and an even more influential input into how and when it was raised and, to a lesser extent, spent. Their advice and complaints therefore carried some considerable weight.

The creation of a substantial sum of money directly in the control of the Estates strengthened their role in the province. The first influence it gave them was the power to repay the subscribers of the loan of 1598; while they were

---

[60] ADIV, C 2647, pp. 268–9, papers of the Estates of 1608.
[61] This matter is treated extensively in Barbiche, *Sully*; in D. Buisseret, *Sully and the Growth of Centralized Government in France* (London, 1968), and in Collins, *Fiscal Limits*, ch. 2.

bound by the rule of 1603, which provided for repayment based on the order of subscription, in practice it is likely that those with influence were repaid most quickly. Payments made before 1603 were not bound by the ordering rule; as we have seen, the most powerful subscribers – Brissac, the Parlement, the Chamber – got their money first.

The Estates could also respond to the needs and desires of the various interest groups within the province because they could spend a great deal of money to make their viewpoint felt. For instance, the Estates could repurchase unwanted new offices, such as the triennial financial offices created in 1616 or the *bureau des finances* (suppressed by payments from the Estates in 1583–8 and again in 1623). They could abolish new officers created to collect new taxes, such as the inspectors of hides and of barrels created by Henry IV. These two activities, tanning and barrel making, were very important to the Breton economy; the Estates' intervention made considerable sense in terms of protecting local manufacturing. They also abolished new taxes on linens, once under Henry IV and twice under Louis XIII. Linen cloth was the most important Breton manufacturing product; its export (to England and Iberia) undergirded the economies of the region around Morlaix and of the Saint-Malo–Rennes urban corridor.[62]

At the same time as the Estates found a newly widened competence, they also had to recognize that their effectiveness in struggles with the Crown would be limited. The king could force them to subrogate themselves to a larger repurchase contract than they desired, as in 1608–9, threaten to create new offices if subsidies were not forthcoming, as in 1616 and 1623, or threaten to quarter troops on the province at the expense of the Estates, as in 1621, in order to obtain more money.

The old role of the Estates as the voter of regular taxation – the *fouage*, the *impôts* – had become ceremonial. In his letters of convocation for the Estates of 1616, Louis XIII noted that he had had nothing to ask the Estates in 1615, so he had not called them. The Estates immediately protested that the king needed to call them each year to approve the following year's taxation; they voted an *ex post facto* approval for the 1616 levies to cover their legal tracks.[63]

Everyone understood why the king did not call the Estates in 1615: he already had his grant for 1615–16, so he had no need to call for a meeting in 1615. The Estates foresaw this problem in 1608, when they first protested against the long repurchase contract. The remonstrances of 1616 complained about the non-adjournment of the Estates as a breach of one of the province's main privileges. They also protested about what they perceived as the Court's general negative attitude toward the Estates:

[62] J. Tanguy, ch. 16 and 17, in *La Bretagne Province* (Morlaix, 1982).
[63] ADIV, C 2753, Estates of 1616.

It happens that their complaints are often received in Your Council with indifference, their deputies sent back to little or no effect . . .[64]

Yet despite such complaints, and contrary to what one might at first imagine, the changed role of the Estates actually *increased* their leverage on the king. The *fouage* and other regular taxes, while they were technically granted as one-year subsidies to the king, were in fact so strongly entrenched in custom that it was impossible for either the Estates or the king to make any changes with respect to them. The vote of the *fouage* hardly provided an effective weapon for the Estates, while the promise of a large yearly subsidy paid from the revenues of a wine tax voted by the Estates offered a very strong incentive for the king to try to satisfy at least some of the requests of the Estates. As long as he got his money, he also had a strong incentive to allow the Estates the greatest of their privileges – the right to choose the form of taxation.

The Estates changed during the early seventeenth century from a defender of provincial privileges to a defender of specific interests within the province. The essential bargain struck between the Estates and the king was that, in return for subsidies from the Estates, the king would allow the Estates to choose the form of taxation. The Estates acted less in defense of some obscure set of privileges than in defense of real economic and political interests. The choice of the form of taxation, sales taxes on wine, speaks volumes about the constellation of political forces in early seventeenth-century Brittany.

The Estates, so poorly attended in the sixteenth century, became vast gatherings in the seventeenth. When the stakes were highest, as in 1608, the gathering was largest: 7 bishops, 5 abbots, 8 cathedral chapters, 146 nobles, deputies from 30 towns. The size of the meetings fluctuated considerably as the century wore on, with a seeming trough in the 1620s, and a very rapid increase after 1649 (on which, see chapter 5).

The tumultuous gatherings of the end of the seventeenth century were the logical extension of the ever-larger meetings of the earlier period. The lesser nobility, particularly the poor rural nobility of the west and north, formed retinues for the Rohans, la Trémoilles, d'Avaugours, and Rosmadecs who dominated the assembly. It is hardly surprising that the members of these families, especially the first three, received considerable gifts from the Estates between 1610 and 1648 (also discussed in chapter 5). These great nobles took their pension money and, in turn, pensioned (and feted) lesser nobles.

The Third Estate was the real loser in the changes. The number of towns represented at the Estates doubled between the 1570s and the early 1600s (in 1614, the Estates ruled that forty-four communities had the right to sit) but the towns could not keep pace with the new mass of the nobility. In the 1560s and 1570s, in most years, some fifteen to twenty nobles and deputies from a roughly

[64] *Ibid.*

equal number of towns attended; in the late 1570s and 1580s, the number of towns stayed the same, but the number of nobles roughly doubled, to some thirty to thirty-five. After the League War, the number of towns jumped to thirty or so but the nobles expanded far more rapidly, up to seventy-five to a hundred at virtually every meeting. While the towns did have some input into the deliberations of the Estates, they were consistently outvoted by the other two orders when it came to important matters of dispute. In 1610, for example, the king sent letters to the Estates responding favorably to their request (made at the urging of the nobility) for jurisdiction over the *octrois* of the towns.

The king granted the Estates the right to check the needs of each town and to tell him if the town needed the taxes it requested to be allowed to levy. The Estates split in their response to the king's approval, with the first two orders approving it and the third rejecting it. The Third Estate refused to deputize anyone to sit on the committee to check the debts of the towns, so the other two orders each deputized two men and went on with the work without the assistance of the third.[65] The practice became permanent after 1613; the papers of the Estates of 1614, for example, show that Nantes, Josselin, Malestroit, and Saint-Pol-de-Léon made requests to the Estates about their *octrois*.[66]

There could hardly be more dramatic proof of noble domination of the Estates than this humiliating and blatant interference with the internal affairs of the towns. The choice of taxes reinforces the point, for urban consumers drank more than rural ones; the wine consumption tax fell disproportionately on the towns. The peasants were protected, with extraordinarily low direct taxes (as we have seen in chapter 3). The low direct taxes meant that the landlord could take a larger share of the surplus production. As landlords, the nobility at the Estates well understood this relationship, particularly since large tenant farmers paid a substantial proportion of total direct taxation. The deputies from the towns, invariably identified as a "sieur de . . .," were also landlords and were usually part of the legal class allied with the landed nobles. Although there was some representation of merchants on town councils, and while a goodly number of those present at electoral assemblies (at least in Nantes) were merchants, virtually no merchants sat as deputies to the Estates.

It was a cozy little relationship among the elite, particularly the noble landlords and the legal class, and the Crown. The military officers of the province continued to collect 5,000 or 6,000 livres each year. The Estates needed to keep on the good side of these individuals, who had in their purview so many positions, sought after by the nobles at the Estates. In 1616, for example, the count of Brissac claimed that he had spent more than 100,000 livres preserving the province from rebels since 1614; he asked that the Estates

---

[65] ADIV, C 3468, description of this affair; see also C 2749–51, papers of the Estates of 1610, when the matter first came up, through 1613, when the matter was settled.
[66] ADIV, C 2752, Estates of 1614.

vote him reimbursement (including a grant of 60,000 livres from the king's grant). He received the money from the king and the Estates came up with another 30,000 livres. In so doing, however, they qualified their magnaminity:

While the said Estates are not in any way responsible for the payment of such expenses, nonetheless, in consideration of the merits of the said *sieur* Count of Brissac and of the affection, good will, care and diligence that he has brought to the conservation of this province in its obedience to the King, they consent and order that there will be paid by their treasurer [to Brissac] the sum of 30,000 livres.[67]

Brissac was not a person whom they could afford to offend. He shared his father's position as lieutenant general and could provide positions as commander of fortresses, as man-at-arms, and as temporary officer. He was also in charge of quartering troops, as we have seen in chapter 3. The other provincial military officers – such as René de Rieux, sieur de Sourdéac, baron d'Avaugour – also received grants throughout the seventeenth century.

The Estates did not forget the royal administration in the pensions list. The *secrétaire du roi* with responsibility for Brittany always got a pension, usually 3,000 livres, and his chief clerk received between 500 and 1,500 livres a year. The *secrétaire* had to countersign all correspondence related to Brittany, so his good offices were essential to the province. The Estates spent a great deal of money on emissaries to Court and on pensions for nobles but almost all of this money went to those in a position whose power had a direct bearing on the business of the members of the Estates.

The king himself was not shy about seeking extra funds from the Estates' own resources. In 1616, he created triennial financial offices and the Estates voted an extra 210,000 livres (in addition to the regular 400,000 livres) to abolish them. Two of the offices had already been sold by the time of the meeting, so the Estates had to act quickly. They borrowed the money from the existing financial officers: 210,200 livres. The officers received 100,000 livres from the king's share of the duty receipts in 1619 and an additional 59,521 livres from the *gages* of the suppressed offices (paid from 1618 to 1620). The rest of the money, set at 74,629 livres in 1621, was paid out slowly from the Estates' own budget. The final repayment came only in 1647.[68]

The king continued his pattern of suggesting how the Estates might spend their money after 1616. In 1618, the Estates had to pay Brissac another 15,000 livres for troops and paid 30,000 livres for the upkeep of troops at Douarnenez. In 1618–19, they also paid 50,000 livres to dismantle various chateaux (here following up an idea originated by the Estates). By 1619, the Estates' budget was in such disarray that they took 80,000 livres from the king's share without

---

[67] ADIV, C 2753, Estates of 1616.
[68] On the rapid sales of the offices, ADLA, B 70, fol. 108 (sale of receiver general), fol. 11 (sale of receiver of *fouages* of Saint-Malo). See ch. 5 for more details; for extreme detail, Collins, "Taxation in Bretagne," ch. 8.

permission. The king subsequently pardoned the Estates, who repaid him in 1620–1.[69]

The Estates of 1618 agreed to repurchase yet another demesne, Rhuys, for 200,000 livres but the king interrupted the repurchase by ordering the money given to Charles Chaunet, holder of a *quittance* from the Central Treasury. The Estates did not have all the money, so their treasurer, Michel Poullain, was arrested and summoned to Paris. He pleaded illness, and the chief syndic took his place; the syndic obtained a six-month extension, allowing the Estates to come up with the money in 1621.[70]

These meetings of 1619–21 showed the Estates and the Crown floundering around once again. The repurchase was over: how would the Crown get more money from the province? In 1619, the king spoke simply of his "urgent necessities." The Estates voted him 400,000 livres over two years but then changed that to three-quarters of the proceeds of the wine duty (in the event, 405,000 livres). The following year it was a grant of 300,000 livres over two years. The Estates also sought to put their own house in order, mandating a balanced budget: they ordered "the deputies named for preparing and attesting the accounts that the said Treasurer must make each year, shall be warned by the *procureur syndic* not to employ in expense an amount greater than that to which the receipts add up and to employ among the expenses, by preference, (reimbursement of) their debts, alms, and gratifications."[71] The following year they ruled that the treasurer could not be legally pursued for monies not listed on the *état* of receipt and expenses, that no one could be paid directly by the tax farmers, and that royal courts were to have no jurisdiction over their duty (there was a special Chamber of Requests at the Parlement with unique jurisdiction over matters relating to the duty – its President always received a substantial pension from the Estates). Their debts were 303,935 livres, chiefly sums due to noble pensioners (32,000 livres), to the repayment of the 1598 loan (45,000 livres), to the financial officers (74,269 livres), and to the king (60,000 livres).

In this desperate climate, the Estates made a momentous decision. In 1620, the Estates violated the principle of the 3:1 division of the proceeds with the king. The proceeds of the duty of 1621–2 were to go to paying the king 150,000 livres per year and to providing the Estates with the rest of the money: 92,000 livres in 1621 and 213,000 livres in 1622. The Estates, somewhat innocently,

---

[69] ADIV, C 2756–8, Estates of 1619–21, notably remonstrance 2 of the *cahiers* of 1620. C 2941, accounts of Michel Poullain for the Estates' share of the money.   [70] ADIV, C 3228.

[71] ADIV, C 2756, Estates of 1619, special ruling on the duties of treasurer. The edict culminated a long series of rulings between 1610 and 1619 about the duties of the treasurer. In 1620 (ADIV, C 2757), the Estates finished a series of rulings about his relationship with the Chamber of Accounts, the Parlement, and other outsiders. I take these extensive rulings as clear evidence of the increased importance of the treasurer's position and as evidence that the Estates needed to institutionalize what was by that point the second largest money-handling position in the province (after the receiver general). By the 1630s, the treasurer of the Estates surpassed the receiver general as the most important Breton fund disburser.

established a principle with this grant that was to cause them great hardship. They did not divide the money on a 3:1 basis but rather gave the king his share and kept the rest. By allowing the king's share to determine how much they received, they opened themselves up to the king taking a higher percentage of the duty receipts than in the past. He did so in 1621.

In 1621, the Estates requested the king's assistance against the pirates of La Rochelle, who were ruining the commerce of the province (to say nothing of their impact on the revenue from the wine duty, severely cut by the loss of Bordeaux wine). The king requested 500,000 livres to arm ships against the Rochelais. The Estates hesitated; the duke of Vendôme threatened to levy the *francs archers* and to quarter several regiments of troops on the province. The Estates quickly voted the money, approving duties of 2.5 livres per pipe in 1622 and of 10 livres per pipe in 1623.[72]

The meeting of 1621 and that of 1626 created the framework of the relationship of the king and the Estates as it would last until 1643 and, in most respects, until 1789. In 1621 three important changes took place in this relationship. First, the needs of the king determined the size of his share of the duty receipts; he took what he needed – 500,000 livres – and left the Estates the rest. Although he was generally less brutal at later sessions, the old 3:1 split was gone forever. Second, the *commissaires du roi* asked the Estates to spend money outside the province. It was typical of the conservative nature of French fiscal policy that the king chose a cause – the naval war against La Rochelle – that was so important to the Bretons; indeed, the Estates themselves had demanded action. In fact, the king probably spent most of the money in the province, as the ships would probably have been outfitted there. The *commissaires* also reverted to an old but seldom used tactic – military extortion – to get the money, the first time since the days of the League that such a tactic had been used.

Third, and most importantly, the *commissaires* demanded an advance on the receipts of the duty. The Estates offered to pay the money when the duties were levied, in 1622 and 1623. The duke of Vendôme replied that "the funds that they have destined for the payment of the sum of 500,000 livres are ridiculous, that the needs of the King being immediate, that it is necessary to have an immediate assistance and not to wait for the years 1622 and 1623."[73] After some bargaining, the Estates agreed to an advance of 160,000 livres: three-fourths now and the rest in November. The principle of paying the proceeds in advance came to be an established part of the relationship between the king and Estates between 1621 and 1626. The advances would prove ruinous in the 1640s, as we shall see in chapter 5.[74]

---

[72] ADIV, C 2757, Estates of 1621. [73] *Ibid.*

[74] Although there are examples of advances against the proceeds of a grant, such as those of 1553, 1597, and 1616, the practice only became institutionalized in the 1620s. The practice of paying entirely in advance, and borrowing the money, began in 1643.

The Estates of 1622–5 proved uneventful. The Estates continued to spend money on the usual expenses: pensions, past debts, abolition of offices, expenses of deputies to Court. The Estates' budget sagged badly in this period because the king took so great a share of the duty receipts; their debts mounted rapidly and they were usually unable to meet their expenses, which had to be passed from one budget to the next. In 1623, the king created a new *bureau des finances*, which cost the Estates 450,000 livres to suppress; this expense forced them to raise the duty to its highest level since the civil war: 15 livres per pipe in 1625.[75] The confusion reached the point at which the Estates of 1625 could not agree on a duty and adjourned without voting anything to the king, leaving the matter up to the deputies to Court. The king heard their grievances in March 1626 and ordered a quick meeting of the Estates, in May. These new Estates voted a grant of 500,000 livres to the king, 150,000 livres to Marie, reserving the rest for themselves. They also changed the form of taxation, to an entry duty on wine.[76]

The arrangement pleased no one: the king wanted more money; Bretons disliked the new tax, which proved impossible to lease. The nobility and legal class must have realized the implications of an entry tax, which would fall on *all* consumers, including them; the existing duty taxed only wine sold retail, and therefore fell disproportionately on the lower classes, who bought their wine in taverns. While the Estates were involved with sorting out their own relationship with the king, the duke of Vendôme conveniently brought matters to a head by joining a conspiracy led by Gaston of Orléans. The king himself resolved to come again to Brittany to settle the Vendôme matter and, simultaneously, to reestablish normal taxing patterns by the Estates.

The August 1626 meeting marked a true watershed in the relationship between the Estates and the king: it was the last of the annual meetings. While the situation was unclear from 1627 to 1629, by 1630 the king had permanently determined that the Estates would meet only every other year, a practice that remained until 1789. The Estates also moved permanently to a higher level of taxation, a duty of 15 livres per pipe over two years. The vote of the two-year duty, which became standard practice, was, of course, the key element in the end of annual assemblies. The year 1626 marked considerable change in France and Brittany. Direct taxation began its rapid increase in France, doubling between 1625 and 1634; the *pays d'Etats* would soon be attacked and, save in Brittany, *élections* introduced; provincial Estates would soon disappear in Normandy, Dauphiné, and Provence; Brittany lost its annual meeting.[77]

If we follow the evolution of the relationship of the Estates and the king in

[75] ADIV, C 2759; C 2941, accounts of M. Poullain.   [76] ADIV, C 2762.
[77] Kettering, *Judicial Politics* and Pillorget, *Mouvements Insurrectionnels* on Provence; Beik, *Absolutism and Society* on Languedoc; Hickey, *Coming of French Absolutism* on Dauphiné; Major, *Representative Government*, ch. 13–16, on the king and the Estates; Bonney, *Political Change*, on the general restructuring taking place under Richelieu and Mazarin; Collins, *Fiscal Limits of Absolutism*, ch. 2 and 3, on fiscal changes.

Brittany between 1532 and 1626, we can see the enormous increase in royal pressure on the Estates and the concommitant growth of the king's power and of that of the Estates. Henry IV redefined the relationship of the king and the province because the large military levies of the sixteenth century became unnecessary after 1597–8. He used the original grants ending the war to pay off war debts and to demobilize the army in Brittany. In 1605, Henry initiated the demesne repurchase that extended the wine duties levied to pay off League debts and did so in a manner acceptable to Breton political society. He also resorted to time-honored pressure tactics, such as new offices and new taxes, to shore up the civic virtue of the Estates.

The Regency government's weakness is clear in Brittany in the period 1610–13, when the king got no new subsidies from the Estates and the great nobles saw their share of the Estates' budget triple. In 1614, in Brittany as in France, the government regained control. In the period 1614–20, the king reaped the advantages of the demesne and alienation repurchase and also obtained additional subsidies of about 200–250,000 livres a year. The Estates' own affairs took a sharp turn for the worse because they allowed the duty to become too small: it dropped from 10 livres per pipe in 1610 to 7.5 livres in 1613, 6 livres in 1617, and 5 livres in 1619.

This reduction in the duty level did not go unnoticed in higher quarters. The government knew that Brittany had supported a much higher level of wine taxation under Henry IV, so that it had a considerable bargaining range in 1619, 1620, and 1621. The increased demands of the king led to a return to the old level, 10 livres per pipe, in 1621 and to an increase to 15 livres per pipe beginning in 1626. The duty level rose sharply thereafter, reaching 40 livres per pipe by 1641 (see chapter 5). The grants to the king rose sharply in the 1620s, particularly after 1625 (following the pattern of direct taxation in the *pays d'élection*).

The practice of granting advances meant that the tax year and the payment year did not usually overlap. The annual return to the king fluctuated sharply in the early 1620s, peaking at 850,000 livres in 1624 (table 19). By way of contrast, the king received only 325,000 livres in 1625 and received nothing in the first eight months of 1626. He spent much of this money in the province, to the extent that we can trace it. The vast majority of the accounts mention only payments by means of *quittances* or *mandements* of the Central Treasury. In 1623, we have one account which lists payments to others of some 211,000 livres: the recipients included the duke of Vendôme, governor of Brittany (88,745 livres – 42 percent), the treasurer of the Marine of Ponant (19,000 livres – 9 percent), the duke of Bouillon (30,000 livres – 14.2 percent), and various military receivers.[78] This was the typical pattern of seventeenth-century

[78] ADIV, C 2942.

Table 19: *Major grants from the Estates of Brittany to the king, 1597–1625 (in livres)*

Year	Grant	Specific purpose (if any)
1597	600,000	King's trip to Brittany
1598	2,400,000	Settlement with Leaguers
1599	300,000	League War debts
1605	808,538	Demesne and alienation repurchase
1608	3,600,000	Demesne and alienation repurchase
1614	450,000	Trip of King and Marie de Médicis to Brittany[a]
1616	400,000	Local military costs
1617	unknown	*Jouissance* of demesnes and alienations[b]
1618	200,000	Demesne repurchase
1619	405,000	"Urgent necessities"
1620	300,000	"Urgent necessities"
1621	500,000	Fighting Rochelais pirates
1622	400,000	"Urgent necessities"
1623	450,000	Abolition of *bureau des finances*
1624	325,000	"Urgent necessities"
1625	none	Put off until 1626 session

Notes:

[a] The king got 400,000 livres; Marie, 50,000 livres.

[b] The king was supposed to allow the Estates to keep the revenue from repurchased demesnes and taxes until 1 January 1619, but they voted to shift this revenue to him on 1 January 1618. The amount would have been several hundred thousand livres.

Sources: AD Ille-et-Vilaine, C 2748–63, assizes of the Estates, 1610–25, C 2748, 2762–3, 2888–9, 2930, 2940–2, 2969, accounts of the Estates for the *trois-quarts*.

French spending: allocating resources, to the greatest extent possible, to local expenses. In Brittany, with the money from the Estates, this meant the navy, some military expenses, local pensions. The rest of the money could be used for the king's general debts.[79] The ratio of Breton to non-Breton expenses varied sharply from year to year particularly as a reflection of military spending in the west. Thus the king spent considerable sums in the province in 1621–2 and 1627–8 because of the naval war with La Rochelle.

The first quarter of the seventeenth century was a period of readjustment for the Estates of Brittany. They created permanent Estates-voted grants to the

[79] There is very little evidence that much cash went to Paris. We have some figures for three years in this period, although they are for regular Breton taxation and do not include the money raised by the Estates. In 1607, 42 percent of the share of the Central Treasury or about 15 percent of the total collection, was shipped in cash to Paris. In 1606, the receiver general shipped 86,678 livres of some 568,624 livres received (15.2 percent). In 1629, there is no record of any cash going to Paris from Brittany, but *mandements* of the Central Treasury accounted for 389,000 livres. AN, P 3438. Reproduced as Table 15 of Collins, *Fiscal Limits of Absolutism*, 129.

king, a large annual budget for themselves, and a tradition of effective action. They prevented the introduction of triennial financial offices and the creation of a *bureau des finances* (Brittany was the only *généralité* without one). The success of 1623 meant that the king could not introduce *élections* into Brittany. Brittany was the only *pays d'Etats* into which the king did not try to introduce *élections* between 1628 and 1632.

The successful continuation of regional Estates in the early seventeenth century required two things: 1) the ability to raise money for the king; 2) the ability to represent accurately the political and socio-economic elite of the province. The Estates of Brittany succeeded on both counts. Between 1598 and 1625, they raised close to 10 million livres for the king and they also freed huge chunks of alienated revenue (adding 400,000 livres to the king's regular annual revenue from Brittany). The king could, and did, realienate such revenues to raise still more money.[80]

In terms of representing local interests, the Estates proved an admirable medium for the landed nobility of the province to protect its interests and those of the regions in which it was powerful. The Estates oversaw a dramatic decline in direct taxation, greatly reducing the competition between direct taxation and land rents. Because the *métayers* and other tenants paid the lion's share of the taxes, the reduction in direct taxation was the primary goal of the landlords (in Brittany and elsewhere).[81] The Estates of Brittany enabled Breton landlords, virtually alone among those of France, to achieve this goal. It was hardly a coincidence that, when royal direct taxes went down, cash entry fees for leases went up (see chapter 1).

The Estates also protected the other interests of the western part of the province. They eliminated taxes on grain exports, on linen production and export, and on tanning. They preserved the uniquely powerful position of Breton officers (and the value of their investments in their offices). They eliminated bothersome taxes on barrel making and other trades; they prevented the horde of petty officers of all kinds (so prevalent in France) from setting foot in Brittany. Local wine was protected in the tax system; regional wine, that is, wine from Nantes, suffered prejudice after 1603. Yet the wine taxes had little impact on wine consumption until the 1630s. Nantais wine exports to Brittany remained substantial until the 1630s and even the 1640s.[82] The period 1600 to

---

[80] For example, the king resold the *greffes* in 1626 for a total of 1.625 million livres, for prices ranging from 60.9 livres for the *greffe* of the fish and game warden of Cornouaille to 327,600 livres for the civil, criminal, and presentation *greffes* of the Parlement. See ADLA, B 2966 for a full listing, summarized in Collins, "Taxation in Bretagne," 399–401.

[81] Collins, *Fiscal Limits of Absolutism*, ch. 4. See below, ch. 6. It must be emphasized that, in much of western Brittany, *tenuyers* not *métayers* were the chief taxpayers. In such cases, that is, in the area of the *domaine congéable*, the landlords did *not* assist tenants in paying taxes (see above, ch. 1; below, ch. 6).   [82] Over 20,000 tons in 1631: ADLA, B 2976.

1635 or so seems a golden age, with the Estates able to satisfy almost all interests within the province.

In another sense, the Estates provided money for the nobility of the province – through pensions for great and small and through the military expenses met through their grants. The pensions for the great often found their way into the hands of clients of the *grands* – that is, into the hands of those who had voted the pensions in the first place. The Estates also provided a major social occasion for the nobility; the poor nobles came in the retinues of the rich, eating and drinking in a style to which they would have liked to become accustomed. The wine bills for the city of Nantes during meetings held there were enormous, as we shall see in chapter 5.

That the interests of the nobility of the western part of the province should have received the most attention is unsurprising, given the dominant position of Henry de Rohan as the president of the Second Estate at eight of the twelve meetings between 1608 and 1620. At the major meetings, such as 1608 and 1609, the other leading nobles of the province also participated: the marquis of Kergroisais (Morlaix), the baron of Nevet (Cornouaille), the marquis of Carman (Cornouaille), the baron of Cahideuc (Saint-Malo) and the marquis of Coëtlogon (Tréguier), members of the Rosmadec family (Vannes, Cornouaille), Cambout-Pontchâteau (Nantes). During the Regency, Rohan, the duke of Retz, the marquis of Guémadeuc, the count of Boiséon, Cahideuc, Rosmadec, and Bordage participated in some or all of the meetings. In 1611, constable Montmorency, as baron of Châteaubriand, also attended, no doubt as part of an effort to reassure the Estates on behalf of the Regency. That meeting had Rohan, Retz, Montmorency, and la Hunandaye (Rosmadec) – an unusually distinguished leadership of the Second Estate. Rohan's unshakeable loyalty to Marie de Médicis in the first several years of the Regency made him a key figure for the government's control of Brittany, even though the duke spent relatively little time there. The only meeting he mentions in his *Mémoires* is that of 1614, when he met with Marie and her advisers before they entered Brittany. He agreed to meet them in Nantes, in order to facilitate the disgrace of the duke of Vendôme. Rohan's subsequent close ties to Luynes (who married his niece) made him an excellent governmental client during the latter's ascendancy (although he does not seem to have respected Luynes, to judge from the *Mémoires*).[83]

The composition of the Estates varied sharply between 1608 and 1626. Between 1608 and 1617 the meetings were quite large, an average of ninety-two nobles per session (median ninety-seven). In the 1620s, the meetings appear to have been much smaller – an average of forty-six nobles are listed at each

---

[83] *Mémoires du duc de Rohan* (Paris, 1822), I, 98–161.

session, but the lists all include the notation "and several others." More concretely, there was a sudden change in the leadership of the Second Estate. In most years before 1617, the duke of Rohan presided (1608, 1609, 1611, 1613–16). In 1617, a rotation began: the duke of la Trémoille in 1617 and 1619, Rohan in 1618 and 1620. Given their later contestation for precedence at the Estates (see chapter 5), the rotation was likely arranged in advance to avoid the thorny matter of whether the baron of Laval (held by la Trémoille) or the baron of Léon (Rohan) was the first ranking nobleman of Brittany. The later contestation was eventually solved by a specific royal imposition of a rotation, so that the 1617–20 solution was probably not serendipitous.[84]

In the early 1620s, the presidency of the Second Estate rotated among a variety of individuals: la Trémoille in 1623 and 1626; the duke of Mercoeur-Penthièvre, son of the duke of Vendôme, governor and chief royal commissioner, in 1624 and 1625; the marquis de Rosmadec in 1621; the marquis d'Assérac (Rieux) in 1622. This constant shifting in the presidency of the Second Estate indicates the inability of any single clientage network to establish itself within the province. Henri de Rohan was obviously no longer a possible choice because of his involvement in the Protestant rebellion: the duke of Rohan would not reappear at the Estates until 1647. In his place, came the duke of la Trémoille, who would preside over the meetings of 1623, 1626, 1628, and all the sessions from 1634 until 1645, as well as those of 1649, 1653, and 1655. From 1598 to 1620, the duke of Rohan presided over the nobility ten times, the duke of la Trémoille a mere twice. From 1623 to 1655, the Rohans appeared only once (1647) and la Trémoille presided a dozen times.

Although the shift from Rohan to la Trémoille happened between 1620 and 1623, the real change in the political climate came between 1626 and 1630. One harbinger of the shift can be seen in 1624: the second-ranked noble at the Estates was one Charles de Cambout, baron of Pontchâteau, cousin of a new member of the king's council, Cardinal Richelieu. Pontchâteau, who had not been a regular participant at the Estates prior to 1624, also attended the meetings of 1625 and 1626. He was part of a small new group of nobles who suddenly appeared at the meetings between 1624 and 1626 and became regulars thereafter. The group included René de Bordage, Anne de Bruslon, the marquis de Goulaine, and several lesser nobles. Several of the regular members of previous Estates, such as Cahideuc and Vauduran, continued to assist at the meetings.

These individuals formed a Richelieu clientele at the Estates. Cambout was Richelieu's cousin and, as we shall see, rose to great prominence in the province: he and another cousin, the duke of la Meilleraye, were Richelieu's chief clients in Brittany. The others had their roles at the Estates; their social life

[84] ADIV, C 3287.

only accentuates the impression that they formed a tightknit group. Anne, count of Bruslon, was the official royal introducer of foreign ambassadors and Richelieu entrusted him with several delicate diplomatic missions, such as ambassador to the bishop of Triers (1631). His grandfather had been president of the Parlement; his father had married the daughter of the governor of Nantes. Through the two sides of this marriage, he was related to the Coëtquen, Gouyon, Rohan, and Rieux families. Sébastien de Cahideuc's father, Artur, was one of Henry IV's main military leaders during the League War. His family, too, was related to the Coëtquens. He married Guyonne de Montbourcher, daughter of René de Montbourcher, marquis of Bordage. Vauduran was a member of the Gouyon family. Vincent du Parc, another of the new clique, married Claude Nevet, widow of the marquis de Goulaine. His seigneurie of Guerrand became a marquisate in 1637. Du Parc attended the Estates of 1620, 1621, 1624, 1625, 1626, and 1629. Another of the Richelieu clients was the sieur of Tréambert (Sesmaisons), who attended his first Estates in 1626 and assisted at six of the next seven meetings. Renée de Sesmaisons married Jean-Baptiste de Becdelièvre, later First President of the Chamber of Accounts. The Becdelièvre family intermarried with the du Bots (a *sieur* du Bot Pilleau was another of the newcomers, attending the meetings of 1626, 1629, 1630, and 1632), with the Harouys and Blanchards (the leading families of Nantes).[85]

The Estates had to adapt to a new role between 1598 and 1626. They had lost their old role of voting the *fouage* and the *impôts* in the 1550s and 1560s. The exigencies of war between 1561 and 1598 meant that the Estates could never establish a stable relationship with the king. The extraordinary military levies of that period meant that the leverage of the Estates on the king was quite small because one of the largest (in some years, the largest) elements of Breton taxation was beyond anyone's control. When the wars ended, the Estates and the king had to achieve a compromise that would protect the main interests of both sides. The Estates wanted to control the form of taxation, while the king wanted to maximize his income. These goals were not mutually exclusive and the compromise worked to the satisfaction of all, even of the lower classes, who had to pay an extraordinarily low level of taxation.

Yet the clouds were on the horizon in 1626. The Estates had to increase substantially their assistance to the king; they had to vote multi-year taxation; they had to increase their pensions lists because the recipients were individuals of much greater national weight; they had to tax, for the first time, beverages other than wine (they added cider and beer to the dutiable beverages in 1626);

---

[85] Saulnier, *Le Parlement de Bretagne*, Becdelièvre family members' biographies; Colbert de Croissy, *La Bretagne en 1665*, references and notes to Bruslon, Bordage, la Trémoille, Gouyon families. See also Abbé Guillotin de Corson, *Les grandes seigneuries de Haute-Bretagne* (Rennes, 1897–8), volumes I and II. In Provence, virtually all judges owned seigneuries, but those from old noble families owned the largest (and most profitable) ones.

they had to pay ever-larger advances to the king. The Estates became more and more familiar with the most pitiless, most onerous of all seventeenth-century governmental expenses: interest. Interest payments would threaten their fiscal viability, and hence their very existence, in the second quarter of the century, as we shall see in chapter 5. The Estates, and Brittany itself, also entered firmly into the clientage network of Cardinal Richelieu. One of his cousins, the duke of la Meilleraye, was lieutenant general of Brittany and one of the king's commissioners to the Estates; another cousin, Charles de Cambout, from a Breton family, was already one of the nine ranking barons of Brittany (Pontchâteau, purchased in 1586), and so one of the leaders of the Second Estate. Cambout's ties to Richelieu only added to his prestige. He became local lieutenant for Lower Brittany and, in 1636, was able to purchase the barony of La Roche Bernard at a judicial auction.

The establishment of Richelieu's clientage network began as soon as he entered the king's council, in 1624. Cambout immediately became a key figure at the Estates, and Bordage could be counted on by the government. The following year Goulaine, Tréambert, and Bruslon added their voices. The rump Estates of 1626, those that failed to achieve any grant, were a who's who of the new clientage network: Cambout, Cahideuc, du Parc, Tréambert, Bordage, du Bot Pilleau, Vauduran, and ten others, several of whom were also regular members of the Estates during Richelieu's ascendancy (la Gaptière, Pontmenard, Trévégat).[86] The new political patterns took firm root in 1626, with Louis XIII's trip to the Estates of Brittany, held that year in Nantes. This meeting led to the removal of César de Vendôme as governor and to the execution of the poor Chalais, one of Vendôme's co-conspirators of 1626. That meeting opens a new chapter in the history of the Estates: it was the last of the annual meetings.

---

[86] ADIV, C 2763, papers of May 1626 Estates.

5

The Estates of Brittany and the Crown, 1626–1675

The first ten years of Richelieu's ministry (1624–34) was one of the most important periods of change in the evolution of the French monarchy. Richelieu did not directly attack Brittany's privileges – he did not try to introduce *élections* into Brittany when he created them in all the other *pays d'Etats* between 1628 and 1632 and he did not send an intendant to Brittany in 1634 – but the province's relationship with the Crown did change fundamentally in the late 1620s and early 1630s. Brittany was not likely to be the site of a conflict between the intendant and the governor, because Richelieu himself was the governor, and the introduction of *élections* was impossible because Brittany, alone among the *pays d'Etats*, did not have a *bureau des finances*. These particularities do much to explain Brittany's exemption from some of the attacks on privilege so common in the late 1620s, yet a true understanding of the relationship between the Crown and the province can come only by examining the interplay of forces at the Estates.

Brittany stood on the front line in the key military problem of the 1620s: the royal assault on La Rochelle. The Estates asked the king to arm ships against the Rochelais and then granted him 500,000 livres for that purpose in 1621. The Estates had periodic difficulties with the wine duty farmers between 1617 and 1628 because of the interruptions of regular traffic by Rochelais pirates (ideally located to disrupt the extensive commerce between Bordeaux and western Brittany); the Estates had to pay very large rebates in 1621–2 and again in 1627–8 because the volume of wine commerce dropped so much lower than normal in those years (in addition to the normal ravages of war, the king forbade trade with the southwest). The dual pressure on the Estates in the 1620s was the demand for more money to combat La Rochelle and the awkward reality that a major portion of their only source of revenue came precisely from the trade most affected by the war, the commerce in Bordeaux wine imported by western Brittany.

Closer to home, the governor of the province, César de Vendôme, caused new trouble. In early 1625, rumors again spread that Vendôme was conspiring against the king. Vendôme sought to combat these rumors by writing directly to Richelieu on 15 January 1625:

I have learned from my brother of the good offices that you have rendered to me with the King, and how vigorously it has pleased you to employ your authority to make known the falseness and nullity of the suspicions that some wish to give the King with respect to me.[1]

A week later, he wrote again to Richelieu, this time detailing his considerable personal expenses for outfitting ships to fight against the Rochelais.[2] The rumors proved true: Vendôme and his friends seized Hennebont, Châteaugiron, and some other towns in the province in 1626, as part of the conspiracy touched off by the marriage of Gaston of Orléans. This miserable plot, the so-called Chalais conspiracy, was quickly crushed by local forces, led by François de Cossé-Brissac, lieutenant general of Upper Brittany.[3]

Despite the resolute and effective action taken by the locals on the king's behalf, Louis XIII decided to come once again to the meeting of the Estates, scheduled for Nantes in August 1626. The king sought to achieve two goals: chastise Vendôme and Gaston and negotiate a new grant from the Estates of Brittany. The October 1625 Estates had been unable to reach any decisions and had taken the extraordinary step of granting their deputies to Court full authority to determine the size of the grant to the king. The king met with the deputies in March 1626, absolved them from all remaining problems left over from the great repurchase contract of 1608–18, and ordered them to demand, in his name, a new grant from the Estates meeting in May 1626. These "Estates" voted 650,000 livres to the king and Marie de Médicis and changed the form of taxation to an entry duty on wine. When the Estates could not lease these new duties, they could not meet their obligations to the king. The Estates of May 1626 were, in fact, a meeting of a small coterie of Richelieu's clients. Although there is no direct proof that the provincial elite balked at a decision taken without serious consultation, the difficulties of implementing the decisions of the May Estates do imply such a connection.

Louis XIII and Marie de Médicis came to Nantes for the second time in August 1626. As in 1614, the city put on a royal festival: building a special theater for the royal pageant (for which the carpenters alone received 415 livres) and providing a sea of refreshments. The king's party received eighty-five *barriques* of wine from Graves, Anjou, and Orléans, while the Estates consumed ninety *barriques* of wine from Graves, Orléans, Anjou, Muscat, and Spain. The total cost of the wine and the 7,537 bottles used in its consumption came to just under 8,000 livres. The city also spent substantial sums on sweets, candles, and other accoutrements.[4]

---

[1] P. Grillon, ed., *Papiers d'état de Richelieu*, I (1624–6) (Paris, 1975), 1625, piece 3 (146–7).
[2] *Ibid.*, 1625, piece 4 (147).
[3] B. Pocquet and A. de la Borderie, *Histoire de la Bretagne*, V (Rennes, 1906). On the affair at Châteaugiron, Brissac to Richelieu, 2 June 1626, Grillon, *Papiers*, 1626, piece 79 (355).
[4] AM de Nantes, CC 161.

In such an atmosphere, it is little wonder that the Estates were quite generous: 850,000 livres over two years for the king; 200,000 livres for Marie de Médicis. The increases in the grants (over those voted in May) came in return for the promise that the Estates would not have to pay an advance. The form of the tax reverted to the traditional levy on wine sold retail, this time set at 15 livres per pipe of imported wine (and pro rata).[5] The Estates themselves were to get at least 100,000 livres, plus whatever monies remained from the duty lease receipts, above those paid to the king and to Marie de Médicis. These actions, apparently so reasonable and well within the normal parameters of the Estates' relationship to the Crown, represented the crystallization of two major changes and the introduction of a third: 1) the permanent move to a higher level of taxation than the original sou/pot (10 livres per pipe) of Henry IV; 2) the determination of the amount needed from the duty receipts by the king's needs, with the Estates getting the leftovers; and 3) the permanent use of multi-year grants. There were no more one-year grants after 1626.

The duty levied in 1627–8 also marked an important new innovation in the progression of the tax itself – the duties now covered beverages other than wine for the first time. The Estates established a tax of 2.5 livres per pipe on cider and beer, thus following the examples of the towns, many of whom had first done so between 1610 and 1625.[6] In 1637, the Estates added a tax on another beverage, eau-de-vie. The two taxes struck very different social levels. The eau-de-vie tax was extremely high, implying that eau-de-vie was a luxury beverage. The cider tax, on the other hand, hit the poorest segments of society. The king himself noted, in his response to Dinan's request for town taxes in 1613, that he would "suppress that of three deniers per pot of cider, as being oppressive for the poor people."[7]

The Estates also had another agenda: the permanent removal of César de Vendôme as governor. He had always been unpopular, if one can judge by the rather paltry pensions voted to him by the Estates (they had also requested his ouster as governor as early as 1614). His involvement in conspiracies in 1614 and again in 1626 did not endear him to the locals, many of whom remembered the catastrophes of the League War and sought to preserve the province from civil war. Louis was equally contented to remove his half-brother, whom he replaced with the aged Marshal Thémines, a professional soldier. Thémines had a most unusual connection to Richelieu: his son had killed Richelieu's beloved older brother, Henri, in a duel, a defining event in the Cardinal's personal life. Despite this unpleasant connection, Richelieu's correspondence shows Thémines to have been a faithful client of the Cardinal.[8]

---

[5] ADIV, C 2765, papers of Estates of 1626.   [6] ADLA, B 69–75 for examples; see also ch. 1.

[7] ADLA, B 69, fols. 342–3.

[8] Their connection antedated 1624: see the correspondence in both the volumes edited by Grillon and by G. d'Avenel, *Lettres, instructions diplomatiques et papiers d'état du cardinal de Richelieu* (Paris, 1853–1877), 8 vols.

Vendôme does not seem to have been paid for the governorship, even though the king did include a special listing of 153,000 livres for Vendôme among the expenses to be paid by his share of the duty receipts. On the accounts (and in the other documents) of the Estates, this amount is listed as being a reimbursement for Vendôme's personal expenditure on ships for the campaigns against La Rochelle. We have seen that Vendôme wrote to Richelieu in 1625 about his expenditures at Saint-Malo, and we also have the testimony of the Estates that he outfitted twelve ships for the king, ten of which he bought and outfitted, at his own expense, in Saint-Malo.[9] There is no mention of a payment for the governorship, although a reimbursement would have been standard practice.

The replacement of Vendôme by Thémines was a temporary expedient, one made more fleeting by Thémines' death in November 1627. Thémines wrote simply and touchingly to Richelieu from his deathbed:

I have always regarded you as the most worthy man of our century and the one most necessary to this State, and as such I assure you, Monseigneur, that when I am before the face of God, you will have a part in my prayers. May those that I leave behind me please have a part in your good graces and receive the effects of your protection, because I have always lived and I die, Monseigneur, your very humble and very obedient servant, Thémines.[10]

In Brittany, Thémines left behind a significant political vacuum. No province could afford to be without a political patron. The absence of a governor meant that the local patronage network could not operate at peak efficiency and that the province would not have a powerful intercessor at Court. In fact, it was precisely this second matter that led the Estates to seek a governor in 1630. In 1629, the Estates had turned to the king's chief commissioner, the prince of Condé, to act as intercessor with the king. To that end, they offered Condé a substantial pension, which he refused. He did accept, however, a payment of 12,000 livres to his guards and one of 6,000 livres to various domestics. In 1630 and again in 1632, Condé attended the Estates as chief royal commissioner; each time the Estates voted the two grants, raising the amounts to 24,000 livres for his guards and 8,100 livres for his domestics.

The 1630 Estates debated the matter of the governorship, wishing first to offer it to Marie de Médicis, but they were dissuaded by the argument that she had too many other duties. They decided that "it is fitting to cast eyes on one of the *grands* of this Kingdom, in the power, affection and good offices of whom the said province can be assured to be protected." The delegates opted for Richelieu, ostensibly because he was already admiral of France and of Brittany, and therefore had many Breton towns within his jurisdiction. The Estates had also been extremely pleased with the Cardinal's efforts to establish a trading

---

[9] ADIV, C 2765.
[10] P. Grillon, ed. *Papiers d'état de Richelieu*, II (1627) (Paris, 1977), piece 741 (614–15).

company at Morbihan and had voted him special thanks for that action in 1629.[11]

The Estates of 1630 had a large contingent of the Richelieu forces, led by Condé himself (Bullion described the prince as "blindly devoted" to Richelieu's wishes on the eve of his departure). The listing of nobles is maddeningly incomplete (the usual "and several others" appended to it). Among those from Richelieu's regular network of supporters we find the duke of Retz, as well as Bot Pilleau, Cahideuc, Kergrois, Vauduran, Bruslon, and Tréambert. After the meeting had already begun, reinforcements arrived. The supplemental list of thirteen new nobles joining the meeting in progress is a who's who of the Cardinal's clients: Goulaine, Bordage, la Gabetière, Plessis Josso, la Hunandaye, Saint-Jouan, Cosnelaye, Francheville. Cambout and la Meilleraye were two of the royal commissioners. In such an atmosphere, it is little wonder that the Estates "offered" Richelieu the governorship. To sweeten the pot, the Estates voted 100,000 livres as a pension for Richelieu, should he decide to accept their offer. He did.

The events of 1626–31 were a watershed in Breton political development; they mirrored similar patterns elsewhere in the kingdom. In the 1620s, the king faced three major sources of independent authority: the great nobles, the Protestants, and, potentially, the *pays d'Etats*. He spent the 1620s and early 1630s eliminating the independence of each group. In hindsight, we can see the relationship between the executions of Chalais (1626) and Montmorency (1633) and the siege of La Rochelle (1627–8). Chalais died on the scaffold of the place du Bouffay at Nantes, shortly after the king had left. The permanent establishment of Richelieu's clientage network also took root in 1626. One of the Cardinal's clients, Henri, duke of la Trémoille, had been president of the Second Estate in 1623; in 1624 and 1625, governor Vendôme had the effrontery to insist that his sons, Louis, duke of Mercoeur (and Penthièvre) and the count of Martigné, both teenagers, should head the nobility (the insult no doubt contributing to the local distaste for the governor).

In 1624, we can see the beginning of the change in the local clientage pattern. Richelieu entered the king's council in the spring; in the fall, at the Estates, Charles de Cambout, baron of Pontchâteau appeared at the meeting, the first time the sitting baron had attended since 1609. Pontchâteau was Richelieu's cousin; his presence at the Estates of 1624 and 1625 was undoubtedly an effort by the Cardinal to keep a close eye on the proceedings by means of a reliable client. Pontchâteau rose quickly in Breton circles; by 1630, he was Richelieu's acting governor in Brest and local military lieutenant for the king in Lower Brittany. In this latter role, he was *ex officio* one of the king's commissioners to the Estates.

---

[11] ADIV, C 2766, 30 April 1629.

In 1626, 1628, 1629, and 1630, Richelieu acted expeditiously to cement his control over the province. The duke of la Trémoille headed the all-important Second Estate in 1626 and 1628 and throughout the 1630s and early 1640s. His ties to Richelieu must have been fairly close, to judge from the fact that the duchess sent Richelieu copies of documents in the la Trémoille family archives relating to the privileges and rights attached to the positions of admiral of Guyenne and Brittany (which a member of the family had held in earlier times).[12] In 1629, Richelieu sent one of his most reliable clients, the prince of Condé, as the chief commissioner of the king; Condé scored a public relations triumph by taking social precedence at the meeting not as first prince of the blood but as the ranking Breton baron in attendance (he had been given the barony of Léon, confiscated from Henri de Rohan because of his rebellion).[13] We can see Richelieu spinning his clientage web around the province. Pontchâteau, attending in 1624, is the first strand, then the removal of Vendôme and the insertion of la Trémoille as president of the nobility, followed by the use of Condé to deal with the Estates during the period in which there was no governor. Finally, Richelieu himself becomes governor (officially, in 1631) and his cousins take over the local military. Richelieu secures his position by obtaining the governorships of several major towns: Nantes, Brest, Redon (of which he was also abbot).

Richelieu took few chances. In 1624, the Estates sent its customary three deputies, one from each order, to Court. For the clergy, the bishop of Cornouaille, Guillaume Le Prestre, replaced Guy Champion, bishop of Tréguier; for the nobility, the new deputy was none other than Charles de Cambout. This pattern continued throughout Richelieu's ascendancy. In 1630, the deputies to court were open clients: the duke of Retz, Bordage, the bishop of Nantes (Cospéau), the abbot of Saint-Jacut (Francheville), and Pierry Henry, *avocat du roi* at the presidial of Rennes. In 1636, it was Cambout again; in 1634, it was Sébastien de Rosmadec, bishop of Vannes (and again in 1641), and Jan Troussier, sieur de la Gabetière (one of the new men of 1624: he attended the Estates in 1624, 1626 (both), 1628, 1629, 1630, 1632, 1634).

Richelieu's most useful client at the Estates was Jean de Bruc, sieur de la Grée. De Bruc was a typical Breton judicial noble; he served as the duke of Retz's intendant before becoming the *procureur syndic* of the Estates. The rules of the Estates required the *procureur syndic* to be a noble. De Bruc was an ideal choice because he was the client of one of the local *grands*, Retz. He became *procureur syndic* before (1619) Richelieu came to power but easily made the transition, along with Retz, into the Cardinal's clientage network. His brother, Guillaume, was one of the two chief members of the Company of Morbihan, the

---

[12] Grillon, *Papiers d'état de Richelieu*, I, 237, piece 80.
[13] The issue of how Condé should take precedence led to a considerable debate among Richelieu and his advisors (Grillon, *Papiers d'état*, IV).

trading company founded under the Cardinal's auspices in 1626.[14] Richelieu also picked up other useful clients, such as Gilles Ruellan. Ruellan had arranged the marriage of Richelieu's nephew, the marquis of Pont Courlay, with a rich Breton heiress (Marie-Françoise de Guémadeuc) and he was an intermediary between Richelieu and his Breton clients, such as Thémines. When Ruellan died in March 1627, Richelieu wrote to Amador de la Porte, his uncle, that "the poor M. du Rocher-Portail has died and I am much put out by it, for several reasons."[15] Clearly, the Cardinal left no stone unturned in his creation of an ample network of clients.

The selection of Richelieu as governor meant that the Estates had to come up with much larger sums of money for their pensions list. This process had begun with Condé in 1629 but the introduction of the Cardinal accelerated the rate of increase. He received 100,000 livres per session, a total of 600,000 livres between 1630 and 1641. His immediate household – guards, secretary, doctor – obtained another 138,000 livres in that period. Richelieu's clients also fared well. His cousin, Charles de la Porte, duke of la Meilleraye, became lieutenant general of Brittany in 1632 and served as chief royal commissioner to the Estates in the 1630s and 1640s; he and his household received 425,000 livres between 1632 and 1645. The other cousin, Pontchâteau, governor of Brest and local military lieutenant of Lower Brittany, received 56,000 livres between 1632 and 1643. As we can see in table 20, other clients, such as superintendant of finance Claude Bouthillier, also received substantial sums; in all, Richelieu and his clients received some 1.2 million livres during his governorship of the province.[16]

The Estates did not forget the other notables of the kingdom from whom they hoped to receive support; many of them were also clients of Richelieu. His client, the prince of Condé, obtained 82,200 livres between 1628 and 1632; the Estates granted the princess of Condé 60,000 livres in 1647, although she had to wait until the 1650s to collect because of the near bankruptcy of the Estates. After the deaths of Richelieu and the king, Anne of Austria quickly seized the opportunity to obtain money from the province, naming herself governor and collecting pensions of 350,000 livres from 1645 to 1648. She also used Breton resources to gratify Gaston of Orléans, voted 50,000 livres in 1645 (although he, too, had to wait several years for his money).[17] The duke of Brissac, following in his father's footsteps, received a regular pension from the Estates. It is indicative of his considerably lower standing in the province's clientage system that he had to wait many years for full restitution of sums voted to him, but he ultimately collected 139,000 livres between 1616 and 1646. The Estates also voted regular

---

[14] Its articles are reproduced in Grillon, *Papiers d'état*, I.
[15] *Ibid.*, I, 125, piece 152. See also pieces 50 and 92.
[16] ADIV, C 2766–72, papers of the Estates; C 2940–1, 2980–1, accounts and auditing of Estates duty receipts.   [17] ADIV, C 2980–1, accounts of Bernardin Poullain for 1645–9.

Table 20: *Pensions of the Estates of Brittany, 1631–48*

Pensioner	Function	Amount in livres	Years
Cardinal Richelieu	Governor	600,000	1630–41
Richelieu's guards		120,000	1632–41
Richelieu's secretary		15,000	1632–43
Richelieu's doctor		3,000	1638–43
Duke de la Meilleraye	Lieutenant general	342,000	1632–45
Meilleraye's domestics		56,000	1634–45
Meilleraye's guards		24,000	1643
Meilleraye's secretary		3,000	1643
Baron of Pontchâteau	*Lt. part.* Lower Brittany	56,000	1630–43
Claude Bouthiller	*Secrétaire d'Etat*	48,000	1630–43
Loménie de Brienne	*Secrétaire d'Etat*	8,000	1645
First clerk of *Secrétaire d'Etat*		19,000	1630–45
Anne of Austria	Governor	350,000	1645–7
Princess of Condé		60,000	1647
Gaston of Orléans		50,000	1645
Dame de Lansac	Wet nurse of the dauphin	20,000	1641
Intendant des finances		20,000	1639–47
First clerk of intendant		3,500	1643–7
Prince of Condé's guards		48,000	1630–2
Conde's domestics		16,200	1630–2
Duke of Brissac	Lt. gen. of Upper and Lower Brittany	100,000	1630–43
Duke of Montbazon	*Lt. part.* Nantes	48,000	1630–43
Prince of Guéméné		12,426	1630
Count of Vertus	*Lt. part.* Upper Brittany	19,000	1630–43
President Marboeuf	Head of Commission on Estates' Duty	12,000	1641
Duke of Retz		26,000	1630–2
Sieur de Châteaubriand		20,000	1641
Dame de Kerholin		10,000	1641

Note:

Lt. part. Lieutenant particulier: Brittany had three such sub-regional commanders, one
    for Lower Brittany (bishoprics of Cornouaille, Léon, Tréguier, and Vannes),
    Upper Brittany (bishoprics of Dol, Rennes, Saint-Brieuc, and Saint-Malo),
    and for Nantes.

Sources: AD Ille-et-Vilaine, C 2766–8; C 2940–1; C 2980–1; AD Ille-et-Vilaine,
C 2982, special account concerning Brissac, Vertus, and Montbazon.

pensions to the two other chief military officers of Brittany, Claude de Bretagne, count of Vertus (governor of Rennes and *lieutenant particulier* of Upper Brittany) and Henry de Rohan, duke of Montbazon (*lieutenant particulier* of Nantes); Vertus and Montbazon had to wait many years for full payment. Another Rohan, Louis, prince of Guémené-Rohan, received grants of 8,500 livres in the 1630s but the Estates took so long to pay him that they granted him an additional 3,926 livres in interest.[18] La Trémoille, yet another client of Richelieu, who presided over the Second Estate, as baron of Laval, in 1634, 1636, 1638, 1640, 1643, and 1645, received 63,000 livres in grants from the Estates in 1634, 1638, and 1643, as well as 30,000 livres voted in 1624 (whose payment was long dragged out) but he, too, waited many years for full payment.

Although the enormous expenditure on pensions may seem to modern eyes to be somewhat frivolous, the Estates were rarely frivolous in their attitude to any matter involving money. Early seventeenth-century French politics revolved around personal influence and it was essential for those participating in politics to have powerful personal protectors. Protection cost money, lots of money. Fortunately for the Estates, they had a great deal of money at their disposal. They spent the money, in order to protect what they viewed as the interests of the province, in two ways. The first part, by far the largest, went directly to the king. They voted money and the king satisfied some of their demands. The king spent a great deal of the money voted to him by the Estates in the province itself, so that even the money granted to the king often ended up in the pockets of local notables (both nobles and merchants). The second expenditure came from the Estates' own share of the tax duty receipts. Most of this money went either to the king (see below) or to powerful protectors/intercessors.

The nature of the protection was fairly straightforward. The governor came first, both because of his (in one case, her) considerable military powers and because of his role as conduit between the king and the province.[19] Richelieu was, in this sense, the ideal governor. He well understood the individual nature of protection in early modern France, and while he sought, as the king's chief minister, to overcome local protectors, he was himself an active practitioner of the ancient art. In 1627, we find him writing to the *élus* of Thouars on behalf of his nephew's villages, seeking a reduction in their *tailles*.[20] In 1637, when the bishopric of Vannes was assessed for the *étapes* of troops who had stayed in Vannes, the town of Redon, of which he was governor, was exempt from the levy.[21] In the case of the province, its peculiar administrative position – it was

---

[18] ADIV, C 2982, special account of overdue amounts due to these nobles.
[19] R. Harding, *Anatomy of a Power Elite: The Provincial Governors of Early Modern France* (New Haven, 1978), uses the term "conduit" and provides an excellent description and analysis of this process. For the slightly different system of the seventeenth century, S. Kettering, *Patrons, Clients, and Brokers in Seventeenth-Century France* (Oxford, 1986) and D. Bergin, *Power and the Pursuit of Wealth* (Cambridge, 1985), on Richelieu's clientage system and his use of it to pursue personal financial goals.   [20] Grillon, *Papiers*, 1627, piece 16.   [21] ADLA, B 77, fol. 191.

the only *généralité* without a *bureau des finances* – made it difficult to impose *élections*, but it remains the case that Brittany was the only province into which Richelieu did not attempt to introduce *élections*. His letter of instructions to la Meilleraye, for the Estates of 1634, told the duke not to interfere in the free debates of the assembly, to make sure that all entitled to sit were allowed in, and generally "to restore to the Estates their ancient liberty." He added that la Meilleraye "was to take the most exact care that the Estates assist the king in his present necessities with the largest sum that the current state of the province will allow."[22] Although the king's demands on the province escalated steadily under the Cardinal, Brittany was able successfully to meet those demands. His successors, as we shall see, quickly drove the province to the brink of bankruptcy.

The lesser military officials – the lieutenants general, the *lieutenants particuliers* – ranked next in importance because of the nature of their responsibilities. They billeted troops and determined the military needs of the province: raising troops, supplying them, supervising their movements. The memoirs of Jean Gangnières, count of Souvigny, who was stationed in the province in 1627 and 1628, detail the process. His regiment went to Lower Brittany; its commander was a close friend of the marquis de Timeur (married to Marie de Sourdéac, daughter of René de Rieux, former governor of Brest). Timeur and his friends – Kergomar, Cludon, Faoûet, Coatjenval – received an exemption for their lands, and those of their friends, from the quartering of troops. Souvigny and the other officers often visited a "beautiful young widow of 22, honored and esteemed for her rare virtues"; this dame de Brézal also received an exemption for her lands.[23]

Everyone viewed troops as a kind of plague, so that everyone in the province wished to stay on the good side of those who could have them billeted elsewhere. The deputies to the Estates acted in self-interest here, particularly in the case of those deputies who sought a military post (also in the purview of the governor or other military officers). There were a goodly number of military positions in the province, and they were a lucrative addition to one's income. The practice of "gratifying" military officers was followed by all (examples in chapter 3). Towns and villages invariably gave "gifts" to military leaders in order to convince them to move their troops elsewhere or, barring that, to get the authorities to keep better order during the troops' visit.[24]

The other pensioners usually occupied positions of specific importance to the Estates. The Estates pensioned the secretary of state with responsibility for

[22] D'Avenel, *Lettres*, VII, 728–9.
[23] J. Gangnières, *Mémoires du Comte de Souvigny, lieutenant général des armées du roi* (Paris, 1906), I, 1613–38, 150.
[24] ADIV, C 3672, account of troops at Saint-Brieuc, 1628, showing 20 *pistollets d'or* paid to Brissac's emissary as a gift.

Brittany because he handled all papers relating to the province going to and from the king. The Estates had to remain in his good graces, lest he inadvertently misplace important missives or perhaps delay his (obligatory) signature, thus stalling the execution of royal orders. The *procureur syndic* of the Estates noted in June 1638 that his most important object was to make sure the relevant *secrétaire d'Etat* got his 3,000 livres on time because "the secretaries of state are those with whom the deputies of the Estates have the most to negotiate."[25]

The Estates paid occasional pensions to Parlementaires, notably to the First President in the early part of the century; in the 1640s, they pensioned President Claude de Marboeuf because he presided over the special Parlementaire session that heard all lawsuits relating to the Estates (and their duties). The great Breton families – Rohan, de la Trémoille, Retz – usually held the major provincial military offices, so that grants to family members served a dual purpose. These families also presided over the Second Estate, so that the 20,000 livres grant to la Trémoille in 1638, when he was president, served to help defray the costs of the dinner parties he threw each night.

The Estates grew substantially larger in the seventeenth century. Very few delegates came in the sixteenth century, whereas the seventeenth-century meetings attracted enormous numbers of people. The number of nobles attending the sessions jumped from about 15 to 25 in the 1560s and 1570s to 50 in the 1580s and to 75 to 150 in the early seventeenth century. The Estates of 1616 and 1617 each had over 100 nobles but the number dropped to 58 in 1618 and 1619. In the 1620s, the attendance seems to have dropped even lower, although the notes of the eighteenth-century scribe of the Estates on whom one must base these calculations unfortunately add, at the end of the list of names of nobles, "and several others." The inadequacy of these figures is highlighted by the listing for the Estates of 1636, which carries 61 names, and the notation "and several others." Dubuisson-Aubenay's diary of that meeting indicates that one dinner party included 36 of the "principal" members of the nobility, implying a much larger overall number. He also tells us that Charles de Cambout arrived with 100 gentlemen in tow, a figure which casts into serious doubt the total of 61 on the register. The apparent massive increase of 1651, when 226 nobles attended, may therefore be misleading.

The deputies from the clergy included several bishops at each session; their number tended to go up after 1650 (in the 1660s, seven of the nine bishops often attended). Each session also had some five to eight abbots and an equal number of cathedral chapters. The Third Estate had an average of sixty deputies, representing some twenty-five to thirty-five towns. The 1651 meeting in Nantes took place in strained circumstances – the duke of Rohan had

---

[25] ADIV, B 631.

assembled a rump Estates of many nobles in Rennes – and the Estates were at great pains to demonstrate their representative quality, so that each deputy signed a notarized statement indicating his presence. We find 2 dukes, 14 marquises, 6 counts, 6 barons, 3 viscounts, and 211 simple nobles. Among the Third Estate, we find the legal class: there were deputies from thirty-one towns, of whom twenty-eight sent lawyers and/or royal officials. Saint-Malo sent a lawyer and the town treasurer (always a merchant), while Lannion and Tréguier each sent a lawyer and a "deputy of the community" (a term usually used for a merchant). There were fifty-two deputies on the list, some of whom were not clearly identified by position, save that of *procureur syndic* (town lawyer) of the town in question: nineteen of the deputies can be clearly identified as royal officers, most of them seneschals in the local court.[26]

The Estates came to be massive multi-week festivals, at which the major nobles feted their noble clients. No session prior to 1621 lasted more than nineteen days, and the typical meeting took only ten to twelve days. Under Richelieu, the meetings tended to last a month, with the general trend toward longer sessions. In the troubled 1640s and 1650s, the meetings lasted longer: in 1645, 1647, 1651, 1655, and 1657, they lasted two months or more. In the 1660s and 1670s, under calmer circumstances, the meetings went back to the one-month sessions, although the noble attendance seems to have gone up sharply (to over 200 at each meeting). The major nobles feting this mob were often the royal commissioners, so that the parties served also as occasions for lobbying for support of royal demands. Richelieu's cousin, Cambout, shows the complex interrelationship between local and royal power; his conduct at the Estates of 1636 reveals the close relationship between feasting and politics. As we have seen, Pontchâteau-Cambout began to attend the Estates in 1624, immediately after Richelieu joined the king's council. Pontchâteau was one of the nine ranking barons of Brittany and often presided, in that capacity, over the meetings of the Second Estate. He was also the local military lieutenant of Lower Brittany, so that he was usually one of the king's commissioners. In 1636, when President la Trémoille was absent, Pontchâteau presided over the Second Estate. The Estates later named him as one of their deputies to Court, to present their remonstrances to the king. Thus he was both the king's representative to the Estates, and the Estates' representative to the king.

As befitted his high station, Cambout arrived at the 1636 Estates with his 100 gentlemen. Two weeks after the start of the meeting, he visited his nearby property of Koëlin, taking a large number of the nobles with him to "passer des festes." His fellow client-relative of Richelieu, the duke of la Meilleraye, was chief commissioner for the king; he, too, gave parties, such as that held on the Epiphany for the commissioners and some forty-five nobles (and three bishops).

[26] ADIV, C 2777.

In December and early January, the Estates remained divided over the size of the grant to the king: the nobles offered 1.8 million livres, the clergy and Third Estate only 1.2 million livres. After intense lobbying, no doubt some of it at the parties offered by Cambout and la Meilleraye, the nobles agreed to offer 2 million livres, and the clergy (remember the three bishops dining with la Meilleraye) went along. The Third Estate remained at 1.2 million livres.

Four days after the great party of la Meilleraye, the duke of la Trémoille gave a speech that convinced the Estates to raise the offer to 1.8 million livres. La Meilleraye, on behalf of the king, thereby offered to lift the recent prohibition against the export of grain and to exempt Breton nobles from the *arrière-ban*. The round of elaborate dinners continued: on the 11th, la Trémoille hosted the commissioners of the king and a few others; on the 12th, the intendant, Valençay-d'Etampes, hosted a dinner for la Meilleraye, Cambout, la Trémoille, the three bishops, the presidents of the Sovereign Courts, the seneschals (likely only those from the four presidial courts), and thirty-six principal nobles. Dubuisson-Aubenay tells us that the meat and fruit alone cost 600 livres. The same day, la Meilleraye lifted the ban on grain exports. Several Dutch and English ships, waiting, laded with grain, at La Vieille-Roche, left as soon as word reached them. In the end, the Third Estate had to give way: the king got his two million livres.[27]

The parties surely assisted the royal commissioners in their efforts to obtain larger grants from the nobility. The towns, too, were generous to the deputies; the host city of Nantes provided some 32,000 liters of Angevin and Graves wines for the deputies. The partying tradition continued until the end of the Ancien Régime. Under Louis XIV, Mme. de Sévigné, a guest at the Estates of 1671, remarked that she had never seen so much food and drink.[28] In the eighteenth century, the parties had become even more of a feature of the Estates. The chief commissioner of the king in 1720, Marshal d'Estrées, kept a table for seventy-two every night of the meeting. One deputy, in his journal of the Estates, claimed that d'Estrées kept a staff of eight chefs and 100 kitchen assistants. This deputy, M. Jacquelot de Boisrouvray, claimed that one of the kitchen assistants told him that d'Estrées went through 10,000 bottles of wine from Burgundy and Champagne in a five-week period. The heads of the First and Second Estates had dinners every evening, as did the intendant, the First President of the Parlement, and the seneschal of Nantes (the latter two rather small, only fifteen to twenty people a night). The Estates rewarded d'Estrées for

[27] F.-N. Baudot, sieur du Buisson et d'Aubenay, "Journal des Etats de Bretagne," *Bulletin de la Société Archéologique et Historique de Nantes* (1927): 339–99; ADIV, C 2769, papers of the 1636–7 Estates; C 2940–1, accounts of M. Poullain.

[28] AM de Nantes, CC 167; *Lettres de Madame de Sévigné*, ed. Gérard-Gailly (Paris, 1953), letters of 5, 9, and 12 August 1671, to Mme. de Grignan, pp. 350–9.

his generosity with a grant of 30,000 livres and, perhaps mindful of their debt to the d'Estrées household, voted his wife 15,000 livres.[29]

The social whirlwind of the Estates (Mme. de Sévigné comments as well on the superior dancing skills of the local nobles) was integrally related to its political functions. How antagonistic were the nobles likely to be toward someone at whose table they dined each evening? The chief commissioner built up enormous good will by his generous dinners; the Estates repaid him by providing a large pension. In a sense, they were paying for their own two-month party. They also helped to create a strong sense of solidarity within the nobility, the dominant group at the Estates. One notices that the guest lists of these dinners were almost exclusively noble; in fact, it is interesting to note that the seneschal of Nantes kept a table in 1720 – was it for deputies from the Third Estate, those not invited to the more socially exalted evenings elsewhere? The poor nobility often arrived in the retinues of the great; it was a rare chance for them to participate in a lifestyle far beyond their meager means. In return, they provided their patrons with a certain critical mass with which to confront the Third Estate at the sessions. This critical mass proved to be very effective, as the nobles won virtually all confrontations between the two orders in the seventeenth century.

What did these nobles seek to accomplish? How did they achieve their goals? Here we must return to the daily workings of the Estates, to see how they functioned. How did they spend their money? What did they get in return for their grants to the king? How did the king spend his share of the money? How did these various elements blend together to help the elites keep control of the province? Let us go back again to the Estates of 1626 and trace their evolution from that point.

The Estates of August 1626 voted the king 850,000 livres and Marie de Médicis a further 200,000 livres. The lease price for the farm of 15 livres per pipe of wine sold in 1627–8 was 1,330,000 livres, so the Estates had a budget of 280,000 livres. Despite the promise that they would not have to pay an advance, the Estates paid the king 47,000 livres in August 1626 and another 200,000 livres in December, before the start of the lease. The Central Treasurer disbursed most of the king's money through simple *mandements* of the Treasury, but obviously local expenses (military costs, payments to the Parlement and local notables) added up to nearly 310,000 livres, above and beyond the grant of 153,000 livres to Vendôme. Total assignations against the grant came to 1,072,178 livres, an overdraft of 218,277 livres.[30] The king shunted off the overdraft onto Vendôme and Marie de Médicis, relieving some pressure on the Estates, but the duty farmers refused to pay 263,593 livres (79 percent) from

---

[29] M. Jacquelot de Boisrouvray, "Journal des Etats d'Ancenis," in *Journal inédit d'un député de l'ordre de la noblesse aux Etats de Bretagne pendant la Régence, 1717–24*, ed. G. de Closmadeuc (Rennes, 1915), 57–132; 60–1 on parties of 1720.   [30] ADIV, C 2942 and C 2765.

their obligations of the final term of the lease. Because the king insisted on the principle that payments to him came from the first seven terms of the lease, the Central Treasurer argued that the Estates would have to absorb the entire shortfall from their own share of the receipts.

The Estates claimed, in contrast, that their share of the final quarter was simply their proportion of the total receipts (roughly 21 percent or a bit more than 70,000 livres). The farmers of the duty went to the king's council to ask for a rebate; he granted one of 200,000 livres.[31] The king's council originally held the Estates responsible for this rebate (and others related to the *impôts*) but the king decided to bail them out in 1632, by granting them 280,050 livres from his own share of the duty receipts. When we go beyond this surface generosity, however, we find that the king was not giving something for nothing: the Estates actually had to pay their own rebate. The king's intervention merely allowed them to put off the payments until they were able to come up with the money. A detailed analysis of the accounts showed that the Estates owed 199,589 livres of unpaid expenses, almost the precise amount of the rebate.[32] In short, the king was allowing the Estates to assume payment of some of his debts (with interest).

The king's generous offer of 1632 allowed the Estates to pay these expenses but they, in return, had to agree to assume some of the king's unpaid expenses (that is, they had to pay the overdraft of 1627–8). The two chief outlays were the 153,000 livres owed to Vendôme and the rebate for the *impôts*. When the king could not pay the 153,000 livres to his half-brother (whose disgrace did not help his chances for a speedy repayment), Louis assigned the payment to the Estates. Vendôme felt he had a right to interest on so large a capital outlay and the Estates of 1630 voted him 198,000 livres for his expenses and interest (the 45,000 livres for interest was the figure set by the king himself).[33]

The Estates levied a special tax of 5 livres per pipe of wine in 1633 to pay the duke. He received the money in 1633 but also sought, and received, two further payments for interest falling due after 1630. In 1632, the Estates voted 25,000 livres for this additional interest. When they could not pay it, they re-voted the grant in 1636, paying it between 1637 and 1639. At the 1638 meeting, Vendôme received a further grant, compensation for all the delays, of 19,281.5 livres, of which he received 12,000 livres by 1641 and the remainder between 1644 and 1646. In all, Vendôme received 242,281.5 livres as his reimbursement for the outlay of 1625–6. In 1651, the king even ordered the Estates to pay Vendôme 330,000 livres more for the damages done to some of his property in 1626.[34]

---

[31] The Estates had guaranteed the king 340,000 livres a year from the *impôts* in return for removing it from the *Aides Générales* farm. When the lease price for 1627–9 was only 337,000 livres a year, they had to to make up the difference (9,000 livres); when the king granted the farmers, notably those of the western bishoprics, a rebate, he claimed the Estates had to pay another 84,250 livres, plus interest. ADIV, C 2980, 2941.   [32] ADIV, C 2942.

[33] ADIV, C 2980, C 2767, Estates of 1630; C 2768, Estates of 1632.

[34] ADIV, C 2757–8, C 2766. Perhaps for the loss of his governorship.

The second matter was not quite so expensive but it, too, necessitated a special tax – 1.67 livres per pipe of wine from 1637 to 1639. The Estates had to pay Guillaume Martin, the receiver general of Brittany, 84,250 livres for the rebate granted to the *impôts* farmers of 1627–8 (Martin had had to advance this sum to the king from his own funds) and an additional 9,000 livres to bring the lease price up to the 340,000 livres that they had guaranteed the king in 1626. Martin also sought and received interest on his outlay, so that the total payment to him came to 120,000 livres. The overall cost to the Estates of the rebate agreement was therefore 362,281 livres, so they gained time to balance their books but at an additional cost of some 82,000 livres.

The interest paid to Vendôme and Martin – a combined 125,000 livres – brings us to the main expense of the Estates in the 1630s and 1640s. The king demanded, and received, advances on his share of the duty receipts. In order to meet these demands, the Estates had either to force the farmers into interest-free advances or to borrow money. In 1629, they got a loan of 100,000 livres from the farmers of 1627–8 (it was a condition of the rebate), one that seems to have carried no interest. In 1629, they borrowed 34,200 livres for their own expenses – the grants to Condé and Bouthillier – but this cost them 3,420 livres. The next year it was 50,000 livres for the same general purpose, but it took two years to repay the principal, so the interest came to 10,000 livres. In 1632, the pattern continued, Michel Poullain, treasurer of the Estates, borrowing 58,000 livres from the *caution* (surety) of the farm and having to pay 10,633.5 livres in interest.

Poullain and his successor-son, Bernardin, managed to keep the Estates afloat through the 1630s by borrowing in their own names and by forming a family association to spread the risks and responsibilities of the office. Being treasurer was a risky business. Michel Poullain was placed under house arrest in 1619 for failure to pay one of the king's creditors. Ten years later, he was imprisoned and his goods seized for non-payment of a royal assignation of 4,800 livres. Royal officers attempted to sell his property and the *procureur syndic* of the Estates had to rush to Paris to get Poullain out of prison. The Estates later voted Poullain 1,800 livres for his court costs of this affair.[35]

Bernardin shared in his father's office by the early 1630s and we find him associating his two sons-in-law, Charles Chaunet, provincial war treasurer of Brittany, and César de Renouard, master of accounts at the Chamber of Accounts of Nantes, in the responsibilities of the office: Chaunet in 1636, Renouard, his eventual successor, in 1645. Bernardin's death in 1648 touched off a long lawsuit, so we can get some sense of how he operated in the 1630s and 1640s. He left forty creditors, including several local merchants owed money for provisions provided to the Poullain family. Most of the creditors, however, were

---

[35] ADIV, C 2766.

people who had something to do with the Estates during the tenures of Bernardin and Michel Poullain. The oldest debts dated from 1622, three sums (totalling 4,508 livres) owed to Jan Guy, the *procureur* of the Estates at the Chamber of Accounts. The other major creditors all held *rentes*; they were individuals who had lent money to Poullain in his capacity as treasurer of the Estates. They included:

Messire Louis de Harrouys,		
First President of the Chamber	1,600 livres	(1635)
René de Pontual,		
procureur du roi at the Chamber	15,152 livres	(1638)
Écuyer Julien Aubin	6,000 livres	(1637)
Charles Chaunet, surrogate for		
écuyer Bonaventure de Santo Domingue,		
receiver of the *fouages* of Saint-Malo	15,000 livres	(1642)
	(remainder of 31,000 livres)	
Louis Sanguin,		
receiver general of Brittany	120,625 livres	(1645)

Sanguin had loaned the money to a consortium of Poullain, Chaunet, and César de Renouard (soon to be treasurer of the Estates).[36] The Estates had to pay Poullain 259,000 livres on the account of 1645–7 to reimburse him for interest he personally had had to pay on the money he had borrowed to pay advances to the king and to Anne of Austria. The rate of interest, 11 percent, was slightly higher than the customary 10 percent; the Estates, and then the Chamber of Accounts, at first refused to allow the higher interest, but Poullain argued successfully that he had been unable to borrow at the customary figure.

The accounts of the deceased treasurers invariably touched off long lawsuits. The family of Gabriel Hus (treasurer until 1608 and father-in-law of Michel Poullain) sued the Estates in 1608 for sums they claimed were past due to their father. The Estates paid Hus' widow 94,704 livres between 1608 and 1615 but she was convinced they owed her for other debts he had contracted during the League War (1589–98).[37] In 1629, a special investigation by the Chamber of Accounts found that the Estates owed the Hus family 38,253.9 livres; the costs of the audit were another 27,000 livres. The Estates could not come up with the money for the Hus family, so they paid interest on it, a total of 27,871 livres from 1637 to 1646. The principal was finally repaid in 1646–7, more than fifty years after some of the debts had been contracted.[38]

These protracted lawsuits involved other Breton financial officials as well. The heirs of Nicolas Fyot, receiver general of Brittany until his death in 1606, had a lawsuit against the Estates that lasted from 1606 until 1632, with the

---

[36] ADLA, E 1188, succession papers of Bernardin Poullain.
[37] ADIV, C 2748–53, papers of Estates; C 2940–1, accounts.   [38] ADIV, C 2980–1.

family getting a judgment of 14,385 livres. They did not get full reimbursement until 1646, this for another debt contracted during the League War.[39] René Sain, also a receiver general, acted as chief of the syndicate of financial officers who had advanced the Estates 210,000 livres for the suppression of triennial financial offices in 1616. Ten years later the Estates still owed them 10,796 livres and the final payment, 18,000 livres (to cover principal and interest) to Sain's widow came only in 1646.[40] The Chamber of Justice of 1661 fined the treasurer of the Estates, César de Renouard, 600,000 livres for irregularities, but he seems to have been able to settle for a payment of 40,000 livres.[41]

The finances of the Estates were fully as confusing as those of the Monarchy. The king's demands on the Estates escalated as his needs grew; those needs were usually military. The money raised in Brittany usually went to local military costs, especially to the royal navy. In most cases, it is difficult to trace the spending of the king's money because the accounts of the Estates list it all simply as paid to the Central Treasurer. Even in those cases for which an *état au vrai* survives, we find that *quittances* and *mandements* of the Central Treasury cover 75 percent of the expenses. On the account of 1629–31, the principal known beneficiaries were the navy treasurer (289,671 livres), Claude Legras, a bourgeois of Paris whose money (136,000 livres) was to be paid "preferable to all others assigned to the *don gratuit*," the duke of Montbazon (22,000 livres), and Bouthillier's chief clerk (22,768 livres). In 1635–6, the account lists 78.6 percent of the money as simply payments to the Central Treasury. In a sharp departure from earlier practice, one finds many non-Breton expenses on the account: troops in Champagne (24,480 livres), honoraria for members of the king's council (17,000 livres), the stipends of two French diplomats in Germany (7,000 livres). The largest single amount was, however, a familiar one: 40,450 livres for the navy.[42]

Once again the papers of Poullain, which cover 1635–6 in detail, demonstrate that all was not as it appeared to be.[43] Poullain kept a factor in Paris, Jean Guilbaud, treasurer of the *mortes-payes* of Brittany. We find that the *caution* of the duty farm was one Louis Le Barbier, *secrétaire du roi* and *maître d'hôtel*. He provided an inventory of *quittances* and *mandements* of the Central Treasury to Guilbaud who, in turn, gave him a blank receipt signed by Poullain. In other words, despite strenuous Breton protests to the contrary, and strict orders to the duty farmers to pay the money directly to the treasurer of the Estates, the farmers in fact paid the money directly to the Central Treasury or its creditors, forcing Poullain to issue a blank receipt through his Paris factor. The accounts presented to the Estates for 1635–6 show that 1.18 million livres in coins (and

---

[39] ADIV, C 2768, C 2980.   [40] ADIV, C 2759, 2763, 2767–8; C 2941, C 2980–1.
[41] D. Dessert, "Finances et société au XVIIe siècle: à propos de la Chambre de Justice de 1661," *Annales E.S.C.* (1974): 847–81 and annexes.
[42] ADIV, C 2942, account of 1635–6.   [43] ADLA, E 1188.

the coins are specified as to type) were received for the duty. Guilbaud, accounting for 1.81 million livres, shows in-coin receipts of only 64,455 livres. The bulk of the money not accounted for by the paper transactions at Paris came to Paris by means of letters of exchange drawn on Rouen, so that the actual shipment of cash was quite minimal. In short, Poullain was, in reality, a banker and the extremely complicated lawsuits and accounts of the Estates were a reflection of the bewildering thicket of paper transactions to which the duty receipts gave rise. It was up to Guilbaud, or someone like him in Paris, to make sure that the farmers did not pay off more of the king's debts than Brittany had contracted to pay.

The problem worsened drastically after Richelieu's death. Just as the finances of the kingdom rapidly collapsed in the 1640s, so too did those of the Estates of Brittany. The main problem was that Breton revenues were so reliable, so that the government (and some Court opportunists, such as Gaston of Orléans) took a special interest in so ready a source of cash revenue. In the *pays d'élection*, the shortfall in tax collection was enormous; entire sections of the country paid half of their assessments or even less.[44] Brittany provided a rare exception in that it paid its taxes. The royal government, desperately short of cash in the late 1640s, forced ever more onerous terms on the Estates of Brittany.

The king obtained advances on the duty receipts as early as 1621 and he increasingly demanded that his share of the money come from the first six (later five) quarters of the receipts. In 1629, for example, the Estates voted the king 700,000 livres and Marie de Médicis 200,000 livres. Richelieu's client, Jean Aubry, wrote to the Cardinal on 8 May 1629 that he had arranged a deal with the chief duty farmer (Launay), by which the farmers would pay 200,000 livres on 15 July, at interest of 10 percent. Aubry expected to arrange rapid payment of the remaining sums, on the best terms available, as soon as possible; he wrote to seek the Cardinal's approval of the deal.[45] Richelieu obtained large advances from the duty farmers but Aubry's letter makes it clear that the king himself paid the interest. The accounts of the Estates do not carry any interest charges for such advances prior to 1645. The Estates did borrow money for other costs; they paid 10 percent interest on these funds.

In 1645, however, Anne of Austria demanded a fundamental change in the nature of the advance money: the Estates would now borrow the money and pay the interest from *their* share of the duty receipts. The king received an advance of 1.05 million livres, forcing the Estates to borrow 325,000 livres: 220,000 livres for two years' interest on the 1.05 million livres, 75,000 livres for interest on the money borrowed to pay the interest on the advance, and 30,000 livres in "losses."[46] In 1647, the Estates had to advance the king and Anne of Austria 1,154,666.67 livres; the costs of these advances consumed 57 percent of the

[44] Collins, *Fiscal Limits*, ch. 3.   [45] Grillon, *Papiers d'état*, IV, piece 252.
[46] ADIV, C 2981, account of 1645–7.

Estates' share of the duty receipts. By the time the 1645 Estates had finished paying for the shipment costs of the money (which were set by percentage, not by real costs of shipment), the *épices* for auditing the account, the *taxe* of their treasurer, the interest, and the grant of 150,000 livres to Anne, they had used up 93.7 percent of their *own* budget.

The 1640s were also a time of troubles with respect to the receipts of the duties. The farmers of 1644–5 received a rebate of 714,000 livres and those of 1648–50 some 165,902 livres. The ratio of receipts to duty level continued to decline, accelerating a process first noticeable in the mid-1630s. The higher the duty became, the fewer pipes of taxable wine were sold. The duty ratio (1611=100) declined from 106 in 1635–6 to 83 in 1639–41, 75 in 1642–3, 69 in 1644–5, and 66 in 1646–7.[47] The duty, which had been 10 livres per pipe under Henry IV and even as late as 1624, rose to 20 livres in 1631, 32.5 livres in 1639, and 40 livres in 1642. The Estates realized that it could go no further, so they turned to another resource in 1643: the *fouage extraordinaire*.

The regular *fouage* and its adjuncts came to roughly 500,000 livres per year in 1643; the new *fouage* added another 800,000 livres spread out over two years.[48] The landlords certainly did not like this greater burden for their tenants, but they realized that the wine tax had gone about as high as it could go. They also worried about the increasing use of fiscal expedients to raise money through the direct tax system. The king sold *affranchissements* in both 1638 and 1640, and he levied the *amortissements* in 1642. In each case, most villages, especially those in the western part of the province – that is, those villages in the area dominated by the landed nobility that, in turn, dominated the Estates – had to pay several times their typical annual direct tax. The *fouage extraordinaire* might well have been an effort to moderate the increase in Breton direct taxes, an increase the Estates viewed as inevitable by 1643. The immediate cause of the levy, however, was the financial crunch on the Estates, whose 1643 grant to the king consumed the entire product of the wine duty; without the *fouage extraordinaire* the Estates would have had no money to spend on their "own" (here using the term own rather loosely; as we have seen, most of this money was spent to make it possible to meet the other demands of the king).

The demands on the Estates, by the king himself and by others seeking money from the share of the Estates, had gone up dramatically since the 1620s. The king received 850,000 livres over two years at the 1626 meeting; this rose to 1.05 million by 1632, 1.5 million in 1634, 2.0 million in 1636; 2.4 million in

[47] The ratio is based on the principal of a lease of 10 livres/pipe of wine producing 400,000 livres, as was the case in 1611. This rate changed little in the period 1605–15, which makes it a solid foundation on which to build the series. The earliest figures, from the duties of 1598–1600, are much lower, because of the aftermath effects of the war and the famine of 1597.

[48] ADIV, C 2777, Estates of 1643; C 2980, accounts; ADLA, B 78, fol. 165, *jussion* of 18 December 1643 at the Chamber; fol. 172v, approval; B 79, fols. 11–12, *jussion* for second year of the levy.

1638, and 2.9 million in 1642. This last grant proved too much when the duty farmers failed to pay the full price; in fact, the king seems to have gotten only 2.2 million. He received a similar amount in 1645, 2.6 million in 1647, but only 1.7 million in 1649. The tax relief of 1649 averted certain bankruptcy by the Estates (table 21).

The Estates' own budget followed the same trend. In 1627–8, they had 284,000 livres but they quickly exceeded 200,000 livres per year. The large settlements with Vendôme and Martin forced them to levy extra taxes in 1633 and again in 1637–9, raising their budgets for those years to new heights: 660,000 livres for the 1636–8 budget (of which 240,000 livres was for the special tax voted to help settle their debts – half of this money went to Martin). In 1644–5, they needed a *fouage extraordinaire* of 800,000 livres and another one in 1647–8. They used this expedient again in 1653, 1655, and 1657; it became a permanent tax in 1661. The budgets became longer and longer in the 1640s, with more and more expenses put off. The carryover from one budget to the next usually ran into hundreds of thousands of livres. Despite these vastly greater resources, the Estates could not balance their budget. Each time their resources increased those with a claim on the resources increased their demands. The pensions list became staggering by the later 1640s – gifts of 50 and 60,000 livres to those of only marginal importance to the Estates (but who were in a position to demand, or to have Anne of Austria demand on their behalf, substantial sums). The only people who were sure to get their money on time were the king, Anne, and those from whom the Estates borrowed at interest.

The late 1640s and early 1650s seem a period of crisis in Brittany, as elsewhere in France. Brittany had no real Fronde, in the sense of the open fighting between partisans of Condé and Mazarin, but the institutional and financial structures of the province fell into disarray. In 1649 and again in 1651, the Estates asked the king *not* to call the Estates for another two years (with the proviso that he respect the Breton privilege of consent to new taxation). The 1649 Estates had been very reticent to vote the sums requested by the government. The deputies of the Third Estate "strongly resisted the proposition that was made for the good of the service of the king" and they refused to vote the normal sums for the various grandees. "This tumultuous order removed the gratifications normally voted to the king's military lieutenants." Only the steadfast support of the deputies from the clergy and nobility saved the day. Séguier's informant, Babin, suggested that one way to keep the deputies of the towns (notably Fougères, Vitré, Dinan, and Saint-Brieuc) in line would be to refuse to grant them permission to levy their *octrois* when those taxes came up for renewal.[49]

---

[49] R. Mousnier, ed., *Lettres et mémoires adressés au chancelier Séguier* (Paris, 1964), 2 vols, piece 384.

Table 21: *Grants from the Estates of Brittany to the king, 1626–75*

Year	Amount in livres	Duties levied to pay gift in livres
1626	850,000	15/pipe, wine in 1627–8
1628	640,000	15/pipe, wine in 1629
		5/pipe, wine in 1630
1629	700,000	10/pipe, wine in 1630
		15/pipe, wine in 1631
1630	900,000	5/pipe, wine in 1631
		20/pipe, wine in 1632
1632	1,050,000	15/pipe, wine in 1633
		20/pipe, wine in 1634
1634	1,500,000	20/pipe, wine in 1635–6
1636–7	2,000,000	20/pipe, wine in 1637–9
1638–9	2,400,000	5/pipe, wine in 1639
		32.5/pipe, wine in 1640–1
		0.3/pot, eau-de-vie, 1639–41
1640–1	2,550,000	40/pipe, wine in 1642–3
		0.3/*pot*, eau-de-vie, 1642–3
1642–3	2,900,000	35/pipe, wine in 1644
		40/pipe, wine in 1645
		0.525/*pot*, eau-de-vie, 1644
		0.6/*pot*, eau-de-vie, 1645
		fouage extraordinaire, 1644–5
		(856,000 livres)
1645	2,200,000	40/pipe, wine in 1646–7
		0.75/*pot*, eau-de-vie, 1646–7
1647	2,600,000	35/pipe, wine in 1648
		40/pipe, wine in 1649
		20/pipe, wine in 1650
		1.25/*pot*, eau-de-vie, 1648–9
		0.625/*pot*, eau-de-vie, 1650
		fouage extraordinaire, 1648–9
		(856,000 livres)
1649	1,700,000	20/pipe, wine in 1650
		40/pipe, wine in 1651
		20/pipe, wine in 1652
		0.625/*pot*, eau-de-vie, 1650, 1652
		1.25/*pot*, eau-de-vie, 1651
1651	1,700,000	20/pipe, wine in 1652; 0.625
		40/pipe, wine in 1653; 1.25
		10/pipe, wine in 1654; 1.15
1653	2,300,000	40/pipe, wine in 1654; 0.95
		40/pipe, wine in 1655; 1.25
		10/pipe, wine in 1656; 0.31
		fouage extraordinaire, 1654–5
		(856,000 livres)

Table 21: *contd*

Year	Amount in livres	Duties levied to pay gift in livres
1655	2,500,000	25/pipe, wine in 1656; 0.775
1657	2,300,000	40/pipe, wine in 1659–60; 1.25 *fouage extraordinaire*, 1658–9 (856,000 livres)
1659	2,300,000	40/pipe, wine in 1661–3; 1.25
1661	3,000,000	40/pipe, wine in 1664–5; 1.25 *fouage extraordinaire*, 1662–5 (1,712,000 livres)
1663	2,000,000	40/pipe, wine in 1966–7; 1.25 *fouage extraordinaire*, 1664–7 (1664–5, 214,000 livres 1666–7, 856,000 livres)
1665	2,200,000	40/pipe, wine in 1668–9; 1.25
1667	2,950,000	40/pipe, wine in 1670–1; 1.25 *fouage extraordinaire*, 1668–9 (856,000 livres)
1669	2,500,000	40/pipe, wine in 1672–3; 1.25 *fouage extraordinaire*, 1670–1 (856,000 livres)
1671	2,200,000	40/pipe, wine in 1674–5; 1.25 *fouage extraordinaire*, 1672–3 (856,000 livres)
1673	2,600,000	40/pipe, wine in 1675–7; 1.25 *fouage extraordinaire*, 1674–5 (856,000 livres)
1673	2,600,000	tax on nobility – 250,000 livres; tax on those eligible for *francs fiefs* and new acquisitions, 520,000 livres; notaries, lawyers, 150,000 livres; *fouage extraordinaire*, 1,284,000 livres in 1674–5; alienation of 26 sous/pipe of the *petit devoir* — 600,000 livres
1675	3,000,000	40/pipe, wine in 1678–9; *fouage extraordinaire*, 1676–7, 1,284,000 livres

Note:
There were periodic grants to the Queen Mother. Marie de Médicis – 200,000 livres (1626 and 1629); Anne of Austria – 150,000 livres (1645), 200,000 livres (1647), 150,000 livres thereafter. In 1667, Louis XIV insisted that the Estates pay Anne's customary pension to him, in addition to his regular share.
Sources: AD Ille-et-Vilaine, C 2940–2, accounts of the Estates; C 2765–86, assizes of the Estates; AD Loire-Atlantique, B 79–83, registration of contracts of Estates and king.

The nobility divided violently over a question of precedence in 1651: the dukes of Rohan and la Trémoille each claimed the right to preside over the nobility. Rohan's followers met at Rennes, and received the full backing of the Parlement, which forbade the Estates from meeting in Nantes. The main body of the nobility, roughly 240 strong (as we have seen above) met in Nantes, along with the clergy and deputies from thirty-one towns. The Estates demanded that the king denounce Rohan's assembly and the Parlement, the latter for interfering in matters outside its jurisdiction. The king responded by banning both Rohan and la Trémoille from the Estates and by fully supporting the Estates against the Parlement.

The Estates thanked the duke of la Meilleraye for his efforts at keeping the peace, and for reassuring "the people of the said town against the fears they have of so extraordinary an assembly." The king wrote to la Meilleraye about the relationship between the grant he expected from the Estates, and the dispute between the assembly and the Parlement:

I can say that there is no other province in the kingdom nor one in any of the kingdoms of Europe that is fortunate and rich like theirs, that it not only does not suffer from the quartering of troops, while others succumb under the weight of them and the evils that they endure from our enemies and from my own forces ... and they [the Bretons] have an entire liberty to continue their commerce, which enriches them ... those who represent them make difficulties over assisting [me] with sums which earlier they would have been ashamed to offer me ... I have taken up their defense against the enterprises of my Parlement, and that it is easy to see that I am more impassioned to maintain them in their privileges than anything else.

The king (Mazarin and Anne of Austria) bluntly told la Meilleraye that one way in which the Estates could be sure of the king's continued support in this matter was to vote the requested monies. They did.[50]

The Estates of 1651 counter-attacked, in their remonstrances, against the Parlement. The usual list of complaints – against new taxes, against granting local benefices to non-Bretons, etc. – took a back seat to several new requests concerning the Parlement. The Estates demanded that Parlement stop evoking cases from lower courts and stop harassing royal sergeants. In 1653, they further demanded that Parlement must be "filled with persons of sufficient age, capacity, experience, and probity," and that the king observe the ordinance prohibitions on underage judges and on close kinship to sitting judges. These requests struck at the very heart of the court, in which the practice of allowing the relatives of sitting judges to assume office before age 25 and with limited experience, was endemic. Indeed, the Estates were willing to make an exception for family members who had served at the bar of Parlement or in "some considerable office of the subsidiary jurisdictions."

[50] ADIV, C 2777, letter of 27 November 1651.

The Estates clearly stated the reason for this attack in the second remonstrance of 1653: Parlement sought to "prendre des avantages sur la noblesse de cette province." The nobility, because of its "prowess" and charity to churches, "merited to be maintained in its preeminences and precedences, which appertain legitimately to it." The nobles stated that Parlementaires demanded preeminences for themselves (and their families), and that Parlementaires had even claimed preeminences in areas in which they did not even own fiefs or lands. Because Parlement caused difficulty about registering the Estates' contract with the king, the Estates asked permission to register it only in the Chamber and in the four presidial courts, as well as asking the king to force Parlement to register recent contracts. In the ultimate assault on the Parlement, remonstrance 5 demanded that Parlement be exempted from the *paulette*, and promised that the Estates themselves would pay the king the 32,000 livres a year he obtained from that source: in other words, the Estates wanted to abolish venality of office at the Parlement. Faced with this threat, the Parlement knuckled under, and the anti-Parlement clauses disappeared; in 1655, the Estates asked that all Breton officers, even the Parlement, be fully paid their *gages*.[51]

The anti-Parlement outbursts of 1651 and 1653 were very atypical. The Estates needed to maintain good relations with the two sovereign courts, because they relied on the courts to assist them in their struggles with the king. As a general rule, the Estates got on well with the Parlement; their relationship with the Chamber of Accounts was often strained by disputes over the procedure by which the accounts of the Estates should be audited. The Chamber insisted that the accounts for the duty of the Estates should be audited in a manner similar to all other accounts, while the Estates argued that the Chamber had no jurisdiction over their money. The two bodies reached a compromise in 1613, by which a joint commission from the two groups would collectively audit the accounts of the Estates, at the expense of the Estates.[52] In general, the Estates and the Parlement and Chamber would work together: the Parlement and Estates cooperated most commonly to protect Bretons from non-Breton jurisdictions; the Chamber often refused, at the request of the Estates, to register edicts creating new taxes or offices.

Breton salt smugglers, whose trade was one of the chief employers in the province, provide the clearest example of the cooperation of the Parlement and the Estates. The battles between the smugglers and the archers of the *gabelle* were a constant source of friction between the Estates and the *gabelle* farm syndicate. After many years of dispute, the 1623 Estates finally got some satisfaction. The king sent them special letters on the matter.

[51] ADIV, C 2778 and 2779.   [52] ADIV, C 2750.

And to make an end to the complaints that we daily receive from our deputies about the inroads that the captains and archers of salt make into the region, to make a specific ruling on this subject.[53]

The king sent the sieur de la Roche Labert to establish new regulations and "to facilitate the execution of our said ruling."[54]

In this matter, the Estates relied on the assistance of the Parlement, which strongly defended its absolute right to hear all cases concerning Bretons; thus Bretons arrested for smuggling salt were supposed to be tried in Breton courts, with final appeals coming to the Parlement at Rennes. The *gabelle* farmers preferred, for obvious reasons, to have appeals heard by the officers of the *gabelle* (that is, the *grenetiers*) rather than by Breton judges. The Estates complained of this abuse in 1624 and received support from the Parlement. It is likely that the Estates received some satisfaction in this matter, as it disappeared from their list of remonstrances in 1625 after more than ten years on the list.[55]

The remonstrances of the Estates contained three basic varieties of complaint: 1) on-going issues, such as the exclusivity of Breton benefices; 2) topical issues, such as opposition to a new tax; and 3) technical issues related to the relationship of the king and Estates, most especially to their wine duty. In the 1620s, the Estates combined these remonstrances and the specific provisions of their grant of money into a written contract, which had to be signed by representatives of the Estates and by the king's commissioners. The deputation of the Estates to Court would then bring the contract to the king for his final approval; they, in turn, would have to approve, in the name of the Estates, any changes made by the king. A contract provided protection from arbitrary royal action, by a method consistent with contemporary views of the meaning of "absolute power" (such as those of Bodin, cited in the introduction): although the king was not bound by the law, he was bound by contracts.[56] The Estates relied on this same principle in their dealings with the king, always referring to the famous contract (treaty) of 1532 and seeking to codify new situations by means of written contracts, duly signed by the king and representatives from the Estates.

The technical clauses in the contracts focused on four matters: 1) exemptions; 2) rebates; 3) the liability of the treasurer of the Estates; and 4) the payment of money by the farmers of the duty directly to the treasurer. The first matter divided local elites somewhat, as the Estates singled out some members of the Parlement and the Chamber of Accounts as frequent violators of the incidence rules. One of the presidents of the Parlement, Pierre Cornulier (earlier a treasurer of France in Brittany and nephew of the bishop of Rennes),

---

[53] ADIV, C 2761.   [54] ADIV, C 2762–3.   [55] ADIV, C 2763.

[56] J. Bodin, *Les six livres de la République* (Paris, 1583, Geneva reimpression of 1961), "le Prince souverain est tenu aux contracts par luy faicts, soit avec son subject, soit avecques l'estranger" (pp. 151–2).

owned a free tavern at Rennes, for which he claimed exemption from all wine taxes. Cornulier was only one of many violators of the clause that stipulated that all selling wine, "either of their harvest or not," had to pay the duty. The Estates argued that religious houses frequently violated the rules, a claim supported by the export figures of Nantes in 1631, which show several abbeys receiving far more wine than the brothers could possibly have drunk.[57]

Rebate questions proved even more volatile, as they involved both financial and jurisdictional disputes. The king frequently granted rebates directly to the farmers, without seeking the advice of the Estates. The farmers took appeals directly to his council, rather than going through the official special chamber of the Parlement set up to hear cases concerning the great duty. This problem of "evocations" was, in Brittany as elsewhere, one of the most important grievances of the Parlements. For the Estates, it was a financial disaster because the king received all of his money before the final payment on the duty, so that last-minute shortfalls (and rebates granted to cover them) fell entirely on the Estates' share of the proceeds. Virtually every contract of the Estates demanded that the king give no rebate

for whatever possible cause or pretext, be it war, famine, pestilence, sterility of harvests, cessation or prohibition of trade or other fortuitous or unforeseen cases, even in the case of the imposition or augmentation of other duties.[58]

The Estates tried every means to guarantee that the farmers would pay. In the contract of 1637, they insisted that the *cautions* had to live in Nantes; in 1641, they insisted that four solvent *cautions* had to live in Nantes.[59] In the 1650s, the Estates tried repeatedly to get the king to agree to the principle that the rebates could only be granted by the dual consent of the king and the Estates.[60]

The final two problems were essentially offshoots of the second. The treasurer of the Estates was forever being dunned for money he did not have. As we have seen, he was often sued, even arrested. He had to borrow money in his own name to meet the Estates' obligations. The Estates tried to protect him, writing in a clause that he could not be constrained for their debts "beyond the funds he had in his hands."[61] In 1634, they added a clause stipulating that creditors other than the king would be paid according to the order specified by the Estates themselves, so that the treasurer could no longer decide such matters on his own (and could legally hide behind the wishes of the Estates when being sued).[62] As we have seen, the fourth matter was not resolved in the

[57] ADLA, B 2976. B 79, fols. 172–4, list of free taverns of Rennes, showing, among other owners, Messire Pierre Cornulier, member of the Parlement, brother of the bishop of Rennes.
[58] ADLA, B 76, fols. 37–41, contract of 1632. ADIV, C 2768.
[59] *Ibid.*, fols. 224–8; B 77, fols. 210v–215.   [60] ADIV, C 2778, 2779, 2780.
[61] ADLA, B 76, fols. 37–41, contract of 1632.
[62] *Ibid.*, fols. 72–6, contract of 1634.

Estates' favor. The farmers regularly paid money directly to the king's creditors (that is, they often paid themselves).[63]

The substantive matters often related to other forms of taxation. The contracts ritually required the king not to levy new taxes in Brittany without the consent of the Estates. In many cases, the Estates referred to specific taxes, such as the *francs fiefs* or military levies. In the contracts of the 1630s and 1640s, the request that no money be raised for troops – "victualling nor other imposition for men of war and their upkeep in the province" in the language of 1637 – occurs in each contract. When the king introduced the levy for winter quarters in 1639, the Estates quickly added it to the list of specific taxes from which Brittany should remain exempt. As we have seen in chapter 3, the Estates largely succeeded in preventing extra military taxation in Brittany but their success had much to do with the province's distance from land fighting, a fact noted by the king himself in his 1651 letter to la Meilleraye (cited above).[64]

The Estates actively protected local merchants and landlords from other forms of taxation. They fought continuously against the imposition of taxes on Nantais eau-de-vie (levied by the farmer of the *Traite d'Anjou*, the proceeds to be used to redeem seigneurial river tolls).[65] This tax remained in force throughout the first half of the century, but the Estates were more successful fighting against other levies. The king constantly sought to tax the sale of linens, especially at Morlaix, the great export center.[66] He briefly levied such a tax from 1606 to 1609, but the Estates paid for its suppression. The tax reappeared in the 1620s, a levy of 37 sous/100 *aunes* of linen exported; once again, the Estates intervened vigorously and obtained the abolition of the tax.

In the 1640s, another *partisan*, André Le Jeune, obtained a levy of 1 sou/*pièce* of linen sold at the town market of Morlaix. The edict required that all linens exported from Morlaix be sold through the town market. The Estates sought the abolition of this tax in 1641 and the end of the selling restriction in 1643. In 1649, the deputies from Morlaix and all the towns from the bishoprics of Léon, Cornouaille, and Tréguier demanded "full liberty to sell their linens" wherever they wished. The deputies of Saint-Pol-de-Léon, Lesneven, and Lannion spoke out particularly against the "abbots" of the confraternity of the Trinity at Morlaix. These "abbots" were the stewards of the weavers guild, seeking to regulate production of linen in the entire region around Morlaix. The Estates supported the "liberty of commerce" against the "abbots" as well as

---

[63] ADLA, E 1188. This was an old problem; one of the duty farmers of the late sixteenth century was André Ruiz.
[64] ADLA, B 77, fols. 210v–215; B 78, fols. 166v–173, contract of 1643.
[65] ADLA, B 73, fols. 236v–242v, lease of *Traite d'Anjou*, 1627. The Estates regularly complained about this matter in the contracts of the 1620s and 1630s.
[66] For example, in 1641, the Estates eliminated such a tax, ADLA, B 77, fols. 210v–215. ADIV, C 2772, papers of Estates of 1641.

against the *traitant* of the market of Morlaix; in both cases, they were successful.[67]

The Estates did not forget other Breton merchants, acting on behalf of those whose goods were seized by the *Traite Foraine* in 1641 (a group including two merchants of Saint-Malo, Louis Petit and Jan Chesnier, singled out in the contract of the Estates). The Estates carried on running battles with the bureaucracies of the *Traite Foraine*, the *gabelle*, and the *Traite d'Anjou*, vigorously defending, with the active assistance of the Parlement, Breton privileges in all three cases. Bretons had a right to special treatment with respect to export duties (and were, of course, suspected of reexporting goods to areas not so privileged) and the province never paid any salt taxes.

Although few merchant deputies attended the Estates, the assembly sensitively responded to mercantile interests. They had a sophisticated understanding of commercial matters. In the 1620s, they argued that the merchants of Saint-Malo (and other towns) had to have the right to export bullion in order to continue their commerce. The Estates told the king that a large volume of Spanish silver came into Saint-Malo and that there were better means (unspecified) to keep money from leaving the country. The king also tried to force the Estates to pay their obligations to him entirely in French money; they argued that foreign, notably Spanish, money had to be accepted as well. The Estates clearly won out, as the accounts of 1635 show Spanish (53,000 livres in *réals*), Flemish (156,000 livres in *patagons*), and Italian (6,000 livres in ducats) money among the receipts. In the 1650s, well over half of the *fouage* receipts in Léon came in in Spanish coins; the position of the Estates on Spanish silver was simply a reflection of everyday reality.[68]

In the 1660s, the Estates again acted vigorously to protect the mercantile interests of the province. They invariably cited the importance of the liberty of commerce. In 1659, they opposed the new duty of 0.5 percent on all French goods entering Spain granted to Malouin merchants acting as "consuls" in Seville, Cadiz, and other Spanish cities. In 1661, and throughout the 1660s, they demanded that the king abolish the tax of 50 sous/ton on foreign ships exporting French goods. In 1663, they told the king that their "commerce with foreigners was the most considerable" of the province. In 1669, the Estates explained to the king that one-third of the "foreign" ships trading in Brittany were, in fact, French, owned by foreign merchants "in order to enter in the ports of Spain with greater liberty during the time of war declared by Spain." Breton ships had to lay off, 8 to 10 leagues from shore, where they were subject to great loss by storms and enemy attacks.[69]

---

[67] ADLA, B 77, fols. 210v–215; B 78, fols. 166v–173; ADIV, C 2772–3. The Estates also stated their opposition to any "imposition nouvelle sur quelque sorte de marchandise que ce soit" in 1634 (ADLA, B 76, fols. 37–41; ADIV, C 2768).

[68] ADIV, C 2942, account of 1635–6; ADLA, E 1188, papers of Poullain.

[69] ADIV, C 2782 (1661 and 1663), and 2784 (1669).

When the king established the Compagnie du Nord and gave it a monopoly on the whale fishery, the Estates argued that all Breton merchants should be able to "commerce in fish oils."[70] In 1669, they opposed the gunpowder monopoly granted to François Berthelot. In the 1670s, they opposed the state tobacco monopoly, telling the king that the edict of 1674 "caused a sadness which closely resembles despair in the hearts of the poor sailors, *laboureurs*, artisans and all the ordinary people who live more from tobacco than from bread and for whom its usage has become either impossible or very difficult because of the great augmentation of its price."[71] In fact, one of the demands of the famous peasant code of 1675 was that tobacco be given out with the *pain bénit* at mass, said tobacco to be purchased with the *fouage* receipts![72]

The nobility often requested very forward looking reforms, as in 1614–15, when the *cahier* of the nobility of Brittany for the Estates General demanded that the king introduce a uniform system of weights and measures throughout the country.[73] The Estates also sought to assist Breton merchants in their dealings with other countries, asking the king's protection against pirates and, in the 1630s, themselves ransoming prisoners taken by the Barbary states.[74] In the late 1660s and early 1670s, they demanded that the king get other countries to respect the rights of French merchants; they cleverly phrased this request in terms of the king protecting his own privileges overseas. In the 1670s, they demanded free trade with the West Indies. When the king sought to ban trade with England in the 1680s, the Estates tried, unsuccessfully, to dissuade him. Their lack of success on this critical issue allowed the ruin of the linen trade of the west.[75] They had forewarned the king of the perils of over-regulation in 1675, claiming that royal regulation of the pewter trade had virtually eliminated pewter exports and nearly ruined the pewter merchants.[76] The Estates also sought to protect Breton merchants from the stamped paper act of 1674, arguing that merchants in Paris and Lyon had not had to use stamped paper for their private ledgers. The Estates told the king that the loss of confidentiality in business, combined with the excessive cost of the paper, would ruin Breton merchants.[77]

The Estates of Brittany, a body composed almost entirely of landowners, with virtually no merchants, often defended the interests of Breton merchants: how

[70] ADIV, C 2782 (1663).
[71] ADIV, C 2784 (1669) and C 2785 (1675), article 4 of remonstrances.
[72] Reproduced in Tanguy, *La Bretagne province*, 109.
[73] Durand, *Cahiers de doléances de la noblesse*, 133. They demanded universal weights and a single measure for all of France within six months.
[74] ADLA, B 76, fols. 72–6, 224–8; B 77, fols. 210v–215. There was considerable discussion of this issue at the Estates, on which see ADIV, C 2768–70.
[75] Tanguy, "Les problèmes de l'économie bretonne," in *La Bretagne province*, 129–31. On the action by the Estates, ADIV, C 2784–6.
[76] ADIV, C 2785; they repeated the claim in 1679, article 3 of their remonstrances.
[77] *Ibid*, special comment against stamped paper act, attached to remonstrances.

do we reconcile such conduct with our modern notions of class conflict between the merchants and landowners? The Estates understood the centrality of mercantile activity to the Breton economy. They often cooperated with merchants in commercial activity, notably the export of Breton grain to Iberia and southwestern France. One of the constant themes of the contracts of the Estates was the abolition of the periodic prohibitions on grain exports, clearly protecting their own economic interest. The king could use the lifting of the grain export prohibition, as in 1636, to extract more money from the Estates. To the Estates' credit, it must be noted that in truly desperate famines, as in 1661, they strongly supported a prohibition on grain export outside the province (although one must recognize that they could still make substantial profits exporting their grain to Nantes).[78]

The Estates stood firmly for freedom of commerce: no monopolies, no special taxes on foreign ships, no restrictions on export of grain (save in emergencies). There was no conflict between the class interests of the merchants and those of the landlords on these issues. The towns often came to the Estates with specific local problems and the Estates frequently came to their aid, even against noblemen.[79] That said, there can be no question that the main interest of the Estates was the protection of the nobility's political and social dominance of the province. The interests of all landlords tended to overlap, and the royal officers who represented the towns invariably owned land. Their interests and those of the old nobility overlapped with respect to low direct taxation, to preventing *affranchissements* (although the officers usually bought up such exemptions when they were offered), and to keeping troops out of the province. No one had any illusions on that last score; the Estates denounced the presence of virtually all troops, whether they were regiments passing through the province or the garrisons regularly stationed there.[80]

The most common complaints of the Estates related to the creation of new offices. The king never wanted for ideas of new positions to fill, from guard of the charters of the castle of Nantes to *huissiers* for each diocese to three guards of the petty seal of each jurisdiction. Sometimes the offices were more than a nuisance, as in the case of the triennial financial officers of 1616 or the *bureau des finances* in 1583 and again in 1623. The Estates remained ever vigilant in such matters, buying up virtually all offices created by the king. The only major exceptions were a creation of new offices at the *prévôté de Nantes* in 1626 and

[78] ADIV, C 2782, action of Estates on 16 September 1661, in response to request from syndics of Vannes, Auray, Hennebont and "other coastal towns" that such export be allowed.

[79] ADIV, C 2778, Estates of 1653, dispute between the town of Malestroit and the *sieur* de Crauhac, over his claim to levy a tax on all goods shipped on the Oud river. The Estates supported Malestroit (and the town of Saint-Malo in a similar dispute), affirming their support for "the public liberty of traffic which is common between all towns of this province."

[80] In 1679, for example, the Estates claimed (remonstrance 4) that troop movements had ruined the entire province. They had special concerns with the damage in large "bourgades" and villages (ADIV, C 2785).

periodic additions to the Parlement (as in 1632). The Estates, despite their frequent disputes with local officers (particularly with the Chamber of Accounts), usually defended the interests of those officers, whether it be an effort to exempt the officers from forced *gages* increases or to exempt them from the *paulette* renewal payments.[81] These demands lasted well into the 1650s, when the Estates argued that paying *gages* at one-fourth their official level was "to deprive your subjects of the fruit of your promises."[82]

The royal officers and the seigneurs shared many economic interests; their class interests were generally quite similar. They did not share order-based interests. We have already seen one case of dispute, that of the attack on the pretensions of the Parlement in the early 1650s. In addition to the rancor of the 1651 conflict, the Estates took umbrage at the efforts of a Parlementaire to take precedence over a nobleman in a village church outside of Rennes, in a parish in which the nobleman held lands (while the Parlementaire was merely a visitor). The Estates attacked the new privileges of the *secrétaires du roi* in 1661, arguing that these privileges had not been consented to by the Estates, "which wounded the ancient privileges and diminished the *éclat* of the ancient nobility of Brittany in giving this quality indifferently to all people." They demanded that the *secrétaires du roi* should not benefit from hereditary nobility. Two years later, the Estates attacked the new privilege of the auditors of accounts, who were to become hereditary nobles, like the masters of accounts. (Here we must remember the very different social origins of the two groups, as spelled out in chapter 2, above.) In a truly extraordinary departure from custom, the Estates agreed to join the plaintiff against the auditors at their *own* expense. Two years later they spelled out their objection to the auditors receiving nobility:

the auditors of the said Chamber will have the quality of noble in the first degree similar to that of barons, [which] will give cause and fear of a notable disorder in the *corps* of the nobility of your province of Brittany by the *mélange* of persons of low birth who do not have the courage and valor that this illustrious nobility has always demonstrated.[83]

The nobility obtained satisfaction: the auditors did not get hereditary nobility.

The sessions of the 1660s and 1670s demonstrate the balance of mercantile as opposed to landlord and noble interests at the Estates. The Estates were certainly active in protecting the liberty of commerce and in defending mercantile interests with respect to free trade with the West Indies and the Great Banks, and in opposing the 50 sous per ton levy on foreign ships. The sheer volume of complaint on such matters, however, pales in comparison to the amount of material on issues of serious importance to the landlords and nobles: the rules governing the *fouage*, the reformation of the nobility, and, above all, the

---

[81] ADLA, B 77, fols. 210v–215, contract of 1641, asking king to restore the one-fourth of their *gages* stripped from the Parlement, Chamber, and other royal officers of the financial and judiciary services.   [82] ADIV, C 2778, article 3 of remonstrances.
[83] ADIV, C 2783, article 10 of remonstrances.

reformation of the king's demesne proposed in the 1670s. The 2.6 million livres grant of 1673 related directly to abolishing the demesne reform, so that the reestablishment of the reform in 1678 touched off a storm of protest. The 1679 remonstrance against the reformation of the demesne was twenty-six and a half pages long; the remonstrances for the liberty of commerce covered scarcely a half page.[84]

The late 1660s and early 1670s were a period of tremendous pressure on the Estates. Louis XIV wanted more money; the Estates responded by making permanent the *fouage extraordinaire*, by confiscating the *petit devoir*, and by steadily increasing the tax on eau-de-vie. The main tax on wine, however, remained the same: 4 sous per *pot* of imported wine.[85] The grants to the king were lower in the early 1650s, only an average of 1.7 million livres at the three Estates between 1649 and 1653; in 1655, however, the king received 2.5 million livres, and the grants between 1657 and 1665 averaged 2.1 million livres. In 1667, the king obtained 2.8 million, but only 2.5 million in 1669 and 2.2 million in 1671. This last amount reflected the extent to which the Estates had gotten ahead of themselves in granting the receipts of their tax money: the *don gratuit* of 1671 was to come from wine taxes levied in 1674 and the first half of 1675, as well as from the *fouage extraordinaire* of 1672 and 1673.[86] All of these grants mask the real amount that the Estates furnished to the king, because they had to pay enormous interest to borrow money in order to pay his debts: the grants of the period 1661–8 totalled 9.0 million livres, but the Estates also paid interest of nearly 2.5 million livres solely for the money borrowed to pay advances to the king and to Anne of Austria.[87]

When, in 1673, the king introduced a broad series of edicts attacking Breton privileges – abolishing notaries and clerkships, investigating cases of false *foi et hommage*, levying the *francs fiefs*, reforming the demesne, new taxes on pewter and tobacco, a stamped paper act – it was merely the first step in the bargaining

---

[84] ADIV, C 2785. They concluded the research into titles of lands would "ruin many families."

[85] A. Rebillon, *Les Etats de Bretagne de 1661 à 1789* (Paris, 1932), covers the period after 1661, but his discussion of financial matters is somewhat confused. The main tax, the *grand devoir*, remained steady at 4 sous per *pot* of imported wine (3 for Nantais wine sold outside the bishopric of Nantes, 2 for wine sold in the bishopric in which it was grown, and 1 for cider and beer). The *petit devoir*, originally a tax of 27,000 livres created to pay extra *gages* to the Parlement (1601), became a separate tax in its own right. The Estates regularly raised the rate of the *petit devoir* after 1653, and even alienated part of its proceeds in the 1670s. By the 1670s, the *petit devoir* lease reached some 33–40 percent of the *grand devoir* lease.

[86] The accounts of the Estates are in ADIV C 2940, 2941, 2980, and 2981. The gift of 1643, 2.9 million livres, may not have been fully paid because of a rebate to the duty farmers. Thereafter the gift declined to 2.2 million in 1645, 2.6 in 1647, and under 2.0 million in 1649 and the early 1650s. In addition to the papers of the Estates of 1661–79 (ADIV, C 2782–6), the accounts are in ADIV, C 2980, 2981, and 2985.

[87] The grants were: 1661 – 3.0 million livres; 1663 – 2.0 million; 1665 – 2.2 million; 1667 – 2.8 million. In 1661, for example, the Estates scheduled interest payments of 510,000 livres on their grants to the king (who was present) and to Anne of Austria.

for the Estates of 1673. These Estates would have much larger resources available to them, because the 1671 Estates had only extended the wine taxes through 30 June 1675. The Estates offered the king a regular *don gratuit* of 2.6 million livres and agreed to purchase the revocation of the edicts for another 2.6 million livres. In addition to the regular taxes, the Estates agreed to a special tax on nobles (250,000 livres), a tax on clerks and lawyers (150,000 livres), a levy on those subject to *francs fiefs* and *nouvelles acquêts* (520,000 livres), and an augmentation of the *fouage extraordinaire* (about 200,000 livres per year). The Estates borrowed 600,000 livres, using the surtax of 26 sous/*pot*, levied with the *petit devoir* as collateral. In addition to voting 5.2 million livres for the king, the Estates anticipated paying 874,619 livres in interest on their grants to him, and they agreed to pay to outfit six warships, at a further cost of 230,000 livres: the real grant to the king was therefore closer to 6.3 million livres than to 5.2 million.[88]

The fiscal consequences of the massive demands of 1673 proved to be even more onerous than the Estates anticipated, because the great Breton rebellions – the Papier Timbré and the Bonnets Rouges – broke out just as the new wine tax lease came into effect. The nobles and other specially taxed individuals chose not to pay much of their share, so that the receipts for the three special taxes were only about 401,000 livres. The peasants refused to pay their direct taxes, so that the budget of the Estates descended into chaos; as late as 1680, the Estates' budget for 1678–80, which carried expenses of 5.1 million livres (this budget had nothing to do with the regular grants to the king), showed non-payment of nearly 2.0 million livres of those expenses.[89] The way out of the financial labyrinth was to borrow money, to follow the example of the Estates of Languedoc by issuing *rentes*.

The Estates sold 1.6 million livres of *rentes* between 1676 and 1679. They did not want for prominent buyers. On 26 June 1677, Antoine Barillon, *maître des requêtes*, paid 20,000 livres in "louis d'or et d'argent et monnoye" for 2,000 livres of *rente*; other purchasers included Auguste de Harlay, another *maître*, Henry de Fourcy, a president of the Parlement of Paris, Honoré Coustin, French ambassador to England, and even one Jacques Cadet, described only as a "bourgeois de Paris," who owned five separate *rentes* worth 49,000 livres of capital.[90] The Estates were soon paying out 160,000 livres for interest each year, above and beyond the interest paid for the advances to the king.

The remonstrances in the 1660s and 1670s focused on topical issues. In the early 1660s, the Estates demanded the preservation of local religious privileges,

---

[88] ADIV, C 2785. The Estates did not raise all of this money; the nobles and other special assessees of 1673 did not pay their due amounts. They estimated the shortfall, in 1675, as 200,000 livres but it was, in fact, much higher: the account for 1673 indicates that 401,248 livres had not been paid as late as March 1677.

[89] ADIV, C 2785, C 2786. Accounts of 1667–77 in ADIV, C 2985.

[90] ADIV, C 2785, receipts from various purchasers included with papers of the Estates.

opposed a new seigneurial tax near Châteaulin and municipal taxes at Rennes and Nantes, demanded full payment of *gages* and *rentes*, stood up for the liberty of commerce, and strongly opposed the new privileges of the auditors of accounts and *secrétaires du roi*. In 1663, for the first time, the Estates seriously discussed the incidence rules for the *fouage*: the matter was newly important because the *fouage extraordinaire* had just become permanent. The Estates demanded that the *fouage* collectors in the villages respect the fact that Brittany was an area of "taille mixte": that is, that both noble persons and noble lands were exempt from direct taxation in Brittany. The remonstrances also included a wide variety of specific requests: repairing the fortifications of Nantes, maintaining the Breton exemption from the *traite foraine*, opposing various new minor taxes, such as the 7 sous per *quintal* on soap from Provence.[91]

The Estates spent some of their money on interesting minor projects. Most of their own budget went to pay interest on advances to the king (and to Anne); the largest other expenses were the usual pensions for the governor (100,000 livres), the lieutenant general (50–60,000 livres), and others. The minor expenses showed the Estates involved in a wide variety of causes. They voted 20,000 livres *cash* to the former queen of England (Louis XIII's sister, Henrietta-Maria) in 1655; the bishop of Rennes, speaking on her behalf, noted that "no one ignores the revolutions having taken place in England in the past 15 years" and reminded the Estates that their peers in Languedoc had voted her a similar gift. The Estates pensioned Irish bishops and expatriate English Catholic nobles, as well as provided small grants (usually 1–2,000 livres) for charitable causes, such as the "girls of good condition but little means" who needed instruction in the Catholic faith. In 1665, they manifested a much less positive attitude toward some of the poor: they voted 6,000 livres "to complete a building destined for the confinement of people of evil ways (*mauvaise vie*)".[92]

In the 1670s, the greatly increased demands of the king and the new fiscal edicts issued in 1669–73 galvanized the Estates into a series of more pointed remonstrances. In 1671, they demanded that all edicts issued since 1669 be sent to Parlement for registration, attacked the broadened powers given to sergeants and clerks (*greffiers*), demanded the lower traditional fees for presentations to courts and the reduction to old levels of the fines for false appeal. Article 7 summed up the general principle: the Estates demanded the abolition of all the edicts on the grounds that there could be no new taxation in Brittany without their consent. Article 8 introduced an issue that would dominate later meetings,

---

[91] ADIV, C 2782. The complaints of the nobles and ecclesiastics focused on the issue of the exemption of noble and church lands, and, in the case of the latter, on tithes. They claimed that the tax assessors assessed both *métairies nobles* and the tithe incomes of collectors, and that the assessors even demanded taxes from those living in noble houses. The nobles claimed this was an effort to introduce the *taille personnelle* "which has never been suffered in Brittany." Even commoners living in noble houses were exempt from the *fouage*.

[92] ADIV, C 2783. Grant of 17 September 1665.

the announced reformation of the king's demesne. In article 11, they requested that high justiciars keep their traditional jurisdiction over cases such as "*rapt* and removal of persons by violence." In 1673, it was much the same list of complaints, although the Estates asked the duchess of Chaulnes to intervene personally with the king to abolish the demesne reform. The main focus in 1673 was the abolition of the many edicts, a goal the Estates achieved by paying the dual grant of 5.2 million livres.[93]

Their success was short-lived; the king reintroduced many of the edicts in 1674–5. The stamped paper edict touched off a rebellion in Rennes and other cities, and contributed to the massive peasant uprising of the Bonnets Rouges. The Estates of 1675 were at great pains to assure the king of the loyalty of the province: the troubles were "caused, for the most part, by people without occupation or goods, carried away more by a spirit of pillage than of revolt and by the fear that His Majesty had conceived some evil suppressions against the general good of the province (which has never gone outside the respect, submission, obedience and fidelity due to His Majesty)." The Estates sent a special delegation – the bishop of Saint-Malo (Sébastien de Guémaduec), the duke of Rohan, and the mayor of Nantes (Jean Charette) – to beg the king's forgiveness. The Estates also solicited the return of the Parlement to Rennes, arguing that the court's exile to Vannes was ruining the members of the court and all the tradespeople of Rennes. The court would spend fifteen years in exile.[94]

The three people in this delegation are an interesting example of change and continuity in Breton politics. The Estates clearly sent the three most eminent statesmen they could muster. Guémadeuc was from an old, prominent family, one intermarried with all of the other major noble clans; he was also, as we will see in chapter 7, one of the two individuals most responsible for putting down the rebellion. Jean Charette was the seneschal and mayor of Nantes. His family had held that office since the late sixteenth century. The Charettes were often at odds with the other leading Nantais families, particularly since the Charettes had supported Henry IV rather than the League in the civil war of 1589–98. Jean Charette had been instrumental in putting down the uprising at Nantes and he was from a family with impeccable royalist credentials.[95]

---

[93] ADIV, C 2785. The Estates had long been an admirer of the duchess; in 1671, they gave her a special purse containing 2,000 gold *louis* as a gift. Mme. de Sévigné discusses at length the important social role of women at the Estates in her letters of late August 1671 to Mme. de Grignan. The Estates were quite grateful for the hospitality they received from various people. In 1669, for example, they began the practice of special grants to the presidents of the three orders and to their wives. The Estates usually granted 14,000 livres to the presidents of the First and Second Estates, 2,000 livres to their households, but only 11,000 livres and 1,000 livres to the head of the Third.

[94] As Mme. de Sévigné put it, "Rennes without that [Parlement] is not worth Vitré" (*Lettres*, I, 892, letter of 27 October 1675 to Mme. de Grignan).

[95] J. Collins, "Police Authority and Local Politics at Nantes, 1550–1680."

The duke of Rohan is another matter. The 1651 conflict between Rohan and la Trémoille is yet another example of the clientage wars after the death of Richelieu. As Sharon Kettering has pointed out, Mazarin was not able to pick up Richelieu's clientage networks intact. He lost control of Provence, Burgundy, and Guyenne, to cite only the three most serious cases.[96] In Brittany, la Meilleraye was briefly named governor but passed the office to Anne of Austria; however, la Meilleraye remained the main instrument of royal power. Pontchâteau had died in 1641; his son was only six at the time.

The power vacuum encouraged a revival of the Rohan–la Trémoille rivalry. La Trémoille won the short-term battle; the king decided in his favor in 1651 and he served again as president of the Second Estate in 1653 and 1655. In the long run, however, the situation shifted considerably in the 1650s and early 1660s. Henri de la Trémoille passed his Breton holdings to a son, Henri-Charles, in 1661; the duke of la Meilleraye had done the same in 1654. Pontchâteau's son, Armand, married to Marie Séguier, daughter of the chancellor, continued the father's meteoric rise; by 1659, he was president of the Second Estate (a position he filled again in 1665). In 1663, his holdings in Coislin and Pontchâteau became the duchy-peerage of Coislin.[97] In the same year, the la Meilleraye family, heirs to the fabulous wealth of Cardinal Mazarin, also received a peerage.

In an atmosphere of such upheaval, it was small wonder that the Rohan family was able to reestablish its preeminence in the province. The la Trémoilles had the misfortune of two generations dying within two years (1672, 1674), so that, in 1675, the duke of Rohan was incontestably the leading noble of Brittany. The family was suddenly on the best of terms with the court. Anne de Soubise, daughter of the aged duchess, Marguerite de Rohan-Chabot, may have been Louis XIV's mistress in the early 1670s. Anne's husband, François, prince of Guéméné and duke of Montbazon, became lieutenant general of the king's armies. Louis XIV's choice of governor fell on the duke of Chaulnes, nephew of Marie de Rohan, duchess of Luynes and later of Chevreuse. Chaulnes's nephew, in turn, married the daughter of Colbert.[98] The lieutenant general for the king in Brittany, replacing la Meilleraye (*fils*) in 1663, was Malo II of Coëtquen; Coëtquen was married to Marguerite II of Rohan-Chabot, another of the duchess' daughters. By 1670, the Rohan family had extremely close ties to the two major Breton military officers (although Chaulnes and Coëtquen detested each other) and an intimate link with the king himself. In such a context, it is little wonder that the Estates of 1675 chose to send the duke of Rohan as their representative to the king.

---

[96] Kettering, *Patrons, Clients and Brokers*, ch. 4.
[97] Guillotin de Corson, *Grandes seigneuries*, III, chapter on barony of Pontchâteau.
[98] This was the same Marie de Rohan so involved both in the Chalais conspiracy of 1626 and in the Fronde.

Mme. de Sévigné wrote to her daughter (17 November 1675) expressing astonishment that Rohan had chosen to make the journey: "Il est sans exemple qu'un président de la noblesse ait jamais fait une pareille voyage." In a second letter (20 November), she mentions that the Estates armed their deputation with 2,000 *pistoles* each, in order to make the necessary bribes at Court. In a series of letters on the outcome of the mission, she first says the bishop of Saint-Malo (Guémadeuc) was "badly received" by the Estates, who felt he had bungled the negotiations at Saint-Germain. The duke of Rohan was reported to be so incensed that he deliberately avoided a simultaneous return with Guémadeuc. The latter presented the king's response to the delegation as a great favor, while Rohan found the "tristesse où est cette province" a poor setting for "the slightest pleasure." As for Guémadeuc, he stated: "vous croyez que c'est les prières de quarante heures? C'est le bal à toutes les dames, et un grand souper: ç'a été un scandale public."[99]

Rohan was closer to the mark; the king had hardly been generous in his response to the situation. If anything, the issuance of *rentes* necessitated by the debacle of 1675 drew the province more tightly into the net of royal finances. The king did not relent in his other pressures; he continued to demand the complete reformation of the royal demesne, with mandatory (written) justification for all alienations made since 1532.

In 1679, the Estates shifted the focus of their remonstrances from the rebellion issues to the demesne reform. This issue was of the greatest possible importance to the landed nobles because the king threatened to demand the return of lands alienated or sold (in the case of heaths and commons) to others since 1532. The king also wanted to investigate the "quality" of lands; that is, he wanted to check on the legitimacy of claims that a given piece of land was "noble" (and thus tax exempt). The remonstrances against the investigation of the demesne ran on for 26.5 pages; the Estates cited the ravages of war and storage for the difficulty of producing written titles, argued that local custom only required forty years of noble ownership to make land noble and that the rule for titles on royal demesne lands was 100 years of proof (an important issue in 1679 because most of the alienations took place in the period 1558–76), and noted that communities would be ruined by the costs of proving their right to communal lands. The subsidiary complaints of 1679 attacked the stamped paper tax, the gunpowder monopoly, the pewter tax, and the usual grounds for complaint (Breton benefices, troops, etc.).[100]

What is one to make of the actions of the Estates in the 1660s and 1670s? First, we must recognize that they often defended the general interests of all in

---

[99] Sévigné, *Lettres*, I, letters of 17 and 20 November 1675 (Letters 366 and 367). Quotation on the dance in letter of 15 December 1675 (letter 374). Guémadeuc was so disgraced that a nephew had to defend the bishop's honor in a duel against an unnamed noble from Lower Brittany.
[100] ADIV, C 2785.

the province. They defended the liberty of commerce, took the side of merchants against new seigneurial and town transit taxes, and acted vigorously to reserve a place for Bretons in the emerging colonial market in the West Indies. They opposed new taxes of any kind and demanded the general maintenance of all Breton privileges: use of Breton courts, exemption from French taxes, the vote of all taxation, the registration of all edicts at the Parlement. In short, they defended what they perceived to be the existing order: not primarily a class interest or an order interest but the interest of all in the maintenance of order, specifically, the system of order in place. If that system of order prospered, the dominant position of the ruling class (and order) would be secure.

They defended the nobles' order-based interests by opposing the extension of hereditary nobility to the auditors of accounts and the *secrétaires du roi* and by opposing the Parlement's claims to precedence in public places. They defended the nobles' class interests by reviewing and defining the incidence rules for the greatly increased direct taxation of the 1660s and 1670s and by opposing so bitterly the reformation of the king's demesne. This last issue was critical to many nobles (and to the Church), because a considerable portion of their lands had been bought or accreted from the royal demesne. An investigation of such frauds and purchases could have ruined many noble families.[101] The Estates also defended the political position of the nobility in the 1670s, when they opposed the shift of jurisdiction over cases of abduction from high justiciars to the presidial courts.

The Estates' most important interest was to keep down the level of direct taxation because the tenants of large landowners (both noble and non-noble) paid the lion's share of the direct taxes. The nobles largely succeeded in achieving the goal of low direct taxation. In some years during the 1660s, the levy came to 2.25 times the old level, and the direct taxes of the 1670s reached 2.5 times the traditional level. Despite such a massive increase, Breton direct taxation remained very low in comparison with such levies in the rest of France. In the middle of the seventeenth century, it is likely that one Frenchman in ten lived in Brittany, yet the province paid less than 3 percent of French direct taxes.[102]

By way of contrast, Breton taxation on wine quadrupled between 1610 and 1640. If we go back to the 1580s, we would find that the wine tax levels of Henry IV were roughly four times those in effect under Henry III. Between 1583 and

---

[101] That is the impression one gets from both the great financial investigation of 1583 (ADLA, B 12,871) and the sale of royal waste lands of 1644–6 (ADLA, B 2461), each of which shows extensive noble (and legal class) possession of royal demesnes and waste lands.

[102] Collins, *Fiscal Limits of Absolutism*, appendix tables on general tax levels, which, in the *pays d'élection*, reached 35 million livres by the mid–1630s: Brittany paid about 500,000 livres at that time. With the increase of 1643, Brittany paid about one million livres in a total collection of about 40 to 42 million livres (including the entire kingdom).

1643 direct taxation declined by an indeterminate amount (certainly by 20 percent or more), while the duty on a pipe of imported wine rose from 2.5 livres to 40 livres. In the 1650s, the Estates changed the nature of the *petit devoir*, from a tiny surtax on wine sales to a substantial levy in its own right (generally leased for 33–40 percent of the *grand devoir* price), and added steadily heavier taxes on eau-de-vie. The nobles kept taxes off other commodities of interest to them, such as grain (as we have seen, the grants of the 1570s included export duties on grain). They also used the Estates to obtain exemption from the *ban et arrière-ban*. New nobles sought and obtained exemption from the *francs fiefs*, which had been levied in Brittany throughout the sixteenth century.[103]

The protection could be even more specific. The duke of la Trémoille, who often (as baron of Laval) presided over the nobility, received the support of the Estates to obtain dispensation from paying the *lods et ventes* for his purchase of the marquisate of Espinay. The Estates even included this matter in their contract with the king in 1647, when they reached an agreement with the king on the matter, and in 1649, when they sought to ensure that he kept the agreement.[104]

The relationship between the Estates and the Crown had two sides. On the one hand, the position of the Estates grew progressively weaker in the second quarter of the seventeenth century. They were less and less able to resist the demands of the king, particularly his demands for advances (forcing them into ruinous interest payments). The debts of the Estates, which had been of the order of 150,000 livres in 1620, rose to over one million livres in the mid 1640s and remained at 800,000 livres even in the mid 1650s.[105] By 1679, the Estates had sold *rentes* of 1.6 million livres and had a shorfall of 1.9 million livres more on their accounts for 1677–8. The Estates of the late 1620s clamored for the king to respect the traditional date for calling the annual meeting – 25 September – and complained that the irregular pattern of meetings between 1626 and 1630 had disrupted normal administrative practice in the province. In 1649 and 1651, the Estates requested that they should *not* be called for another two years.

On the other hand, the Estates saw their resources increase greatly in this period and they continued to be able to set the form of Breton taxation. They successfully avoided the introduction of standard French bureaucratic forms into the province and maintained the local officer elite at a remarkably small size. Breton offices, precisely for that reason, usually sold at a premium: a treasurer of France, worth some 50,000 livres in most jurisdictions in the 1630s, was worth 130,000 livres in Brittany. The two Breton Sovereign Courts

---

[103] Levied most recently in 1566 and 1539. See the contracts of 1638, 1641, and 1643. The 1645 and 1649 contracts (ADLA, B 79, fols. 5–11 and 307–10v), as well as papers of the Estates (ADIV, C 2778, 2779) on the grain export requests.

[104] ADLA, B 78, fols. 166v–173; B 79, fols. 5–11.

[105] ADIV, C 2757, special report of the treasurer; C 2980–1, accounts of the late 1630s, 1640s, and 1650s.

remained closely integrated into local elites. The landed nobility dominated the Parlement and turned it increasingly into a closed oligarchy.

The Breton solution worked well for both parties. The king got more money and, what was more important in the 1640s and 1650s, he got a reliable source of money. The Breton elites maintained control of the province, protecting their clients, and thus their own financial interests. The system broke down in the 1670s, perhaps because of division among the elites or because of the actions of the governor, the duke de Chaulnes, whom the bishop of Dol accused of taking a bribe (*pot de vin*) of 700,000 livres from the great duty farmers.[106] The landlords exacted relentless contributions from the peasants. The wine taxes of the king struck hard at the towns and the wine-growing regions. The Breton economy, in part because of the heavy indirect taxation, began to suffer in the 1640s. The combination of factors – economic slump, ineffective political leadership, draconian seigneurial practices, heavy royal indirect taxes – led to a cataclysm, the revolts of 1675.

There were two revolts in 1675, the Papier Timbré of the towns and the Bonnets Rouges of the countryside. The town revolt, against yet another royal tax, needs little explanation: it was one more in the series of endemic anti-tax rebellions of seventeenth-century France (although it was the last major one). The upper classes, as was so often the case, provided active support to the lower in their rebellion against the king. The king certainly believed that the Breton elite had a hand in the matter: he banished the Parlement to Vannes for fifteen years, the most severe exile ever enforced on any Parlement, for its ineffectiveness in dealing with the rebels at Rennes. Indeed, his anger was so great at the rebellions that he ordered all court records related to them to be destroyed. It is a tribute to the administrative monarchy's ability to execute effectively a limited action such as this one that very few records of the rebellion have come down to us, so that it is the least known of all the great seventeenth-century rebellions. Even in the papers of the Estates, there are few mentions of so great a rebellion.

The Bonnets Rouges rebellion, while it came under the same administrative order concerning destruction of records, was a separate revolt, although it, too, began as a demonstration against the new indirect taxes. In Cornouaille especially, the peasants burned chateaux, destroyed seigneurial records, demanded access to woods and water, to common grazing lands, and protested against misappropriation of tithes. They also attacked the towns, particularly Carhaix, at the center of the heaths of inner Cornouaille. The peasants

---

[106] Pocquet, *Histoire de Bretagne*, V, gives the details of the letter by the bishop accusing de Chaulnes. The duke has not fared well in Breton folklore. P. Hélias, *The Horse of Pride* (New Haven, 1978), 281, relates that: "Whenever he told that family story, to serve as guidance for us all, my grandfather never failed to explain his ancestor's behavior, recalling two other uncles or cousins of old who had been hung from the Guilguiffin trees after the 'Bonnets Rouges' rebellion – hung by the Duc de Chaulnes, the cursed duke, may he never cease boiling in hell-fire, even after Doomsday, the bastard!"

especially directed their animosity against the legal professionals of the towns. In a group of peasant articles, drawn up in the Concarneau region, the two main targets of complaint stand out: the justice system and the seigneurs.

With the exception of the wine tax, which the peasants wanted to be cut by 75 percent, they offered no complaints against royal taxes other than the newly introduced stamped paper and pewter levies (the former listed among the high costs of justice), and the tobacco monopoly. They made no serious complaints against royal direct taxation, a remarkable contrast to all other seventeenth-century French peasant rebellions. The Bonnets Rouges was the only major seventeenth-century French peasant rebellion aimed against the seigneurs rather than the king. The peasants, in this eloquent manner, tell us of the success of the Breton elite in preserving its power, even in the day of the Sun King.

6

The burden of Breton taxation

Who benefited from this system? That question is easily answered: the king and the local elite, especially noble landlords. Who paid for it – the reverse side of the issue – is a more complex question. The contribution per *feu* and the number of *feux* had both become fixed in custom by the middle of the sixteenth century, so that any increases in direct taxation had to come from immediate military necessities. The king often levied military taxes between 1562 and 1598, peaking in the period 1589–97, but in the seventeenth century, save for local levies between 1614 and 1617 and again in 1628, he rarely did so.

Brittany had some 35,000 *feux* but the forced sales of *feux* in 1577, 1638, and 1640 sharply reduced that number.[1] In 1577, the sales did not include the western part of the province – no sales took place in Léon, Tréguier, and Cornouaille – so the sales of 1638 fell disproportionately there. We can compare the evolution of the number of *feux* between 1577 and 1640 in table 22.[2] The example of the lawsuits over the tax assessments of Gévezé (see chapter 3) indicates that, by the seventeenth century, Bretons believed that a *feu* represented a given amount of cultivable land, rather than a fixed number (three) of actual households. Such an interpretation may have existed from the start, because a *ménage* could well have been interpreted to mean a *manse*, defined as a given area of land, rather than as an actual household. However one chooses to define the *feu*, it is clear that a *feu* bore no relationship to population after 1550.

A fair number of tax rolls from the sixteenth and seventeenth centuries survive, for both Breton rural and urban parishes, so that we can see who among our original economic groups or classes paid the taxes. Breton villages had a markedly more equal tax distribution than French ones. In Brittany, the top quartile paid an average of 60 percent of the taxes, whereas in France, it was 70–5 percent.[3] The broad comparison is misleading, however, because of several factors creating a more equal division in Brittany. The total amount levied was much smaller, so that the highest assessments (usually in the range 7–15 livres) were much closer to the bottom (1 or 2 sous) than was the case in

---

[1] ADLA, B 3009, *feux* count in 1617.
[2] ADLA, B 3009, B 2987 (1630), B 713 (1589), B 3010 (1652), B 2994, sale of 1638, B 2990 (1645). [3] J. Collins, *Fiscal Limits of Absolutism* (Berkeley, 1988), ch. 4.

Table 22: Feux *sales of 1577, 1638, 1640; total* feux, *1640*

Bishopric	1577 sale	1638 sale	1640 sale	1640 *feux*
Rennes	139	162	138	2,833
Fougères-Vitré	83	49	63	1,245
Nantes	111	296	286	5,693
Vannes	271	56	228	4,502
Cornouaille	0	363	201	4,023
Léon	0	181	102	1,885
Treguir	0	251	182	3,520
Saint-Brieuc	233	14	184	3,599
Saint-Malo	297	30	211	4,316
Dol	59	45	40	824
Totals	1,193	1,447	1,635	32,440

Sources: AD Loire-Atlantique, B 3009; B 2987; B 713; B 3010.

France, where the top assessments could be several hundred livres.[4] Custom fixed the Breton levies, offering less likelihood of variation. The *domaine congéable* leasing systems of much of the province tended to even out assessments: the large-scale tenants (*tenuyers*) of *domaines congéables* paid less than *métayers* would have done because the landlord, receiving one-third of the *gross* production, had no share in costs (seed, tithe, tax).

Let us examine several individual parishes and then come back to the general issues at hand. The parish of Audierne, a fishing town and associated hamlets, had 235 taxpayers in 1616, assessed for a median contribution of 7 sous; 196 of 242 taxpayers paid less than 1 livre.[5] The parish was typical in most other respects: the top quartile paid 60.9 percent of the taxes, the bottom 6.1 percent (this last figure a bit higher than normal – see table 23). Audierne had a large number of women on the roll: 14.7 percent of the taxpayers, paying 11.3 percent of the taxes. The highest assessment fell to a woman, Anne Le Deuffic; she and her son-in-law paid 8 livres.

The roll for 1619 also survives and we see another typical phenomenon, the annual disappearance of many of the taxpayers: 11.6 percent disappeared, 15.3 percent if we count the nine known deaths.[6] Those who disappeared came

---

[4] In the 1640s, assessments of 100–250 livres were quite common in Saint-Ouen-de-Breuil (Normandy) and Augé (Poitou); it is likely that such assessments were not paid, or not paid in full, in many parishes. J. Jacquart, *La crise rurale en Ile-de-France, 1550–1670* (Paris, 1974), gives similar figures for the *laboureurs* of that region in the 1640s to 1660s.

[5] ADF, 16 G 1.

[6] The civil registers for Audierne do not survive; the known deaths are those on the roll in 1616 but whose places are taken by their widows or heirs in 1619.

Table 23: *Quartile distribution; tax rolls of selected parishes*

Tax distribution by quartile	I	II	III	IV
Massérac	63.9	21.5	10.3	4.3
Lannion	61.9	22.0	10.9	5.2
Carhaix (1603)	61.0	25.3	10.8	3.0
Audierne	60.9	20.2	12.8	6.1
Loc Eguiner	58.9	20.3	13.3	7.4
Carhaix (1668)	58.2	21.4	13.8	6.7
Langourla	56.6	25.9	12.8	4.8
Assérac	55.0	22.0	14.6	8.5
Lanvaudan	52.1	26.9	16.9	4.1
Muzillac	51.2	31.4	14.1	3.4
Nantes Saint-Nicholas	78.0	15.1	5.9	1.0

Note: All percentages rounded to nearest tenth, thus some totals do not add up to 100.0.

Sources: Massérac (ADLA, G 440); Lannion (ADIV, 1 F, de la Borderie papers); Carhaix (ADF, 2 E 1501–2); Audierne (ADF, 16 G 1); Loc Eguiner (ADF, 125 G 2); Langourla (ADF, 1 F 1640); Assérac (ADLA, G 348); Lanvaudan (ADM, G 853); Muzillac (ADM, B 2782); Nantes (AM de Nantes, GG 743–4 – 1586; CC 86 – 1593).

overwhelmingly from the bottom quartiles; sixteen of the twenty-eight disappeared individuals paid less than 5 sous and only three more than 20 sous. As in Carhaix or Massérac, the disappeared tended to be the only person of their surname in the parish. Of the 136 taxpayers who shared a surname with someone else, only seven disappeared (5.1 percent); of the 105 taxpayers who did not share their surname, 21 disappeared (20 percent). Rural taxpayers had lower assessments than those who lived in the bourg of Audierne; in fact, only one person living outside of Audierne itself paid more than 1 livre.

The same patterns recur in the other parishes, both rural and urban. Using a sample of nine parishes (table 23), we find that all but one lay in the range 55–64 percent of their tax burden on the first quartile. In fact, this figure probably warps the true distribution of land and income even among the taxpayers. In the west, there is the problem of the *domaine congéable*, and the reduced rates of the *tenuyers*.[7] As the largest parts of the parishes lay under this form of tenure, the largest blocks of land were substantially under-assessed. In the three rural

---

[7] T. J. A. Le Goff, *Vannes and Its Region* (Oxford, 1981).

parishes clearly in the region of the *domaine congéable* – Loc Eguiner, Langourla, and Lanvaudan – the first quartile paid under 59 percent of the taxes. By way of contrast, in the one full parish outside of the *domaine congéable* region, Massérac, the first quartile paid 63.9 percent of the taxes.[8]

The remarkably low average assessments also contributed to the relatively equal tax distribution. When we get to a tax not bound by custom, such as the poor relief assessment in Nantes in 1586, we find the top quartile of the parish of Saint-Nicolas (a mixed area of rich and poor) paying 78.1 percent of the taxes.[9] Even within balanced Breton villages, the richer peasants (often, indeed usually, tenants) paid the lion's share. Thus in the *frairie* of Tréhiguier in the parish of Assérac (bishopric of Nantes), the three "métairies roturières" paid 3.4, 6.25, and 8.7 livres, respectively: in all, some 9 percent of the tax burden. Two belonged to a "sieur de" and the third to "honourable homme" François Guillory, who also possessed the "héritages roturières appartenant au sieur du Bezit," assessed at another 3.15 livres, and a third piece of land assessed at 3.55 livres. The *métayers* of these landlords were often quite rich in their own right: Guillaume le Bolhet, *métayer* of the *sieur* de Carmallo, paid 9 livres for his own possessions. At the parish of La Fontenelle, in the bishopric of Rennes, the roll of a 1679 "extraordinary *taille*" lists eighteen *métayers* among the taxpayers. On average, they were assessed for just under 3.5 sous for their own property but for 17.8 sous for the lands they held in *métayage*.[10]

In terms of our original groups, we can see the rich had a fairly complex relationship to the tax system. For those landlords whose lands were held in *domaines congéables*, there was no tax burden. Landlords in the *pays Nantais* or other parts of the province in which *métayage* was common, likely paid a share of their tenants' taxes: in the case of *métayage*, an equal split was common in many parts of France.[11] In all cases, however, the tenant's tax obligations interfered with his or her ability to pay rent. Entry fees presented the most direct conflict, because they, like royal taxes, had to be paid in cash. The legal profession landlords shared the concerns of noble landlords; the lower level members of this group, like the notaries of Massérac, often had to contribute to the direct taxes in their own name. The lists from the sale of exemptions in 1638 and 1640, when legal men or their widows bought many of the exemptions, here strengthen the evidence from the tax rolls.

The merchants often held exemptions from the *fouage* because they lived in towns, such as Nantes or Rennes, that did not have to pay. The merchants and legal class paid the lion's share of direct taxes in the towns, such as the levies for the 50,000 infantrymen in the sixteenth century, the special collections for poor relief, and the enormous military taxes of the 1590s. In the seventeenth century,

---

[8] ADF, 125 G 2 (Loc Eguiner), ADIV 1 F 1640 (Langourla); ADM, G 853 (Lanvaudan); ADLA, G 440 (Massérac).   [9] AM de Nantes, GG 743.   [10] ADIV, G La Fontanelle.
[11] Collins, *Fiscal Limits of Absolutism*, 187–94.

such expedients seem to have been less common, because the towns had much greater permanent resources and had less recourse to extraordinary levies. The small tradesmen, therefore, had few direct taxes to pay in a town such as Nantes or Vitré. The only town exempt from the *fouage* which seems to have used substantial direct taxes in the seventeenth century was Rennes; much of this money went to cover the enormous expense of building the Palais de Justice for the Parlement.[12]

In the countryside, the richer peasants – the *laboureurs*, *tenuyers*, and *métayers* – paid most of the taxes, just as they did in France. The top quartile invariably consisted of such peasants and of the non-exempt members of the legal professions, and the occasional merchant. In small Breton towns, such as Carhaix or Audierne, merchants and legal people made up a more considerable block of the first quartile. The small occupiers filled the bottom half of the first quartile and all of the second. The landless, and perhaps a few of the poorer small occupiers, made up the bottom half of the roll. Along with these basic class divisions, however, we must also consider the gender division of the taxpayers, because women formed 15 to 25 percent of the taxpayers in virtually all parishes.

The role of women in these parishes is difficult to assess because of the vagaries of the rolls (table 24). A woman could be listed in a variety of different ways. At Lannion, in 1641, for example, we find: Marguerite Le dautec (single or a widow?); Jacquette Le mogueron, widow of Penhuel; the widow of Hervé Berthou (her own name not given); Yvon Bodeveur and Janne Bizich, his wife (why is this particular woman listed, when most wives are not?); Martin Auti, husband of Catherine Le Rueult (why is he listed as her husband and not, as in all other cases, she as his wife?); and Marie Queraulen and her son-in-law (was she a widow?). The listings often raise as many questions as they answer. It is often unclear why a married woman is listed, although one suspects that the woman in question had established herself as a "marchande publique."[13] In a rural parish, she might very well have co-signed the lease of their tenancy, a practice increasingly common in the seventeenth century. In the case of Mme. Le Rueult, her occupation may well have been more lucrative than that of M. Auti, her husband, so the roll duly noted her preeminence; it is likely that she followed this profession *before* their marriage.

In following a practice of counting as widows only women listed as widows, we find many hearths headed by single, never-married women. The towns had far more such hearths than the countryside. At Carhaix, for example, the 1603 roll listed thirty-two widows and thirty-three single women among the 266 taxpayers (24.4 percent). These women paid 16.6 percent of the taxes.[14] The roll shows three large clusters of women – fifteen of fifty taxpayers in the opening group,

---

[12] ADLA, B 79, fols. 256–7v, renewal of duties of 1649, is one example among many of their complaints on this score. See also Croix, *La Bretagne*, I, ch. X.
[13] ADIV, 1 F 1640, special sub-series, papers of A. de la Borderie.   [14] ADF, 2 E 1501.

Table 24: *Percentages of Women on the tax rolls of selected parishes*

Parish	Percentage of women	Percentage of women's assessment
Carhaix (1603)	24.4	16.6
Langourla (1652)	21.0	18.5
Massérac (1665)	19.0	7.0
Loc Eguiner (1672)	15.3	14.0
Audierne (1616)	14.7	11.3
Lanvaudan (1635)	14.2	10.0
Lannion (1641)	13.4	10.4
Lannion (1651)	10.3	9.7
Muzillac (1558)	10.3	6.0
Nantes		
Saint-Léonard (1593)	21.6	n.a.
Saint-Laurent (1597)	20.4	23.4
Saint-Denis (1586)	14.0	9.0
Saint-Nicolas (1586)	11.4	7.5
Ten parishes (1586)	10.0	n.a.
Seven parishes (1593)	9.0	n.a.

Sources: Massérac (ADLA, G 440); Lannion (ADIV, 1 F, de la Borderie papers); Carhaix (ADF, 2 E 1501); Audierne (ADF, 16 G 1); Loc Eguiner (ADIV, 125 G 2); Langourla (ADIV, 1 F 1640); Assérac (ADLA, G 348); Lanvaudan (ADM, G 853); Muzillac (ADM, B 2782); Nantes (AM de Nantes, GG 743 – 1586; CC 86 – 1593).

eight of twenty-four (seven of fifteen in one stretch) on the rue Saint-Augustin, and nine of twenty-seven (eight of sixteen in one area) on the place aux Charbons. In these last two clusters, thirteen of seventeen women belonged to the fourth quartile. The clusters suggest an employment pattern, perhaps one related to textiles (much produced in the region).

The rural parish of Langourla, in the bishopric of Saint-Brieuc, provides a more thorough, albeit also confusing, presentation of the issues related to women. Langourla had 283 taxpayers, of whom fifty-nine (21 percent) were women. The roll only identifies nine of these women as widows. In addition, another forty-two assessments listed a woman: thirty-six husband–wife combinations, three men listed with their mother, two with a daughter, and one with a sister-in-law. The women listed alone paid an average of 12 sous, 5 below the parish-wide figure, yet the averages mask the reality: forty-one of the fifty-nine women paid less than the 12-sous average.[15] The households co-listing a

[15] ADIV, 1 F 1640.

woman with a man paid 22.5 percent of the taxes, so that households listing a woman paid 41 percent of the taxes. The large number of women co-listed almost certainly reflects the presence of *domaines congéables*, which could not be subdivided; the widow received one-half of the land of the couple, so that widows were frequently partners of surviving children. In Breton inheritance customs for *roturiers*, daughters also had rights equal to those of sons, so that many women inherited land or shares in a *domaine congéable*.[16]

The parishes show two groups of women: rich or middling widows and a large group of extremely poor women clustered at the bottom of the roll. In a rural parish, single women almost always belonged to this second group; in towns, they often had the same distribution within the roll as widows. A substantial portion of the widows, usually half or so, could also be found in this poor cluster. Lanvaudan had the typical pattern: fifteen widows and seven single women among 154 taxpayers. The widows spread out among the quartiles; the single women included six members of the fourth quartile, five of whom paid either one or two sous in taxes.[17] The general distribution of women heads of households, in Brittany as elsewhere in France, was that some 20 percent of the women were well off, another 30 percent at the middling level, and 50 percent in desperate poverty.[18] Poor women are always found at the bottom, not the top of the fourth quartile.

We can get a better sense of these poor women in the remarkable documentation preserved for Nantais relief efforts in the 1580s, which include a number of parish relief tax rolls for the city itself, as well as considerable information on a number of the rural parishes receiving such relief.[19] In the city, the relief roll of the parish of Sainte-Radégonde, near the port, shows that women headed eleven of the seventeen households on relief: six widows, three single women, and two abandoned wives.[20] In a sample of seven rural parishes, in which the relief effort focused on families with children, however, women made up 20.2 percent of the heads of households on relief. Just over 13 percent of the listed children lived in a household headed by a woman. An eighth parish, Carquefou, has a more detailed roll than any other. Women headed 30 percent of the poor households of Carquefou; 91 percent of these households had an adult woman. The younger widows had fewer children than the couples, roughly 2.7 as against 3.2 per couple.[21]

The relief tax rolls of Nantes for 1586 reinforce the picture of the large numbers of women living in poverty. We find a lower number of women heads of households on these rolls because they exclude the poor (who are, of course,

[16] *Coutume générale des pays et duché de Bretagne* (Rennes, 1581), article 587. See also Le Goff, *Vannes*, 235.   [17] ADM, G 853.
[18] J. Collins, "The Economic Role of Women in Seventeenth-Century France," *French Historical Studies*, 16, (2) (Fall 1989): 436–70, tables 1 and 2.   [19] AM de Nantes, GG 743.
[20] AM de Nantes, CC 86.   [21] AM de Nantes, GG 743.

the object of the relief being collected from those assessed on the roll). At Saint-Clément, likely the poorest parish of Nantes, women headed only 6 of 68 households; at Saint-Saturnin, a mixed parish of rich and poor, it was 22 of 177, yet 5 of these women paid nothing. In the city as a whole, there were 66 women among the 667 people on the list; of these women, 13 were listed as paying "nothing" or listed with a blank amount: 19.7 percent. By way of contrast, only 38 of the 601 men were so listed: 6.3 percent. Eighteen of the women belonged to the first quartile (11.6 percent), including the widow Perrin in Saint-Saturnin, assessed at 24 livres, third highest on the existing rolls.[22]

The implication of these rolls is that widows headed roughly one household in five in Nantes. If we accept the typical division of widows on a tax roll as normative for Nantes, that is, roughly half of the widows in the bottom quartile, we would expect to find a much lower level of widows heading households among the remaining groups. The rolls of 1586 do not include all households; indeed, there is only one parish in which the number of heads of households equals half the number on the 1593 fortifications tax. The highest percentages are in Notre-Dame, 36 of 80 (45 percent), and Saint-Saturnin, 160 of 307 (52 percent); the lowest in Saint-Léonard, 21 of 124 (17 percent) and Saint-Nicolas, 108 of 688 (16 percent).[23] Although many of those missing were quite well off (some parishes listed notable absentees at the end of the roll), the roll obviously under-represents the poor by a considerable amount. The number of assessees in 1586 was only 26.6 percent of the total listed (for the same parishes) in 1593. The poor parishes either left off most of their inhabitants, as was the case in Saint-Léonard and Saint-Nicolas, or assessed them for a pittance, as in Saint-Clément, where 41 of the 68 assessees paid 1 sou or less. Saint-Clément was the only parish to list people paying under 1 sou: twenty-eight of the sixty-seven people assessed for an actual amount paid 6 deniers or less. Aside from two people in the first quartile within the city, together paying 5 livres, the remaining sixty-six individuals in Saint-Clément paid a *total* of 6.55 livres. Twenty-six individuals in Nantes paid more for their personal assessment than the sixty-six parishioners of Saint-Clément combined.

In other parishes, these poor people were left off entirely; we would expect that they were often women. This conclusion is strengthened by the relief roll of Sainte-Radégonde (1580), on which 64.5 percent of the relief recipients were women.[24] The fortifications tax of 1593 provides a fuller picture, showing both the extent to which poor women could be excluded from the roll of a given parish, and the numbers of such women in parishes which did not exclude them. In the close-in suburbs of Nantes – Piremil, the Petite Biesse – we find virtually no women taxpayers in 1593. Even inside the walls, there were suspiciously few women in many parishes: in Sainte-Croix, there were twenty-eight women

---

[22] A. Croix, *Nantes et le pays nantais* (Paris, 1974), 207; rolls in AM de Nantes, GG 743.
[23] AM de Nantes, GG 743.   [24] AM de Nantes, CC 86.

among 270 taxpayers. Of these 28 women, two were exempt (reason not given), nine were well off (assessed at 30 livres or more), nine were assessed for between 6 and 24 livres, and eight for less than 5 livres. This is hardly the pattern with which we are familiar, with a large cluster of women at the bottom of the roll. The obvious question is: did the roll simply exclude poor women?

The roll for the poor parish of Saint-Léonard entirely confirms these suspicions. The roll listed 169 people, some of whom were absent from the parish or otherwise exempt, such as the Regent of the Collège Saint-Jean and his wife. The tax collectors specified at the end of the preamble to the roll that "the said commissioners have indiscriminately listed all people." The roll listed thirty-six women, ranging from Mlle. de la Fontaine Bonfilz, listed among the elite at the beginning of the roll but assessed for nothing, to the three poor widows, surviving by selling candles and washing clothes, who lived together in the house of Mathurin Nouzillan (along with Nouzillan and three other tenants). The three widows collectively paid 3 sous. In the parish as a whole, two women were exempt, two paid 6 livres each, one paid 18 livres, and the rest less than 3 livres. We find eleven *revendeuses* or candle sellers, six washerwomen, a teacher, a nursemaid, and a nurse among the thirty-four non-exempt women. Several women lived in attics – two poor women mercifully assessed for nothing shared one on the rue Saint-Léonard. We get a very different picture in Saint-Léonard: twelve widows, five wives, and sixteen other women (likely single). Among these sixteen, thirteen worked as laundresses, *revendeuses*, or candle sellers. The quartile distribution is also quite striking: ten women exempt due to poverty (including three soldiers' wives), fifteen women in the fourth quartile, two in the third, three each in the top two. Counting only those assessed for an actual amount, there were twenty-three women among the 121 taxpayers, 19 percent, yet they were assessed for only 3.5 percent of the taxes.

The figures from Saint-Léonard are a bit skewed, because three of the richest women in the parish were not assessed and because it was mainly a poor working-class area. The low percentage of the total paid by the women reflects the tremendously skewed general distribution: two people were assessed for 37 percent of the taxes, and the ten richest for two-thirds of the total. Of the 121 assessees, 75 were to pay a day's wages (10 sous) or less; 20 of these 75 were women. The overall image we receive at Nantes is that some 10 percent of the viable households were headed by women, but that an additional 10 to 15 percent of the households, as defined by the tax rolls, were female. This second group consisted primarily of women living alone, or with other, unrelated adult women, but it included some women (usually widows) with children.

In 1622, Saint-Malo assessed every inhabitant, "without exception," for a special tax to be used to pay for the upkeep of the poor of the hospital and those stricken by the "contagion" in the city. The roll is incomplete, in that it includes only 911 names, but it provides a broad cross section of another city's population. The first listing is for the city's clergy (excluding the bishop), who were assessed collectively for 900 livres. The total for the 911 named individuals was 7,630 livres. The 188 women on the roll (20.6 percent) were assessed for 1,474 livres or 19.3 percent of the total. As at Nantes, we see a broad mixture of women, both married and single. Only 58 of the 188 women are clearly identified as widows, although another 25 to 30 are listed in such a way as to imply that they were or had been married. Such women included people like Bertranne Crosmer and her daughters, assessed for 2 livres, or Lorance Boullaine, "wife of Thomas Ourson," assessed for 8 livres, or Guillemette Frotet, dame de la Vignette, assessed for 12.8 livres. She was part of the richest family of Saint-Malo, if the tax roll is any guide: the two largest assessments were for Nicolas Frotet and his son, Jean, 180 livres, and for Ollivier Frotet, *sieur* de la Touche, 100 livres. The largest woman's assessment fell to *demoiselle* Bertranne Frotet, 64 livres. Nicolas and Jean Frotet contributed more by themselves than the the 233 members of the fourth quartile. Indeed, two families, the Frotets and the Gravés, contributed more than the 400 smallest contributors combined.[25]

The roll irregularly lists occupation: 74 of the 911 taxpayers are identified by trade (seventy-three men and one woman). The roll identifies eight surgeons (a group no doubt singled out because of their possible utility in fighting the contagion), nine hatmakers, seven carpenters, and a wide variety of other artisans. These people were generally quite poor: thirty-one of the seventy-four paid 1 livre or less in taxes. These poor people were typically the hatmakers, carpenters, shoemakers, porters or weavers. The surgeons were better off, most notably Pierre Boullain, a member of a powerful Malouin mercantile family (Richard Boullain paid the fourth highest assessment, 72 livres), but François Jambon contributed only 1.6 livres and François Langlais a mere 2 livres. The highest contribution among these individuals was for another professional, Monsieur Sallazin, a doctor, who paid 12.8 livres. The highest contributions came from the great merchants – Frotet, Gravé, Boullain, Davy. The royal officers charged with the collection seem to have been extremely indulgent to their own purses: the seneschal, André Pepin, contributed only 24 livres, while Pierre Pepin, the *procureur fiscal*, paid only 16 livres and Michel Porée, the *alloué*, 32 livres. Robert Heurtant, the *procureur syndic* (and fourth collector), paid 60 livres, an amount more in keeping with the fortunes these men likely possessed.

The villages had a somewhat different pattern, as we have seen. There were fewer single women, therefore women headed a lower percentage of overall households. Rather than one household in five, it was more usually the case that women headed one household in seven. The general patterns in Breton villages, on this and other issues, are well represented by the situation in the parish of

---

[25] ADIV, citation lost.

Massérac, in the Vilaine valley near Redon. Massérac had a slightly more skewed tax distribution than typical Breton villages (it lies outside the *domaine congéable* region) but in most other respects it was quite typical: percentage of women heads of households, percentage of annual disappearances, overall levels of assessment. Alain Croix has estimated that the parish had some 450–500 people in 1600, perhaps 600 or more by the middle of the century. In Massérac, we have the tax rolls for 1665 to 1668, the civil registers for most of the seventeenth century, and many accounts of the *fabrique*, especially between 1600 and 1630.[26] There had been 20 *feux* at Massérac in the late fifteenth century; the duchess reduced the count to 19.5 *feux* in 1501. In 1645, the parish had 17.1 *feux*.[27] In 1665, the levies were 243.9 livres, which would be 14 livres 5 sous 3.5 deniers per *feu*, an accurate assessment of the levies of the time (excluding the *fouage extraordinaire*).

Massérac had eighteen tracts of lands or hamlets and the parish commons. The smallest tract, "La Bas la Peut," contributed nothing in 1665 and a small sum thereafter; the smallest regular contributor was Bas-Paimbien (4.75 livres in 1665), the largest, Paimbien (42.65 livres). The parish had a large number of shared surnames: thirteen surnames had five or more taxpayers. The average contribution was about 1.15 livres but the median contribution was closer to 15 sous. In fact, nearly two-thirds of the parishioners paid less than 1 livre, a remarkably light burden given that a day's wages were about 10 shillings, that a pound of grey bread went for a sou (at Nantes), and that a *pot* (1.8 liters) of Nantais wine sold for 6 sous – indeed, for as little as 3 in the taverns defrauding the duty farmers.[28]

We see all of our familiar patterns. The tenants of large landowners paid the largest assessments: *métayers* of the *sieur* de Boutaye, of the *sieur* Doumaine, and of the *sieur* de Grand Pré. Some of the most important villagers received scarcely a mention on the roll, as we see in the comparison of the civil registers and the roll. *Noble homme* Guillaume Macé, *sieur* de la Porte, whom we have met in chapter 2, is listed for 4.8 livres in 1665 and for 5.9 livres in 1666 and 1667. Macé was the seneschal of Massérac. One wonders about his assessment, should it have been higher? Similarly, was the 18-sous assessment of Jullien Hurtel, *procureur fiscal* of Massérac, too low? And what of Me. Benjamin Legendre, notary, assessed at 1.35 livres? What of *honourable homme* Jacques

[26] Croix, *Nantes et le pays nantais*, 215.
[27] ADLA, G 440; *fabrique* accounts in G 441; civil registers at town hall, unclassified. On hearth counts, ADLA, B 3009 and 3010. It should be emphasized that short-term military levies could substantially raise the annual burden. In 1614, Massérac spent 130 livres on troops; in 1615, it was 532 livres; in 1616, they borrowed 734 livres for this purpose. The records do not survive as to how they paid off this money, but most of it must have come from surtaxes on the *fouage*. As the regular *fouage* burden was some 245 livres a year, a one-shot levy to pay back the loans of 1615 would triple the regular burden and a levy for 1616's loans would more than quadruple it (raising the top assessments into the range 20–25 livres – still quite reasonable by French standards).
[28] Prices from AM de Nantes, CC 151 ff., accounts of the city government.

Thébaud, *greffier* of Massérac, assessed at 2.2 livres, while Pierre Thébaud, *laboureur*, paid 5.65 livres (perhaps even 8.75 livres)?[29]

The *rôle rentier* of 1608 offers some intriguing insights into the relationship between direct taxation and landholding, although the distance between the *rentier* and the first tax roll is considerable (fifty-seven years). The tax roll has 238 assessments but only 208 names (it is impossible to determine if some people are taxed in different locations or if it is simply a case of two or more people with the same name: the likely answer is a mixture of the two). The *rentier* lists 123 parcels, paying feudal rent of just over 23.5 livres. The leading landowners of Massérac in 1608 were Me. Mathurin Thomas, who paid 1.6 livres, Me. Guillaume Macé, who paid 1.25 livres, Me. Sébastien Thébaud, who paid 1.2 livres (along with Julien Amosse), and Jan Thébaud, who paid 1.55 livres. The ten richest individuals – from the Thébaud, Macé, De Rennes, Guerin, Rochedreux, Lebrun, Joubier, Legendre, and Thomas families – paid just under half of the total feudal rent. Nine of these ten families (Lebrun was the exception) were on the 1665 tax roll. The ten richest taxpayers contributed less than 15 percent of the total in 1665. The implication is that those in real control of the village – Macé, Thomas, Thébaud – paid substantially less than they should have done.

The intermarriage pattern within the village enhances our suspicions. As noted above in chapter 2, the village elite was thoroughly integrated: Thébaud, Thomas, Leclerc, Legendre, De Rennes, Hurtel, Provost – all intermarried. At the baptism of Marie Macé, daughter of Guillaume Macé and *damoiselle* Marguerite Landays, on 17 January 1663, however, we see a series of families who do not show up on the tax roll: Landays, Guichon (Guyschon), Rolland (there are no families of that name on the roll, but one of the hamlets is called Rolland), Blanchard, as well as priests from two of the major local families, De Rennes and Jullaud. These families, with the exception of Macé, De Rennes, and Jullaud, do not appear on the civil registers either. Macé belongs to an elite group of notaries and landowners; his witnesses come from that group, not from among the locals. The signatures of the witnesses, including those of two women – Marie Guyhard, widow of *noble homme* Roland Landays, and Janne Landais – are sharp, clear, and numerous (fifteen plus the *curé*).[30] Literacy was one of the hallmarks of this ruling village elite, a line of demarcation between the small town or village notable and even the richest peasants.

Macé belonged to this regional elite, and therefore stood well above regular village society, along with his cronies Hurtel and Thomas. The other major local families – De Rennes, Rochedreux – intermarried heavily and paid the bulk of the taxes. The twelve richest families paid about half of the tax burden in 1665, despite what would appear to be their clear under-assessment. In 1608, they

---

[29] ADLA, G 440.
[30] Civil registers of Massérac, list of 1663. Civil registers at town hall of Massérac, unclassified.

controlled about 60 percent of the land assessed for feudal rent; several of the substantial families of 1608 (such as Amosse and Canault) had disappeared by 1665, so that the land share of the twelve richest families in 1665 was likely closer to 80 than to 60 percent. At the other end of the scale, we find individuals such as Jan Mischert, paying 3 sous (and gone from the roll in 1666) or the six individuals listed as paying nothing in 1665 (some of whom paid a small amount in 1666). All told, about 38 percent of the taxpayers paid less than a day's wages in taxes.

Not all Breton parishes had the same tax distribution. The parish of Gévezé, about 15 kilometers north of Rennes on the road toward Dinan, shows a distribution much more similar to that of French parishes. Gévezé was a classic Breton large parish; in 1584, the *fouage* roll listed 530 assessments. In 1660, there were only 492 taxpayers, although there were 123 additional listings for people already on the roll (one listing for their own property, another listing for lands they farmed, perhaps a third for land over which they had tutorial responsibility). This "rural" parish therefore had some 2,500 inhabitants.[31] In 1584, the top quartile paid 79.5 percent of the taxes; in 1660, the figure had dropped to 74.6 percent. One problem for the villagers was that two of the richest families in the parish, Biet and Chauvin, had purchased *affranchissements* equivalent to two *feux*.[32]

Gévezé is somewhat atypical in others ways as well. The percentage of women declined slightly, from 16.2 to 14.8 percent, and their share of the taxes dropped more sharply, from 15.2 to 9.9 percent. In both cases, these declines are a contrast to the situation elsewhere in Brittany and France as a whole.[33] The 1660 roll may give evidence of a decline of the local textile industry, which would have employed many women. The highest assessments on the roll, for 9, 8.35, and 8 livres, respectively (two of them, Ollivier Chenart and Julien Larcher, described as "honourable homme," a phrase most often used for merchants), would imply annual assessments for all direct taxes of 30 to 35 livres.

The parishes varied when it came to such matters; at Assérac, in the *frairie* of Tréhiguier, the *lowest* assessment was 8 sous. The larger assessments were much higher than in Massérac – Marie Davy, widow of Guillaume Nicolas, 15.4 livres; *honourable homme* François Guillory, holder of three parcels, 13 livres – and more in line with those of Gévezé.[34] As we have seen, Audierne represented the other extreme, with its infinitesimal assessments. The reason for the discrepancies was the arbitrary nature of the *feux* count; a parish such as Massérac, assessed as if it had 51 real hearths, was obviously well off because it had over 200. In contrast, the *frairie* of Tréhiguier had 18.5 *feux*, that is, was assumed to have 55.5 real hearths, and, in fact, had only 61. The entire province

---

[31] ADIV, G Gévezé, number 16, roll of 1584.   [32] *Ibid*, special account of 1599.
[33] Collins, *Fiscal Limits*, ch. 4 on French parishes.   [34] ADLA, G 348.

had such inequities, so that, while the overall picture was quite a positive one, there were certain parishes, and individuals, that bore relatively high assessments (although quite reasonable by French standards). We must also consider the implications of the practice of Gévezé, in which a *feu* represented a given amount of tillable land, rather than having to do with hearths.

The overall impression is clear enough, wherever we turn. Breton peasants paid a remarkably small amount in direct taxation. Assessments of a day or two's wages were quite typical everywhere; the larger tenant farmers and non-exempt landowners (like Macé), who paid most of the taxes, rarely carried assessments of more than 10 or 15 livres. After 1643, with the doubling of the tax burden, these assessments rose to 20 to 30 livres, still a very modest sum in comparison to French assessments of the time. The only exceptions to the light-handed treatment were the special sales of 1638, 1640, and 1642, when assessments, notably in Léon, Cornouaille, and Tréguier, rose to two to three times their normal amount, and the highly localized levies of troops in the field. The surviving peasant complaints from 1675 make it clear that the peasants cared little about direct taxation. Some complaints make no mention at all of direct taxation, and the most famous of the collections, the articles of the fourteen parishes of the Douarnenez region, treats the *fouage* as something of a lark: "article 8: that the money from the old *fouage* be employed to purchase tobacco, which will be distributed at the parish masses along with the *pain bénit* for the satisfaction of the parishioners."[35]

The serious matters related to landlords – *champarts*, *corvées*, hunting rights, mills, local justice. In the articles drawn up between the inhabitants of La Motte L'Abbé and the surrounding villages, the emphasis was on the legal profession – limiting costs for inventories, legal audiences, attacks on use of stamped paper – as well as on the usual complaints (*champarts*, pigeons, hunting) against the nobles. The only real complaint against the royal fisc concerned the wine tax, which the Douarnenez area articles sought to cut by three-fourths, to 20 livres per ton of wine (article 7), so that wine could be sold for 5 sous per *pinte* of non-Breton wine and 3 sous per *pinte* of Breton wine. The Motte l'Abbé articles wanted wine sold at a maximum of 10 sous per *pot*.[36]

Here we encounter the serious element of royal finance in Brittany: the wine tax. Who paid the wine tax? How was it assessed within the province? The key factor in the relationship between population and direct taxation was population and economic growth after 1500, that is, after the last serious adjustment of the *feux* count. As we have seen in chapter 1, the serious discrepancies between the

---

[35] Typical French assessments in the *pays d'élection* were on the order of 1 or 2 livres for poorer peasants, 5 to 15 livres for middling peasants, and 25 to 50 livres for the richer peasants. The exceptions to this pattern are in the 1640s, when, for example, fourteen of fifteen *laboureurs* in the parish of Saint-Martin-les-Melle were assessed for 50 livres or more (AD Deux-Sèvres, C 145). Articles reprinted in *La Bretagne province* (Morlaix, 1986), 109.

[36] ADIV, 1 F 692, papers of de la Borderie.

feux count and the population would have been in the bishoprics of Rennes (−1.7), Vannes (−1.1), Léon (−1.9), Tréguier (+3.1), and Saint-Brieuc (+1.4). It would seem that the north coast lost population in this period, whereas Léon, Rennes, and Vannes all gained population relative to the rest of the province.[37]

The bishoprics of Saint-Brieuc and Tréguier clearly got the worst of the deal on direct taxation, as their percentages of *feux* were much higher than their percentages of population. The overall impression is that the relationship between percentage of population and percentage of direct taxes was quite fair for Nantes, Vannes, Cornouaille, Saint-Malo, and Dol, that Rennes and Léon were sharply under-assessed, and that Tréguier and Saint-Brieuc were over-assessed. Given the rather low average assessments in all parishes, it is most unlikely that the discrepancies led to serious inequities. Certainly the peasants of nearby Normandy did not find the north Breton coast inhospitable: there was a steady stream of emigrants from the heavily taxed Cotentin into northern Brittany.[38]

If we turn from direct taxes to indirect taxes, we find again that Saint-Brieuc was in decline. Just as its percentage of population was much lower than its percentage of *feux*, implying relative population loss in comparison to other areas, so, too, its share of both the wine duties of the Estates and the *impôts* declined sharply between the 1580s and 1650s (tables 25 and 26). By way of contrast, Léon was growing rapidly, both in terms of its excess of population over *feux* and in terms of its percentage of the wine duties and *impôts*. Léon was, by any measure, the richest of the dioceses in the seventeenth century.

The measures are somewhat inexact in terms of their relationship to population because the authorities did not tax all beverages at the same rate. Thus cider-drinking areas, such as Saint-Malo and Rennes, might show a different rate of payment for the great duty of the Estates (which taxed cider) than for the *impôts*, which taxed only wine and would therefore show the bishopric's percentage of wine consumption. In fact, we see that both Dol and Saint-Malo paid much less of the great duty than of the *impôts* but at Rennes, alas, it was precisely the other way around. Nantes made out well on all beverage taxes because of its privileged position in both systems: Nantais wine had a special low rate in the bishopric, so Nantes' percentage of the wine taxes remained substantially lower than its percentage of population. In Brittany, as elsewhere in France, we see the basic Ancien Régime pattern of low taxation of a given commodity in its region of production. Given the impossibility of policing fraud in such regions, this policy was the most rational one available (far more rational than a policy of uniform taxation of commodities).

---

[37] Croix, *La Bretagne*, 123–83, esp. 152, table 18a, and map 37; ADLA, B 3009, B 2990.
[38] M. Le Pésant, "Un centre d'émigration en Normandie sous l'ancien régime. Le cas de Percy," *Bibliothèque de l'Ecole des Chartes* (1972): 163–225.

Table 25: *Comparison of population and wine tax receipt percentages, by bishopric*

	Population 1660	Wine duty 1620s	Wine duty 1650s	*Impôts* 1575–9	*Impôts* 1640
Rennes	14.3	11.9	14.3	12.6	10.6
Nantes	17.1	12.9	13.8	11.8	13.4
Vannes	14.6	15.6	14.6	15.5	14.1
Cornouaille	13.0	15.6	14.6	12.6	16.4
Léon	8.0	9.5	11.2	6.7	9.1
Tréguier	8.0	11.2	11.2	11.0	10.4
Saint-Brieuc	9.3	9.5	7.1	11.0	8.3
Saint-Malo	12.9	12.1	11.5	14.8	15.4
Dol	2.8	1.7	1.7	4.0	2.4

Note:
These figures could vary sharply from year to year, hence the use of averages from the wine duties of the 1620s and 1650s and from the *impôts* of 1578 and 1579. The figure of 1640 is for the alienation of the *impôts*, done on the basis of an average lease price for each jurisdiction (typically, the government used the previous three leases).
Sources: Croix, *La Bretagne*, table 18a; ADIV, C 2765–7; ADLA B 2973.

Table 26: *Wine tax receipts by bishopric (in percentages)*

Bishopric	1600	1627	1629	1646	1648	1652	1656
Vannes	34.3	15.8	30.8	15.2	14.6	29.2	29.2
Cornouaille	45.8	15.8	—	15.2	15.0	—	—
Léon	—	8.8	10.1	12.2	33.8	23.2	21.5
Tréguier	—	11.4	11.1	12.6	—	—	—
Saint-Brieuc	—	9.4	9.5	7.0	—	7.0	7.2
Saint-Malo	15.3	12.0	12.3	13.0	13.2	11.9	11.2
Dol	—	1.7	1.8	1.5	—	1.6	1.8
Rennes	—	12.0	11.8	11.8	11.7	14.1	14.5
Nantes	4.7	13.1	12.7	11.4	11.7	13.0	14.5

Note:
A blank in a given column indicates that the bishopric in question was leased along with the bishopric(s) immediately above it, for which a figure is listed. Thus, in 1600, Cornouaille, Léon, Tréguier, and Saint-Brieuc were all leased together for 45.8 percent of the total.
Sources: ADIV, C 2645, 2765–7, 2778, 2779, 2781, 2783.

The burden of Breton taxation

Léon drank primarily non-Breton wine, taxed at the highest rate, so its percentage of wine taxes was substantially higher than its share of population. On the great duty, for example, a *pot* of non-Breton wine paid 4 sous, whereas a *pot* of Nantais wine sold in the bishopric itself paid only 2 sous. Nonetheless, Léon shows obvious growth – up about 36 percent in its share of the duty and about 18 percent on the *impôts* – while Saint-Brieuc shows the most severe decline – down about 25 percent on each. If we take the first figure, the *impôts* of 1578–9 and compare it to the last, the great duty in the 1650s, we find that the share of Saint-Brieuc declined 54 percent, that of Léon increased about 67 percent.

The pattern of taxation in its entirety indicates that the peasants of Léon, Vannes, and Rennes were strongly protected by the *fouage* system, those of Tréguier, Saint-Brieuc, and, to a lesser extent, Nantes, disadvantaged. By way of contrast, the wine tax duties struck hardest, in the 1640s, at Léon, Cornouaille, and Tréguier, protecting Nantes. Tréguier got much the worst of things in terms of overall tax burden per capita. Was this a reflection of the area's prosperity? There is no direct evidence to suggest that the Estates took that into account, and the main area of prosperity was Léon, not Tréguier (even though the town that profited the most, Morlaix, was partly in Tréguier).

The direct and indirect taxes struck different populations: the former lay on peasants, the latter more heavily on townspeople. One of the lingering problems of the direct tax system was that areas that had been important in the fifteenth century tended to be over-assessed, whereas those whose importance had grown tended to be under-assessed. Breton (and French) taxation followed very traditional lines; the percentage of a given area's assessment usually remained fairly stable over long periods of time. This pattern did not pose a problem with the wine taxes, as the farmer syndicates subleased the duties by bishopric or groups of bishoprics. The farmers kept entirely up to date with a given area's ability to pay because the penalty for a poor forecast was bankruptcy.

Within the bishoprics, we must distinguish between urban and rural taxpayers. The direct taxes fell almost exclusively on rural dwellers, the wine taxes fell more heavily (although by no means exclusively) on urban dwellers. Upper Brittany, notably the area between Rennes and Saint-Malo, was much more urban than Lower Brittany, whose only real towns were the ports. We can examine tax distribution from two perspectives: first, the relationship of the direct tax burden to rural population; second, the relationship of wine tax burden to urban population. On the first matter there can be little question that almost everyone was well off because the overall burden was so low. Until 1635, the per capita annual direct tax burden was in the order of 7 or 8 sous; this burden doubled between 1638 and 1642 and gradually settled into a level of 15 sous or so after 1643. Those best off lived in the bishopric of Léon; those living in Rennes and Vannes also made out well. There were parishes, such as

245

Assérac, where the burden was much higher; in general, it was worst in the extreme north, the bishopric of Tréguier. As for the indirect tax burden, the west paid the lion's share because of the discrepancy in the rate of taxation on different varieties of wine. The urban consumers of western Brittany paid a disproportionate share of royal taxes: the four bishoprics of Lower Brittany (Vannes, Cornouaille, Léon, and Tréguier) paid about 60 percent more of the wine taxes than their share of urban population would seem to warrant. By way of contrast, Rennes and Nantes paid 40 percent less than their urban population would have indicated.

The solution to the province's need to raise money was therefore more complex than it would first appear. The landlords did protect their tenants, so that direct taxes, levied almost exclusively on the countryside and paid in large measure by tenants of rich landlords, stayed quite low, allowing rents and dues to stay very high. But the indirect tax burden that allowed the low level of direct taxation was assessed not against the most powerful Breton towns, Rennes and Nantes, but against the far western towns, far from the center of political power. The beverages of the lower classes of Rennes (cider) and Nantes (Nantais wine) were protected from heavy taxes; the beverage of urban consumption in the west (Bordeaux wine) was heavily taxed. One notices immediately that the most protected area of the province was the bishopric of Rennes, its political capital. Yet even the bourgeoisie of the west were protected, because the tax fell only on retail wine sales, not on wholesale ones. The one effort to introduce an entry duty on wine, to replace the sales tax, failed in 1626, due to universal opposition from constituents and supposed difficulties leasing the farm (the farmers, of course, were members of the mercantile elite).

The revolts of 1675 fit in perfectly with this pattern. The revolt in the towns, especially Rennes, was touched off by a new royal tax – stamped paper – that hit the elite, particularly the legal profession (see chapter 7). The revolt in the countryside was aimed at the landlords; the peasants paid relatively little in royal taxation, so they had little need to attack it. The peasants asked that the price of wine (that is, the tax on wine) be reduced but there was no mention in any surviving document of a reduction in direct taxes. What did they wish to change? They wanted to abolish *champarts*, *corvées*, and milling monopolies, and to reform hunting rights, both in terms of limiting the rights of the nobility and of extending their own hunting rights.

How can seventeenth-century Brittany, alone among French provinces of the period, have been the site of a peasant rebellion aimed at the nobility, not at the Crown? There can be little doubt. The local institutions, dominated by an elite of landlords and lawyer-landlords, both noble and *roturier*, kept royal taxes on their tenants at a remarkably low level. They also kept taxes in the two largest, and potentially most politically volatile, towns at a reasonable level, thereby defusing the two major possible powder kegs. (Here one can note that the rebellions of 1675 began with disturbances at Rennes and Nantes.) The lower-class and middling wine consumers of other Breton towns, such as Morlaix or Vannes, had to pay the price for the favoritism shown to the peasants and to the Nantais and Rennais. One of the principal responses to the taxing policy of the elite was a shift in the beverage of lower-class consumption, from local and Nantais wine to cider.

The towns themselves aided and abetted this process because they all shifted their duties from a package of indirect taxes – on grain, cloth, fish, wine, meat, butter, iron, and various other commodities – into taxes on retail wine sales. Breton wine taxes, levied by the Estates or the towns, fell on retail, not wholesale commerce, on wine sold "au détail", that is, in a tavern. The middle classes must have escaped much of this taxation, as they would have purchased wine for their private consumption from a wholesale merchant. The lower classes bought wine both by the glass or pint and by the jug, for home consumption; the duties taxed both sorts of consumption. In the case of wine from outside the province, either from the Loire Valley or from Bordeaux (much less often, La Rochelle), the tax was 4 sous a *pot* (1.8 liters) by 1642, plus the duties of the given town (usually another sou) and a sou for the *impôts*. In the case of Angevin wine, this more than doubled its original price; in the case of Bordeaux wine, it raised the price about 70 or 75 percent.[39] By 1642, the various governing authorities in the province obtained between 2.0 and 2.5 million livres a year from taxes on wine, as against only 0.5 million livres from direct taxation. In 1643, and most years thereafter, the amount of direct taxation rose to about 1 million livres, but duties on alcohol, if not always the revenues from those duties, also went up.

How much did this taxation cost a typical Breton? The implications of the wine duty figures are that per capita consumption was some 50 liters in the countryside, perhaps two to three times as much in the towns.[40] A family consuming 100 liters of cider would pay as little as 3 or 4 livres of taxation a year; a family consuming 250 liters of Bordeaux wine would pay 15 or even 20 livres of taxation by the 1660s. An artisan drinking a half liter a day (a minimal amount, judging from the records), was paying a sou a day in wine taxes (roughly

---

[39] The duty of the Estates was, by the 1640s: 4 sous per *pot* of wine from outside the province, 3 sous per *pot* of wine grown in one bishopric but sold in another, 2 sous per *pot* of wine consumed in the bishopric in which it was grown, and 1 sou per *pot* of beer or cider. Angevin wine typically sold for 30 to 50 livres per pipe (of 200 *pots*), while Bordeaux wine sold for 80 to 100 livres per pipe. Prices from AM de Nantes, CC 164–70, accounts of the city of Nantes. In 1634, for example, Angevin wine went for 30 to 36 livres per pipe, Bordeaux wine for 80 to 90 livres. In 1642, Angevin wine went for 41 livres per pipe, Bordeaux wine for 93 livres (in 1641, prices had been much higher, 65 and 135 livres, respectively); in 1647, Bordeaux wine was 75 livres a pipe, Angevin wine 45 livres. A pipe of Bordeaux wine contained about 450 liters; a pipe of Angevin (or Nantais) wine held only 380.

[40] The tax in 1583 was 2.5 livres per pipe, in 1610, 10 livres per pipe, in 1641, 40 livres/pipe. Consumption figures are based on the tax records and known population totals. At Nantes, for example, wine consumption ranged from 110 to 200 liters a year per capita.

5 to 10 percent of his income, depending on his occupation).[41] Given that the middle classes paid a fairly low percentage of the retail taxes on wine, we can understand why the tax levels of the 1630s and 1640s had such a dramatic impact on the rate of return.[42] Those purchasing much of the retail wine, and thus paying the bulk of the taxes, had a very low level of discretionary spending; when the wine taxes went up sharply, many Bretons had little choice but to switch beverage, to cider.

The authorities were caught in a guaranteed losing position after 1640. Every time the tax on wine went up, consumption went down (see chapter 1). The ratio between the duty per ton and the total lease price for the duty of the Estates declined continuously from 1635 to 1655. Wine shipping figures dropped everywhere, especially in the Loire Valley. When the expected return from higher taxes did not materialize, the various governing bodies raised taxes again, to cover revenue shortfall. This increase only accelerated the declining consumption. The Estates recognized the problem in 1643, voting the extra *fouage*; yet it would seem likely that they voted the extra *fouage* in part because of their dissatisfaction with the *ad hoc* levies of the king in 1638, 1640, and 1642. By 1661, the extra *fouage* had become a regular part of their offering to the king, buttressing the declining wine duty receipts. Those declining wine sales, however, affected more than the duty receipts; they also meant economic stagnation and eventually depression for several parts of the province.

The key shift in Breton tax policy after 1640 was the increased attack on peasant stocks of cash. The need for more direct taxation coincided with a rapid rise in rents, especially cash entry fees, and more rigorous tithe collection. The strain on peasant taxpayers must have been substantial, but their actions in 1675 made it obvious that royal taxes did not provide the main burden on their resources. Alone among the great French peasant rebellions of the seventeenth century, the revolt of the Bonnets Rouges attacked the seigneurs and the royal courts, rather than the direct tax system. An examination of the events of 1675 is an appropriate conclusion for a study of order in Brittany, because order disintegrated as never before in the late spring and early summer of 1675; the fault lines of society are never so visible as they are in such periods of disarray.

---

[41] The artisan's wages ranged from 10–12 sous per day, based on hospital accounts and other records. A *pot* of wine (1.8 liters) paid rates that ranged from 0.25 sous to 4 sous for the main duty of the Estates (depending on the time and type of wine). A *pot* of local wine at Nantes, for example, would have paid 2 sous after 1640; we must add to this another sou (at least) for the town duty, the *impôts et billots*, and the *petit devoir*. Two sous per *pot*, a half *pot* per day, is roughly a sou a day (about 10 percent of a laborer's income for that day, although a higher percentage of his total income divided by 365). The much higher rates of the western towns would drive up the rate closer to 20 percent of daily income going to wine taxes.

[42] ADIV, C 5979, sales of wine by a wholesaler of Morlaix, 1682–4.

248

The problem of order

What was order to a seventeenth-century Breton? The ruling elites sought always to impose their version of order, yet they themselves often disagreed as to what order they would impose. The traditional formulation, the society of orders, of the three orders of prayers, fighters, and workers, continued to define the legal and political system, but a new political formulation, revolving around the divinely anointed king, increasingly competed with it. Order meant one religion; it meant respect for property; it meant the continued social and political preeminence of landed nobles; it meant strengthened male control of women (and, by extension, of families). Order was political and social but also moral. The authorities and the other forces of order had to restrict popular political action. Because they defined the moral as political, they believed that they had to supervise morality closely to preserve the political (and social) order.

The authorities relied on a broad social coalition to preserve order: on all those with a stake in the system. The coalition included the nobles, legal people, and merchants but also a wide range of humbler citizens – guild members and shopkeepers in the towns, the ploughmen in the villages. The one element that united all members of the forces of order was property. The purpose of society, as John Locke said in 1679, was the preservation of property – of lives, liberties, and estates. Whether we look with Foucault at the "insane" or with Muchembled at the moral and then legal "criminalization" of certain forms of behavior, everywhere we see the intense concern with the connection between immoral behavior, social and political dissolution, and the preservation of property. As Sébastien de Guémadeuc, bishop of Saint-Malo wrote to Colbert (20 April 1675) of the burghers of Saint-Malo: "les bourgeois et principaux habitans sont très bien intentionnés tant pour le service du Roy que pour la conservation de leurs biens." The good bishop reminded them that the two went hand in hand, that the king was, in Bossuet's phrase, the "invincible defender of order," that is, of property.

Nearly 100 years earlier, on 8 August 1583, a special meeting of the town council of Saint-Malo ordered the captains of the town militia to choose two men "from their roll of artisan reserves" to guard the town gates, in order to prevent unauthorized entries. Nine months later, another meeting sought to raise money because of the "number of poor and vagabonds who are in this town"; the town fathers wanted to prevent these poor people from "begging in church and in houses."[1] In December 1584, they decided to hire "beggar chasers" to drive out the "able-bodied poor beggars and to prevent the poor from going by the churches." The clerk must have reconsidered this formula, because he subsequently crossed out the word "able-bodied" ("vallid").

The good mothers and fathers of Saint-Malo took particular care of the poor during periods of real or possible infestation by "plague" (as in 1583–4). In 1645–6, they tried to establish a permanent solution to the problem: a "maison de charrité" (poor house) like the one at Lyon. The town council recognized the zeal of several "pious and charitable souls of this town" who wanted to stop the widespread begging and to bring a remedy to the "present necessity of the poor." Their goal was to "instruct them [the poor] in the catholic faith and religion, the fear of God and the observance of his holy commandments." These pious souls also wanted "to put those capable of work in suitable occupations and, to that end, to give them masters and mistresses to avoid the laziness and idleness of the said poor and to remove them from the vice into which they have fallen due to a lack of occupation and of instruction." The council recognized the utility of such a poor house, not only for its immediate practical benefits but because it would "bring from heaven ... all sorts of benedictions" for the city.[2]

The town council of Saint-Malo brings together in its deliberations all of the basic considerations of the *gens de bien* about their society. They believed in maintaining order, which meant giving the poor a combination of religious instruction, work, and a definable master/mistress, as well as forcing on them a sort of public discipline. Public begging, notably in front of churches, and the general rowdiness of a port population, threatened this discipline. In 1654, the town council explained why the city needed a police force.

These policemen ["polliciers"] are very necessary in the town of Saint-Malo because it has a great commerce and is filled with many seamen ["gens de mer"], who are ordinarily very rude ... the infinity of persons of different nations and professions ... leads to small differences among them at every moment about the fulfilment of their agreements, particularly those among artisans, porters, and sailors ... these little contestations can lead to disorder and to blows.

The policemen ("commis") always carried "a cane in their hands, both as a sign of their authority and because it is sometimes necessary to reestablish order."[3]

The line between ordinary rowdiness and the breakdown of civil order was a murky one. Historians have typically concentrated on large revolts, such as the Papier Timbré and Bonnets Rouges of 1675, in their analyses of order in early

---

[1] AM de Saint-Malo, BB 7.   [2] *Ibid.*, BB 12.   [3] *Ibid.*, FF 3, piece 113.

modern France, yet the ongoing difficulties of maintaining a stable civic order formed a far more serious concern for the authorities of the day. To get a clearer sense of the context of the 1675 events, we must turn first to the patterns of social discontent in early modern Brittany. Only by examining the earlier civil disturbances and the running battles between the police and the people can we understand the 1675 revolts because of contemporaries' conviction that moral order formed the strongest barrier to social and political disorder.

PATTERNS OF SOCIAL DISCONTENT

Dubuisson-Aubenay's drunken and seditious *gars de Rennes* and people like them throughout the province constantly threatened the forces of order, although Brittany had a relative low level of political violence prior to 1675. The most obvious form of social discontent was open rebellion. The greatest Breton rebellions, the revolts of the Papier Timbré and the Bonnets Rouges, took place in 1675, but there were other, smaller revolts. The most notable of these were grain riots at Morlaix (1631) and Hennebont (1642) and the uprising of northern parishes against the royal army in 1628.[4] There were small-scale riots in Saint-Pol-de-Léon, Guingamp, Saint-Brieuc, and elsewhere in 1631, as local consumers protested against shipments of grain to Nantes.[5] The largest single "émotion populaire" was that at Rennes in 1636, for which the city lost its right to preside over the Third Estate, and, indeed, for which it had to beg the right to be seated at the Estates. We know little about it, save the information from Dubuisson-Aubenay and Valençay, and from the records of the Estates about its consequences.[6] Alain Croix has counted about twenty grain riots between 1566 and 1662, of which eleven date from 1630–1 and 1661–2. This small number alerts us again to the province's relatively favorable position with respect to grain, which was rarely wanting in the entire province. The Parlement and the king usually acted to prevent the export of grain in famine years, such as 1643, but enterprising merchants found ways to circumvent the passport system and ship grain abroad despite the restrictions.[7] The riots of Hennebont and Morlaix are perhaps typical in their developments. In the former, we read of "several tumults and seditions" and of bands of inhabitants threatening to "kill, loot, and burn." The local officers noted that they acted quickly to maintain a reasonable supply of grain and that the "grain price list was done at a very reasonable price." They arrested three ringleaders – Louys Bahuc, Marie

---

[4] The rising against the army is discussed in ch. 3.
[5] On the problems of the Sauvaget brothers, who had an agreement with the city of Nantes to furnish grain during the famine of 1630–1, see AM de Nantes, FF 176 and ADIV, 1 Bh 8.
[6] Dubuisson-Aubenay, "Journal des Etats." This revolt is discussed in greater detail below.
[7] ADIV, 1 Bh 8, papers of the Parlement, December 1643 investigation showing Breton merchants using English passports to smuggle grain to Spain.

Malecoste, and "petit Jan," a shoemaker – who had shouted from the prison windows that the people should "break the head of the officers."[8]

The revolt at Morlaix is even more interesting, because we have a more detailed report from the seneschal of Morlaix, Guy Le Levyer. He claimed that 500–600 people, both men and women, marched on the city hall to protest the illegal, nighttime shipment of 25 tons of grain by a Gascon merchant on 3 June 1631. The assembled masses, who feared neither "God, the king, nor justice," threatened to introduce those infected with the plague, then at the Parc au Duc in the suburb of Saint-Melaine, into the city "to infect and contaminate everyone in the said town."[9] An armed troop of well-heeled and well-armed men protected the boat. Croix sees this as a clear-cut case of class hatred, the rich protecting the boat (and the "liberty" of commerce), the poor ("un tas de quenaille" as they are called by the merchant) protecting their right to grain. The suggestion that the seditious respected neither God, king, nor justice demonstrates, as well, the manner in which contemporaries connected the moral and the political, as well as the moral and the economic.[10] The authorities were not insensitive to the moral outrage of the community. We see the success of the crowd at Morlaix, which has tacit support from some of the "bourgeois" of the town; we see the emphasis of the royal officers of Hennebont on the fact that grain was reasonably priced, implying that were the grain outrageously expensive, the rioters would have had a legitimate reason to rise up. In fact, the officers argued that the riot was a ruse by those wishing to steal under cover of the disorders.

Riots and rebellions, while attractive to the historian because they are so active (and leave so many records), were not the main form of social discontent. The real discontent was a kind of smoldering resentment of authority: of tax collectors, of policemen closing taverns on Sunday morning, of the *gabelle* archers and clerks of the transit duties, of the elite who ran the town or village. One of the most striking elements of the peasant rebellion of 1675 was its anti-urbanism, aimed especially at judicial officers, as well as its anti-seigneurialism. The peasants knew full well who ran the towns, and they often aimed their complaints directly at such people (who were often heavily invested in the countryside). The peasants even attacked certain towns, taking over Carhaix and Châteaulin, while failing to take Guingamp, Morlaix, and Brest. In the well-known articles of the fourteen parishes near Douarnenez, article 11 stated that the inhabitants of Quimper must ratify the accord between peasants and seigneurs, under pain of being economically quarantined by the peasants.[11] Other peasants signed peace treaties with the tiny towns they captured, and demanded reduced prices for wine and for "inventaires." Their key opponents, however, were the judicial system and the nobles – the governor noted that "all

[8] ADM, B 2794.   [9] ADF, 2 E 5; Croix, *La Bretagne*, 409.
[10] ADIV, 1 F 692, papers of A. de la Borderie.   [11] Tanguy, *La Bretagne province*, 108.

of their rage is against the gentlemen, from whom they have received ill treatment."[12]

Contemporaries were doubtless struck by stories such as that concerning M. de Kersalaun, murdered by his "own parishioners" as he left high mass on Sunday, 23 June, or the case of the marquis de la Coste, whose arm was disabled by a peasant using a flail. The peasants did not forget the judiciary – the peasants of the region around Concarneau, for example, claimed that they were oppressed by all sorts of new exactions and that was why "we were obliged to defend ourselves against justice [i.e., the judicial system] and against the nobility." Their list of complaints began with the statement that, while the king had issued many good ordinances, the judges had no consideration "either for the poor, for minors, or for the poor people. They burden them on all occasions, stringing out their lawsuits as long as their [the peasants'] estate lasts, and keep them always in anguish; that is why we cry mercy against justice."[13] The great 1675 rebellion, or even the rising against the royal army in 1628 (see chapter 3), were only a small part of the picture. The real discontent comes through most clearly in police archives, where we see the general surliness of the population, particularly the poor, toward the authorities. If we come back to the records of the provost of Nantes, we can see this antagonism in its many aspects. We have seen (in chapter 2) the antagonism in the taverns of Bastard, Plessis, and Marcan; let us examine more closely those cases, and others, to get a clearer perspective on social discontent.

The provost bore down hard on some of the "gens comme il faut," notably the bakers and grain traders, but he aimed most of his other activities at the poor. He ordered all vagabonds out of the city on various occasions, such as June 1633 and May 1636; the city officials often claimed that the *chasse-gueux* were not assiduous enough, as in 1632.[14] The penalty for vagabondage was whipping and having one's head shaved. The city authorities worried particularly about the poor in times of plague, as in 1626, when they called an emergency meeting of the city assembly for the "police of the poor"; the council wanted authority to "keep them closed up."[15] The assembly wanted to enclose the poor to keep them away from "doors of houses" and churches. Five years later, during a dispute over how to fund poor relief, Jan Charette, sub-mayor, noted: "There is nothing more agreable to God, important to the public, favorable and salutory in itself, than this affair that concerns the feeding of the poor sick people."[16]

The provost also sought to restrain the lackeys of the rich, banning them from

---

[12] ADIV, 1 F 692, papers of A. de la Borderie. J. Lemoine, "La révolte dite du Papier Timbré ou des Bonnets Rouges," *Annales de Bretagne*, 12–14 (1894–7), document LXIV (on de la Coste) and LXXXIX (on Kersalaun).   [13] Lemoine, "La révolte," document LXVI.

[14] ADLA, B 6655.   [15] AM de Nantes, BB 31, meeting of 8 June 1626.

[16] AM de Nantes, BB 34, fol. 153v, meeting of 12 May 1631.

bearing "swords, batons, and other arms" in the city and suburbs: he held their masters personally responsible for violations.[17] Labor peace came under the provost's scrutiny, as in the case, cited above, in which porters demanded higher wages; the provost fixed such wages as 18 deniers per 150 lb. load within the city, 2 sous for a load carried from the Fosse to the city.[18] The penalties for violations included imprisonment, whipping, branding, and banishment. The first of these, while seemingly the mildest (three days on bread and water) could turn out to be a nightmare, as happened to Amboise Demeury, who spent six months in prison without facing any charges. He finally obtained his release, noting that he had no friends to help and that he suffered terribly from "the vermin that eat him because he does not change linen."[19]

In the second case, the journeymen tailors striking in 1644 and again in 1650, the provost again vigorously reacted against the strikers. They had sent a handbill around, telling their confreres to meet at the tavern of the Croix Blanche on the rue Saint-Léonard. The provost arrested the ringleaders but we do not know their fate.[20] In 1667, "several apprentice tailors rose up [smudge] on the shops of the masters; they did not wish to work and assembled in a place called the Fontenelle on the rue des Carmes where they carry on debaucheries." The masters banded together and sought "a prohibition against the said journeymen to gather together, to debauch, or to make any assemblies and to enjoin them to go work at their masters' shops." The apprentices and journeymen brandished swords in the street and the provost investigated their gathering place, seeking firearms.

The matter particularly involved master tailor Henry Fumet, who had declared bankruptcy and thereby cheated his journeymen of their wages. Fumet was back in business, with new employees, when some of his former workers paid a visit to the shop. They swore at Fumet, grabbed his new journeyman by the hair and throat, pummeled and kicked him, and even twice struck Fumet's wife, who led the shop's defense. The witnesses specified a group ranging from six to twenty; the provost took depositions from ten workers and from five eyewitnesses and the beaten journeyman, André Rohan. Interestingly, the one worker in the group of witnesses, Antoine Bonnet, "carleur de souliers," said nothing about the incident, while Catherine Rousseau, wife of Philippe Cassouet, clerk at the *prévôté*, and Me. Jan Le Figuer, a student (*escollier*) of 16, gave detailed condemnations of the workers. Once again, we do not know the final outcome of the case.[21] The provost intervened constantly against the poor and those outside the bounds of middle-class society: vagabonds, porters, journeymen and apprentice tailors, independent producers, foreigners. One notes with interest the meeting place of the workers in 1650: the tavern of the

[17] ADLA, B 6655, 31 March 1634, one among many such prohibitions.
[18] ADLA, B 6649 (1615). [19] ADLA, B 6651, 18 June 1627.
[20] ADLA, B 6662. [21] ADLA, B 6671.

Croix Blanche in Saint-Léonard. In this parish, one of the poorest in the city, in 1593, more than 60 percent of its households paid less than 1 livre in taxes. A working parish, it had a wide variety of shopkeepers, as well as a substantial number of indigents, including many poor women.[22] In 1586, the city taxed roughly one household in seven for poor relief, very similar to the percentage in the poor suburb of Saint-Clément (12.5 percent). The intervention in a tavern, here in a workers' section of town, shows the provost supervising in the social life of the workers – their free time, their amusements. Although the case of the journeymen was clearly political (and economic), the presence of the provost at the Croix Blanche shows one incident among many involving the police and the taverns. The antagonism against the kind of intrusion represented by the visits to the taverns of Bastard or Menard can well be imagined. In January 1636, the wife of François Desvignes expelled the wine duty clerks "avec viollence" when they wanted to see her cellar. They got in by the side entrance and found three or four pipes of unregistered wine. Eleven years earlier, Charles Contaret, clerk of the *impôts et billots*, had his arm "slashed to ribbons" by an irate tavern keeper. Contaret claimed to have spent 1,000 livres on doctors and medications, in a vain attempt to regain use of his arm.[23]

Contaret was luckier than some; in 1669, there was a general rising at Nantes against the wine duty clerks and at least one was killed.[24] In 1668 and 1669, the working districts of the city were in constant upheaval against the wine duty collectors. The town council registers note, in the summer of 1669, that "the clerks and bailiffs have been beaten and exceeded in divers encounters and several of them wounded unto death." The tax farmers complained of the "rebellions that have been made against their clerks" and asked that the town authorities see to it that "the inhabitants submit to the carrying out of the said farms without troubling the said clerks, even less to beat and importune them." They complained that the impunity of one rebellion led to another, and then another.

The farmers were so overwhelmed by popular resistance that they abandoned, as of 3 July 1669, all efforts to collect wine taxes. On 23 July, they informed the mayor that they were abandoning the farm itself "for the surety of their persons." They also obtained a royal judgment ordering the mayor and councilmen to pay the city the lease price. Although the town council issued a defense arguing that Legendre and Symon (the tax farmers) issued a "false and calumnious" statement, the records of the provost and seneschal of Nantes entirely support the claims of the tax farmers.[25]

These claims might, at first, seem to be against isolated individuals, against tavern keepers too zealous in defense of their fraudulent activities, but it would seem unlikely that the tavern keepers alone could have brought the tax farm to a

---

[22] Croix, *La Bretagne*, 730–4. Roll in AM de Nantes, CC 86.   [23] ADLA, B 6652.
[24] AM de Nantes, CC 2.   [25] AM de Nantes, BB 46, fol. 31.

halt. Indeed, the police records bear out such an interpretation. On 7 June 1668, for example, the wine duty clerks burst into the tavern of Jan Priou and his wife, on the rue Saint-Léonard. They claimed he owed them 119.65 livres in past due tax payments; when he refused to pay, they tried to bring him to prison. Priou seized a knife and struck out at the *commis*; his wife ran into the street, rousing the neighbors. She rallied Le Bourguignon, a *couvreur d'ardoise*, several women of the neighborhood – La Camille, La Pryou, the widow Magente, the wife of an unnamed merchant – M. Deramie, master carpenter, M. Pasquier, *couvreur*, Laurens Gallos, baker, Clément Lucas, *savetier*, Nicolas Lelieur, *blanchisseur*, M. Buissonière, master mason, Pierre —, *menusier*, journeyman of master carpenter Doreceveur, and Adrien —, armor maker: in short, the entire population of the district. They removed Priou by "force and violence" from the hands of the *commis*. He was later fined for selling three pipes of wine without paying duty (May 1669). In December 1668, at the tavern of Jan Minereau and Julienne Gauchard (his wife), also in Saint-Léonard, the *commis* fled for their lives from a crowd that "wished to throw itself against us to mistreat us." In August 1669, Sebastien Contenu went to prison because he caused an "émotion populaire"; in fact, his wife had followed the *commis* down the street, calling them "thieves of *malthoters*" – Contenu paid for her audacity.

In another working district, the rue de la Boucherie, the situation was even worse. There, on 27 November 1668, at the tavern of the widow Henriette Legallois, we find "the said persons [customers] with the other inhabitants of the said place, who started to cry in a loud voice, haro, haro, against those buggers of *maltosters* with many other injurious remarks; seeing that daily there are committed against us insults and rebellions by the butchers of the said rue de la Boucherie, because of which there are several lawsuits, both civil and criminal, in progress ... that in the said place we were not in surety of our persons." The *commis* fled. In the sailors' district it was much the same, the *commis* being physically thrown out of the tavern of Double and his wife in March 1668. The boatmen had little respect for anyone; in the presence of the seneschal of Nantes himself (May 1668), they forcibly ejected the *commis* from the tavern of Mathurin Vinet and his wife. The final blow came in November 1669, when a crowd murdered Pierre Roussy while he investigated a tavern near the Piremil tower of the Fosse. A large crowd attacked two *commis*, Roussy and Ragot, with swords and batons; Ragot staggered away "half-dead," Roussy was not so fortunate. The king eventually made resistance to the *commis* a capital offense.[26]

We see all the basic patterns in our earlier cases, at the taverns of Anne Plessis and Claude Marcan and his wife. At Anne Plessis' tavern, in Saint-Nicolas (again, the port), the clerks were verbally abused by Mme. Plessis and by her

---

[26] ADLA, B 6785, on all these separate incidents.

neighbor, Henry de la Haye, tailor. De la Haye was followed by eight or ten men, "swearing and blaspheming the holy name of God, saying there are those thieves of *malthoters* and markers of wine that we must beat." Amid shouts of "buggers of markers" and cries "tending to move the people to sedition, he was already followed by a number of people" leading the clerks "to avoid a greater scandal" and fleeing "in order not to lose our lives."[27] Once again, we see the blending of the political – sedition – and the moral – blaspheming the holy name of God.

At Marcan's place, it was more of the same. Here we find the clients identified: shoemakers, porters, weavers, tilers. They had all come for cheap wine. A lengthy conversation ensued, with Marcan claiming they were all his friends, paying nothing for their drinks. The four clerks searched the tavern, finding barrels, meat, bread, plates, cups, and other utensils; when they tried to cart some of this off as evidence, Marcan's wife, with the help of some of those drinking, assaulted them and attacked them with a sword. The clerks fled.[28]

The workers met even the efforts to close down taverns during high mass with disdain. On Sunday 12 March 1634, the provost found the tavern of Jan Maurat "practically filled with people" eating and drinking; at the tavern of the widow Mortain, it was full as if "a working day"; at Guillaume Bourjon's place (in the port), he had at least twenty-five clients; at that of the widow of Sébastien Meneust, more than thirty people carried on. The list goes on and on. In January of the same year, the provost found more than forty-four taverns open between 10.00 and 11.30 a.m. on a holy day.[29] These figures are hardly stirring testimony to the regular church attendance of a substantial part of the population; more specifically, they are hardly such testimony for the *working* population.

Nantes was in no way exceptional in such matters. Along the Loire, upstream from Nantes, we find an unidentified woman commanding a crew of armed men, smuggling 4.25 tons of eau-de-vie past the royal duty barrier at Ingrande.[30] We have evidence of riots against the wine duties everywhere, from the bishopric of Nantes in 1564, when the town of Clisson refused to keep statistics on wine sold and when all of the area of the *terroir* of Guérande, including Le Croisic and Pihiriac, refused to pay the duty and threatened to sack

---

[27] ADLA, B 6784. De la Haye was a master tailor.

[28] Nor was such conduct exceptional; in 1663, we find Pierre Caron, tavern keeper, fined 200 livres for beating up the duty clerks; in the same year, François de Bas threatened a clerk with a musket and swore at him, receiving a two *écus* fine (B 6782, piece 2).

[29] ADLA, B 6655–6. On 13 February 1633, there were sixteen taverns fined; seven on 1 January 1633; on 18 May 1636, six; on 8 March 1642, the provost issued an ordinance against selling wine and allowing *boules* to be played during mass – the fine was 100 livres. The episcopal visitation records of 1665 show that the rural parishes were not much better with respect to drinking during high mass. At Cordemais, the curé himself drank too often (ADLA, G 49).

[30] ADLA, B 6782. In 1659, the duty farmers drew up a list of nearly fifty tavern keepers who refused to allow them to inspect their cellars.

the offices of the wine duty clerks and the royal officers of Guérande, to western Brittany in the 1720s.[31] In 1725, in Fouesnant, four clerks of the wine duties – René Gourhael, Sébastien Corantin, Pierre Le Prendour, and René Macé (the last three of whom had been employed by the farm for thirty years!) – went out to investigate frauds and met with resistance from a blacksmith who sold eau-de-vie on the side. They quickly withdrew, noting that "in a country in which few people are in surety against the eruptions of a mutinous population," discretion, in this case a return to the bourg of Perguet, was the better part of valor.[32]

From Corentin Le Calvez smashing the eau-de-vie pot, and cutting the hand of the clerk at Fouesnant, to Desvignes or Bastard at Nantes, the same "insolence" and ill-will is everywhere in these confrontations of the police and the people. The taverns were more than a place to socialize; they were a place to escape the strictures of upper-class moral controls. How unfair it must have seemed to have the taverns closed much of Sunday and on holy days, the only days of rest for the worker. This moral police surely galled the workers, particularly as it was connected to a system of justice so blatantly class-conscious. The vagrants, the porters, the butchers of the poor parish of Saint-Clément, the heads of households unable to afford a fine of 500 livres – all were threatened with whipping, corporal punishment. Little wonder that when the authorities ventured into the poor quarters of the city or the isolated rural districts, the workers met them with open hostility and a constant refrain of what the authorities viewed as insolence and disrespect. The tavern visits came most often during Lent, perhaps because the taverns could do little trade during the week at that season, but perhaps because, in such a religious season, upper-class opinion was more shocked by open disregard of what it considered respectable, moral behavior.

Early modern elites, in Brittany as elsewhere, consciously sought to control political, social, and moral behavior. For them, political control meant careful regulation of popular morality. It meant that the political elite had to run the church, the hospital, the royal government. The apex of the ruling elite consisted almost exclusively of those who owned one particular element of the means of production – land – but, in a large town such as Nantes, the landlord–legal profession group also had to give great consideration to the needs of the merchants. To see these two groups as locked in some sort of early modern class struggle makes little sense. They shared a common primary goal – the preservation of order. All those with a place in the society of orders, including the small occupiers, possessed some stake in the system, some inclination to preserve order. So long as the rulers maintained the sense of belonging in the large groups who had so tenuous a stake in the system, they

---

[31] AM de Nantes, CC 479, piece 2.   [32] ADF, B 1289.

could preserve order. When they lost the support of people such as the shopkeepers of Saint-Léonard, they could not. In Brittany, the authorities lost this support most seriously in the spring of 1675.

THE REVOLTS OF 1675

In April 1675, the mounting tensions in Breton life led to one of the largest, most sustained rebellions in the history of the Ancien Régime. The precipitant, in the eyes of contemporaries, was the news of a revolt against new taxes in Bordeaux. M. Morel, a *procureur* at the presidial of Rennes, tells us that the director of the stamped paper tax office of Bordeaux was "burned alive on that same stamped paper that he wished disdainfully to distribute."[33] At Rennes, there were murmurs against the tax farmers on 3 April; on 18 April, the crowd stormed the tax offices in the Champ Jacquart. The following day, the *procureur du roi* told the Parlement:

that it is of public notoriety that this afternoon several vagabonds and persons unknown and without occupation, of which the greater part were from foreign provinces, who had entered into this city and suburbs, tumultuously gathered together, first pillaging the office of the tobacco monopoly and that of the marking of pewter, and then the offices of land registers, deeds, and suits over lands, and of the stamped paper, and prepared themselves to pillage several houses of individuals and to commit other great disorders and violences.[34]

In fact, the grocers (*épiciers*) had done much to foment the rebellion by announcing that they would once again sell tobacco, as they had done before the tax edict (issued 1673 but just recently registered by the Parlement) creating a tobacco monopoly. The predictable public response was the pillaging of the tobacco monopoly offices.[35]

Several of the upper-class witnesses to the April events emphasized the avariciousness of the participants. René de la Monneraye (member of an officer family that included several of the king's secretaries at Rennes) called the participants the "canaille" and the "dregs of the people" ("gens de la lie du peuple"). He claimed they stole and pillaged everything in the tobacco tax office, right down to the "utenciles."[36] Maître Tondeau, a notary of Rennes, believed that the participants were the "menue populace" of the faubourgs. He claimed that they did 20,000 livres of damages at the tobacco office. When their "temerity" led them to attack the offices of the "*sieur* Ferret, banker, and the

---

[33] ADIV, 1 F 307, papers of de la Borderie, description of Rennes events by M. Morel, *procureur* at the presidial of Rennes; eighteenth-century copy of original.
[34] BN, Mss. Fr. 11,537, secret registers of the Parlement of Brittany, fols. 460v–461v.
[35] Lemoine, "La revolte," document III, Coëtlogon (son) to Louvois, 19 April 1675. Coëtlogon reported that he took a group of twenty to thirty gentlemen to the Champ Jacquart and attacked the crowd, killing twelve and wounding nearly fifty. [36] ADIV, 1 F 691.

farmers of the great duty [of the Estates] . . . in the rue des Foulons," the forces of order, led by Coëtlogon, *fils*, killed or wounded twelve of them.[37]

From Rennes, disorder spread to Saint-Malo, where the bishop alertly told the tobacco monopolists to allow the free sale of tobacco until after the ships left for Newfoundland (less than a week later), and to Nantes, where serious disturbances broke out on the 20th. The crowd pillaged the tobacco and pewter offices, but the combined efforts of the leading royal officials and the bishop convinced them not to do the same to the stamped paper and wine tax bureaux.[38] The arrest of the supposed leaders of the uprising – two female and two male artisans – led to the seizure of the bishop as a hostage. The governor released the four artisans, but when the king officially promulgated a general pardon for all of the revolts in February 1676, he specifically exempted l'Eveillonne and her three companions from his grace.[39]

When it came time to chastise the Nantais for their action, the authorities adopted a typical measure of the time: they hanged an outsider, Goulven Salaun, a poor tavern boy from Châteaulin. During his execution, the governor heard the crowd grumbling "among themselves that he had done well to attack a Bas-Breton, that if he had tried to arrest the *gars* of the town, to put them to death, as he had done to this *valet*, that they [the *gars*] would sooner all be hanged than to suffer it and for that they would all have sacrificed."[40]

These events opened the famous revolts of Papier Timbré (stamped paper), in the Breton towns, and of the Bonnets Rouges, in the countryside. The rebellions lasted until mid-September, when the marquis of Montgaillard killed the leader of the peasants of Cornouaille, Sébastien Le Balp. Brittany had had relatively few examples of political and social unrest during the first three quarters of the seventeenth century, so how can we explain so massive a rebellion?

The basic structural indices changed course after 1650 or so. The population grew rapidly from the late fifteenth to the late seventeenth century. After 1660 or 1680, depending on the locality, the increase slowed and often reversed. In the eighteenth century, the population stagnated and, in certain periods, even declined.[41] The economy, save that of Nantes, also stagnated after 1640–80. Breton agriculture weakened, particularly the wine and livestock sectors. Breton internal commerce slowed, and with it the various economic sectors tied to that commerce – fishing, shipbuilding (save for the royal navy), wine.[42] Here the

---

[37] *Ibid.*, journal of Tondeau.

[38] Lemoine, document VI, Guémadeuc to Colbert, 20 April 1675.

[39] *Ibid.*, document VII, Jonville (commissioner of war in Brittany) to Louvois, 20 April 1675. See also documents IX (Morveaux, governor of the chateau of Nantes to Louvois, 23 April) and X (Jonville to Louvois, 23 April).

[40] *Ibid.*, document LXIV, Jonville to Louvois, 28 June 1675.

[41] Croix, *La Bretagne*, I, 183–222.

[42] *La Bretagne province*, ch. 18; on the wine trade, J. Collins, "Les impôts et le commerce du vin en Bretagne au XVIIe siècle," *Actes du 107e Congrès National des Sociétés Savantes* (Brest, 1984), I,

distinction between Léon and Tréguier, which continued to enjoy prosperity in the 1670s, and Cornouaille, whose economy slumped after 1660, is quite clear: the peasants of Cornouaille joined the rebellion, those of Léon and Tréguier did not.

In the eighteenth century, the province became a classic example of two-track development: a modernizing, flourishing sector such as the colonial trade of Nantes; a decaying traditional sector in places such as the Vannetais or Léon. Brittany, perhaps the most developed region of France in the middle of the seventeenth century, became one of the least developed by the middle of the eighteenth. One of the reasons for the decline was the interrelationship between the social and political structures of the province and its economy.

On the eve of the great rebellions, we find demographic stagnation, economic downturn, and, as we have seen in the examples from Nantes, increased social unrest.[43] Politically, the ruling classes of the province – the seigneurs and the legal men – felt themselves under attack from the Crown. The royal demesne reformation of 1673 assaulted all landlords; the stamped paper edict had an immediate impact on the professional interests of the legal class. The new tax on pewter probably hit hardest at lower class consumers and at those in the food and beverage trades, while the tobacco monopoly raised substantially the price of a commodity of universal consumption. Was it a coincidence that the rebellions broke out in the immediate aftermath of edicts attacking the two ruling classes of the province? Their anger at the king was all the greater in that he had just revoked these edicts in return for a grant of 2.6 million livres; the king's behavior on this score was, by any contemporary definition, unjust. Perhaps those charged with upholding his justice, then, had a hand in starting the rebellion?

The governor, the duke de Chaulnes, had no illusions on that score. He wrote several times to Colbert that the Parlement directed the revolt at Rennes. On 15 June 1675, he wrote that: "the Parlement conducts all of this revolt, and they advise the people not to give up their arms right away, that it is necessary that they come to the Parlement to demand the revocation of the Edicts, particularly that of stamped paper, and from the *procureurs* to the presidents *à mortier*, the largest number [of them] are going to combat the authority of the King. That is the pure truth and one here does not have to be very enlightened to know it."[44]

The comparison of the 1675 events at Rennes with what little we know of those of 1636 is enlightening. As we have seen, Dubuisson-Aubenay, accompanying the intendant, Valençay, attributed the disturbances to the drunken and

155–68. On the connection between economic downturn and the revolts, see J. Tanguy, "Les révoltes de 1675 et la conjoncture en Basse-Bretagne," *MSHAB* (1975), special issue devoted to the 300th anniversary of the revolts.

[43] Although resistance to the wine duty tax collectors was endemic in the 1630s and 1640s, the level of violence was much higher in the 1660s.

[44] Lemoine, "La révolte," document XLI.

seditious "gars" of the poor district across the Vilaine from the Parlement. Valençay wrote to chancellor Séguier that "a furious sedition" lasted for three days (12 September 1636). There were "assemblies of the people, day and night, with arms and once even with drums [*tambour*]"; these assemblies numbered 100, then even 400 to 500. They cried: "Kill the commissioner" and "Vive le Roy and monsieur the duke of Brissac without the *gabelle*, we will all have a piece of the commissioner." Two men were arrested but released on Brissac's advice, to prevent further disorder. Valençay credited Brissac with saving the day, because of the "belief the people have in him." He also suggested that the city be punished by quartering 4,000 infantry there. He asked to be named first royal commissioner to the Estates, citing the need to preserve his "honor in this province."[45] The apparent precipitant of this revolt was a demand to the Parlement that they offer the king a sizeable "loan." Valençay had no doubts: he believed the Parlement was behind the 1636 revolt and even suggested their temporary removal from the city. The parallels with the events of 1675 are striking, particularly given Valençay's specific connection of the revolt to the presence of an intendant ("commissaire extraordinaire") in the province.

We come back to the original description of the events of 18–19 April 1675, given by the *procureur du roi*; what truly alarmed the Parlement was the idea that the crowd was going to sack the houses of individuals. Indeed, a week after the original pillaging on the Champ Jacquart, the crowd, led, it would seem, by the students of the Jesuit *collège*, turned its wrath on the local Protestant community, burning their church in the suburb of Clerne. The son of the governor, Coëtlogon, with a small troop of nobles, rode to the rescue of the Protestants, but the crowd scattered along routes "inaccessible to cavalry." Coëtlogon managed to arrest two people, one a student (soon released because he was only 14), the other a baker. The crowd then marched on the prison, threatening to burn it down; Coëtlogon responded by calling out the bourgeois militia, to protect the jail. Two days later, the Parlement told the lieutenant general of the province, the marquis of Lavardin, that "one could scarcely imagine to what extremity fury had carried this mutinous *canaille* that they prepared nothing less than a universal pillage of the richest individuals of the city and of the bureaux in which they believed they would find money."[46] "Universal pillage" of the rich – here the Parlement had to draw the line. Like the leaders of Nîmes in 1645, those of Rennes in 1675 learned that local elites who encouraged rebellions could find that the lower classes might turn on their upper-class allies to follow an independent agenda. In Rennes, there was a clear split between the Parlement, at least part of which supported the rebellions, and the "bons bourgeois," that is, the merchants. The list of those arrested and held for trial in

[45] R. Mousnier, ed., *Lettres et mémoires adressés au chancelier Séguier* (Paris, 1964), I, 347–9.
[46] BN, Mss. Fr. 11,537, fols. 465–65v.

Rennes, and the list of those exempted from the amnesty of 1676 are quite revealing in this respect: those exempted (forty-four or more) included twelve people in the court system (*procureurs*, clerks, a notary, and a sergeant), thirteen artisans (eight of them butchers), five hoteliers, two women artisans, and an unknown number of fishwives; the list of prisoners held in 1675 includes nine *procureurs*, a sergeant, a mason, and a blacksmith.[47] When the Parlement reopened at Vannes in spring 1676, thirteen of the councilors failed to attend the sessions and had their *gages* withheld.

The lower classes had an agenda of their own (although a universal pillage was likely not it). The rebels were rarely unknown people, as we have seen from the occupations of those arrested or charged with complicity in the rebellion. The "leaders" of the rebellion were publicly executed. The "chief of the seditious" was one Jean Rive, a hotelier; among the others put to death we find a goldsmith and his wife, Jacques Miguet and Perrine Dubois, and a merchant seller of old clothes, Pierre Trehol.[48] The leader of the second sedition (of 17 July), was held to be one Pierre Daligault, a violinist; this poor soul was broken, drawn and quartered, and the sections of his body displayed at the four main gates of the city. Here we see the king and the duke de Chaulnes following the advice of Sébastien de Guémadeuc, the bishop of Saint-Malo, that what was needed was to "have done here some striking punishment that will imprint terror in the spirits of the people."[49]

The list of those implicated in the rebellions shows that the participants were people with an immediate interest in repealing the edicts: legal officials opposed to the stamped paper tax, those in the food trades opposed to the pewter and stamped paper taxes. The rebellion at Rennes did not represent a simple case of fury. The attacks were too continuous, too well organized to be the work of the infamous "unknown persons," to be a case of the "libertinage of some vagabonds and persons without occupation." The seditious did not fool the "noble bourgeois and inhabitants of Rennes." Feeling the "honor" of their city violated by so brazen a deed, they demanded that the Parlement punish the authors of the insurrection of 17 July:

certain armed individuals threw themselves into the Palace and there, with a hardened and temerarious insolence, pillaged the place in which the stamped paper was distributed ... the facility with which the wrongdoers executed, at high noon, a violence of this consequence and the effrontery with which they dared to form such a design makes the supplicants presume that it was a thing framed, conceived, and prepared well in advance, it seeming unlikely that it fell into the spirit of some individuals to form so perilous an enterprise without having taken advance preparations for its execution.[50]

---

[47] Lemoine, "La révolte," documents CXXXIX–CXL. List of Parlementaires absent from the sessions in BN, Mss. Fr. 11,537, fol. 515. [48] ADIV, 1 F 307, description of Morel (p. 35).
[49] Lemoine, "La révolte," document XCIII, Guémadeuc to Colbert, 23 July 1675.
[50] BN, Mss. Fr. 11,537, fols. 481ff.

There can be little doubt that some in the Parlement played a hand in organizing the daring raid. Although the merchants of the city may have "been so afraid of the tumultuous crowd that they dared not leave their houses, menaced as they were by a seditious cohort of a vagabond and libertine populace," the legal professionals played an integral role in the organization and execution of the various rebellions. The duke de Chaulnes told Colbert on 30 June 1675 that: "it is the *procureurs* who are most to be feared. Those of this city [Rennes] ... as well as those of Nantes, were the first authors of the seditions."[51] The king accepted this argument, disarming the bourgeois militia of Rennes and exiling the Parlement to Vannes for fifteen years.[52]

In the countryside, it was a different matter. There, too, the rebellion began at the bureaux of the stamped paper, tobacco, and pewter taxes. The news from Rennes made many tax clerks nervous, in Guingamp, in Quimper, and in Lamballe, where the clerk fired shots into his own office to make people think he had been attacked. The original disturbance at Guingamp took place on 24 May; the town militia held firm, arresting the ringleaders and hanging them a fortnight later. On 9 June, a more serious uprising took place in Châteaulin, in Cornouaille. The *lieutenant particulier* of Lower Brittany, the marquis de la Coste, killed an insolent local sergeant and was, in turn, shot in the shoulder by an angry crowd. The crowd surrounded the house in which de la Coste and his entourage took refuge, threatening to burn it down and kill them all unless de la Coste abolished the recent edicts. He agreed to do so.[53] In late July, the bishop of Saint-Malo told Colbert that all of the stamped paper offices in the small towns and bourgs had been closed (the owners of the houses fearing that they would be burned, like those in Carhaix), and that the nobility had everywhere fled to the enclosed towns.[54]

The troubles of Lower Brittany certainly began in response to events at Rennes and Nantes, and because of popular discontent with the new taxes, but they soon turned into something very like class warfare: the tillers of the soil against its owners. The bishop of Saint-Malo, in that same letter of 23 July, told Colbert that the peasants exercised cruelties on individuals from the towns and "still more on the nobility and the Church, in which it even seems that they have no further belief, as they had in the past, indicating to all gentlemen and ecclesiastics that they cannot henceforth claim either rents or tithes from them."[55] A month earlier, the duke de Chaulnes had written to Colbert that:

It is only in the bishopric of Quimper where the peasants gather every day, and all of their rage is currently against the gentlemen, from whom they received bad treatment. It is

---

[51] Lemoine, "La révolte," document LXVI.
[52] ADIV, 1 F 307, description of Morel. The governor disarmed the militia in stages: on 15–16 October, he disarmed all but fifty of the militiamen; on 24 October, he disarmed the rest.
[53] Lemoine, "La révolte," document LXIV, Jonville to Louvois, 29 June 1675.
[54] *Ibid.*, document XCIII, 23 July 1675.   [55] *Ibid.*

certain that the nobility has very rudely treated the peasants, who currently revenge themselves and who have already acted against five or six [nobles] of very great barbarisms, having wounded them, pillaged their houses, and even burned some of them.[56]

As Allain Le Moign, one of the leaders of the sack of the chateau of la Bouexière, was reported to have said when firing a shot through one of its windows: "I see one of the nobles and we must burn them all."[57]

De Chaulnes remained consistent in all his letters to Colbert about the mistreatment that the peasants had suffered from the nobility. In early July, he was quite specific about the nature of these complaints: "the exactions that their seigneurs have made against them and the ill treatment that they have received from them [the seigneurs], as much by the money that they [the seigneurs] have taken from them as by the work that they [the seigneurs] continually make them do on their lands, having no more consideration for them than for horses."[58]

Here we see something more than simple class warfare; we see populist demands for justice. The peasants struck out at the unholy three mentioned by the baron of Nevet: they "demand justice from the evil nobility, judges, and tax farmers."[59] The evidence of the bishop of Saint-Malo notwithstanding, most peasants demanded the abolition (or moderation) of seigneurial obligations; they did not attack rents or entry fees.[60] They also wanted judicial reform, particularly lower court costs (including the abolition of the use of stamped paper), and lower indirect taxes (on wine, tobacco, pewter, stamped paper). The focus of the rebellions became the towns: the nobility had taken refuge in the enclosed towns, the strongholds of the lawyers and notaries. Peasant bands (one might even call them armies) looted tax offices and some houses in Carhaix and Pontivy (neither enclosed); another band besieged Concarneau. The largest band, led by Le Balp, three times considered an attack on Morlaix, a town of more than 10,000 inhabitants and one of the richest ports in France.[61]

Again, the lists of those punished or pardoned for participation in the revolts show that the rebellion involved all of the lower classes. The crowd at Carhaix included many women (fishwives, servants, wives of artisans), as well as millers, *laboureurs*, *métayers*, farm workers, artisans of every sort (blacksmiths, polishers,

---

[56] *Ibid.*, document LXVI.
[57] *Ibid.*, document CXLVII, testimony of Jean Le Quere, *laboureur* of Keraliez. Le Moign refused money and insisted that he wanted the three nobles (de la Coste and two others) and other "gabeleurs"; he then beat the woman (*gouvernante*) in charge of the house. One of the shots from Le Moign's gun started a fire in the stables that spread to the house. Le Moign was publicly broken and strangled in Carhaix, his body returned to the parish of Briec and placed on scaffolding eight feet high, in front of the chateau of la Bouexière, where it remained until fully decomposed (document CXLVII, sentence against Le Moign).
[58] Lemoine, "La révolte," document LXXX, letter of 13 July.
[59] *Ibid.*, document LXXXIX, Nevet to de Chaulnes, 19 July.
[60] *Ibid.*, document LXXXIII, agreement between Abbey of Langonnet and their "vassals."
[61] *Ibid.*, 523–30, 544–50.

couturiers, bakers, butchers, tailors, saddlers), hoteliers, even a merchant of horses. Leaving aside the class composition of the crowds, we often find women in the forefront: l'Eveillonne at Nantes; an unidentified woman of Guingamp, hanged for leading the insurrection there; the large crowds of women who surrounded the Palace of the Parlement at Rennes in June 1675. The soldiers were reticent to fire on women: as the duke de Chaulnes said in his report to Colbert on the June events, "there is no honor in killing women and children."[62]

Much as the historian wishes for a simple explanation of these events, there is none. We see class antagonism, gender differentiation, populist demands for justice, immediate economic interest (of *procureurs*, of tavern keepers and hoteliers), and order antagonisms. The events of 1675 show precisely the impact of the massive coalition of lower classes so feared by the ruling classes. Virtually every member of the ruling classes speaks of the loss of the "authority of the king" and of the necessity to maintain the integrity of that most essential underpinning of society. The class war element seems strongest in the countryside, in the demands of some peasants that their landlords obey a "law" drawn up by the peasants. Yet the majority of agreements between landlords and peasants did not abolish rents or dues; the peasants usually insisted that the seigneur take only the customary dues and services. Those most severely punished by the peasants seem to have been those who abused the system (especially seigneurs who demanded excessive *corvées*).[63] The more one studies the peasants' actions, the more they seem to be a demand for justice, as defined by the peasants' perceptions of customary relations between seigneurs and peasants.

The immediate, selfish economic interest of specific people cannot be ignored as a cause of the revolts. Those in the legal profession strongly resented the stamped paper act; the hoteliers and cabaret owners resented both the wine taxes and the new tax on pewter. As for tobacco, all agreed that the people "could not do without it" and that the new tax made it too expensive for them to buy.[64] The substantial role of women in the revolts, especially the urban ones, had economic roots as well as legal ones (women's more lenient treatment from the criminal justice system). Women often ran wine shops and cabarets, and they handled the paperwork of many a small business.[65] Although one would be hard put to find a document that specifically assigned women the primary role of

---

[62] *Ibid.*, document XLI, 15 June.
[63] For example, the marquis of Trevigny, whose chateau of Kergoet was reportedly built entirely by *corvée* labor. Lemoine, "La révolte," document LXXII, de Chaulnes to Louvois, 13 July. Lemoine discusses the extremely bad relationship between Trevigny and his "vassals," which had led to sedition in 1668 and even to an attempted murder of the marquis on 10 June 1668, for which the authorities executed a local tailor in Carhaix shortly thereafter.
[64] ADIV, C 2785, remonstrance 4 of the Estates of Brittany, 1675.
[65] Collins, "The economic role of women."

guardians of moral justice in the community, the evidence from the revolts makes it quite clear that women did play such a role.[66]

As for the system of orders, we can see both solidarity and division. The old nobles – de Chaulnes, Guémadeuc, Lavardin – all blamed the judicial nobles, and the legal class as a whole, for instigating and supporting the 1675 rebellions. Before we see this as a simple matter of order-based conflict, however, we must admit that their accusations ring true in the light of other evidence. We must also admit that de Chaulnes and the others castigated the seigneurs of Lower Brittany for their harsh treatment of the peasants, and claimed that the injustices of the seigneurs provided the main cause of the rural rebellion. Again, other evidence from the peasants themselves supports their assertions. De Chaulnes' main support at Rennes came from the merchants, from the "bons bourgeois," who acted both to support the authority of the king and to protect their own goods.[67]

The peasants' sense of frustration must have been heightened by the impression that everywhere they looked, they saw the same people bearing down on them. The landlords were the deputies to the Estates: the bishops, abbots, and canons of the First Estate; the nobles for the Second; the lawyers for the Third. The legal men included the notaries lending them money and foreclosing on the mortgages; the same legal men or their relatives, serving as Cathedral canons, farmed the tithes. In the 1640s, around Nantes, the tithe farmers included notaries (at La Chapelle Basse Mer, at Saint-Erblain, at Carquefou), officer families from the Chamber, minor officers at the Chamber (including the *huissier*), and canon-rectors from prominent Nantais officer families (Fourche, Guischard, Robin). One of the most interesting cases is that of Assérac, where the tithe collector was *maître* François Guillory, a *procureur* at the presidial of Nantes. We have seen Guillory before, assessed for three separate parcels on the *fouage* roll of 1620: he paid the second largest tax in the village.[68]

The concentration of the elements of power into the hands of one group made popular rebellion less likely in Brittany because there was relatively little division within the ruling elite. The exclusivity of power also explains the very high level of disgruntlement and surliness on the part of the lower classes. The peasants' complaints of 1675 were quite specific about the perceived abuses of the existing system: the exactions of the nobles and the injustice of the court system. The complaints against the nobles were traditional ones: the peasants demanded an end to *corvées*, *champarts*, hunting restrictions and noble hunting rights.[69] The peasants also complained about the abuses of judges and the high

---

[66] In most cases, a women – either the noblewoman herself, or a *gouvernante* or even a *métayère* – provided the first line of defense of the chateau under attack.
[67] The phrase comes from Guémadeuc, writing to Colbert, about the positive attitude of the bourgeois of Saint-Malo. (Lemoine, document VI.)
[68] ADLA, G 244–5. See ch. 6 on Guillory.   [69] Peasants' articles in ADIV, 1 F 1640.

costs of justice: the twelve articles of the peasants assembled at Pont l'Abbé included one against soldiers, three on seigneurial rights (*corvées* and *champarts*, hunting, pigeons), one against priests charging too much for masses and burials, one against the wine tax, and six against the high costs of justice.

The peasant codes imply a strong reaction against two distinct forces: the seigneurs and the state legal system. In the rest of France, of course, peasant rebellions generally focused on the state fiscal system, which was much more onerous than it was in Brittany.[70] The complaints of the peasants of Cornouaille spoke to the remnants, real and important, of feudalism: seigneurial obligations. The peasants did not fight against obligations arising from property as such, that is, rent. They also objected to the political, that is, judicial, system, although here their focus was not *seigneurial* but *royal* courts. In the light of the practical realities of life in the region near Quimper, the two demands make perfect sense. First, the main form of land tenure was the *domaine congéable*, which carried everywhere seigneurial obligations in addition to rent and entry fees. Second, the city of Quimper had a presidial court and a Jesuit *collège*; Colbert de Croissy, visiting in 1665, commented that the decline of the local commerce was due to the children of the merchants attending the *collège* and following legal careers.[71] Jurisdictional disputes were endemic in the region because of extensive overlapping among high justiciars, and the presence of two royal and one ecclesiastical court at Quimper itself.[72]

The peasant codes provide an interesting indicator of discontent in the period of decline. Who drew them up? The internal evidence of the documents seems abundantly clear: the rich peasants surely authored these codes and provided the force behind the rebellions of 1675. Why would poor peasants be concerned about the tax on imported wine and not mention that on cider? What were the concerns of rich peasants? They objected to the heavy *champarts* and to the principle of *corvée*; they objected to the cash drain on their resources; they objected to abuses related to hunting and pigeons. The second category of complaint – the costs of justice – also related most to the richer peasants, the ones who had to have recourse to the courts (leases, etc.).[73] The traditional view that the stamped paper tax affected only urban dwellers makes little sense in the light of the peasant codes; the rich peasants associated the stamped paper with the hated legal men, those who already had their fingers in every pie – buying up

[70] Y.-M. Bercé, *Histoire des Croquants* (Paris, 1974); M. Foisil, *La révolte des nu-pieds* (Paris, 1970); M. Pillorget, *Les mouvements insurrectionnels en Provence entre 1595 et 1715* (Paris, 1975); B. Porchnev, *Les soulèvements populaires en France avant la Fronde, 1623–1648* (Paris, 1963).

[71] Colbert de Croissy, *La Bretagne en 1665*, 212–13. Although one can hardly accept this explanation for the local economic decline, it does point out the growing number of legal professionals in the region (and thus the likely greater demand for legal services).

[72] *Ibid.*, 204–10.

[73] In the region of the *domaine congéable*, the peasant displacing the sitting *tenuyer* (one removed by a legal action), had to pay the court costs. The landlord did not pay the fees.

peasant land (which, in the Vannetais, had virtually ceased to exist by 1690), lending at interest and foreclosing, leasing tithes at much higher rates (and presumably collecting more rigorously to cover the difference), buying tax exemptions in 1638 and 1640 (thereby sharply driving up the rates paid by the rich peasants), buying up common lands from the king and the high nobility, charging high fees for legal transactions, giving themselves (and likely their clients) a break on the tax rolls.[74]

There was little elite support or direction for the rural rebellion. The correspondence of de Chaulnes, Lavardin, and Guémadeuc shows a certain contempt for the peasants of Cornouaille, who, they often note, did not even understand French. There was a touch of cultural chauvinism involved here: the Breton-speaking peasants were, to those running the province, an inferior race of "brutal and savage" people. De Chaulnes, on 26 June, wrote to Colbert that "he [the governor of Quimper] assures me that the misery is so great among these people that we must greatly fear the results of their rage and their brutality."[75] Lavardin spoke even more directly: "Perhaps this regiment and the *maréchaussée* will be even more necessary in Lower Brittany; it is a rude and ferocious country, which produces inhabitants that resemble it. They poorly understand French and scarcely better reason."[76] The artisans of the towns, while often dismissed as a *canaille*, seemed to pose a more serious threat, because they could ally with the classes immediately above them to overturn authority. That was the worst nightmare of de Chaulnes and his assistants, one that came true in Rennes during June, when the bourgeois militia barred royal troops from the town.

The king needed the cooperation of local elites to carry out his policies, so that their needs, to some extent, dictated the limits of his policies. In Brittany, the local elite meant the seigneurs and the legal professionals. The mechanism

---

[74] Goubert, *French Peasantry*, ch. 9 on the activities of such people all over France. In Burgundy, for example, virtually every sale of land in the parish of Alligny-en-Morvan from 1659 to 1666 involved payment of a debt to a moneylender (often a notary) of Saulieu. (AD Côte d'Or, 4 E 49, 12–15)   [75] Lemoine, "La révolte," document LXXII.

[76] *Ibid.*, document LXXI. Guémadeuc to Colbert (document XCIII), wrote that: "If, among this people so gross and brutal, there was someone capable of understanding reason, there would be hope that the happy return of the King to Paris would terrorize them and make them go back to their duty, but as they do not even understand the French language, I think that only the chastisement and punishment of their crimes can henceforth prevent them from committing new ones and that one will at last be obliged to make rigorous examples for the good of the service of the King and the reestablishment of his authority in this province." The government pardoned all but a "few" of the rebels and sentenced relatively few people to death in the main towns, but several sources reported that the trees along the roads near Quimper were heavy with peasants, and we have seen the terrible punishment meted out to Le Moign (note 57 above), one relatively typical for those condemned to death for the rebellion. ADIV 1 F 1640 includes the printed list (contemporary to events) of those not covered under the general pardon. The duke de Chaulnes specifically exempted three entire villages near Quimper from the pardon (Lemoine, "La révolte," 188).

of cooperation was relatively simple because Breton elite structure was uncomplicated by the presence of a politically potent bourgeoisie or of its financial bureaucratic offshoot. The king got obedience and he got a steady and reliable source of income. The elites got royal backing for the preservation of their political and economic position, as well as a considerable share of the money raised in the king's name. The peasants got a seigneurial system of great harshness and a pattern of exploitation that deprived them of the resources – notably *cash* – needed to improve their economic condition. The long-term result was the desolation of the richest province in France and the creation of the impoverished, backward Brittany of the eighteenth and nineteenth centuries.

Conclusion

Henri de Rohan, baron of Léon, duke of Rohan and so often president of the nobility at the Estates of Brittany between 1600 and 1620, wrote in 1617 that: "It is certain that in every kingdom the authority of the King diminishes that of the *grands*, just as the increase of theirs reduces the royal power; it is a balance that cannot remain equal, one of the sides must have superiority."[1] Rohan suggested that the power of the *grands* was more deleterious to public order but added: "I do not mean to speak against the *grands*, I would be speaking against myself. The more means they have, the more effective instruments they are for serving well the King. I know that those who have a well-ordered intelligence [*esprit bien réglé*], judge that their grandeur is that of their King; the *grands* are happier and more assured under a great King, than under those little sovereigns who fear everything."

Early modern France was a society of contradictions, just as Rohan implies. He sees the struggle between the *grands* and the king for power, yet argues (from extensive personal experience) that what the *grands* really need is a great, not a weak king. Everywhere we turn, we find the same reality of "this and that at the same time" rather than one that conforms to our utopian belief in "this *or* that" as the reality of social life.[2] The transition to modernity – from feudal to sovereign government, from family to individual, from "violent, dirty, *méchant*" creatures to rational beings – created an insecure, terrifying world, one impossible to order even in hindsight.[3] Just as the chronological web of history is seamless, so, too, are its social hierarchies.[4] However much Loyseau and other seventeenth-century French people wanted to describe, and in describing proscribe, a society of finite immutable orders, they could not.

We can posit three basic truths about early modern French society. First, we must accept two hierarchies: the society of orders (the legal and social hierarchy); and the society of classes (the economic hierarchy). The political hierarchy combined the two elements. The top rung belonged to those who owned the main means of production, land. These people were both the ruling

[1] H. de Rohan, *Mémoires* (Paris, 1822), I, 174–5.
[2] L. Febvre, *The Problem of Unbelief in the Sixteenth Century: The Religion of Rabelais* (Cambridge, Mass., 1982), 100.
[3] The term "méchant" is that of R. Muchembled, *L'invention de l'homme moderne* (Paris, 1988).
[4] M. Raeff, *The Well-Ordered Police State* (New Haven, 1983), 11.

class, the landlords, and the ruling order, the nobility. To be accurate, we must admit that the ruling class, or classes, included many who were members of another ruling order, the judiciary.

Second, we must recognize that Ancien Régime France was a mobile rather than an immobile society. At the higher levels of society, there was substantial social mobility, by means of purchase of land, combined with the proper (legal) education and entry into the legal profession. The family could then aspire to office in the royal judiciary and obtain, if fortunate, fully fledged legal nobility. The highest ranks of this legal nobility contained, at least in the provinces, many people from the old seigneurial families. Some of the new families also received seigneurial privileges, either through purchase or royal grant.[5]

Third, we need to redefine absolutism. The contemporary meaning of absolutism, that the king had unlimited authority to make law, is quite clear.[6] Its historical meaning is less evident. Absolutism was not simply the last stage of the feudal monarchy, nor was it a mechanism by which the king allied with the bourgeoisie to destroy the power of the nobility.[7] The second model assumes that the legal class were the bourgeoisie, and that the king either used the bourgeoisie to break the power of the nobility or that he systematically played the two classes off against each other to expand his own power.[8] Both of these assumptions are dubious. The Parlements and other sovereign courts were landlords, not bourgeois; they shared a class interest with other landlords, such as old nobles, not with merchants. These rising *sieurs* were those who most threatened the old system of orders, who most acted as individuals (and who most often sought repression of women), yet they were also those on the first line of defense of the existing system of order. They had the uneviable task of defending order while redefining it. Before we start to argue that the king used the state apparatus to attack the old nobility, we would do well to remember that a key element in assuring obedience to the state was the royal army, commanded by that same nobility. The empirical limits on the king's ability to act were substantial, in every aspect of government. In short, "absolutism," as historians

[5] Breton examples in F. Saulnier, *Le Parlement de Bretagne* (Rennes, 1909), 3 vols.; in Colbert de Croissy, *La Bretagne en 1665*, and in the papers of the Chamber of Accounts, ADLA, B 66–79.
[6] See Keohane, *Philosophy and the State in France* and S. Hanley, *The Lit de Justice of the Kings of France* (Princeton, 1983) on lawmaking ability and absolutism. As noted above, Bodin also used this definition.
[7] Beik, *Absolutism and Society*, conclusion, as well as Anderson, *Lineages of the Absolutist State* and Brenner.
[8] This model is most closely associated with Mousnier, but it goes back to the work of G. Pagès, perhaps best summarized in his "Essai sur l'évolution des institutions administratives en France du commencement du XVIe siècle à la fin du XVIIe siècle," *Revue d'Histoire Moderne* (1935): 8–57, 113–38. Another recent presentation of such ideas can be found in P. Deyon, "Rapports entre la noblesse française et la monarchie absolue," *Revue Historique* 231 (1964): 341–56. Perhaps the most extreme statement is that of Mousnier, "Monarchie contre aristocratie dans la France du XVIIe siècle," *XVIIe Siècle* 31 (1956): 377–81.

use the term, is meaningless. How then can we best describe the early modern French state and its society?

The common point of the three elements – the nature of the social hierarchy, the (in)stability of society itself, and the rise of the modern state – was an obsession with order. The primary purpose of the state was to preserve order, which, to elites, seemed to mean the society of orders and its theoretically immobile population. The social reality was quite different. Society was not stable and immobile but unstable and fluid, in both hierarchical and geographic terms. In Brittany, there was less access to the top in the seventeenth century, the Parlement of Brittany became a closed corporation after 1650 or so, but exceptionally wealthy financiers could always advance up the ladder. At the Chamber of Accounts, for example, at least 120 families joined between 1590 and 1650, 36 of them between 1640 and 1650. The nobility and officer class needed new members, as families died out and as other families gradually moved up the social scale, leaving room in the middle for others to follow.

Below the top, Brittany (and France) had a remarkably fluid society. The rapid turnover of population in all areas, urban and rural, meant that a static society was impossible. At the lower levels of the ordered society – in the tavern trade and bakers' guild of Nantes or the mercers' guild of Rennes – many people changed residence and status on a regular basis.[9] In the villages, the occasional new face made its way into the ranks of the large-scale tenant farmers, although mobility seems slowest in this category. The guilds could not become closed corporations because their constant need for new members was so pressing; the village could not become a closed entity because of its permanent need for itinerant labor and because its land distribution meant that a large portion of the population, indeed the majority of it, could not hope to aspire to a land holding large enough in itself to support a family.[10] In most cases, social mobility required geographic movement. If we consider female as well as male lines, social mobility would appear even more striking.

Elite social mobility in Brittany, because of the absence of a financial bureaucracy, revolved around the legal profession: training at a *collège*, work for a legal man, purchase of a notary's study or the practice of a lawyer, purchase of a low-level legal office, followed by gradual ascent up the ladder of offices. In the process, the social climber bought land and removed his investments from commerce. Rarely, in Brittany, did he invest in tax farms or financial office. Social climbing was a slow process, one involving the purchase of land right at the start. Many Nantais families rose up from the legal profession, into the Chamber, and, in some cases, to the Parlement. The 1539 *francs fiefs* list of the bishopric of Nantes shows how long successful families had been at it: Bernard

[9] AM de Rennes, "Livre des Merciers."
[10] J. Collins, "Geographic and Social Mobility in Early-Modern France," *Journal of Social History*, 24, (3) (1990): 563–77.

d'Espinoze (family reaches Parlement in the late sixteenth century), Benjamin Rocaz (the same), Ollivier de Harouys (family has a First President of the Chamber in the early seventeenth century), and many other Chamber families – Davy, Chenu, Du Val, Hus (also Parlementaires around 1600), Morin, Avril, Bernard, Le Breton, Lescaut, Richard, Roger.[11] Those purchasing land near Nantes, as elsewhere in Brittany, were overwhelmingly from the legal class, not merchants. The only exceptions to this pattern were those cities, such as Morlaix or Saint-Malo, that had very rich merchants but no important royal court. In those cities, the merchants did buy land in the surrounding countryside.[12]

When the king sold the tax exemptions in 1638 and 1640, we see the legal men and royal officers in the front of the line; when he sold waste lands in the 1640s, the purchasers were the same individuals. In Nantes, it was our old friends from the Chamber – Le Lou, Madeleneau, Robin, Berthelot, Harouys; in Rennes, it was the descendants of Gilles Ruellan, in conjunction with old nobles, such as the Harcourt, and with other Parlementaires; in Vannes, it was René de Montigny, *avocat général* of the Parlement, as well as other Parlementaire families; in Cornouaille, more Parlementaires and the seneschal of Pontslorf; at Saint-Malo, it was the governor of the city, Talhouet.[13] The Estates argued against selling the common land, in 1643, claiming that the king should rescind sales of all marshes and commons not fully enclosed or attached to forests, because the lack of access to commons would ruin the poorer peasants.[14] Yet many landlords were simultaneously selling or dividing and leasing their own common lands. The extent to which the nobility and legal families had bought up or usurped the royal demesne is clear from the actions of the demesne reformation of the 1670s and 1680s, and from the extraordinarily violent reaction against the commission by the Estates and the Parlement.

Brittany is a valid microcosm of France, if we do not try to push the analogies too far. The administrative system of early modern France took local peculiarities into consideration not only because France had been constructed over a period of centuries, but also because the central government needed local elites to govern the country. In an "exceptional" area, like Languedoc, the "absolute" monarchy seems fundamentally "feudal" because its local allies were the seigneurs and the legal class.[15] The king respected the privileges of these people not because of some arcane sense of obligation (although that was part of his motivation) but because they alone held the ability to get things done in the local area. Most merchants could not directly enter this system because there was no

[11] BN, Mss. Fr. 22,342, fols. 193v and ff. In 1566, it was the same group paying the *francs fiefs*: Bernard and Yvon Rocaz, Jan Picault, François and Anne Menardeau, Guillaume and Pierre Bernard, Mathurin André, Marguerite and Michel Poullain, Pierre Le Breton, François Salomon – all families that would move on to the Chamber, most before 1600 (ADLA, B 3023)
[12] Colbert de Croissy, *La Bretagne en 1665*; see above, ch. 1.   [13] ADLA, B 2461.
[14] ADIV, C 2774.   [15] Beik, *Absolutism and Society*, calls it a "late feudal society" (335).

real financial bureaucracy in such areas (Brittany, Burgundy, Languedoc, Provence); they had to launder their money and themselves by buying land and becoming part of the legal class. The only exceptions were the very richest merchants and financiers, men like Ruellan or the Languedocian bankers of the late seventeenth and eighteenth centuries.[16]

In Brittany, as in Languedoc, the king allied with the landlords, because they held all the power. But does this mean the state was "feudal"? Part of the problem lies with the definition of feudal: we must take it to mean, like Beik or Perry Anderson, a state in which the dominant class is the seigneurs – landlords who retained political (feudal) rights over their tenants.[17] In fact, we should be more specific: the real ruling class was the great *seigneurs*. The more one examines any aspect of early modern France, the more the same, small elite sticks out. We have seen, in chapter 1, that very few nobles had a large landed income. In all of Brittany, fewer than a hundred families (indeed more like sixty) had landed annual incomes of more than 30,000 livres. These families invariably held superior seigneurial jurisdictions and virtually all significant military posts (royal lieutenancies, town governorships, commands in the local noble militia or the royal army). The leading judges in the Parlement, the presidials, and the main seneschalsies, were all large-scale landowners, although rarely seigneurs. The great seigneurs also dominated the Estates; again and again, as we have seen in chapters 4 and 5, a prominent noble (Condé, Rohan, la Trémoille, Pontchâteau) brokered a deal between the royal government and the Estates. The real business of the Estates of Brittany took place not in the assembly hall, but at the dinner table of a great lord, such as la Trémoille. The political ruling class was the great nobles, invariably those with a title (marquis, count, viscount, or duke).

If the state were truly feudal, it would seek to further their interests above all else. Did it? In a political sense, the king maintained the *grands* in many positions of power, notably in the military, but he increasingly gave effective authority to others, to the *sieurs* or the rising legal elite. Here we come back to our original definitions of classes, seeing the seigneurs and the *sieurs* as two separate groups, groups whose economic relationship to the means of production was very similar, but whose political relationship to the means of production was quite different. The king expressed his power through both groups: the seigneurs dominated the military, the *sieurs* ran the civil administration.[18] Even among the seigneurs, only a small elite received a substantial portion of their income from political (feudal) sources.

[16] Y. Durand, *Les fermiers généraux au XVIIIe siècle* (Paris, 1971).
[17] "Absolutism was the political manifestation of a system of domination protecting the interests of a privileged class of officers and landed lords," Beik, *Absolutism and Society*, 335.
[18] Not all seigneurs were military nobles; many Parlementaires, often with generations of both nobility and judicial service, held seigneuries. On Brittany – Saulnier, *Le Parlement de Bretagne*; on Paris – F. Bluche, *Les magistrats du Parlement de Paris au XVIIIe siècle* (Paris, 1960); on

Classes, estates, and order in early modern Brittany

The primary interests of the ruling classes in early modern France were the effective accumulation of the surplus (above subsistence) produced by the lower classes and the maintenance of order. The landlords and the state were directly opposed on the first issue: the landlords wanted low direct taxes so that they could obtain higher rents; the state wanted more tax money. On the most fundamental economic issue of the time, therefore, the state and the larger class of which it was supposedly the agent were often at odds. The smaller elite, however, received enormous sums of money from the proceeds of the tax money: in payments for military or civil service, in pensions and gifts, in interest. The particularist financial institutions of the *pays d'Etats*, such as Brittany, mitigated this conflict because, at least in Brittany, direct taxes were so much lower than they were in France. The fact remains, however, that landlords opposed, often violently, higher direct taxation.

Here we come back to the identity of the rural rebels: the critical role of the better-off peasants. Why did they rebel precisely in 1675? The duke de Chaulnes offers one possible explanation:

That which animates these spirits, this year, against the Edicts and particularly that of stamped paper, is that it is certain that cash is in short supply in the Province and that this Edict takes the clearest money ["l'argent le plus net" i.e., cash] while the people suffer greatly from necessity. That the country people have never opposed this Edict until a few months ago proves it.[19]

Who received the lion's share of Breton tax money? The Rohans, la Trémoilles, Rieux, Coëtlogons, Coëtquens, Brissacs – in short, those at the peak of the feudal hierarchy. They kept direct taxes on their tenants at very low levels, thus maintaining the integrity of their landed income, yet they also received massive payments from the royal treasury (whose Breton income came primarily from townspeople technically free of the control of these great feudatories). If we concentrate on the *grands*, instead of on the nobility as a whole, Brittany can seem another case of the essentially feudal nature of early modern France.

If we shift from the economic to the political, we again find that the state was the mechanism by which the landlords secured their position, just as the landlords were the agents through whom the state acted. Order depended on the cooperation of the state and the landlords, a fact that each understood. In the centralized core of France, with its vast financial bureaucracy, the state had a different mix of interests to satisfy. The king needed the capital of the financiers and of those from whom they could obtain support capital (that is, the *rentiers*,

Provence – S. Kettering, *Judicial Politics and Urban Revolt: The Parlement of Aix-en-Provence, 1629–1659* (Princeton, 1978) and Bohanon, *Old and New Nobility*; on Normandy – J. Dewald, *The Formation of a Provincial Nobility: The Magistrates of the Parlement of Rouen, 1499–1610* (Princeton, 1980).

[19] Chaulnes to Colbert, 26 June 1675, in Lemoine, "La révolte," document LIX.

especially women, and some merchants). He had to be sensitive, to some degree, to the interests of these financiers and their backers. Mercantilism was an effort to appeal to these financiers, who often profited from the monopolies granted by the king. Mercantilism in France was not, however, evidence of rising bourgeois influence in the state; in fact, it was quite the reverse. The mercantile bourgeoisie overwhelmingly opposed mercantilism, to judge from the reactions of Breton and Norman merchants to royal monopolies in the second half of the seventeenth century.[20]

The gradual movement to a more capital-intensive economy did not bypass the state; the king, too, needed more and more capital. There is little evidence that he allied with the "bourgeoisie," however defined, *against* the nobility, in an effort to obtain this capital.[21] He resorted to mechanisms well within the social and political framework: he sold, privatized if you will, governmental functions, such as offices and tax collection rights. French mercantilism was an economic extension of the sale of public functions into private hands: the extension of the basic political element of feudalism, the combination of private and public power, into the economic sphere, by granting of monopolies to those from whom the king borrowed money.

The king was trying to preserve the existing social and political order, not to destroy it. He sought not to replace the nobility with a new ruling class, but to preserve the system by obtaining the most dynamic and essential element of the new economy: capital. He combined these goals by improvising mechanisms – sales of offices, tax farming, monopolies – structurally and intellectually compatible with the existing system. The sale of public power into private hands, the sharing of public revenue with those who collected it, the granting of economic exclusivity to given individuals or corporations: are these not the very foundation stones of the Ancien Régime? Can we best describe these foundations as feudal?

Feudal society was largely corporative. The dominant corporations were the king, the Church, the seigneurs, the financiers, and the legal men but the corporate pyramid rested on a base of towns, provinces, guilds, and parishes. In the *pays d'élection*, where the financiers were strongest, the king had to assure the return on their investments. This meant no more assaults on the *paulette*, more regular payment of *gages* and other obligations, and a revised direct tax system. Louis XIV changed the structure of the direct tax system, so that it became more a set of tax farms given out to specific officers (the receivers of the *tailles*) than the official bureaucratic structure it had been in the first half of the century. By

---

[20] J. Collins, "La flotte normande au début du XVIIe siècle: le mémoire de Nicolas Langlois (1627)," *Annales de Normandie* (1984): 161–80. Norman merchants vigorously protested against whaling and other monopolies. Breton merchants did the same (see above, ch. 5).

[21] D. Dessert, *Argent, pouvoir et société au grand siècle* (Paris, 1984), on the extensive use of capital from the nobility to finance the tax farm syndicates of the 1640s and after.

making one person responsible for each collection district, while simultaneously making the taxpayers collectively responsible for the parish contribution, the king coopted the most active element of the financial elite. The others accepted the loss of their power along with the concomitant gain in financial security to some of their investments.[22] The threat to these investments, more than the loss of power, ignited the officers' Fronde in 1648. The Fronde demonstrates the corporate nature of these officials; they acted together, as a corporation, to protect their individual property. The king viewed both officers and financiers as parts of a corporation: the collective fines against financiers in the Chambres de Justice are a clear example of this mentality.

The noble corporation received enormous benefits from its connection to the monarchy but its members had to give up illusions of independent political power. The process was a gradual one, perhaps best symbolized by the end of the *compagnies d'ordonnance*, those aristocratic bands of personal retainers of the great that formed the core of the French army in the sixteenth century. The aristocrats still dominated the army, even in its regimental structure, and they filled local command posts – castles, town garrisons – with loyal clients just as before.[23] But they did not oppose the form of government; as Jouhaud has said of the Mazarinades, "this Fronde of words was not a Fronde of ideas."[24] The Mazarinades did not call for a different political system but for a realignment of political leadership. Louis XIV gave these people what they wanted: reassurance of their social and political supremacy, positions in the royal army, support for their control of local areas, money. They, in turn, gave their cooperation in getting more money from the population as a whole and in strengthening the king's power, which was, after all, expressed through *them*.[25]

With so many feudal elements so evident in the state construct, why should we be reticent to label the seventeenth-century state the last stage of the feudal monarchy, one we can call absolutism? To the extent that the ethos of the warrior nobility was the ethos of the king himself (as was particularly the case with Henry IV), it cannot be surprising that the state evolved institutions

---

[22] Dessert, *Argent* and E. Esmonin, *La taille en Normandie au temps de Colbert* (Paris, 1913), on the changes in the manner of levying the direct taxes.

[23] R. Harding, *Anatomy of a Provincial Elite: The Royal Governors of Renaissance France* (New Haven, 1980), examines these networks in the sixteenth century. K. Neuschel, *Word of Honor*, offers several correctives to the one-way perspective we often take to such relationships. See her chapters 3 and 5 for an extensive analysis of the reality of the Condé family's clientage system. As for the military in the seventeenth century, *avocat général* Millotet of Burgundy claimed in 1651 that every governor of a fortress or a town, every military officer in Burgundy (indeed every abbot and most of the Parlement) were clients of Condé: M.-A. Millotet, *Mémoire des choses qui se sont passés en Bourgogne depuis 1650 jusqu'à 1668* (Dijon, 1866), 3–4.

[24] C. Jouhaud, *Mazarinades: La Fronde des mots* (Paris, 1986), 237, 239.

[25] "Libre discours sur le temps présent, 1617," by the duke of Rohan, in *Mémoires*, 173–82.

modeled on feudal principles (monopoly, private ownership of public power).[26] The early modern state, like all states, existed in a given social reality; if the state did not reflect that reality – the economic, social, and political dominance of landlords – it would not survive.

At the same time that the king acted in such a manner as to defend the interests of feudal landlords, however, he also acted vigorously to establish the modern principle of united sovereignty; nothing could be more foreign to the feudal order than the rejection of divided sovereignty. To the extent that seventeenth-century France was a society of orders, it was still a feudal monarchy. The king sought to maintain the existing order; that order preserved the dominant position of the warrior nobility (the ruling class of the feudal order). To the extent that seventeenth-century France was a society of classes, it was not a feudal monarchy. The state's insistence on higher direct taxation directly attacked the fundamental economic interest of the ruling feudal class, maximizing their share of the surplus production of the peasantry. The long-term trend in landed revenue, away from feudal sources (particularly judicial rights) and towards land rent, also mitigated against the preservation of a feudal state. Politically, the state also attacked the feudal basis of society. The king's courts expanded their jurisdictions at the expense of seigneurial and urban authorities. The state sought to destroy the independent political power of these authorities, not to destroy their power itself. The state wanted them to express their power through state mechanisms – royal courts, the royal army – instead of through feudal ones such as seigneurial courts. The state did not seek to displace the ruling class, the landlords, but to redefine the basis of their power.

In a broader sense, there were several conflicting elements of early modern life that make a "feudal" state an inadequate description of political reality. The conflict about order centered on two different conceptions of order. The elites wanted to maintain the traditional "divine cosmos" of the ordered society.[27] In this divine cosmos, God sanctioned the entire social edifice. Protestantism's obvious threat to social order (as in 1525) helped exacerbate conflicts about that order. The early modern social order rested on a hierarchy of orders, on a family-based patriarchy, on the principle that everyone was unequal, and on the corporatist protections of group contracts. The Renaissance and the Reformation helped to create the individualism that attacked each of these fundamental principles of social order.

The ultimate guarantor of the social order was, of course, the king, yet the king was also the first individual. The lawmaking king acted *as an individual*,

---

[26] J.-P. Babelon, "Compte rendu du Colloque Henri IV," in *Quatrième Centenaire d'Henri IV, Colloque de Pau*, ed. P. Tucoo-Chala (Pau, 1990), has presented the first systematic exposition of the idea that the military training of Henry IV and Sully formed a key element in their conception of royal administration.   [27] S. Collins, *From Divine Cosmos*, ch. 1 and 4.

deliberately moving society *outside* of the realm of corporatism. The king's absolute authority to make law posed a dramatic threat to the divine cosmos. The king, in the imagery of Bodin and so many others, became the father of the national family; indeed, for Bodin the state was nothing more than the collection of its families. Those families, too, had an absolute authority: the father. To suggest that those subjected to these absolute authorities willingly accepted them is to misunderstand fundamentally the dynamic of early modern society. Corporations resisted royal absolutism, women resisted male "tyranny."[28]

The woman choosing her own husband, the poor man changing residence, the artisan drinking or playing cards on a work day or during high mass – all of them, acting as individuals, threatened the social order of groups. The king, too, threatened this order when he introduced so many *commissaires* into the administrative framework. The ambiguity of the relationships between individuals and groups dominated seventeenth- and eighteenth-century French society. The ruling authorities – state, Church, local – slowly "criminalized" much of traditional behavior.[29] At Troyes, for example, the police ordinance of 25 November 1665 forbade artisans from hanging about "idly and vagabondly, especially in the streets and public places, during work days." The ordinance also prohibited artisan banquets, "on pretext of confraternities," "public, scandalous or dissolute dancing," and charivaris. Artisans were not to "demand any money from newlyweds, nor from their families" or "to make any cries or clamors, nor to offer any 'deshonnestes' words, to sing illicit or defamatory songs in front of the doors of newlyweds." As for the "debauched and scandalous girls and women of ill life ('mauvais vie')," they were to leave town immediately, on pain of the iron collar and a shaven head.[30]

Breton authorities took a similarly dim view of "unrestrained" human conduct. In 1581, the police bureau (town council and royal officers) of Nantes complained that the "artisans and craftspeople of the town and faubourgs ... pass the greater part of working days in taverns, gambling and getting drunk, rather than everyone sticking to his work to gain his living and serve the public and individuals." Various workers – bargemen, porters, carters and others – refused to work, and demanded "illegitimate" wages. They formed "cabals and monopolies" to make themselves masters of their salaries, and spoke insolently to those who offered less than they demanded. The police forbade gambling and debauching on work days, as well as banding together in public, insolent and injurious speech, and any demands for higher wages.[31]

In the countryside and in smaller towns, the Church authorities stepped up the pressure. At Batz and Le Croisic, the episcopal visitor of 1665 (Jean-

---

[28] S. Hanley, "Engendering the State: Family Formation and State Building in Early Modern France," *French Historical Studies*, 16, (1) (Spring 1989): 4–27.
[29] Muchembled, *L'invention de l'homme moderne*, ch. III.
[30] AD Aube, E supplément 5340.   [31] AM de Nantes, FF 119.

Baptiste Coupperie, archdeacon of Nantes and member of a long-established officer family) noted that "mothers bring their small children into the church and have no respect for the holiness of the place." He banned mothers from bringing their small children to mass. At Assérac and Campbon, he forbade the inhabitants to go to the tavern after baptisms and burials, "a very pernicious custom." At Saint-Donatien (a poor suburb of Nantes), Carquefou, Sucé-sur-Erdre, Grandchamp, and elsewhere, he ordered taverns to close during high mass.[32] In 1669, the episcopal visitor attacked a wide variety of paganisms. At Saint-Etienne-de-Montluc and elsewhere, he banned the "ringing of bells on all souls' night" and on St. John's Eve; at Campbon, in 1675, the parishioners held a wild party on All Saints' Night in the church itself. At Coueron, Saint-Nazaire, Pontchâteau (and elsewhere), he forbade the *veillées*, the night-time social get-togethers centered on yarn and cloth production. At Mesquer, the parishioners were to stop playing *boules* in the cemetery "or making other profanations." Everywhere, the peasants used the cemetery to dry their laundry or to hold markets. In 1665, 1669 or 1675, the clergymen denounced the practice of giving "blows to enfianced" couples or "parading newlyweds through the parish." At Campbon, the curé even noted that "the young people pass too long a time between their engagement and marriage and sometimes live together, despite the Church's prohibition." The Campbonnais were not alone: at "Guenrat" (Guenrouet?), the priest limited engagements to two months and ordered the young people not to "frequent each other in a familiar manner during the said time of the engagement."[33]

The authorities reserved special harshness for vagabonds. As one ordinance put it, "several foreign and unknown persons" have entered the cities of the kingdom (in 1618) who might "engender and bring an alteration in the amity, concord, society, and good morals among the former inhabitants of the said towns." Vagabonds had to be well known in their "lives, morals, and conditions," lest they bring anything untoward, such as change, to the city in question.[34] These vagabonds threatened order precisely because they were individuals, acting outside the parameters of the corporate society, as defined by the elites. The *gars* of Nantes of 1675 shouted that the authorities had done well to hang a Bas-Breton, because had the victim been a *real* Nantais, there would have been a revolt. The *gars* of Nantes, of course, were overwhelmingly immigrants themselves. Everywhere we turn, we will see this same contradiction between the perception that the society of orders had to remain intact, and the reality of staggering social and geographic mobility.

The reality of social and geographic mobility exacerbated fears of individualism. Again, we see two contradictory movements. The Renaissance legacy emphasized man as the meaning of all things; Pico della Mirandola argued that

---

[32] ADLA, G 49.   [33] ADLA, G 47 (1638), G 48 (1640), G 50 (1669) and G 51 (1675).
[34] AD Aube, E supplément 5340.

man was superior to the angels precisely *because* man was changeable. Man acted; he willed his fate. The new state, the one we call absolutism in its French manifestation, was built around this revolutionary concept: that man – in France, the king – willed the social and political order. As Stephen Collins says of the English case:

Hobbes' metaphor compared the created state to created man and thus man the creator to God the creator. The Leviathan was contracted to do man's will and to fulfil man's purposes and needs; and man fashioned and willed his own order, his own efficient means to peace and satisfaction, his own meaning for activity and existence, and consequently, by extended metaphorical suggestion, his own means of salvation.[35]

The Reformation legacy provided the apparently contradictory element: man had to act but because he could act, he had to be restrained. The church investigators like Coupperie demanded the extirpation of "bestial" activity. The Reformation (and Counter Reformation) instituted a thorough-going, although not entirely successful, effort to eliminate natural liberty. Certain people, because they were too emotional or too bestial, could not be allowed to have such liberty. The apparent contradiction between the Renaissance and Reformation legacies was resolved by the role of reason; reason enabled man to act and that same reason, if properly developed, would control "natural" urges. This civilizing process can be seen everywhere in seventeenth-century France, whether in the creation of a "court society," in the sanitized rural images of Le Nain, or in the strictures of Jean-Baptiste Coupperie.[36]

There were four major elements that had to be integrated into the new order. First, society had to reconcile the spreading notion that all men were equal with the "necessity" for "inequality among men."[37] Early modern society rested on this second belief. Each man sought to protect the privileges of his group, seeing those privileges as his fundamental shield against others, particularly (in the seventeenth century) against the state. Second, society had to find a way to lessen the social implications of individualism. The individual, "sovereign over his own body," is a phrase best applied to the king himself. He was sovereign over his own body and over the bodies of all others. Society had, first of all, to seek protection from royal individualism. In England, men sought such protection by means of guarantees of their own individual sovereignty; in France, they sought protection, prior to 1789, through their group's privileges. In an increasingly individualist society, the French pattern was sure to fail, as it did.

Third, society had to protect property. Whether it was Bodin, Hobbes, Locke or Bossuet, the primary goal of political philosophers was to protect order and

[35] S. Collins, *From Divine Cosmos*, 29.
[36] N. Elias, *The Court Society* (Oxford, 1983), esp. ch. 3 and 7.
[37] The phrase is from B. Pascal, *Pensées* (Paris, 1954), 1149.

property. This protection went hand in hand with the need to restrain the savage in man, in part by the criminalization process described by Muchembled. Bossuet wrote that:

> Looking at men as they are naturally, before there is any established government, we find only anarchy, that is to say, in all men a ferocious and savage liberty ... there is no property, no rulership, no good [*bien*], no assured repose, truth be told, no right other than that of the strongest.[38]

Bossuet argued that only the king, the "invincible defender" of order, would assume the protection of property.[39] As Delumeau says, for early modern people, "the greatest evil of life was insecurity of life and goods."[40]

The fourth disharmonious element was the redefinition of gender roles demanded by the creation of a mixed individualist–group society. Women had had considerable economic, social, and even political power within the framework of the traditional patriarchal society. That society rested on the patriarchal family, not on individuals. Women could run these families (even kingdoms) without threatening the patriarchal order itself. When the focus began to shift to the individual, women became a threat in a new sense. The *individual* woman, acting independently, was a threat to the individualist patriarchal society in ways that she had not been a threat to the patriarchal family. The royal (and social) response to this threat was to require women to submit themselves to ever more rigorous control by the patriarchal family.[41] The steadily rising curve of exogenous marriage, particularly noticeable in the early eighteenth century, is only one example of the failure of this repression of women.

The king sought the cooperation of relevant elites of any given area in the governing process, so that the process would work. The only exception to this pattern came between 1634 and 1654, when the state as an ordinary instrument of governance collapsed; in those years, the French monarchy moved from expedient to expedient, relying as never before (or after) on the army to collect its taxes. The compromise of Louis XIV protected the vital interests of everyone: greater security for investors in royal debt; reduced direct taxes; a more stable tax leasing environment; clear support for the traditional social, moral, and political order of the localities. It is this last that so confuses us, because the local political order was not everywhere the same. What made Brittany typical of France as a whole was the respect for the interests of its elite, not the absolute commonality of those interests with those of other local elites.

---

[38] J. Delumeau, *Rassurer et protéger. Le sentiment de sécurité dans l'Occident d'autrefois* (Paris, 1989), 24, citing Bossuet, *Cinquième avertissement aux protestants* (1690).   [39] *Ibid.*, 25.

[40] *Ibid.*, 23. Delumeau later (28) writes: "Le besoin de sécurité, incluant la protection sociale et le droit au travail, a pris dans notre civilisation une telle importance qu'il y est devenu une obsession." The roots of this obsession, as he argues, lie in early modern times.

[41] Hanley, "Engendering the State," 9–13.

Some of these interests were commonly held; the king everywhere buttressed such interests. The clearest example of such support was the increasingly draconian legislation against women. Women guild members saw their rights curtailed; adult, never-married women found their ability to choose marriage partners eliminated; noble women found themselves increasingly cut off from public political power. The state, and society itself, enhanced the female role in the moral sphere, by means of an extensive literature devoted to women's role as the guardian of morality and by practical action by upper-class women, such as the poor relief supervisors of Nantes.[42]

Here we see the limits of state action against the trends in underlying structures: women's legal economic rights declined, but women's economic activity seems to have gone up; women lost legal authority to choose marriage partners, yet, in practice, increasingly chose their own husbands.[43] Despite strong theoretical support from men for the curtailment of female economic roles, the practical exigencies of individual households (which needed the resources provided by the adult woman) meant that legal restrictions against women would often be ineffective. Men might support economic restrictions against "women," but were unlikely to support such restrictions against their own wives.

The political role of women cannot be ignored. Breton women frequently led the resistance to the police in the ordinary disturbances of civil life and they also played a key role in popular rebellions (at Nantes, at Guingamp, at Rennes in July 1675). Upper-class women, too, were active political figures. We have seen, in chapter 5, that the Estates of Brittany asked the *duchess* de Chaulnes to intervene personally with the king to overturn the new edicts. The Rennais crowd similarly thought the duchess worthy of special attention. They showered her with rocks on one occasion, kept her from leaving the city (although not a prisoner, a rather nice distinction as Mme. de Sévigné points out), and even attacked her carriage. One group of women importuned the duchess to stand as godmother to a newborn, that is, to take the traditional role of the seigneur's wife. When she agreed, they hurled the rotting corpse of a cat into her carriage; at the same moment, a shot from the crowd struck one of her pages in the shoulder.[44] Was the choice of a cat accidental? It would hardly seem likely, given the special allegorical role of the cat in early modern society.[45] Surely the crowd believed that the duchess de Chaulnes was a powerful political figure in her own right, even if she had no official position.

We must also avoid the either–or mentality when we turn to male political

---

[42] That of 1579 at Nantes seems to be the first time they played the role there: AM de Nantes, GG 726.   [43] Collins, "Economic Role of Women."

[44] P. Clément, *Histoire de Colbert et de son administration* (Paris, 1874), 270. The story also appears in Tardeau's journal, ADIV, 1 F 691, 65. Mme. de Sévigné, *Lettres*, I, 777, letter of 26 July 1675 to Mme. de Grignan.   [45] Darnton, "Great Cat Massacre," esp. 82–9.

elites.[46] J. Russell Major has argued that sixteenth-century Estates were an integral part of the French "Renaissance" monarchy, and that such Estates played a valuable role as conduits of public opinion. Major sees the Crown shifting its attitude toward Estates under Henry IV (and Sully), and progressively growing less interested in public opinion. The culmination of this contempt for public opinion (and, by extension, Estates) is absolutism: the king (Louis XIV) without limits.[47] One aspect of this "absolutism" is the elimination of provincial Estates: in the southwest, in Normandy, in Dauphiné, and Provence.

Why did the king preserve Estates in Languedoc and Burgundy, both of which revolted against the *élus* in the early 1630s? Why did he preserve the Estates of Brittany in 1675? In fact, the duke de Chaulnes specifically recommended the Estates as a mechanism by which the king could reestablish complete order in the province. De Chaulnes understood perfectly the dual nature of Estates; in a letter of 26 June 1675 to Colbert, he wrote:

> I think that it is important that noone in Paris know when you have sent me the letters of convocation for the Estates, it will even be necessary to send them in a little case by messenger. The reason is, Monsieur, that if it is in the interest of this province and even for the good of the king's affairs to advance [the date of] the Estates, it could be that it will be convenient to put them off a bit so that the king can come during the time when they are held, because I know that those who were defeated in their hopes by the calming of the troubles in this city [Rennes] wish to take their revenge at the Estates and to put irons in the fire in order to take out a *fronde*.[48]

The Estates could serve the ends of local elite malcontents but, if carefully managed, could even better serve the needs of the king. De Chaulnes then went into a detailed discussion of why the Estates should be held at Dinan, rather than Nantes; the king took his advice. The Estates of Brittany (and those of Languedoc) survived because they were useful to the king *and* to the local ruling classes; the Estates that perished served no serious function.

Each side had certain vital interests to protect but those interests were by no means irreconcilable. The king wanted money, the Estates wanted to protect their own income. The compromise on that central issue was simple: make someone else pay. This policy had serious negative effects on the Breton (and Angevin) economy but it seemed to preserve the economic and political position of those who dominated the Estates: the landlords.

The intendant of 1636, Valençay, wrote to Séguier about the difficulties he was having in Rennes (and feared to have elsewhere). One of those from whom he sought advice was Richelieu's cousin, Charles de Cambout, baron of Pontchâteau. As we have seen, Cambout was one of the king's commissioners to

---

[46] Keohane, *Philosophy and the State*, on the general principle of reconciliation of apparent opposites in early modern French political thinking.   [47] Major, *Representative Government*.

[48] Lemoine, "La révolte," document LVIII.

the Estates of 1636, but he also sat with the Second Estate (at times as its president) and acted as one of the Estates' own deputies to Court. Valençay offers a remarkable insight into the mixed emotions of people such as Cambout:

I find myself greatly fortified in that such is the advice of monsieur de Pontchâteau, with whom I have conferred while at Quimpercorentin. He, like a good *compatriote*, cares as much as anyone in the world for the preservation of the privileges of the province but as a good and zealous servant of the King desires also that the royal dignity not be violated and that His subjects obey Him.[49]

The Estates of Brittany were not an assembly of feeble-minded, backward-looking, obstructionist bumpkins, fighting a last stand for privilege against a modernizing, centralizing monarchy. They were a group of powerful landlords, including some nobles of national stature, who used the Estates to protect not obscure privileges but very real economic interests. They protected their tenants from direct taxation, thereby preserving rental income, protecting particularly the cash resources needed to pay the higher entry fees; they voted themselves pensions (and paid for a lengthy social extravaganza every two years); they provided the king with enough money to convince him to let them continue to run the province. The problem for the province was that their interests were not those of other Bretons. For those who had to pay the higher rents, taxes, and tithes, the uncontested power of the landed elite proved an unmitigated disaster. For the landlords themselves, the solution preserved their political power, but likely worsened their economic position (rents declined or stabilized after 1660).

What was the nature of the French state, of French society, in the seventeenth century? First, the stronger state was not the manifestation of something called absolutism but of individualism. The state's unlimited ability to act, to make law, made the king the first individual. As French society moved toward individualism, the political elite believed it needed a strong, centralized state to overcome the immediate disorder of rampant individualism. In a society in which people had not yet internalized the new self-restrictive values of reason, social institutions, above all the state and the Church, had to serve as the restraint on individual action. At the end of the eighteenth century, believing people to have sufficiently developed their reason to check themselves (the Rousseauian ideal that "freedom is obedience to law of one's own making" – laws made, of course, through reason), the political elite overthrew both the state and the Church.

The principle that all men are equal was an inherent attack on the principle of order, as seventeenth-century people understood it. Order presupposed hierarchy; equality meant a lack of ordering, and thus of order itself. The emphasis on reason automatically disqualified certain people from individualism. The largest group so disqualified was women. Men were rational, women were

---

[49] B. Porshnev, *Les soulèvements populaires en France avant la Fronde, 1623–1648* (Paris, 1963), appendix document 16.

emotional; reason had to restrain emotion; therefore, men had to be given expanded powers to control women.[50]

Similarly, man the beast could not be allowed individual liberty. How often have we read in these pages the opinion of a member of the elite that the artisans, workers, and peasants are beasts, that they are brutal, that they scarcely understand either French or reason, in Lavardin's telling phrase? The state and the Church together would tame these wild beasts by political and moral repression. The state would do all this in the name of order, by protecting against attacks on the holy trinity of king, justice, and God.

The lower classes understood the dissonance of their interests and those of the landlords but it was difficult effectively to do much to advance their agendas. The elite controlled all the levers of power. There were rarely the sort of factional fights that caused so many problems in Provence and Languedoc in the first half of the seventeenth century; the only Breton examples are the brief dispute about the Estates in 1651 and the revolts of 1675.[51] The lower classes could only create a general atmosphere in which the elites lived in constant fear and insecurity – "a country in which few people are in surety against the eruptions of a mutinous populace" to reprise the phrase of Sebastien Corantin (wine duty clerk, Fouesnant, 1725).

The elites acted within this climate of insecurity and sought to supervise every conceivable aspect of life. They kept a close watch on lower class morality; they monopolized every position in every important institution – town government, royal government, church, hospital, seigneuries; they intermarried and developed clientage networks based on family and on patronage; they allowed considerable social mobility to those with money and a willingness to spend it in socially respectable ways; they enacted legal restrictions against all threats to the emerging order of individualism, whether those threats were women or lower-class men. For the mass of the population, both urban and rural, life was a constant struggle against the forces of order, a struggle for women and men to express themselves as individuals. For most of them, such expression was possible by means of everyday action: they simply moved. They also sought increasingly to organize themselves into groups to protect their individual needs.

The lower classes resented the forces of order, as much for social and political as for economic reasons. It is misleading to single out one aspect of the relationship, to say, for instance, that the critical factor in rich–poor relations

---

[50] Such was the argument of the male-dominant side of the "querelle des femmes." The opposing side took a new stance in mid-century, with the work of the Cartesian François Poullain de la Barre, *De l'égalité des deux sexes* (Paris, 1673). The contemporary English translation, *The Woman as Good as the Man. Or the Equality of the Two Sexes*, is available in a reprint edition (Detroit, 1988). Poullain de la Barre took the then-revolutionary position that women and men are equal because they each have reason.

[51] The Midi had endemic factional fighting, to judge from the works of Kettering, *Judicial Politics* and Beik, *Absolutism and Society*.

was the nature of economic exploitation. In the long run, that was likely true, but in the short run of everyday life, what mattered more was the personal detestation of the wine duty clerk or the provost's deputy visiting the tavern to disrupt the life of ordinary people.

We have seen, in chapter 7, the often violent confrontations between the forces of order and the lower classes, particularly in taverns. I am reminded here of the words of Henry de la Haye, as he led the crowd routing the wine duty clerks visiting the tavern of Anne Plessis. The clerks tell us that he blasphemed the holy name of God, incited the crowd to riot, and urged violence against the wine clerks. When they fled into and down the street, he followed, shouting as they escaped, that "everyone was like him." I believe he was right and, more importantly, that the forces of order of seventeenth-century France also believed he was right. The early modern beliefs that society was insecure, unstable, and too mobile, and that men (and, even more, women) were savages who had to be disciplined through laws determined by human reason, lay at the core of the development of the French state, of its relationship to French society, and of their common search for a definable order to defend.

Appendix

Income of major Breton families, 1665 – the estimates of Colbert de Croissy

Family	Income	Military Office	Superior seigneurial jurisdiction	Highest title
Income 35,000 livres or more				
Rohan	200,000	national	yes	prince
Rohan	133,000	national	yes	prince
Guéméné	65,000	national	yes	prince
Rieux†	160,000	national	yes	
Asséract†	100,000	unknown	yes	count
Sourdéac†	60,000	national	yes	marquis
Trévigny†	80,000	local	yes	marquis
Carman†	80,000	regional	yes	marquis
Rosmadec‡	76,000	regional	yes	marquis
Coëtquen†	61,000	national	yes	marquis
Espinay	60,000	local	yes	marquis
Cludon†	60,000	local	yes	marquis
Brissac	50,000	national	yes	duke
La Moussaye†	40,000	regional	yes	marquis
Pontcallec†	40,000	local	yes	marquis
Coëtjunval	35,000	regional	yes	unknown
Kernezné	35,000	local	yes	marquis
Carné‡	35,000	local	yes	viscount
Very powerful families listed without income estimate				
Avaugour	n.g.	regional	yes	count
Boiséon	n.g.	national	yes	count
Bréhant	"very rich"	national	yes	count
Cambout†	n.g.	national	yes	duke
Goulaine	n.g.	national	yes	marquis

Family	Income	Military Office	Superior seigneurial jurisdiction	Highest title
Very powerful families listed without income estimate — contd				
Lannion‡	n.g.	local	unknown	count
La Trémoille	n.g.	national	yes	duke
Locmaria†	n.g.	national	yes	marquis
Monbourcher†	n.g.	unknown	unknown	marquis
Retz	n.g.	national	yes	duke
Vendôme	n.g.	national	yes	duke
Volviret†	n.g.	local	yes	count
Very powerful families with partial income listing				
Acigné†	22,000+	local	yes	count
Coëtlogon† (wife)	n.g. 15,000	regional	yes	marquis
Guémadeuc†	22,000+	regional	yes	count
Nevet	8,000+	regional	yes	marquis
Income of 20–32,000 livres				
Kerjean	32,000	unknown	unknown	marquis
Cahideuc	30,000	local	yes	baron
Penmarc'h	30,000	unknown	unknown	baron
Poulpry*	30,000	none	no	–
Quengo	30,000	regional	yes	viscount
Penfentyao*	28,000	none	no	–
La Coste	25,000	regional	unknown	marquis
Kerouartz	25,000	unknown	unknown	–
Kergroadez	20,000	unknown	unknown	marquis
Keroual	20,000	unknown	unknown	–
Mortemar	20,000	unknown	yes	duke
Visdelou*	14,000+	local	no	–

Notes:

n.g. not given

* indicates judicial family

† ranked among "first class" in bishopric of Vannes

‡ ranked among "second class" in bishopric of Vannes

Military offices are divided into three categories:

Appendix

National – royal army commands, governor of province, lieutenant general of province

Regional – *lieutenants particuliers*, command of major fortresses (Nantes, Rennes, Saint-Malo, Morlaix)

Local – governors of lesser towns, commanders of local noble militia or seacoast guard.

Titles

The five families marked [–] are simply *sieurs* (although it is likely all five were, in fact, seigneurs). The Coëtjunval family has no titles listed, but one of its members was, in 1665, bishop of Quimper, which makes it likely that the family possessed more than simple nobility. The family had intermarried with other leading local families, such as Rosmadec, Carné, and Nevet (*La Bretagne en 1665*, p. 193, n. 16).
Source: J. Kerhervé, F. Roudaut, J. Tanguy, eds., *La Bretagne en 1665 d'après le rapport de Colbert de Croissy* (Brest, 1978).

Note

Colbert de Croissy is not always consistent with respect to reporting the income of individuals; for example, the income of the duchess of Rohan is reported as 100,000 livres in one place, yet as 133,000 livres when one adds up the totals for her individual holdings. Certain very powerful families, such as la Trémoille, are listed as owning seigneuries but no income figures are provided. The nine families listed in that category, with the possible exception of the count of Lannion, governor of both Vannes and Auray, all had landed incomes of 50,000 livres or more. Lannion was married to Thérèse Huteau de Cadillac, no doubt either the daughter or sister of François Huteau de Cadillac, a Parlementaire (and a high justiciar in the region near Vannes). The other branch of the Huteau family had, early in the seventeenth century, a *trésorier de France*, later president of the Chamber. Colbert de Croissy listed both Huteau de Cadillac and Lannion among the second rank of the nobility of Vannes. Most of the people so listed were judicial nobles.

The partial listings exclude a wide variety of lands, including those in the bishoprics of Rennes (Nevet had large holdings there) and Nantes. The holdings of the Retz and Goulaine families, in the bishopric of Nantes, are not discussed in the report at all, although Colbert de Croissy does mention both families in the context of marriages and of lands they have inherited in various regions (both within and outside Brittany).

Bibliography

ARCHIVAL SOURCES

Archives nationales

P 3438   List of cash shipped to Central Treasury, 1629
120 AP   Family papers of Maximilien de Béthune, duke of Sully

Bibliothèque nationale

Cinq Cents Colbert
16   Finances, 1599, whole kingdom
41   *Rentes* on clergy, 1567–76; charges, 1570s and 1580s; documents on Assembly of Notables, 1596
106   Receipts and expenses, including shipping costs, 1609
203   Documents on *Compagnie de Morbihan*
256   *Paulette* assessments, 1604
289   Direct taxes, 1600, whole kingdom
491   Shipping costs, Nantes to Paris, late sixteenth century

Manuscrits français
3411   Military sutlering contracts, Poitou and Brittany, 1578
3558   *Etapes*, 1597, Brittany
7736   Direct taxation, 1636–40
10,839   *Etat au vrai*, Brittany, 1606; demesne, 1606
11,537   Secret registers of the Parlement of Brittany, 1670s
14,399   List of all officers ever accepted into Chamber of Accounts of Nantes (some inadvertent omissions)
16,622   *Etat de la valeur*, 1620, Brittany
16,626   1607 finances, entire kingdom
17,321   1596 memoir on finances, entire kingdom
18,490   Receipts and expenses, 1636–40, entire kingdom
18,510   *Etat au vrai*, 1610; 1643 and 1647, direct taxation; direct taxes, 1649, entire kingdom
18,592   Seizures protested by Dutch merchants, middle of seventeenth century; lawsuit of Dutch and Nantais merchants, 1644

Bibliography

18,598	Revolt at Vannes, 1643; grain trade, 1643
21,479	*Décimes*, 1578; various financial documents; *état de la valeur*, Brittany, 1618
22,311	Repairs of Douarnenez in 1615–17; Rohan family pensions to noble servants (early seventeenth century); 1587 troops costs; bread purchases for army, 1592
22,330	*Etats de la valeur*, 1533, 1535, Brittany
22,342	*Francs fiefs*, 1539; *état au vrai*, 1535, Brittany

Manuscripts Dupuy

89	Finances, 1607, whole kingdom
233	Memoir on trade, 1584; estimate of debts, 1580; list of *mortes payes*, 1571
824	1611 *état des finances* (probably an *état au vrai*)
848	Extracts from the Central Treasury accounts, 1522–1604

Nouvelles acquisitions françaises

172	1647, receipts and expenses, whole kingdom
200	1634, 1643, *brevets* for direct taxes, whole kingdom
21,878	Account of duke of Mercoeur's treasurer, 1586

Archives départementales (Brittany)

Côtes du Nord

B 107	Wine duties, 1650s
B 1135	Tithe case about flax, seventeenth century

Finistère

B 1289	Resistance to wine duty farmers, 1725
2 E 5	Civil disturbance at Morlaix, 1631
2 E 1501	Special direct tax, Carhaix, 1603, 1604, tax roll
2 E 1505	
1 G 335	Tithes of Gourin
16 G 1	*Fouage* roll, Audierne, 1616, 1619
66 G 60	Tithes of Plouvara
125 G 2	*Fouage* roll, Loc Eguiner
151 G 94	
232 G 4	La Roche Maurice, *amortissements*, 1642
267 G 8	Sizun, *feux* sale, 1640–1
5 H 37	Tithes, middle of seventeenth century
5 H 115	Tithes of Chambrières

Ille-et-Vilaine

Two sources provide the largest share of information about the Estates of Brittany: the *assises*, C 2749–86, covering the period 1610 through 1679; and the accounts of the treasurer of the Estates, C 2887 and following.

Bibliography

Series 1 B are the papers of the Parlement; the records of the Estates of Brittany form the core of Series C. Because of the heavy reliance on Series C, it is listed separately from the others.

Series C

631	Report of *procureur syndic*, 1638
2645–58	Eighteenth-century copies of papers of the Estates, meetings of 1597 to 1680
2744–5	Inventory of papers of the Estates (eighteenth century)
2748–86	*Assises* of Estates, 1610–79
2887–9	Accounts of Gabriel Hus, treasurer of Estates to 1608, grant of 600,000 livres (1597)
2915	War accounts, 1596–8
2920	Accounts of treasurer of the Estates, 600,000 livres grant, through 1609
2922–3	Supporting documentation for accounts of the treasurer of the Estates, early seventeenth century
2930	Account of king's share of duty, 1608–14
2940–2	Audits of the accounts of the Estates, king's share of duty receipts, 1610–36
2967	Account of king's share of duty, 1618
2969	Account of king's share of duty, 1614–17
2980–1	Accounts of king's share of duty, 1640s–1650s
2982	Account of overdue payments to Vertus, Montbazon, Brissac
2985	Accounts of king's share of duty, 1660–1670s
2987–9	Accounts of 2.4 million livres grant, to 1609
3265	*Billots*
3227	Levies for troops, 1614–16
3228	Report from treasurers of France on demesne, 1605
3287	Documents on conflict over precedence between Rohans and la Trémoilles
3300	Collected documents on textile manufacture and taxation
3467	Documents on wine duties
3468	Commission on town debts, 1613
3672	Levies for troops, Saint-Brieuc, 1628
5979	Wine sales of wholesale merchant of Morlaix, 1682–4

Other series

1 Ba	List of all officers who served at the presidial of Nantes (including the seneschals and provosts)
1 Bh 8	Grain purchases by Nantes, 1630–1
B 3276	Glorious accession tax for Louis XIII, 1611

Series 1 F, papers of Artur de la Borderie, a late nineteenth-century historian who collected primary documents and left his collection to the AD of the Ille-et-Vilaine, contains an unusually diverse group of documents, related only by their common possession in the hands of M. de la Borderie.

1 F 36	An eighteenth-century copy of a list of "terres nobles" in Léon in 1536

Bibliography

1 F 307	Journal of Morel, 1675 events at Rennes
1 F 691	Journal of Tardeau, 1675 events at Rennes
1 F 692	Copies of peasant codes of 1675
1 F 1640	*Fouage* roll, Langourla
4 Fc 7	Guérande, housing of troops 1640
G 274	Bishop's taxes on commerce at Saint-Malo
G Acigné	Parish papers of Acigné
G Ercé	Parish papers of Ercé
G Gévezé	Parish papers of Gévezé
G La Fonta-nelle	Parish papers of La Fontanelle

Loire-Atlantique

The papers of the Chamber of Accounts formed the main source in these archives. The registers of the Chamber, which listed most major forms of business (new officers, requests for renewal of town duties, tax leases, contracts of the Estates, etc.) provide the centerpiece of the research. The most important group of registers are those in B 53 through B 85.

B 2	Special duties granted to Rohan family, 1462
B 3	Creation of Parlement, 1550s
B 7	Special duties granted to Rohan family, 1476, as part of dowry for Marie de Bretagne, daughter of duke François II
B 8	Special duties granted to Rohan family, 1477
B 53–85	Registers of the Chamber of Accounts, 1550s–1670s
B 151	Factional division, Chamber of Accounts, 1591
B 713	Finances, 1589, report of treasurers of France; various other financial documents
B 715	Investigation of demesne, 1613
B 720	Investigation of demesne, 1643
B 790	*Pancarte* of duties of *prévôté de Nantes*
B 2461	Sale of "terres vaines et vagues" in 1640–1
B 2966	Sale of *greffes*, 1626
B 2968	*Etat de la valeur*, 1601, Brittany; revenues in Brittany, 1628, 1630
B 2972	Accounts of *prévôté de Nantes*, 1591
B 2973	Sale of *impôts*, 1641
B 2975	Town duties of Nantes, 1595–6, register
B 2976	Port register (*registre de la prévôté*), 1631
B 2987	Finances, 1628, 1630; information on *feux*, 1500–57
B 2990	*Feux* count, 1645
B 2994	Sale of *affranchissements*, 1638, Léon
B 3009	*Feux* count, 1617
B 3010	*Feux* count, 1652
B 3011	Sales of exemptions, Léon, 1640
B 3023	*Francs fiefs*, 1566
B 6649 to B 6670	"Registre de la police" of provost and seneschal of Nantes, 1610 through 1670s

B 6782 to
  B 6784   Police records, primarily related to wine taxes
B 6685   Port register of Nantes, 1643 (partial)
B 8610 to
  B 8612   Grain prices at Nantes, 1650s–1670s, intermittent years
B 9230   Registers of the seneschal of Guérande, intermittent for most of the seventeenth century
B 12,871   Investigation of finances (including royal demesne), 1583
B 12,882   Investigation of nobility, 1660s
B 12,901   Port register of Nantes, 1644 (partial)
C 414–16   Eighteenth-century copies of records of the Estates, 1567–89
C 633   Bread prices, 1694 ruling
C 675   Export rules, 1617 ruling
C 696   Levy of 900,000 livres on towns, 1693
C 700   Charter of *Compagnie de Nantes*, 1646
C 701   Lawsuit of Dutch and Nantais, 1643
C 780   *Pancartes* of various transit and sales taxes
C 781   Duties levied for the *bêtes vives*
C 788   *Pancarte* of *ports et havres*
C 790   *Pancartes* of *prévôte de Nantes*, 1537, 1571
E 212   Breton finances, 1480s; 1503
E 1188   Poullain family succession papers
G 47–51   Episcopal visitations, 1630s to 1670s
G 87   Papers of cathedral chapter of Nantes, concerning their duty of 5 sous/pipe of wine passing under the Loire bridge
G 244–5   Tithe farming, approximately 1600–1720, in the *pays Nantais*, holdings of cathedral chapter
G 348   Tax roll, Assérac
G 440   Tax rolls, Massérac, 1665–8
G 441   Papers of the *fabrique* of Massérac
H 9   Prieury of La Magdelaine, leases on rural property
H 144   Prieury of Sainte-Croix, property leases
H 158   Leases on ecclesiastical property, Carmelites of Nantes
H 162   Leases on property, Abbey of Saint-Gildas of Rhuys
H 242   Loire river duty of Carmelites of Nantes
H 263-5   Leases, properties of Charterhouse of Nantes
H 267   Leases, fishing rights in Loire marshes, Charterhouse
H 275   Prieury of Izeron, Charterhouse, leases on *métairies*
The citations from Series 4 E II are taken from notes compiled by Jean Tanguy, not from my personal consultation of these records.
4 E II 20   Notarial copies of tax leases
4 E II 98   Notarial copies of tax leases
4 E II 100   Notarial copies of tax leases
4 E II 1713   Notarial copies of tax leases

Bibliography

Morbihan

B 820	Papers of merchant Felot (Vannes)
B 2778	*Prisage* of 1634, *laboureur* near Hennebont
B 2780	Bail of *métairie* of Kersalic; inventory after death, 1634
B 2789	Grain sales, region of Hennebont, 1640
B 2794	Papers of *sénéchaussée* of Hennebont, revolt of 1643
G 43	Tithes
G 131	Tithes
G 853	*Fouage* roll, Lanvaudan
38 G 5	Tithes, region of Sarzeau, 1620s to 1670s

Archives départementales (outside Brittany)

Aube
E *supplément* 5340 Police of Troyes, seventeenth century

Côte d'Or
Series C, tax rolls of various Burgundian parishes (C 6194, Alligny-en-Morvan, for example)

4 E 49, 12–15	Papers of notary Goujard, 1650s–1600s

Deux-Sèvres

C 145	Tax rolls, Saint-Martin-les-Melle, 1640s

Gironde

6 B 213	Port register of Bordeaux, 1640
B 4832	Investigation of riots in Quercy, 1624

Municipal and communal archives

Nantes

AA 23	Royal letters for tax on walled towns, various years, sixteenth century
AA 72	Documents on Estates of Brittany
AA 75	List of some town deputies to Estates
BB 4–49	Council deliberations, 1555 to 1680
CC 2	Wine duties, assorted papers
CC 72	Tax on walled towns, various years, sixteenth century
CC 75	Tax documents; 1575 levy for infantry
CC 78	Tax on walled towns, 1575
CC 86	Tax rolls, 1593; relief tax, 1580
CC 150 to CC 179	Accounts of treasurer (*miseur*) late sixteenth and seventeenth centuries
CC 478	Resistance to wine duty collection, 1570s
CC 479	Resistance to collection of wine duties, assorted pieces
DD 30	Accounts 1–3 of New Hospital, 1650s

Bibliography

EE 221 Outfitting ship for king, 1570s

FF 50 Police fines, 1568

FF 52 Police, 1560s

FF 54–6 Police, 1560s

FF 119 "La Police Générale de la Ville, Fauxbourgs, Banlieue et Comté de Nantes," (Nantes: Nicolas Verger, 1721)

FF 152 Grain and bread prices at Nantes, isolated years

FF 154 Grain and bread prices at Nantes, isolated years

FF 176 Grain markets, especially 1630–1

FF 186 1590s, investigations of grain stocks

FF 187 Grain merchants, 1596

FF 188 Grain imports, 1630–1, purchases on behalf of town government by Sauvaget brothers and others

GG 1–10 Parish of Notre-Dame, civil registers

GG 137 to Parish of Saint-Laurent, civil registers
GG 150

I also consulted the civil registers of Sainte-Croix, Saint-Denis, Saint-Laurent, Saint-Nicolas, and most of the other Nantais parishes. Although that material is not cited here, it would be misleading to imply that I have formed ideas about marriage patterns merely on the basis of two parishes. The more detailed analysis of the registers will appear in a book on Nantes, currently in progress (co-authored with Jean Tanguy).

GG 726 Relief of 1579-80

GG 743 Relief tax roll, 1586

HH 1 Prices, isolated years, especially in 1570s, 1630s, 1640s

HH 31 Payment to municipal workers, 1646

HH 137 Wine merchants of 1609

Rennes (catalogued only by number, not by series)
"Livres des merciers" (annual account books of confraternity of mercers)

447 Testament of Gilles Ruellan

1035 Tax roll, 1629

1061–78 Accounts of treasurer, sixteenth and seventeenth centuries

Hennebont
CC 2 Accounts, intermittent

Massérac
Civil registers, to 1668, unclassified

Quimperlé (classified by number, not series)
2 Grain prices in 1680

Saint-Malo
BB 7 Town council deliberations, 1580s

BB 12 Town council deliberations, 1640s

FF 3 Police problems, 1650s

Bibliography

Vannes
BB 4   Complaint about troops in 1653
CC 3–10   Accounts, intermittent, early and mid seventeenth century
HH 1   Grain stocks, 1598

Bibliothèque municipale de Nantes
Manuscrits français
1560   Special duties granted to Rohan family, 1549
1722   Special duties granted to Rohan family, 1467 and 1471

PUBLISHED SOURCES

The following abbreviations are used throughout.
MSHAB   Mémoires de la Société d'Histoire et d'Archéologie de Bretagne
BMSAIV   Bulletin et Mémoire de la Société des Antiquitaires d'Ille-et-Vilaine

PUBLISHED PRIMARY SOURCES

Anger, P., "Cartulaire de l'abbaye de St-Suplice-la-Forêt," *Bulletin et Mémoire de la Société des Antiquitaires d'Ille-et-Vilaine*, 34 (1905): 165–262; 35 (1906): 325–88; 37 (1907): 3–160; 38 (1908): 203–80; 39 (1909): 1–207; 40, n. 1 (1910): 33–192; and 40, n. 2 (1911): 1–89

Audren de Kerdrel, A., "Documents relatifs à l'histoire de la Ligue en Bretagne," *BMSAIV*, 1 (1881): 236–43

d'Avenel, G., *Lettres, instructions diplomatiques et papiers d'état du cardinal de Richelieu* (Paris, 1853–77), 8 vols.

Barthélemy, A. de., *Choix de documents inédits sur l'histoire de la Ligue en Bretagne* (Nantes, 1880)

Baudot, F.-N., sieur du Buisson et d'Aubenay, *Itinéraire de Bretagne en 1636* (Nantes, 1898, 1902), 2 vols., II, 241
  "Journal des Etats de Bretagne en 1636," ed. N. Bourdeaut, *Bulletin de la Société Archéologique de Nantes* (1927): 339–99

Béchameil de Nointel, L., *La Bretagne de la fin du 17e siècle d'après le mémoire de Béchameil de Nointel*. ed. J. Berenger and J. Meyer (Paris, 1976)

Belordeau, P., *Controverses agitées en la cour de Parlement de Bretagne et décidées par arrets du mesme parlement* (Paris, 1619, 1620), 2 vols.

Bernard, D., "Rôle des fouages à Audierne en 1616," *Bulletin et Mémoire de la Société des Antiquitaires du Finistère*, 38 (1909): 158–66

Blanchard, R., "Le cartulaire des sires de Rays," *Mémoires de la Société des Antiquitaires de Poitou*, xxviii, xxx (1898, 1900)
  Lettres et mandements de Jean V (Nantes, 1889–95), 5 vols.

Bodin, J., *Les six livres de la République* (Paris, 1583, Geneva reimpression of 1961)

Boislisle, A., *Correspondance des contrôleurs généraux avec les intendants des provinces* (Paris, 1874–9), 3 vols.

Burke, E., *Reflections on the Revolution in France* (New York, 1973)
Cahiers des plaintes et doléances de la Loire-Atlantique (Nantes, 1983)

Bibliography

Colbert de Croissy, Charles, *La Bretagne en 1665 d'après le rapport de Colbert de Croissy*, ed. J. Kerhervé, F. Roudaut, and J. Tanguy (Brest, 1978)

Coutume générale des pays et duché de Bretagne (Rennes, 1581)

Doucet, R., "L'état des finances de 1523," *Bulletin Philologique et Historique* (1920): 5–123

Durand, Y., *Cahiers de doléances de la noblesse des gouvernements d'Orléanais, Normandie et Bretagne* (Nantes, 1971)

"Emotion populaire à Morlaix en 1631," *Bulletin et Mémoire de la Société des Antiquitaires du Finistère*, 37 (1908): 8–26

"Eon, J." (Mathias de Saint-Jean?), *Le commerce honourable* (Nantes, 1646)

Fontanon, A., *Les édits et ordonnances des rois de France* (Paris, 1611), 3 vols.

Forbonnais, F., *Recherches et considerations sur les finances de France depuis l'année 1595 jusqu'à 1721* (Liège, 1758)

Gangnières, J., *Mémoires du Comte de Souvigny, lieutenant général des armées du roi* (Paris, 1906), 2 vols.

Grillon, P., ed., *Les papiers d'état de Richelieu* (Paris, 1975–85), 6 vols.

Isambert, F. *et al.*, *Recueil général des anciennes lois françaises* (Paris, 1822–33), 29 vols.

Jacquelot de Boisrouvray, M., "Journal des Etats d'Ancenis," in *Journal inédit d'un député de l'ordre de la noblesse aux Etats de Bretagne pendant la Régence, 1717–24*, ed. G. de Closmadeuc (Rennes, 1915)

la Bigne Villeneuve, P. de, "Documents inédits concernant la fondation du couvent de Bonne-Nouvelle de Rennes," *Bulletin et Mémoire de la Société des Antiquitaires d'Ille-et-Vilaine*, 3 (1883): 221–38

la Borderie, A. de, "Le plus ancien rôle des comptes du duché," *MSHAB*, xxvi (1946): 49–68

"Recueil d'actes inédits des ducs et princes de Bretagne," *BMSAIV*, 19 (1899): 155–285

"Recueil des actes inédites d'Anne de Bretagne," *BMSAIV*, 6 (1886): 243–9

la Lande de Calan, C. de, *Documents inédits relatifs aux Etats de Bretagne de 1491 à 1589* (Nantes, 1898), 2 vols.

la Mare, N. de, *Traicté de la police* (Paris, 1705)

la Nicollière-Teijeiro, S. de, *Privilèges accordés par les ducs de Bretagne . . . à . . . la ville de Nantes* (Nantes, 1883)

Lemoine, J., "La révolte dite du Papier Timbré ou des Bonnets Rouges en Bretagne en 1675," *Annales de Bretagne*, 12 (1894): 315–59, 523–50; 13 (1895): 180–259, 346–408, 524–59; 14 (1896): 109–40, 189–223, and 438–71

Leroux, A., *Inventaire sommaire des registres de la jurade de Bordeaux* (Bordeaux, 1916), t. 11

Loyseau, C., *Cinq livres du droit des offices; les seigneuries; les ordres* (Paris, 1613, 1644)

Mallet, J.-R., *Comptes rendus de l'administration des finances de la France (1600–1715)* (Paris, London, 1789)

Ménétra, J. L., *Journal de ma vie*, ed. D. Roche, (Paris, 1982), translated as *Journal of My Life* (New York, 1986)

Meuret, F.-E., *Annales de Nantes*, vol. II (Nantes, Paris, 1830–1)

Millotet, M.-A., *Mémoire des choses qui se sont passés en Bourgogne depuis 1650 jusqu'à 1668* (Dijon, 1866)

Bibliography

Moreau, J., *Histoire de ce qui s'est passé en Bretagne durant les Guerres de la Ligue* (Saint-Brieuc, 1857)

Morice, P.-H., *Preuves pour servir à l'histoire de Bretagne* (Paris, 1744)

Mousnier, R., ed. *Lettres et mémoires adressés au chancelier Séguier* (Paris, 1964), 2 vols.

Ogée, *Nouveau dictionnaire historique et géographique de la Bretagne*, 2 vols. (Rennes, 1843, 1853) (re-edition of eighteenth-century work)

Ordonnances des rois de France de la troisième race (Paris, 1722–1848), 14 vols.

Pascal, B., *Pensées* (Paris, 1954)

Pertuis, A. and de la Nicollière-Teijeiro, S. eds., *Le livre doré de l'hotel de ville de Nantes* (Nantes, 1873)

Poullain de la Barre, F., *Of the Equality of the Two Sexes* (Detroit, 1988, reimpression of English translation of 1677)

Robillard de Beaurepaire, C. de, *Cahiers des Etats de Normandie, règnes Louis XIII et Louis XIV* (Rouen, 1877, 1888)

Rohan, H. de, *Mémoires* (Paris, 1822), I, 174–5

Sée, H., "Cheptels de métairies au début du XVIe siècle," *Annales de Bretagne* (1931): 523–4

"Les comptes de recettes et de dépenses pour la Bretagne en 1495 et 1496," *Annales de Bretagne*, 9 (1891): 544–9

"Un bail de métayage dans le pays de Rennes en 1537," *Annales de Bretagne*, 49 (1931): 297–300

Sévigné, M. de Rabutin de, *Correspondance* (Paris, 1978), vol. III, ed. R. and J. Duchêne *Lettres de Madame de Sévigné*, ed. Gérard-Gailly (Paris, 1953, 1960), 2 vols.

Tallemant de Réaux, G., *Les Historiettes*, 2 vols. (Paris, 1960–1)

Valois, N., ed., *Inventaire des arrêts de conseil d'Etat, règne d'Henri IV* (Paris, 1886)

SECONDARY SOURCES

France and Europe

Amussen, S., *An Ordered Society: Gender and Class in Early Modern England* (New York, 1988)

Anderson, P., *Lineages of the Absolutist State* (London, 1974, 1979)

Antoine, M., "L'administration centrale des finances en France du XVIe siècle au XVIIIe siècle," in *Histoire comparée de l'administration. IVe–XVIIIe siècles* (Munich, 1980)

Asher, E., *The Survival of Feudalism in the France of Colbert. The Resistance to the Maritime Classes* (Berkeley, 1960)

Aston, T. H. and Philpin, C. H. E., eds., *The Brenner Debate. Agrarian Class Structure and Economic Development in Pre-Industrial Europe* (Cambridge, 1985, 1987)

Babelon, J.-P., "Compte rendu du Colloque Henri IV," in *Avènement d'Henri IV Quatrième Centenaire, Colloque de Pau*, ed. P. Tucoo-Chala (Pau, 1990)

Baehrel, R., *Une croissance: La Basse-Provence rurale (fin du XVIe siècle–1789)* (Paris, 1961)

Barbiche, B., *Sully* (Paris, 1978)

Bart, J., *La liberté ou la terre* (Dijon, 1985)

Bibliography

Bayard, F., *Le monde des financiers au XVIIe siècle* (Paris, 1988)

"Manière d'habiter des financiers de la première moitié du XVIIe siècle," *XVIIe Siècle*, 162 (1989): 53–65

Beik, W., *Absolutism and Society in Seventeenth-Century France. State Power and Provincial Aristocracy in Languedoc* (Cambridge, 1985)

Benabou, E.-M., *La prostitution et la police des moeurs au XVIIIe siècle* (Paris, 1987)

Benedict, P., *Rouen during the Wars of Religion* (Cambridge, 1981)

Bercé, Y.-M., *Histoire des Croquants* (Paris, 1974), 2 vols.

Bluche, F., *Les magistrats du Parlement de Paris au XVIIIe siècle* (Paris, 1960)

Bohanon, D., *Old and New Nobility in Aix-en-Provence, 1600–1696* (Baton Rouge, 1992)

Bonney, R., "Absolutism: What's in a Name?" *French History* 1 (1987): 93–117

L'absolutisme (Paris, 1989)

Political Change in France under Richelieu and Mazarin (Oxford, 1976)

The King's Debts (Oxford, 1981)

Brennan, T., *Public Drinking and Popular Culture in Eighteenth-Century Paris* (Princeton, 1988)

Buisseret, D., *Sully and the Growth of Centralized Government in France* (London, 1968)

Busquet, R., *Histoire des institutions de la Provence de 1482 à 1790* (Marseille, 1920)

Cardenal, L. de, "Les dernières réunions des trois ordres de Périgord avant la Révolution," *Studies Presented to the International Commission for the History of Assemblées d'Etats*, vol. II (Louvain, n.d.), 113–28

"Les Etats de Périgord sous Henri IV," *Studies Presented to the International Commission for the History of Assemblées d'Etats*, vol. III (Louvain, n.d.), 163–181

Charmeil, J.-P., *Les trésoriers de France à l'époque de la Fronde* (Paris, 1963)

Chartier, R. and Richet, D., *Représentation et pouvoir politique: autour des Etats-Généraux de 1614* (Paris, 1982)

Clément, P., *Histoire de Colbert et de son administration* (Paris, 1874)

Collins, J., *Fiscal Limits of Absolutism: Direct Taxation in Seventeenth-Century France* (Berkeley, 1988)

"Geographic and Social Mobility in Early-Modern France," *Journal of Social History*, 24, (3) (1990): 563–77

"La flotte normande au début du XVIIe siècle: le mémoire de Nicolas Langlois (1627)," *Annales de Normandie* (1984): 161–80

"The Economic Role of Women in Seventeenth-Century France," *French Historical Studies*, 16, (2) (Fall 1989): 436–70

Collins, S., *From Divine Cosmos to Sovereign State. An Intellectual History of Consciousness and the Idea of Order in Renaissance England* (New York, Oxford, 1989)

Contamine, P., *Guerre, état et société à la fin du Moyen Age* (Paris, 1972)

Coriolis, Abbé de, *Dissertation sur les Etats de Provence* (Aix, 1867)

Corvisier, A., "La noblesse militaire: aspects militaires de la noblesse française du XVe au XVIIIe siècles: état des questions," *Histoire Sociale – Social History*, 11 (1978): 336–55

Couturier, M., *Recherches sur les structures sociales de Châteaudun* (Paris, 1969)

Darnton, R., *The Great Cat Massacre and Other Essays* (New York, 1984)

Davis, N., *Society and Culture in Early-Modern France* (Stanford, 1975)

Bibliography

Delumeau, J., *Rassurer et protéger. Le sentiment de sécurité dans l'Occident d'autrefois* (Paris, 1989)

Dessert, D., *Argent, pouvoir et société au grand siècle* (Paris, 1984)

"Finances et société au XVIIe siècle: à propos de la Chambre de Justice de 1661," *Annales E.S.C.* (1974): 847–81.

Fouquet (Paris, 1987)

Devic, Dom C., and Vaissette, Dom J., *Histoire générale de Languedoc* (Toulouse, 1876–89), 14 vols., notably vols. xii–xiv

Dewald, J., *The Formation of a Provincial Nobility: The Magistrates of the Parlement of Rouen, 1499–1610* (Princeton, 1980)

Pont St-Pierre, 1389–1789 (Berkeley, 1987)

Deyon, P., "Rapports entre la noblesse française et la monarchie absolue," *Revue Historique* 231 (1964): 341–56

Dognon, P., *Les institutions politiques et administratives du pays de Languedoc du XIIIe siècle aux guerres de religion* (Toulouse, 1986)

Doucet, R., *Les institutions de la France au XVIe siècle* (Paris, 1948), 2 vols.

Drouot, H. *Mayenne et la Bourgogne* (Paris, 1937), 2 vols.

Notes sur la Bourgogne et son esprit public au début du règne de Henri III, 1574–89 (Dijon, 1937)

Duby, G., "La carte, instrument de recherche: les communes de France," *Annales* (1958)

Dupaquier, J., *La population de la France au XVIIe et XVIIIe siècles* (Paris, 1979)

Durand, Y., *Les fermiers généraux au XVIIIe siècle* (Paris, 1971)

Elias, N., *The Court Society* (Oxford, 1983)

Esmonin, E., *La taille en Normandie au temps de Colbert* (Paris, 1913)

Farr, J., *Hands of Honor. Artisans and Their World in Dijon, 1550–1650* (Cornell, 1989)

Febvre, L., *The Problem of Unbelief in the Sixteenth Century: The Religion of Rabelais* (Cambridge, Mass., 1982)

Finlay-Crosswhite, A., "Henri IV et les villes," in *Quatrième Centenaire d'Henri IV. Colloque de Pau*, ed. P. Tucoo-Chala (Pau, 1990)

Foisil, M., *La révolte des nu-pieds* (Paris, 1970)

Gay, J.-L., "Fiscalité royale et Etats Généraux de Bourgogne," *Travaux et Recherche de la Faculté de Droit . . . de Paris*, 8 (1961): 179–210

Gentil da Silva, J., *Stratégies d'affaires à Lisbonne entre 1595 et 1607* (Paris, 1956)

Goubert, P. *Beauvais et le Beauvaisis, 1600–1715* (Paris, 1960)

The Ancien Régime (New York, 1970)

The French Peasantry in the Seventeenth Century (Cambridge, 1986)

Goubert, P. and Roche, D., *Les Français et l'Ancien Régime*, 2 vols. (Paris, 1984)

Hamscher, A., *The Parlement of Paris after the Fronde* (Pittsburgh, 1976)

Hanley, S., "Engendering the State: Family Formation and State Building in Early Modern France," *French Historical Studies*, 16, (1) (Spring 1989): 4–27

The Lit de Justice of the Kings of France (Princeton, 1983)

Harding, R., *Anatomy of a Power Elite: The Provincial Governors of Early Modern France* (New Haven, 1978)

Hayden, J. M., *France and the Estates General of 1614* (Cambridge, 1974)

303

Bibliography

Hickey, D., *The Coming of French Absolutism: The Struggle for Tax Reform in the Province of Dauphiné, 1540–1640* (Toronto, 1986)

Huetz de Lemps, C., *Géographie du commerce de Bordeaux à la fin du règne de Louis XIV* (Paris, 1974)

"Le commerce maritime des vins d'Aquitaine," *Revue Historique de Bordeaux* (1965): 25–44

Huppert, G., *Les bourgeois gentilshommes* (Chicago, 1977)

Jackson, R., *Vive le Roi! A History of the French Coronation from Charles V to Charles X* (Chapel Hill, 1984)

Jacquart, J., *La crise rurale en Ile-de-France, 1550–1670* (Paris, 1974)

Jouhaud, C., *Mazarinades: La Fronde des mots* (Paris, 1986)

Keohane, N., *Philosophy and the State in France. The Renaissance to the Enlightenment* (Princeton, 1980)

Kettering, S., *Judicial Politics and Urban Revolt: The Parlement of Aix-en-Provence, 1629–59* (Princeton, 1978)

Patrons, Brokers, and Clients in Seventeenth-Century France (Oxford, 1986)

Labatut, J.-P., *Les ducs et pairs de France au XVIIe siècle* (Paris, 1974)

Labrousse, E., ed., *Histoire sociale et économique de la France* (Paris, 1965)

Le Pésant, M., "Un centre d'émigration en Normandie sous l'ancien régime. Le cas de Percy," *Bibliothèque de l'Ecole des Chartes* (1972): 163–225

Le Roy Ladurie, E., *Carnival in Romans* (New York, 1974)

Les Paysans de Languedoc (Paris, 1966), 2 vols.

Major, J. R., "Henry IV and Guyenne: A Study Concerning the Origins of Royal Absolutism," *French Historical Studies*, 4 (1966): 363–84

Representative Government in Early Modern France (New Haven, 1980)

"The Renaissance Monarchy: A Contribution to the Periodization of History," *Emory University Quarterly* (1956): 112–24

Marion, M., *Dictionnaires des institutions de la France aux XVIIe et XVIIIe siècles* (Paris, 1923), 2 vols.

Merle, L., *La métairie dans la Gâtine poitevine* (Paris, 1956)

Mettam, R., *Power and Faction in Louis XIV's France* (London, 1988)

Meuvret, J., *Etudes d'histoire économique* (Paris, 1971)

Le problème des subsistances à l'époque de Louis XIV (Paris, 1977, 1989), 2 vols.

Moote, L., *Louis XIII. The Just.* (Berkeley 1989)

Mousnier, R., *Fureurs paysans* (Paris, 1967)

La plume, la faucille et le marteau (Paris, 1970)

La vénalité des offices (Paris, 1945, 1971)

Les institutions de la France sous la monarchie absolue, 1598–1789 (Paris, 1974, 1980), translated as *The Institutions of France under the Absolute Monarchy, 1598–1789* (Chicago, 1979, 1984), 2 vols.

"Monarchie contre aristocratie dans la France du XVIIe siècle," *XVIIe Siècle* (1956): 377–81

Recherches sur la stratification sociale à Paris aux XVIIe et XVIIIe siècles (Paris, 1976)

Muchembled, R., *L'invention de l'homme moderne* (Paris, 1988)

Neuschel, K., *Word of Honor. Interpreting Noble Culture in Sixteenth-Century France* (Ithaca, 1988)

Bibliography

Pagès, G., "Essai sur l'évolution des institutions administratives en France du commencement du XVIe siècle à la fin du XVIIe siècle," *Revue d'Histoire Moderne* (1935): 8–57, 113–38

La guerre de Trente Ans (Paris, 1939)

"La vénalité des offices dans l'ancienne France," *Revue Historique*, 169 (1932): 477–95

"Le conseil du roi et la vénalité des offices pendants les premières années du ministère de Richelieu," *Revue Historique*, 180 (1938): 245–82

"Richelieu et Marillac: deux politiques," *Revue Historique*, 179 (1937): 63–97

Pillorget, R., *Les mouvements insurrectionnels en Provence entre 1595 et 1715* (Paris, 1975)

Porchnev, B., *Les soulèvements populaires en France avant la Fronde, 1623–1648* (Paris, 1963)

Poussou, J. P., *Bordeaux et le sud-ouest au XVIIIe siècle. Croissance économique et attraction urbaine* (Paris, 1983)

Prentout, H., *Histoire des Etats de Normandie* (Rouen, 1925), 3 vols.

Raeff, M., *The Well-Ordered Police State* (New Haven, 1983)

Root, H., *Peasants and King in Burgundy. Agrarian Foundations of French Absolutism* (Berkeley, 1987)

Rowan, H., *The King's State. Proprietary Dynasticism in Early Modern France* (New Brunswick, 1980)

Saint-Jacob, P. de, *Les paysans de la Bourgogne du nord au dernier siècle de l'ancien régime* (Paris, 1960)

Sawyer, J., *Printed Poison* (Berkeley, 1990)

Schalk, E., *From Valor to Pedigree* (Princeton, 1986)

Shennan, J. H., *The Parlement of Paris* (Ithaca, 1968)

Trocmé, E. and Delafosse, M. *Le commerce rochelais de la fin du XVe siècle au début du XVIIe* (Paris, 1952)

Troyansky, D., *Old Age in the Old Regime* (Ithaca, 1989)

Weill, G., "Les Etats de Bourgogne sous Henri III," *Mémoires de la Société Bourguignonne de Géographie et d'Histoire* (1893): 121–48

Brittany

Abgrall, J.-M., "La peste de 1639 à Quimper," *Bulletin de la Société des Antiquitaires de Finistère*, 21 (1894): 329–40

Aubry, M., "Le port de Roscoff. Les mutations d'un site," *Norois* (1969): 24–35

Bellier, Dumaine C., "L'administration du duché de Bretagne sous le règne de Jean V," *Annales de Bretagne* (1899–1901)

Bougouin, E., "Le navigation sur la Basse-Loire au milieu du XIVe siècle," *Revue Historique* (1935): 482–96

"Nantes port du sel au XVIe siècle, de la légende à l'enquête," *Annales de Bretagne* (1936): 140–50

Bourde de la Rogerie, H., "Introduction," in *Inventaire sommaire des archives départementales du Finistère*, series B, III (Quimper, 1902)

"Liste des juridictions exercées au XVIIe et au XVIIIe siècle dans le ressort du présidial de Quimper," *Bulletin de la Société Archéologique de Finistère*, (1910): 243–91

Bibliography

Canal, S. de, *Les origines de l'intendance en Bretagne* (Paris, 1911)

Carré, H. *Essai sur le fonctionnement du parlement de Bretagne après la Ligue (1598–1610)* (Paris, 1888)

Les Etats de Bretagne et l'administration de cette province jusqu'en 1789 (Paris, 1868) 2 vols.

"Reception d'un procureur général au Parlement de Bretagne en 1603," *Annales de Bretagne* (1889): 161–89

Recherches sur l'administration municipale de Rennes au temps de Henri IV (Paris 1888)

Collins, J., "Les impôts et le commerce du vin en Bretagne," *Actes du 107e Congrès National des Sociétés Savantes* (Brest, 1984), I, 155–68

"Taxation in Bretagne, 1598–1648," (Ph.D. dissertation, Columbia, 1978)

"Sully et la Bretagne," *XVIIe Siècle* (Jan–Mar 1992): 57–74

"The Role of Atlantic France in the Baltic Trade: Dutch Traders and Polish Grain at Nantes, 1625–1675," *Journal of European Economic History* (1984): 231–80

Couffon, R., "La terreur au pays de Guingamp en 1660. La bande de Kermelquel," *Bulletin et Mémoire de la Société d'Emulation de la Côtes-du-Nord* (1960): 20–9

Croix, A., *La Bretagne au XVIe et XVIIe siècles* (Paris, 1981), 2 vols.

Nantes et le pays nantais au XVIe siècle (Paris, 1974)

Darsel, J., "La paroisse de Mestin au XVIe et XVIIe siècles," *Bulletin et Mémoire de la Société d'Histoire et d'Archéologie de Bretagne* (1969): 77–91

"La pêche sous l'ancien régime dans l'évêché de Saint-Brieuc," *Bulletin et Mémoire de la Société d'Emulation du Côtes-du-Nord* (1962): 69–95

Davis, W., *Small Worlds. The Village Community in Early Medieval Brittany* (Berkeley, 1988)

Delafosse, M., "Marins et marchands bretons à La Rochelle au XVe et XVIe siècles," *MSHAB* (1953): 53–71

Delumeau, J., *Histoire de Bretagne* (Toulouse, 1969)

Delumeau, J., et al., *Le mouvement du port de Saint-Malo, 1681–1720* (Rennes, 1966)

Duval, M. "Erections de seigneuries et institutions de foires en Bretagne sous le règne de Louis XIV (1643–75)," *MSHAB* (1975–6): 69–94

"Erections et constitutions des foires et marchés en Bretagne sous les règnes de Henri IV et de Louis XIII," *MSHAB*, 52 (1974): 83–105

Fourmont, H. de, *Histoire de la Chambre des Comptes de Bretagne* (Paris, 1854)

Gabory, E., "La marine et le commerce de Nantes au XVIIe et au commencement du XVIIIe siècles," *Annales de Bretagne* (1901): 1–44; 235–90; 341–98

Gallet, J., *La seigneurie bretonne, 1450–1680. Le cas du Vannetais* (Paris, 1983)

"Recherches sur les seigneuries à foire et marchés dans le Vannetais du XVIe au XVIIIe siècles," *MSHAB*, 52 (1974): 133–66

Goubert, J.-P., *Malades et médecins en Bretagne, 1770–1790* (Paris, 1974)

Guillotin de Courson, Abbé, *Les grandes seigneuries de Haute-Bretagne* (Rennes, 1897–8)

Hélias, P., *The Horse of Pride* (New Haven, 1978)

Hurt, J., "Les offices au parlement de Bretagne sous le règne de Louis XIV: aspects financiers," *Revue d'Histoire Moderne et Contemporaine*, 23 (1976): 3–31

"La politique du parlement de Bretagne (1661–1675)," *Annales de Bretagne*, 81 (1974): 105–30

"The Parliament of Brittany and the Crown, 1665–1675," *French Historical Studies*, 4 (1964–5): 411–33

Bibliography

Jeulin, P., "Aperçus sur la Contractation de Nantes," *Annales de Bretagne* (1932): 284–331, 457–505

L'évolution du port de Nantes (Paris, 1929)

Jones, M., "Aristocratie, faction et Etat dans la Bretagne du XVe siècle," in *L'état et les aristocraties (France, Angleterre, Ecosse) XIIe–XVe siècles*, ed. P. Contamine (Paris, 1989), 129–60

Ducal Brittany (Oxford, 1970)

The Creation of Brittany (London, 1987)

"Les finances de Jean IV, duc de Bretagne (1364–1399)," *Mémoires de la Société d'Histoire et d'Archéologie en Bretagne*, lii (1972): 26–53

Kerhervé, J., *L'Etat breton aux XIVe et XVe siècles, les ducs, l'argent et les hommes* (Paris, 1987), 2 vols.

L'Abbé, Y., "Les débuts d'une ville bretonne: Vitré au XVe et XVIe siècles," *MSHAB*, 23 (1944): 65–105

la Borderie, A. de, "Armaments maritimes des Malouins au XVIe siècle," *BMSAIV*, 4 (1885): 298–312

la Borderie, A. de, and Pocquet, B., *Histoire de la Bretagne* (Rennes, 1896–1904), 6 vols.

Lapeyre, H., *Une famille des marchands: les Ruiz* (Paris, 1953)

Lebrun, F., "L'évolution de la population de Rennes au XVIIe siècle," *Annales de Bretagne* 93 (1986): 249–56

Le Carguet, H., "La flotte d'Audierne," *Bulletin de la Société des Antiquaires du Finistère*, 26 (1899): 39–40

"Le Cap-Sizun, la morue du Raz de Fonteroy," *Bulletin de la Société des Antiquaires du Finistère*, 37 (1908): 8–26

Le Goff, T. J. A., *Vannes and Its Region in the Eighteenth Century* (Oxford, 1981)

Leguay, J.-P., *La ville de Rennes au XVe siècle à travers les comptes des Miseurs* (Rennes, 1968)

"Les fouages en Bretagne ducale aux XIVe et XVe siècles," (D.E.S., Rennes, 1961)

Leprohon, R., *Vie et mort des Bretons sous Louis XIV* (Brest, 1984)

Lobineau, G.-A., *Histoire de Bretagne* (Paris, 1707), 2 vols.

Mauny, M. de, *1532 – Le grand traité franco-breton* (Paris, 1971)

Meyer, J., *La noblesse bretonne au XVIIIe siècle* (Paris, 1966), 2 vols.

L'armement nantais au XVIIIe siècle (Paris, 1976)

Minois, G., *Les religieux en Bretagne sous l'Ancien Régime* (Rennes, 1989)

Montigny, J.-L., *Essai sur les institutions du duché de Bretagne à l'époque de Pierre Mauclerc* (Paris, 1959)

Moret, H., *Le Croisic* (Rennes, 1917)

Morice, P.-H., *Histoire ecclésiastique et civile de Bretagne* (Paris, 1750), 2 vols.

Pougéard, M., "Le Bretagne au XVe siècle: Etude démographique," (Rennes, 1965, D.E.S., unpublished)

Rebillon, A., *Les Etats de Bretagne, de 1661 à 1789* (Paris, 1932)

Rouzeau, L., *Répétoire numérique des archives notariales sous-série 4 E* (Nantes, 1988)

Saulnier, F., *Le Parlement de Bretagne de 1554 à 1790* (Rennes, 1909), 3 vols.

Sée, H., *Les classes rurales en Bretagne du XVIe siècle à la Révolution* (Paris, 1906)

Les Etats de Bretagne au XVIe siècle (Paris, 1895) and *Annales de Bretagne* (1894): 3–38, 189–207, 365–93, 550–69

Tanguy, J., "La production et le commerce des toiles 'Bretagne' du 16e au 18e siècles," *Actes du 91e Congrès National des Sociétés Savantes* (1966): 105–41

Le commerce du port de Nantes au milieu du XVIe siècle (Paris, 1956)

"Le commerce nantais à la fin du XVIe et au commencement du XVIIe siècle," (Rennes, 1965, thèse de troisième cycle)

"Les révoltes de 1675 et la conjoncture en Basse-Bretagne," *MSHAB* (1975)

"L'essor de la Bretagne aux XVIe et XVIIe siècles," in *La Bretagne province, 1532–1789*, vol. III of *Histoire de la Bretagne et des pays celtiques* (Morlaix, 1986)

Touchard, H., *Le commerce maritime breton à la fin du Moyen Age* (Paris, 1967)

Travers, Abbé, *Histoire civile, politique et réligieuse de la ville et du comté de Nantes*, 3 vols. (Nantes, 1837–41)

Trévedy, J., "Etats de l'armée royale en Bretagne, 1595, 1610," *Bulletin de la Société des Antiquitaires de Finistère* (1895): 107–33; 185–215

"Le couvent de Saint-François de Quimper," *Bulletin de la Société des Antiquitaires de Finistère* (1894): 236–50

Wacquet, H., "Comment étaient traité les prisonniers-de-guerre en Bretagne à l'époque de la Guerre de Trente Ans," *Bulletin de la Société des Antiquitaires de Finistère*, 44 (1917): 133–43

"Le siège de Concarneau (1619)," *Bulletin de la Société des Antiquitaires de Finistère*, 19 (1892): 14–41

Index

affranchissements, 121, 132, 146–8, 152, 206
amortissements, 148, 206
Anjou, 45, 57, 59, 126, 188, 214, 215
Anne, duchess of Brittany, 30, 122, 158
Anne of Austria (governor of Brittany, 1644–66), 193, 203, 205, 207, 210, 219, 221, 223
artisans, 8, 9, 17, 61, 72, 80, 247, 249, 279; see also Nantes
Assérac, 98, 115, 267
Audierne, 49, 50, 81, 82, 230, 231, 233–4, 241, 269

Barrin de la Galissonnière family, 5, 109, 110
Beik, William, 4, 24, 26, 274
bishops, 73, 98, 117, 160, 174, 192, 197–9, 221, 267
Bonnets Rouges, 24, 28, 220, 222, 227, 228, 248, 250, 251, 259–70
Bordeaux, 1, 41–3, 48, 49, 52, 68, 80, 101, 163, 178, 187, 246, 247, 259
Brissac family, 5, 116; Brissac, Charles I de Cossé, duke of, 66, 68, 116, 139, 140, 162, 165, 168–71, 173, 188, 193, 262, 276; Brissac, Charles II de Cossé, count, later duke of, 69, 81, 109, 142, 144, 175–6
bureau des finances, 75, 173, 179, 182, 186, 196, 217
butter, 35, 37–40, 63, 69, 131, 247
Cambout, Charles de, baron of Pontchâteau, 91, 184, 186, 191–3, 197–9, 285–6
Cambout-Coislin (Pontchâteau) family, 5, 66, 69, 74, 117, 162, 183, 289
capitation, 7–9, 65
Carquefou, 235, 267, 281
Central Treasury, 127, 139, 177, 180, 204
Chamber of Accounts, 7, 8, 21, 72, 140, 154, 165, 202, 203, 211, 212, 218, 272; functions of, 75–7, 114, 118, 135; League division of, 129–30; members of, 88–98, 109, 110, 129, 185, 202, 203, 211, 212, 218, 272; role in governance,

75–7, 114, 118, 135, 139, 142, 148, 202, 203, 211, 212, 218, 272
Charette family (Nantes), 77, 222, 253
Chaulnes, Charles d'Albert d'Ailly, duke of (governor of Brittany, 1666–95), 43, 53, 67, 223, 227, 261, 263–7, 269, 276, 285
Chaulnes, Elisabeth Le Feron, duchess of, 22, 284
cider, 36, 40, 44, 45, 53, 57, 62, 119, 185, 189, 243, 246, 247, 248, 268
cloth, 40, 46, 48–9, 58, 63, 101, 104, 173, 247, 281; see also linen
colonial goods, 50, 58, 59, 64, 225, 261
Condé, Henry, prince of, 171, 190–4, 202
Cornouaille, bishopric of, Bonnets Rouges in, 227–8, 260–1, 264–5, 268–9, 274; economy of, 32–5, 37–8, 41, 44, 46, 50, 59, 94–5, 214; League War in, 131–2; nobles of, 65, 67, 79, 183; taxes of, 131, 141–2, 147, 152, 229–31, 242–3, 245–6
Croix, Alain, 30–2, 35, 97, 99–100, 239, 251, 252

D'Espinoze (family of Nantes), 78, 88, 89, 93, 273–4
De Rennes (family of Massérac), 82–6, 240
debts, town, 76, 100, 133–5, 145, 172, 175; see also specific town names
demesne (royal), 41, 45, 125, 130, 161, 273; reform of (1670s), 219, 222, 224–5, 261; repurchase of (1605–18), 151, 168–72, 177, 180
Dinan, 31, 37, 48, 111, 116, 120, 133, 145, 163, 189, 207, 241, 285
Dol, bishopric of, 36, 53, 67, 79, 95, 96, 114, 115, 121, 145, 227, 243

England, 4, 34, 47–9, 59, 60, 173, 216, 220, 221, 281
Estates General, 12; meeting of 1576, 91, 161, 162; meeting of 1614, 7, 91, 171, 172, 216
Estates of Brittany, 1–3, 72–4, 96, 138–9,

262, 271, 274; debts of, 133, 177,
179–81, 201–7, 213, 219, 226; financial
role of, 22–3, 25, 40, 45, 47–8, 52–3,
59–60, 64, 68–70, 118–19, 122–8,
130–3, 135–6, 141–2, 148–9, 154–228,
243, 245, 247–8, 260, 271, 274, 286–7;
members of, 5–7, 9–10, 25, 40, 68–70,
72–4, 98, 117, 122, 123–8, 130–3, 135,
136, 138, 139, 141, 193, 215, 223, 251,
267, 271, 274, 286–7; political role of,
5–7, 11, 15, 25, 40, 45, 59–60, 64,
68–70, 135, 138–9, 143, 151–3, 271,
274–5, 284–7; Richelieu and, 148, 149,
151–93, 198, 285–6; role in protecting
local privileges, 1–3, 11, 15, 22–3, 25,
26, 40, 47, 48, 59, 60, 64, 68–70, 136,
138, 139, 154–64, 170–6, 182–6, 187,
189–90, 195–207, 210–22, 224–7, 267,
271, 274–5, 284–7; treasurer of, 89, 92,
95, 142, 202–4, 212–14

financial officers, 3, 7–9, 12, 75, 176, 177,
204, 217
fish, commerce in, 39, 50, 58, 60, 62, 216,
247
fouage, 30, 45, 74, 75, 118–25, 127, 128, 130,
131, 139–41, 143, 144, 146, 148, 151,
152, 157, 159, 163, 165, 170, 173, 174,
185, 206, 215, 216, 218, 219, 220, 221,
232, 233, 239, 241, 248; Bishopric share
of, 122, 142, 215, 242–5; individual
share of, 81–6, 229–42; parish share of,
146–8, 151–2, 229, 231, 245, 248
fouage extraordinaire, 148, 151, 152, 206, 207,
219–21, 239
fouage receivers, 75, 93–6, 139, 142, 143, 165
Fougères, 31, 37, 48, 120, 134, 137, 163;
fouage receiving district of, 118, 122, 146,
230
Fouquet, Nicolas, 87, 109
Francis I, 13, 122, 123, 125, 158, 159
francs fiefs, 6 (n. 13), 170, 214, 219, 220, 226,
273

gens de bien, 17, 99, 250
Goulaine family, 5, 38, 66, 68, 98, 116, 117,
162, 163, 184, 185, 186, 191, 289
governors of the province, 7, 171, 172, 221;
see also duke of Mercoeur, duke of
Vendôme, marshal Thémines, Richelieu,
Anne of Austria, and duke of Chaulnes
grain, commerce of, 13, 22, 23, 34, 37,
39–43, 45, 46, 50, 52, 58, 59, 61, 62–4,
68, 72, 75, 76, 79, 93, 94, 102, 104, 105,
106, 107, 113, 119, 128, 138, 150, 153,

161, 163, 182, 199, 217, 226, 247, 251–3
Guingamp, 32, 42, 44, 99, 251, 252, 264,
266, 284

Hamburg, 48–50
Harouys family (Nantes), 76, 77, 185, 274
Hennebont, 30, 41, 42, 49, 56, 144, 145, 149,
163, 188, 251, 252
Henry II, 75, 107, 111, 124, 125, 159
Henry III, 69, 117, 127–9, 164, 170, 172, 225
Henry IV, 48, 77, 127, 129, 130, 139, 171–2,
185, 189, 206, 222, 225, 278, 285; and
Estates, 141, 153–6, 164–9, 173; visit to
Brittany, 1598, 164–9, 171
hides, commerce in, 23, 37, 39, 40, 170, 173
Holland, 43, 48, 49, 57
hospitals, 76, 98, 99
Hus family, 95–6, 203, 274; Gabriel Hus
(treasure of Estates), 77, 89

imposition foraine, 124, 125, 159
Ireland, 38, 43

Jean V, duke of Brittany, 39, 40, 119
judicial officers, 3, 6–9, 23, 24, 65, 66, 72, 75,
77–9, 84, 87, 88, 90, 91, 94, 97, 98,
106–10, 113, 114, 116, 117, 136, 150,
151, 186, 192, 252, 253, 265, 267, 268,
279

La Haye, Henry de (tailor of Nantes), 101,
257, 288
La Meilleraye, Armande de la Porte, duke of,
69, 117, 143, 184, 186, 191, 193, 196,
198, 199, 210, 214, 223
La Moussaye family, 66, 112, 115–16, 289
La Rochelle, 41–3, 48, 52, 68, 105, 126, 151,
178, 181, 187, 190, 191, 247
La Trémoille family, 5, 65–7, 69, 74, 91, 115,
117, 162, 174, 184, 192, 195, 197–9,
210, 223, 226, 275–6, 290
laboureur, 83, 240
landlords, 4–7, 10–13, 16, 21–4, 26, 27, 29,
39, 40, 43, 45, 60, 61, 63–5, 67–70, 72,
73, 79, 91, 126, 135, 152, 153, 175, 182,
206, 214, 217, 218, 227, 228, 232, 242,
246, 261, 266, 267, 272, 274–6, 279,
285–7
Langourla, 232, 234
Languedoc, 4, 22, 24, 25, 70, 153–8, 220,
221, 274, 275, 285, 287
Lannion, 41, 48, 67, 81, 163, 198, 214, 233
Lanvaudan, 232, 235
Lavardin, Henri-Charles de Beaumanoir,
marquis of, 262, 267, 269, 287

Index

Le Croisic, 163, 257, 280
Le Lou (family of Nantes), 88, 89, 93, 124,
    136, 274
League (War of the), 46, 50, 76, 84, 97, 113,
    128–33, 135, 141, 152, 158, 160, 164,
    166, 167, 170, 175, 178, 180, 185, 189,
    203, 204, 222
Léon, bishopric of, 31, 79, 114, 115, 117,
    121, 122, 142–5, 146, 162, 163, 230
    242–6, 251; economy of, 32–3, 35–6, 42,
    44, 46, 49, 66–7, 214
lieutenant general of the province, see duke of
    Brissac, duke of La Meilleraye, marquis
    of Lavardin
linen, 23, 31, 33, 34, 43–8, 59–61, 63, 79,
    105, 163, 173, 182, 214, 216, 254
Louis XIII, 23, 48, 147, 155, 173, 186, 188,
    221
Louis XIV, 16, 24, 27, 29, 34, 109, 199, 219,
    223, 276, 277, 282, 284

Macé (family of Massérac), 82–6, 240–2, 244
Marie de Médicis, 21, 69, 171, 183, 188–90,
    196, 200, 205, 223
Massérac, 81–7, 143, 231–4, 239–41
Mazarin, Jules, cardinal, 207, 210, 223
merchants, 9, 37, 60, 64, 68, 73, 76, 77, 88,
    89, 94–7, 106, 109, 164, 198, 215, 233,
    247, 252, 256, 263, 266
Mercoeur, Emmanuel de Lorraine, duke of
    (governor of Brittany, 1582–1602), 68,
    69, 97, 115, 116, 128, 129, 133, 164,
    167, 184, 191
military, 3, 5, 6, 8, 13, 16, 21, 24, 25, 27,
    65–8, 75, 91, 94, 108–10, 117–19, 126,
    127, 129, 130, 132, 139, 141–3, 148,
    160–2, 170, 171, 175, 176, 178, 180,
    181, 183, 185, 187, 191–3, 195–8, 200,
    204, 207, 214, 223, 228, 232, 274, 275
Morlaix, 3, 5, 7, 30, 63, 66, 67, 73, 78, 99,
    100, 104, 106, 111, 116, 146, 148, 163,
    183, 247, 251, 252, 265, 273; economy
    of, 33–5, 44, 46–9, 59, 105, 173, 214–5,
    245

Nantes, 1, 31, 33, 37, 56–9, 109, 119, 120,
    129, 132, 135, 139, 143, 150, 191, 195,
    202, 217, 221, 232, 233, 239, 273, 274,
    280–1, 284–5; commerce of, 36, 37,
    42–3, 48–52, 56–9, 182, 213–14, 261;
    and Estates, 73, 74, 161–4, 167, 171,
    175, 183, 186, 188, 197, 199–200, 210,
    213–14, 221–2, 285; mayor of, 9, 15,
    76–8, 86–9, 91, 113, 133, 154, 222;
    police of, 15, 19, 20, 107, 113, 133, 251,
    253–8, 260, 264, 266, 280, 281; taverns

of, 61–2, 101–3, 253; ruling elite of,
    86–9, 91–8, 109–11, 185, 221, 222,
    273–4, 285
Nantes, bishopric of, 66–7, 115–17, 122,
    141–2, 146, 149, 167, 182–3, 185,
    230–1, 243–7, 265, 267; economy of,
    35–9, 41–3, 45–6, 56–9
Nevet family, 66, 67, 141, 183, 185, 265
nobles, 3, 4, 6, 7, 9–13, 15, 16, 21, 24–6, 70,
    73, 79, 90–2, 97, 98, 108–10, 112, 113,
    118, 121, 133, 135, 140–2, 150, 242,
    248, 249, 252, 262, 265, 267, 272,
    274–5; economic role of, 39–40, 65,
    68–9; at Estates, 157, 160–3, 168, 170,
    174–6, 180, 183–4, 191, 195, 197–200,
    211, 218, 220–1, 224–6

order, 1, 2, 4, 7–13, 15–21, 23–5, 27, 29, 34,
    67, 68, 72, 73, 74, 91, 107, 113, 119,
    124, 127, 133, 142, 144, 145, 153, 158,
    162, 165, 171–3, 176, 177, 183, 192,
    195, 196, 202, 207, 213, 215, 218, 219,
    224, 225–7, 245, 248–51, 257–60, 266,
    267, 271–3, 276–7, 279–83, 285–8

Parlement, 1, 21, 52, 68, 72, 106, 108–10,
    125, 127, 136, 142, 154, 159, 165, 173,
    177, 272–4; cost of, 127, 139–40, 155,
    170, 200, 233; and Estates, 162–4, 198,
    210; and economy, 173, 222; and Papier
    Timbré revolt, 222, 227, 259–64, 266;
    members of, 3, 6–9, 66, 68–70, 74, 75,
    76, 81, 87–99, 106–11, 129, 138, 164,
    169, 199, 218, 225, 273–5; role in
    governance, 1, 3, 6–9, 13, 21, 52, 66,
    68–70, 72, 74–6, 81, 87–99, 106–11,
    114, 118, 125, 145, 151, 164, 171,
    210–13, 215, 218, 221, 251, 259, 261–4
pays d'Etats, 20, 23–4, 151–2, 154–8, 179,
    182, 187
peasants, 8, 10, 12, 23, 26, 28, 112–14, 153,
    245, 274, 281; economic role of, 31, 34,
    36, 42–6, 58–65, 67–8, 73, 78–80, 104,
    150; resistance of, 145, 152, 220, 227–8,
    246–8, 252–3, 260–1, 264–70, 276, 287;
    taxes on, 121, 126, 130–1, 145, 148, 152,
    175, 229–35, 239–43
Pierre II, duke of Brittany, 29, 107
police, 11, 15, 19, 20, 23, 24, 28, 42, 76, 100,
    101, 112, 113, 250, 251, 253, 255, 256,
    258, 280, 284
Pontivy, 35, 36, 39, 44, 265
ports et havres, 36, 39, 43, 51, 119, 149
Poullain family, 77–8, 89, 93–7; Bernardin
    Poullain, treasurer of Estates, 142,
    202–5; Michel Poullain, treasurer of

Index

Estates, 142, 177, 202–5
presidial courts, 9, 73–7, 87, 89, 94, 98, 106, 111, 112, 114, 118, 126, 136, 163, 164, 192, 199, 211, 225, 259, 267, 268
procureur syndic of Estates, 73, 145, 163, 177, 192, 197, 198, 202, 238

Quimper, 33, 35, 37, 40, 41, 44, 46, 67, 75, 80, 98, 105, 106, 111, 112, 119, 120, 130, 163, 252, 264, 268–9

Redon, 35, 38, 40, 41, 46, 49, 58, 82, 83, 85, 143, 144, 192, 195, 239
Rennes, 6, 7, 9, 62, 65, 67, 73, 74–6, 79, 95, 96, 98, 111, 118, 120, 121, 133, 192, 195, 212, 213, 218, 221, 232, 233, 243, 273, 274; economy of, 31–3, 35–8, 45, 46, 48, 69, 78, 106–8, 173; and Estates, 162–4, 198, 210; Papier Timbré revolt in, 222, 227, 251, 259–64, 266–7, 269, 284–5
Rennes, bishopric of, 31–3, 48, 118, 230; economy of, 35, 37–8, 45; taxation in, 129, 142, 243–7
Renouard family, 89, 92, 110, 202–4; César de Renouard, treasurer of the Estate, 92, 202–4
Retz family, 5, 41, 74, 117, 141, 163, 170, 183, 191, 192, 197, 290
Richelieu, Armand du Plessis, cardinal, 13, 23, 24, 117, 223, 284; clientage network of, 69, 91, 144, 184, 185–93, 195, 196, 198; and Estates, 144, 184–93, 195, 196, 198, 205
Rieux family, 5, 65–9, 131, 163, 176, 184, 185, 276, 289; René de Rieux, *sieur* de Sourdéac, 66, 131, 163, 176, 196
Rocaz (family of Nantes), 88, 89, 93–5, 100, 124, 129, 274
Rohan family, 5, 7, 39, 40, 65–9, 74, 78, 91, 116–18, 139, 140, 142, 151, 162, 170, 185, 195, 197, 210, 222–4, 254, 289; Henri, duke of Rohan, 171, 183–4, 192, 271, 275
Rosmadec family, 5, 66, 67, 74, 78, 114, 116, 162, 183, 184, 192, 289
Ruellan, Gilles I, sieur of Rocher-Portal, 5, 25, 66, 68, 80, 88, 109, 116, 169, 170, 193, 273, 274
Ruiz, André, 25, 43, 88, 93, 100, 109, 124, 129

Saint-Brieuc, 36, 42, 44, 46, 49, 134, 143–5, 163, 207, 251
Saint-Brieuc, bishopric of, 32, 33, 35, 46, 66, 67, 79, 114, 115, 117, 121, 122, 142–5, 146, 150, 162, 230, 234, 243–5
Saint-Malo, 2, 5, 7, 33, 35–7, 59, 67, 78, 79, 95, 98, 99, 104–6, 119, 121, 134, 141, 146, 162, 163, 173, 183, 190, 198, 215, 222–4, 237, 238, 249, 250, 260, 263, 264, 265, 274; economy of, 3, 46–9, 59, 63
Saint-Malo, bishopric of, 31, 114–16, 121, 122, 142, 169, 203, 230, 243–5; economy of 32–3, 36–7, 46–9, 59, 63, 66–7, 79
salt, 22, 33, 39, 45, 46, 49, 50, 56, 59, 60, 125, 150, 156, 166, 211, 212, 215
seigneurial estates and courts, 5–7, 9, 14, 22–4, 27, 39, 40, 43, 65–8, 70, 78, 79, 80, 83, 84, 112–15, 117, 118, 136, 159, 214, 221, 225, 227, 265, 268, 271, 272, 275, 279
seigneurs, 6, 10, 14, 22, 26–8, 40, 61, 65, 67, 72, 73, 75, 79, 117, 118, 160, 162, 165, 218, 228, 248, 252, 261, 265–9, 274–5, 277
seneschal of Nantes, 1, 73, 135, 199, 200, 256
seneschalsy courts, 94, 110, 111
shipbuilding, 48, 260
sieurs, 6, 22, 26, 61, 64, 65, 68, 79, 106, 271, 274
society of classes, 1, 2, 4, 270, 278
society of orders, 1, 2, 4, 11, 14, 24, 25, 28, 70, 72, 248, 258, 270, 272, 278, 280
Spain, 18, 37, 49, 129, 166, 188, 215

taille, 10, 123, 155, 157, 221, 232
taverns, 20, 61, 62, 72, 84, 100–2, 135, 179, 239, 252, 253, 255–8, 280–1, 288
Thémines, Pons de, marshal of France, governor of Brittany (1626–7), 189–90
Thomas (family of Massérac), 83–6, 238, 240
tithes, 41, 42, 57, 59, 227, 264, 267, 269, 285
tobacco, 216, 219, 228, 242, 259–61, 264–6
towns, 98–100, 110, 120, 121, 122, 123, 141, 142, 188, 192, 196, 233, 235; and Estates, 25, 72–5, 91, 121–3, 126, 133, 135, 160–5, 167, 174, 175, 189–90, 197, 198, 199, 207, 210, 215, 217, 245–7; debts of, 133–5; economies of, 35, 37, 39, 40, 42, 44–9, 56, 58, 61–2, 65, 113, 135, 145, 146, 167, 214–15, 217, 233, 245–7; lower classes of, 17–19, 27, 61–4, 269; police of, 20–1, 28, 61–4, 76, 78, 113, 145, 146, 227, 228, 249, 251–2, 260–6, 269, 281–2; political power in, 3, 78, 105, 113, 120–3, 281–2; population of, 30–3, 35, 81, 107 (n. 91); *see also* specific town names
treasurers of France, 75, 92, 118, 130, 149, 168, 170

Index

Tréquier, bishopric of, 31–4, 36, 45–6, 79, 115–16, 121–2, 146, 150, 152, 183, 214, 230, 242–6

Upper Brittany, 5, 44, 65, 115, 162, 188, 195, 245

Vannes, 31, 41, 49, 56, 58, 67, 68, 75, 80, 95, 98, 100, 105–7, 111, 120, 133, 146, 149, 162–4, 183, 192, 222, 227, 263, 264, 274
Vannes, bishopric of, 32–3, 57, 114, 116, 146; economy of, 34–5, 38, 42, 44, 45, 79; taxes of, 121–2, 142–4, 146, 195, 230, 243–7
Vendôme, César, duke of, governor of Brittany (1602–26), 5, 115, 139–40, 142, 167, 170–1, 178–80, 183–4, 186–91, 200–2, 207

Vitré, 31, 37, 48, 111, 120, 134, 137, 163

wine, 8, 10, 20–3, 32, 34, 36, 39, 40, 43–6, 48, 50, 52, 56, 57–60, 62–4, 68, 69, 74, 76, 79, 93, 94, 99, 100, 101, 104–6, 113, 119, 122, 124, 126, 130, 131, 132, 133, 135, 136, 141–4, 148, 150, 152, 157, 159, 161, 163–7, 169, 171, 174, 175, 177, 178, 179, 180, 182, 183, 185, 187–9, 199–202, 206, 212, 213, 219, 220, 225–8, 239, 242, 243, 245–8, 252, 255–8, 260, 265, 266, 268, 287–8
women, economic role of, 61, 69, 106, 255–6, 277–8, 284; political role of, 16–18, 69, 72, 88, 97, 98, 99–101, 199–200, 223, 249, 251–2, 254–6, 260, 263, 265–7, 272, 280, 283–7; on relief rolls, 97–101, 235–7; as taxpayers, 81, 106, 230, 233–41

CAMBRIDGE STUDIES IN EARLY MODERN HISTORY

*The Old World and the New**
J. H. ELLIOTT
*The Army of Flanders and the Spanish Road, 1567–1659: The Logistics of Spanish Victory and Defeat in the Low Countries Wars**
GEOFFREY PARKER
Neostoicism and the Early Modern State
GERHARD OESTREICH
Prussian Society and the German Order: An Aristocratic Corporation in Crisis c. 1410–1466
MICHAEL BURLEIGH
*Richelieu and Olivares**
J. H. ELLIOTT
Society and Religious Toleration in Hamburg 1529–1819
JOACHIM WHALEY
*Absolutism and Society in Seventeenth-Century France: State Power and Provincial Aristocracy in Languedoc**
WILLIAM BEIK
Turning Swiss: Cities and Empire 1450–1550
THOMAS A BRADY JR
The Duke of Anjou and the Politique Struggle during the Wars of Religion
MACK P. HOLT
Neighbourhood and Community in Paris
DAVID GARRIOCH
Renaissance and Revolt: Essays in the Intellectual and Social History of Modern France
J. H. M. SALMON
Louis XIV and the Origins of the Dutch War
PAUL SONNINO
*The Princes of Orange: The Stadholders in the Dutch Republic**
HERBERT H. ROWEN
The Changing Face of Empire: Charles V, Philip II and Habsburg Authority, 1551–1559
M. J. RODRIGUEZ-SALGADO
Frontiers of Heresy: The Spanish Inquisition from the Basque Lands to Sicily
WILLIAM MONTER
Rome in the Age of Enlightenment: The Post-Tridentine Syndrome and the Ancien Régime
HANNS GROSS
The Cost of Empire: The Finances of the Kingdom of Naples during the period of Spanish Rule
ANTONIO CALABRIA
Lille and the Dutch Revolt: Urban Stability in an Era of Revolution
ROBERT S. DUPLESSIS
The Armada of Flanders: Spanish Maritime Policy and European War, 1568–1668
R. A. STRADLING
The Continuity of Feudal Power: the Caracciolo di Brienza in Spanish Naples
TOMMASO ASTARITA
After the Deluge: Poland and the Second Northern War 1655–1660
ROBERT FROST

The Nobility of Holland: From Knights to Regents, 1500–1650
H. F. K. VAN NIEROP
Classes, Estates and Order in Early Modern Brittany
JAMES B. COLLINS

Titles available in paperback marked with an asterisk*

The following titles are now out of print
French Finances, 1770–1795: From Business to Bureaucracy
J. F. BOSHER
Chronicle into History: An Essay on the Interpretation of History in Florentine Fourteenth-Century Chronicles
LOUIS GREEN
France and the Estates General of 1614
J. MICHAEL HAYDEN
Reform and Revolution in Mainz, 1743–1803
T. C. W. BLANNING
Altopascio: A Study in Tuscan Society 1587–1784
FRANK MCARDLE
Gunpowder and Galleys: Changing Technology and Mediterranean Warfare at Sea in the Sixteenth Century
JOHN FRANCIS GUILMARTIN JR.
The State, War and Peace: Spanish Political Thought in the Renaissance 1516–1559
J. A. FERNANDEZ-SANTAMARIA
Calvinist Preaching and Iconoclasm in the Netherlands, 1544–1569
PHYLLIS MACK CREW
The Kingdom of Valencia in the Seventeenth Century
JAMES CASEY
Filoppo Strozzi and the Medici: Favor and Finance in Sixteenth-Century Florence and Rome
MELISSA MERIAM BULLARD
Rouen during the Wars of Religion
PHILIP BENEDICT
The Emperor and his Chancellor: A Study of the Imperial Chancellery under Gattinara
JOHN M. HEADLEY
The Military Organisation of a Renaissance State: Venice c. 1400–1617
M. E. MALLETT and J. R. HALE